OPERATION MUSK

THE SUEZ CANAL CRISIS OF 1956

THE STORIES AND PHOTOGRAPHS FROM THOSE WHO WERE THERE

E A PEGG

To Reg with best wishes.

E A Pegg

STELN PUBLISHING

First published in November 2013 by
StelnPublishing
8 Kinross Crescent
Blackpool FY44PE

ISBN 978-0-9926742-0-5

Produced by the Choir Press, Gloucester GL1 1SP.
Printed in Great Britain.

DEDICATION

To the memory of all those on both sides of the Suez Canal conflict, especially those innocent civilian Egyptian men, women and children of Port Said and Port Fuad, who lost their lives or suffered needlessly because of the corruptly conceived Operation Musketeer

ACKNOWLEDGEMENTS

I thank all the British newspapers and magazines which published my appeal, those who responded to it, and the many people and organisations who gave me permission to use copyright material.

Books consulted during the compilation of the book included:

Suez 1956: Operation Musketeer by Robert Jackson, published by Ian Allan Ltd, 1980.

Crises Do Happen. The Royal Navy and Operation Musketeer, Suez 1956 by Geoffrey Carter, published by Maritime Books, 2006.

Suez The Double War by Roy Fullick and Geoffrey Powell, published by Hamish Hamilton, 1979.

Airborne to Suez by Sandy Cavenagh, published by Gludy Publications, 1996.

Thanks to Maritime Books and Geoffrey Carter for their kind permission to use the diagram of the blockship positions at Port Said shown in their book *Crisis Do Happen*.

Thanks to Roy Fullick and Geoffrey Powell for use of the map, *Port Said and Port Fuad,* in their book *Suez the Double War*, published by Hamish Hamilton Ltd in 1979.

Thanks to Captain Dr Sandy Cavenagh, Medical Officer with 3 Para during the parachute drop on El Gamil Airfield, for his loan to me, and generous permission to use, his personal collection of Suez Crisis photographs, many of which were not used in his own book *Airborne to Suez.*

Thanks to the wonderful website Wikipedia, and various other sites on the Internet too numerous to mention individually, for all the information I gleaned that I felt relevant to the book.

Thanks to Mr C Blackburn and the Internet's *Britain's Small Wars* webmasters for permission to reproduce the list of those who died owing to their involvement in the Suez Canal crisis.

Thanks Dr Yahia Al Shaer for generous permission to access, on the Internet, his collection of photographs of Port Said in the aftermath of the invasion.

Thanks to Mr Ted Sparrow of the Internet web site, *www.royalmarinesonline.com*, for his information on the Marines at Port Said.

Thanks to Hansard for permission to reproduce various exchanges in Parliament pertinent to the Suez Crisis

Thanks to Mrs Pat Tarrant for permission to reproduce her 2006 Saga Magazine article about her late brother Lt A G Moorhouse who was abducted and died in Port Said.

Thanks to the Ordnance Survey for permission to use an extract from its one-inch map of Southampton and Marchwood current in the 1950s.

Thanks to Mr Dick Woolley for permission to use his map of the 1950 to 1955 Canal Zone postings.

Thanks to the Royal Marines Association and Tony Davie for permission to reproduce the photograph of the burial service for Marine Michael John Fowler aboard HMS *Theseus*.

Thanks to Joan McCool and Ann Harrison for the loan of their Suez Canal and ship photos.

Thanks to Elsie Hodge for the photographs of Port Said belonging to her late father Ron Colwell RE.

Thanks to Captain Rex Cooper for use of the photograph of HMS *Roberts*.

Thanks to Mr Gill Morgan, who was aboard the ship *Salvestor,* for his selection of excellent photos.

Thanks to Mr Ronnie Hulton for his contribution of excellent photographs.

Thanks to the generous contributor, whoever he is, who donated his small collection of photographs for use in the book without providing a name or a return address.

Thanks to my son Stewart Pegg for all his technical help, advice, and repairing of the many pigs' ears, in the computer preparation of this book. Without his expertise I would have struggled.

LIST OF NARRATIVE AND PHOTOGRAPH CONTRIBUTORS

Surname	Christian name	Branch of Forces	Unit or ship	Page
Adams	Brian	Navy	HMS *Eagle*	106
Ainscow	Peter	Navy	HMS *Bulwark*	128
Ainsworth	Sam	Army	RE Port Operations Squadron	270
Alma	Roger	Army	RA 33 Field Parachute Regiment	33
Alty	Stan	Navy	HMS *Eagle*	114
Applegate	Ken	Navy	42 Commando Battalion	65
Arden	Maurice	Army	REME	290
Avis	W. Bill	Army	RE 165 Port Operations Squadron.	275
Baker	Geoffrey	RAF	Radar unit	21
Ball	Gordon H	Army	Army Catering Corps (ACC)	303
Bentham	Harold	Army	RE 3 Field Squadron	209
Bowden	John	Army	RE 16 Field Squadron	224
Bowes	Bill	Navy	HMS *Eagle*	101
Brandish	Neville	Navy	RFA *Salvestor*	195
Brewer	David	Army	RE Movement Control	218
Brown	Alan	Navy	40 Commando Battalion	52
Burn	John	Army	RE 35 Engineer Regiment.	220
Campbell	Robert	Army	Royal Army Medical Corps (RAMC)	46
Carne	Keith	Navy	HMS *Sallyport*	194
Cavenagh	Sandy	Army	3 Parachute Battalion	36
Challis	John	Army	RE 8 Squadron. Movement Control	213
Church	Frank	Army	RE 3 Field Squadron	211
Clare	Roger	Army	3 Parachute Battalion	30
Clark	Jim	Army	RE 24 Field Squadron	230
Clark	Michael A	Navy	HMS *Ceylon*	171
Clowes	John	Navy	40 Commando Battalion	56
Coleborn	Edgar G	Navy	45 Commando Battalion	80
Cook	Trevor	Navy	HMS *Alamein*	174
Cragg	Roy	Navy	HMS *Decoy*	177
Croot	Peter	Navy	HMS *Bulwark*	123
Cross	Mike	Navy	HMS *Dalrymple*	158
Dagwell	Keith	RAF	Joint Helicopter Unit	22
Dando	Tom	Navy	42 Commando Battalion	71
Davies	John G	Navy	HMS *Letterston*	167
Eastlake	John	Navy	HMS *Anzio*	186
Eke	Gordon	Navy	HMS *Tyne*	146
Elliott	Malcolm	Army	23 Para Field Ambulance. (RAMC)	43
Essam	Richard	Navy	HMS *Theseus*	116
Evans	Colin	Navy	HMS *Diana*	174
Farrar	Charles	Army	RE 82 Port Operations. Squadron	270
Frampton	Les	Army	Queens Own West Kent Regiment	309
French	John	Navy	HMS *Albion*	131
Gant	Norman	Army	Royal Signals	297
Gathercole	Anthony	Army	RE Z-craft operator	278
Gilkes	Thomas George	Army	6 Royal Tank Regiment	286
Green	Dave	Army	Royal Army Service Corps (RASC)	301
Green	Malcolm	Army	RE 3 Field. Squadron	202
Hallett	Albert	Army	RE 42 Field Squadron	227

Surname	Christian name	Branch of Forces	Unit or ship	Page
Halliday	Jack H	RAMC	Operating Theatre Assistant	48
Hartley	Stephen	Army	West Yorkshire Light Infantry	311
Hett	K Stewart	Navy	HMS *Manxman*	137
Hodkinson	Brian	Navy	HMS *Eagle*	112
Hulton,	Ronnie	Merchant Navy	Various ships	200
Hunt	Jim	Navy	HMS *Theseus*	121
Irvine	James 'Danny'	Navy	HMS *Dalrymple*	160
Jacobs	Alan	Navy	845 Squadron Fleet Air Arm	135
Jones	Ken	Army	Royal Signals	294
Jordan	P R (Bob)	Army	RE Port Operations Squadron.	280
Light	Terry	Army	3 Parachute Battalion	24
Lockyer	Maurice	Army	RE 323 Elec. & Mech. Squadron	262
MacGregor	Angus L M	Army	RE 16 Field Squadron.	219
Mallinson	Victor	Navy	HMS *Striker*	182
Manning	David	Navy	HMS *Eagle*	99
Mayoh	Ronny	Navy	HMS *Shavington*	168
Mee	John	Navy	42 Commando Battalion.	60
Mepham	John	Army	RE postal Unit	269
Moorhouse	Anthony G	Army	West York Light Infantry	313
Packer	David	Navy	HMS *Striker*	180
Page	Alan John	Army	RE 3 Field Squadron	205
Pegg	Eric A	Army	RE 33 Field Squadron	240
Phelan	Allan	Army	RE 33 Field Squadron	253
Pickering	Chris	Navy	45 Commando Battalion	75
Ponsonby	Geoffrey	Army	RE, 51 Port Operations Squadron	272
Ramsay	Andrew	Army	RE 36 Engineer Regiment	260
Robinson	Trevor John	Navy	HMS *Forth*	136
Rose	Norman	Army	RE 33 Field Squadron	236
Rudkin	Ray A	Army	RE 57 Field Squadron	254
Salts	Mike J	Navy	HMS *Manxman*	141
Sims	Brian	Navy	HMS *Floriston*	169
Smeath	Pat	Navy	HMS *Ravager*	184
Smith	Guy	Navy	HMS *Eagle*	88
Smith	Keith	Navy	HMS *Jamaica*	172
Spearen	Brian	Army	Royal Army Ordnance Corps	293
Stidwell	Brian	Navy	45 Commando Battalion	85
Talbot	John B	Army	RE 51 Port Operations Squadron	284
Thomson	Derek	Army	Army Catering Corps (ACC)	307
Tuckey	Derek	Army	Royal Army Service Corps (RASC)	300
Tyzack	Dave (Tilly)	Navy	Diver	198
Walters	Huy	Navy	45 Commando Battalion	82
Watt	Alec	Navy	HMS *Parapet*	190
Wernham	Vic	Army	RE, 167 Port Operations Squadron	276
Wild	Norman	Navy	HMS *Theseus*	119
Willey	Neville	Navy	HMS *Dalrymple*	153
Williams	Ben	RAF	No.12 Canberra Squadron	19
Williams	Roy	Navy	HMS *Tyne*	152
Wilson	Brian	Army	2 Parachute Battalion	32

AUTHOR'S PREFACE

This book evolved, belatedly, from two others I put together about a decade ago. During my National Service with the Royal Engineers I either took or acquired quite a number of photos of places I visited which were Cyprus, and Port Said during the 1956 Suez Canal crisis. Years later I became involved in my family history and in 1999 during a visit to the Royal Engineers' Museum and Library at Chatham I enquired about possible photos and accounts of National Service days in the Royal Engineers, specifically of Cyprus and the Suez Canal Crisis to supplement my own material. I was appalled to discover that the library had no such records and all I was shown were a few photos of married families on a gala Saturday afternoon at a sapper camp somewhere in the UK. The only history they had, so it seemed, was several volumes of ten-yearly updates of where each of the different regiments of the corps had served and briefly what it had been doing. There was little about individuals and I assumed, rightly or wrongly, that the same applied throughout the whole of the services. With national servicemen by now getting quite long in the tooth I realised that the knowledge of their experiences and their photographs were soon going to be lost for all time. Consequently I decided to do something about the situation.

I found a list of British newspapers on an Internet site and sent an appeal to all of them asking for National Service sappers to get in touch and to tell me their stories. I received a rewarding response and the finished book contained the contributions of some 140 sappers who wrote the stories of where and when they were born, what they did before the age of call up, whether deferred or not, where trained, where posted and their duties, and how National Service affected the rest of their lives. Overseas postings covered at that time included Germany, Belgium, Austria, Trieste, Gibraltar, Libya, Egypt, Cyprus, Jordan, Palestine, Kenya, Aden, Singapore, Malaya, Hong Kong, Korea, Japan, Christmas Island, Bermuda and Jamaica.

In addition to the stories I received a large number of unsolicited photographs taken by the sappers during their service. With the realisation that there were vast numbers of service photos residing in cupboards and lofts around the country which would eventually end up in skips I decided to put out another appeal, this time for sapper photos from any period of service, just to ensure that they were saved for posterity. The result was an A4-sized book one inch thick just like the first volume, containing 489 pages which included photos of Hitler's death trench and a pit full of dead bodies at Belson. I felt that the Royal Engineers now had a history representing actual individuals and what they had done, and that my job was finished.

I let another seven years elapse until, for some reason, I began thinking about all the Suez Canal crisis photographs that must still be out there belonging to those of us still alive and now even longer in the tooth. Any 18-year-olds involved in the crisis would then be 73 so there was no time to waste if I were to compile another military record. I contacted about 600 newspapers and magazines throughout the British Isles inviting the veterans of all services who had had anything to do with *Operation Musketeer* to get in touch with me. As a result of this I acquired a collection of some 2,500 photos of varying quality which I scanned into the computer. All were returned to their owners except occasionally when widows asked me to find a worthy home for them.

There was much duplication of course since those without cameras had obtained copies from those that did. In fact I was told that the members of some units sent to Port Said were ordered not to take cameras with them. Fortunately, many of the lads ignored this order. Large numbers of these photos have never seen the light of day until now and others, of old Port Said and the Suez Canal, are of postcards acquired at various postcard and stamp fairs.

I have adopted the same format as that used in the previous compilations so that we have recorded a social history of the times as well as a military one. Most of the photos are accompanied by personal accounts of the contributors' adventures and because of this we have learned for the first time a great deal that has never been revealed before in previous publications concerning the so-called Suez Crisis. Suez, of course, is a town about one hundred miles south of Port Said. Since it was at Port Said where most of the 'crisis' action took place the word 'Suez' without the word 'Canal' must seem a rather misleading geographical term to the present generation.

Eric A Pegg

SETTING THE SCENE

In 1832 the Frenchman Ferdinand de Lesseps, son of Mathieu de Lesseps a career diplomat, was appointed as the vice-consul at Alexandria in Egypt. While there his chief, Consul-General Mimaut, loaned him a number of books among which was a memoir on the feasibility of constructing a canal to connect the Red Sea to the Mediterranean, a distance of 101 miles. This had been written back in 1798 by the civil engineer Jacques-Marie Le Pèrere on the instructions of Napoleon Bonaparte.

The project was not pursued because Le Pèrere miscalculated the surface of the Red Sea to be some ten metres (33 feet) higher than the Mediterranean which meant that after the two seas were connected much of northern Egypt would be flooded. It is difficult to understand his believing that the earth's gravity could act so differently on the sea at two different locations and that then he failed to consult the scientific establishment on such a possibility.

The surface of the Red Sea at Port Suez is now known to be about 1.2 m. higher than the eastern Mediterranean, possibly because of the funnelling effect of the Gulf of Suez coastlines. There is also a height difference here of up to 1.9m at spring tides. Yet Despite La Pèrere's findings the concept fired de Lesseps' imagination and the urge to create a short cut from the Mediterranean to the Red Sea was never far from his mind.

De Lesseps remained in Egypt for the next five years, first becoming the Consul in Cairo and then at Alexandria. During this time, through the strong friendship of his father with Mehemet Ali, the Viceroy of Egypt, Ferdinand too became a friend of the viceroy, and of his French-educated son Said Pasha.

In 1837 de Lesseps returned to France and went on to serve in various countries until he retired in 1851. In 1854 his young friend Said Pasha became the Turkish Ottoman Empire's Viceroy of Egypt. Said Pasha sent de Lesseps an invitation to visit him. De Lesseps arrived in Egypt early in November and by the last day of the month had been given the initial go-ahead in the form of a firman (edict or permit) by Said Pasha to eventually establish a Compaignie Universalle du Canal Maritime de Suez to carry out the construction and running of the proposed canal.

All this was carried out without the actual permission of the Sultan in Constantinople who was heavily involved with his allies the British and French in the Crimean War against Russia which had its eyes on the territories of the fading Ottoman Empire at this time. However, Said covered himself by including a codicil to the grant which stated that before construction of a canal could commence the 'concession must be ratified by His Imperial Majesty the Sultan.'

De Lesseps quickly obtained the services of two French civil engineers working in Egypt, Linant Bey and Mougal Bey and had them carry out a survey of the route of the proposed canal and provide extensive answers to a number of concerns which he knew would eventually have to be met. The survey, using more modern equipment than that available to Pèrere half a century earlier and carried out under better conditions, found that the levels of the Red Sea and the Mediterranean were virtually the same.

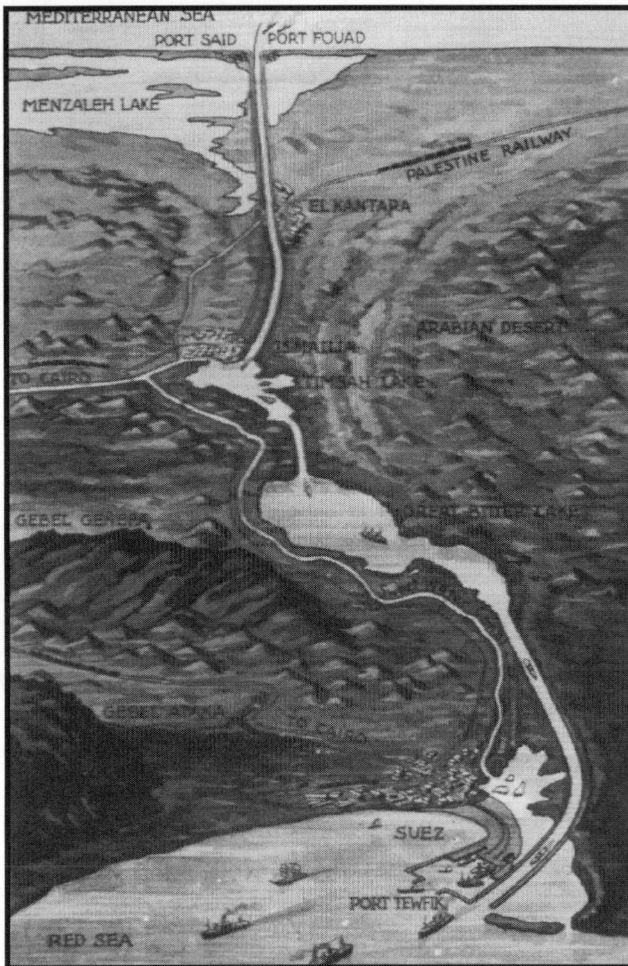

The Suez Canal route.

On 5 January 1856 Viceroy Said issued a second firman which would eventually find its way into the statutes of the Canal Company. Two important points of the document were, subject to the Sultan's ratification and, provided the fees were paid, that the canal was to be open to ships of all nations in peace and in war, and that after 100 years from the opening of the canal, which was sufficient time for the shareholders to reap the benefit of their investment, the canal would become the property of Egypt.

The project was strongly supported by the French and initially by the ruling Ottoman Sultan Abdul 1 until he was persuaded to do an about-face by his ally the British Prime Minister Palmerston who feared possible French control over the canal despite the benefits of its speeding up access to Britain's vast empire to the east. Said's approval for the scheme, of course, depended on the Sultan's approved.

To counter these highly disappointing political and diplomatic setbacks de Lesseps decided that if he could demonstrate the validity of his scheme he would have a better chance of gaining wider support. Consequently he turned once again to his friend Said Pasha with the result that an International Scientific Commission was invited to report on the findings of the survey that de Lesseps had had carried out.

Later in the year the plan, which also included the construction of a freshwater canal, was adopted after some amendments by the commission. The freshwater canal would be required initially for the needs of the vast workforce operating in the desert.

In 1857 the Commission's findings were published in a document entitled: Isthmus of Suez Ship Canal Report and Plan of the International Scientific Committee, London. This was published by John Weale. 59 High Holborn, in 1857.

The Introduction explained that 'We have been invited by his Highness the Viceroy of Egypt, Mahommed Said, to give an opinion upon the design for the junction of the Red Sea and the Mediterranean, presented to him by his Engineers, in obedience to his commands, and upon the proposal of M. Ferdinand de Lesseps...'

With the report in hand de Lesseps travelled throughout Europe lobbying anyone of influence who he thought could put pressure on the Sultan in Constantinople. He was growing impatient. In 1858 he approached the Rothschild banking family for a loan to start building the canal but the rate of interest attached to such a loan was so high that it was out of the question. Instead he decided to float a company and issue shares. Although the company headquarters would be established in Paris the company was registered in Alexandria, Egypt, on 15 December 1858 under the name Compagnie Universelle du Canal Maritime de Suez. This made it an Egyptian company.

It was calculated that capital of two hundred million French francs would be needed for the construction half of which was raised in France. Britain failed to subscribe. A further eighty million francs worth of shares, some 40% of the total, was bought by Said Pasha on behalf of the Egyptian Government despite the shaky finances of the country. He was able to foresee the eventual value of such an asset to the country.

De Lesseps also persuaded Said to find the workers for the canal's excavation. Said provided them from the pool of peasant forced labour known as the corvée. This use of labour was a practice that had been employed to build the pyramids millennia before and was still in operation. Although the some 30,000 Egyptian peasants who would work on the project at any one time during the construction were not considered to be slaves as such and would be paid, this was at the barest minimum. The Canal Company would however provide their food and shelter.

Perhaps a similar parallel to this in more recent times was British National Service. In the mid-1950s a tradesman conscript at the age of 21, having just finished his apprenticeship, began earning £12 a week. Upon conscription he was forced to provide his labour to the government for just £1.8s per week, back to his starting wage upon leaving school at the age of fifteen six years earlier. This was a considerable loss of income over two years at a time when a new semi-detached house could be bought for £2,000.

On 25 April 1859, despite opposition from the Ottoman Sultan, Britain, and varied vested interests in the financial and political world, de Lesseps made the symbolic first scrape in the ground at the small settlement of what was to become Port Said. Named for his close friend Said Pasha this was situated on a piece of Mediterranean beach backed by the lagoon of Lake Manzala. Gradually it grew into a small town of French colonial architecture as it serviced the traffic associated with the canal's excavation.

For years during the construction de Lesseps had to battle against strong opposition to the project which included British payments to Bedouins to ferment trouble among the corvée labour force. There were many periods when work had to be suspended. However, on 19 March 1866, after years of infighting and much political lobbying in Europe, de Lesseps, now with the personal support of the French Emperor Napoleon III behind him, was able to force the Ottoman Sultan to ratify the canal-building concession made earlier by Said Pasha. By this time the canal was only three years away from completion and therefore virtually a fait accompli anyway, so in some respects the Sultan's permission was no more than a face-saving gesture.

Construction of the canal with dredgers and elevators.

In 1867 Said Pasha died and was succeeded as Viceroy of Egypt by his nephew Ismail Pasha. The Sultan conferred the title of Khedive or Prince on Ismail which had the effect of increasing the degree of his autonomy considerably.

Ismail came to power at an unfortunate time. Exports of cotton to Lancashire from the American southern plantations had fallen dramatically during the American Civil war (1861-1865) and Egypt had invested heavily to fill this void in cotton supplies. With the end of the American conflict European importers returned to the cheaper American slave cotton. Egypt, despite the loss of its cotton markets, still had its loans to pay back. However, this situation failed to kerb Khedive Ismail's lavish lifestyle and in July 1869, with the completion of the Suez Canal in sight, he went off on a tour of Europe for the purpose of inviting the continent's royal families and many hundreds of celebrities together with over 1,000 cooks and servants to wait on the guests, all at Egypt's expense, to the canal's grand opening.

On 17 November 1869 Ismail Pasha officially opened the new canal in an extravagant ceremony. The French imperial yacht *Aigle* with the Empress Eugenie aboard was the first official vessel

The Port Said quay in the early days of the canal's operation. The lighthouse, the first reinforced concrete structure in the world, was a copy of a stone lighthouse on the Isle de Re in western France. It came into operation in October 1869, one month before the canal's official opening. Note, there are no buildings beyond it. (Illustrated London News, Saturday 22 July, 1882).

to traverse the canal followed by the British P&O liner SS *Delta*. Ships also entered the canal from the southern end. Afterwards a ball was held which was attended, so it is recorded, by some 6,000 guests. Ismail also had a new palace built in the capital Cairo, all this despite the parlous state of the country's economy.

Local boats on the canal.

Sailing ships on the canal.

The transition from sail to steam.

Also finding itself in financial difficulties was the Suez Canal Company with the cost of the canal's construction having become double the

The Suez Canal Company Offices.

original estimate and with two more years of work still being needed to fully complete the project. However, although the expected volume of traffic and revenue was somewhat slow to pick up initially, the presence of the canal soon began to have a dramatic impact on world shipping. During that first year something like three-quarters of the traffic using the canal was British with its far-flung empire now at its mightiest.

By the middle of the 1870s Egypt was bankrupt and the Khedive was forced to put Egypt's 172,602 Suez Canal Company shares on the market at an asking price of £4 million. In November 1875, during a recess in Parliament, the British Prime Minister, now Benjamin Disraeli, took it upon himself to purchase the shares on behalf of Britain by borrowing the money from the Rothschild family until the Government and Civil Service reconvened. This large single purchase later led to three British representatives being added to the Canal Company's board of directors.

Meanwhile, with Egypt falling more and more into debt to the Europeans, the country's leaders found themselves becoming less and less independent and subject to increasing western influence and dependence. In 1876 the Khedive had to submit to international financial control over the country which led to growing opposition and unrest among politicians, civil servants, and the Army.

In 1879 a prominent army general, Ahmed Urabi, together with a strong following from the Army and other protesters, formed the Egyptian Nationalist Party. In September 1881 an army rebellion led by Urbi initiated a period of high tension in the country resulting in the rebels trying to take power which led to Khedive Tewfiq asking for assistance from the Sultan in Turkey, and then the British, to protect the government. In April

1882 both the British and the French despatched warships to the port of Alexandria which is where Tewfiq had flown. The British were particularly concerned that Urabi would renege on the country's massive debts, and possibly take over the Suez Canal Company.

Despite this intervention however, within two months the country had fallen into the hands of the Nationalists. Britain's response was to send an expeditionary force to Egypt with elements going ashore at both ends of the canal which, in September, resulted in the defeat of Urabi's forces at Tel El Kebir and the surrender in Cairo of the rebel leaders. Although the Khedive was restored to his position of nominal power the British from then on continued to retain a presence in the country for the next 72 years when the 'Canal Zoners' were finally withdrawn in 1954.

Inauguration of the de Lesseps statue on 17 November 1899, thirty years after the opening of the canal.

Port Said's western breakwater prior to the construction of the fishing harbour behind it which would begin at the statue and extend seawards.

People promenading along the western breakwater during the early years of the canal.

Post Statue times. View towards the sea from the top of the lighthouse. Public gardens and buildings, including the Casino Palace Hotel, now extend beyond the lighthouse. These are the gardens where No.3 Field Squadron of the Royal Engineers made a bivouac on the night of 6 November 1956.

As Port Said grew it became, except perhaps for the Shanty Town and parts of the Arab Quarter, an attractive highly cosmopolitan settlement built, naturally enough, in the French Colonial style with verandas and balconies adding charm to the old timber buildings.

A considerable proportion of the population of Port Said has always belonged to a range of ethnic groups from around the Mediterranean basin together with the British and the French all living in harmony and religious tolerance. According to Yahia Al Shaer, the Port Said historian, '...this made the Port Said citizen quite different from his counterpart in other parts of Egypt in that he could frequently speak a range of languages because of this contact with people from other cultures.'

Existing cheek by jowl with the town's mosques was a cathedral, a synagogue, several schools for the children of the various nationalities living in Port Said, and a number of consulates providing their services to the range of international passengers travelling the canal.

The cathedral and mosque. Rue Du Vingt Trois Juillet.

Port Said has long been a brief stopping place for the many ships passing through the canal on journeys between north-western Europe and the Far East with passengers emigrating, going to or returning from, positions in the colonies such as soldiers, civil servants, plantation managers, miners, surveyors, and the like. Photographs and postcards of this stepping stone to the Orient and the Antipodes, with its Simon Arzt department store, shops, waterfront traders and other sights of the town, have found their way into the photo albums of numerous numbers of travellers for well over a century.

The Simon Arzt department store on the waterfront. It was built in 1923-24

This is a view of the Casino Palace Hotel and its verandah-covered open restaurant against what at the time was the promenade which, before the fish harbour was built and reclamation of land took place, had the Mediterranean Sea lapping against it. The photo was taken from near the de Lesseps' statue.

View from the canal side.

Under the verandah of the Casino Palace Hotel. View towards the side of the canal.

Rue de Commerce off the canal side.

The Boulevard Fouard I.

Prince Farouk Street between 1920 and 1936.

A street in Arab Town.

Prince Farouk Street again.

Sultan Osman Street.

With the declaration of the Great War in 1914 the Ottoman Turkish Empire joined forces with Germany which made it an enemy of Great Britain who seized the opportunity to take over in Egypt and make it a protectorate. This finally brought to an end the idea that Egypt was still part of the now defunct Ottoman Empire.

The Khedive of Egypt at this time was the anti-British Abbas II. Britain, fearing his loyalties lay with the Ottomans, deposed him and put in his place his uncle Hussein Kamel who adopted the title of sultan. Hussein Kamel died in 1917 and was succeeded by Fuad I.

In 1919, following the end of the war another wave of nationalism swept across Egypt with considerable violence. This led, on 28 February 1922, to Britain granting the country its independence upon which it became the Kingdom of Egypt. On 15 March Fuad proclaimed himself to be the king of Egypt.

However, despite this so-called Independence, the British continued to maintain an army presence in the canal zone of Egypt perhaps under the pretext that it was there to safeguard the usual smooth-running of the canal and inhibit any attempts by nationalist factions to interrupt these operations.

Ann's signed *Otranto* postcard of the Australia-bound team: Percy Chapman (capt.), Jack White (vice-captain), Douglas Jardine, Jack Hobbs, Herbert Sutcliffe, Wally Hammond, Patsy Hendren, Ernest Tyldesley, Phil Mead, Maurice Leyland, Maurice Tate, George Geary, George Duckworth, Les Ames, Harold Larwood, 'Tich' Freeman, Sam Staples.

In October 1928 Ann Harrison was travelling to Australia aboard the RMS *Otranto*. Also aboard the ship was the English MCC cricket team going down under for the 1928-29 Ashes series. Ann, now living in Scotland, sent the author some items of memorabilia to scan including a postcard of the *Otranto* signed with the names of the English cricket team which went on to win the series comprehensively by four tests to one.

Wally Hammond of Gloucestershire scored an aggregate of 905 runs on the tour and the famous Don Bradman replied with 468 runs during the various games played.

A busy day at Port Said.

The RMS *Otranto* at Port Said on passage to Australia.

More ships tied up at Port Said.

A ship returning from the east and passing the waterworks at the southern end of Port Said which is the source of the Sweetwater Canal. This can be seen making its way southwards parallel to the western bank of the Suez Canal.

Meanwhile King Fuad reigned until his death on 28 April 1936 when he was succeeded by his son Farouk. Farouk, fearing for his country's safety following the recent Italian invasion of Abyssinia, sought British help and soon afterwards, on 26 August, Britain and Egypt signed the Anglo-Egyptian Treaty, an alliance in which Britain would protect Egypt in time of war, train the Egyptian army, and agree to pull its own army out of Egypt except for a maximum of 10,000 personnel required to protect the Suez Canal. The treaty, to last 20 years, would expire, coincidentally, in August 1956.

However, during the WWII action in North Africa against the German Army, the British military returned to Egypt, being forced, out of necessity, to use it as a base for their fight against the German Army in the Western Desert. In 1947, with the war over, its forces were withdrawn into the narrow strip of the Canal Zone.

With the creation of the state of Israel in 1948 the Egyptian Government, in contravention of the Suez Canal statutes, began to search Israeli shipping using the Suez Canal which brought the usual ineffectual protests from the United Nations Organisation.

In October 1951, following Egyptian elections the previous year, the returned Wafd party reneged on the 1936 20-year Anglo-Egyptian treaty but were unable to persuade the British to move out which led to the party quickly losing its popularity.

On 23 July 1952 a group of Egyptian army officers led by a highly respected and educated major-general, Muhammad Neguib, and a colonel, Gamal Abdul Nasser, carried out a coup d'état in which king Farouk and his government were deposed. Because of his seniority and influence Neguib became Commander-in-Chief of the Army and, shortly afterwards, the Prime Minister. Nasser was appointed to the Minister of the Interior post.

Initially King Farouk's six-months-old son Prince Ahmed Fuad was made King under a regent for the purpose of indicating to the British that there had been no quarrel with the monarchy, only with Fuad's corrupt father. However, once the new regime was established without any protests or apparent action being taken by the British government this pretext was dropped and on 18 June 1953 the Egyptian monarchy was abolished, the young king deposed, and the country declared a republic with Neguib becoming Egypt's first president.

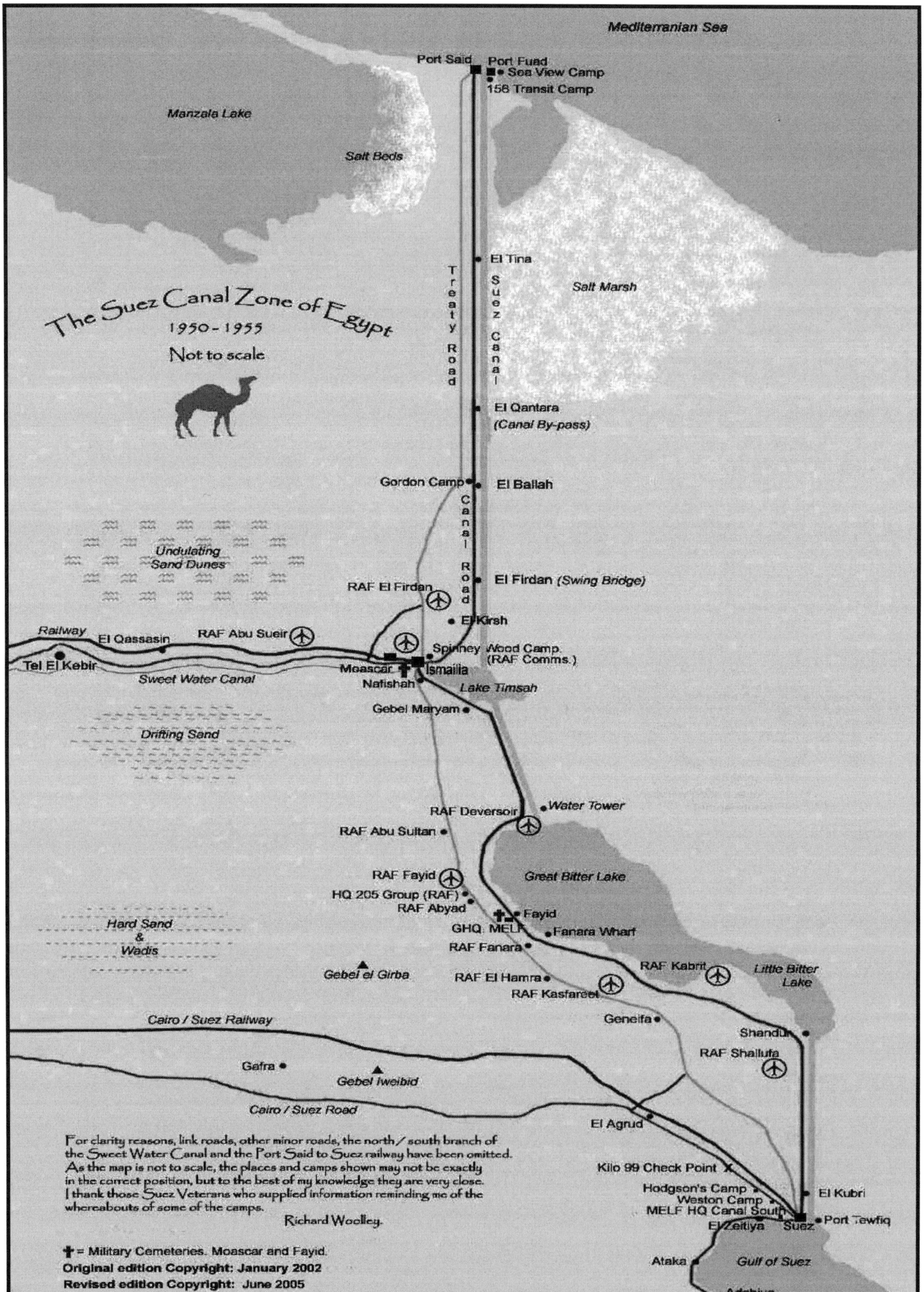

Map of the Canal Zone, 1951 - 1955. First published in Britain's Small Wars on the Internet. With many thanks to Dick Woolley, a member of the RAF at that time, for permission to use his excellent map.

King Farouk.

Major General Mohammad Neguib.

Colonel Gamal Abdel Nasser.

It wasn't long before the new regime began putting pressure on the British to finally withdraw from Egyptian territory. The British in response, once they had decided that they could relocate the headquarters of the Middle East Land Forces (MELF) from Fayid to Cyprus, finally agreed. In October 1954 the Minister of State for Foreign Affairs Harold Anthony Nutting on behalf of the British Government signed an agreement to gradually withdraw all of its troops from Egypt by 18 July 1956, which was more or less the date agreed upon in the original 1936 treaty.

It was Neguib's intention to quickly form an elected democracy but Nasser and his cohorts wanted to retain a military regime and on 14 November 1954 Neguib was deposed and put under house-arrest where he was to remain for the next 18 years. Colonel Nasser immediately took over as head of state.

Following the British Government's decision to pull its troops out of Egypt in 1954 a group of Conservative back-benchers led by Julian Amery created the Suez Group, a behind-the-scenes faction strongly opposed to this decision and privately in touch with Egyptian subversives, ousted royals, and disaffected military officers in a campaign to remove Nasser from power.

Also plotting Nasser's downfall at this time was MI6. Its intelligence at this time led it to believe that there were sufficient dissidents in Egypt, in Cairo particularly, to make this possible, especially if the British were to invade Egypt and destroy its Army. The reality of Nasser allowing this to happen however was just about nil, such was his overall popularity.

One of the items on Nasser's agenda for bringing Egypt into the twentieth century was the construction of the Aswan High Dam on the River Nile. This was intended to generate electrical power and also control flood waters for irrigating the Nile delta region. Another scheme was to modernise the country's armed forces so that it could defend itself and, Nasser dreamed, liberate Arab Palestine from the Jews who had seized a large part of that country in 1948.

The United States was approached and agreed to sell arms to Egypt but Nasser refused to accept the strings attached. Instead he went to the Eastern Block countries which led the Americans in particular to become extremely concerned about a relationship developing between Egypt and the Communists in the cold war climate beginning to escalate at that time between the NATO countries and the Soviet Union.

In September 1955 Egypt signed an arms deal with Czechoslovakia, yet two months later, despite this, the British and Americans, together with the World Bank, agreed to loan Egypt $70 million to help finance the dam project. In June 1956 the Soviets offered Egypt a loan of $1,200 million at an extremely favourable interest rate.

By now, however, Egypt's recognition of the Communist regime that had taken over in China had also become of considerable concern in the West and on 19 July the Americans and the British offer was withdrawn as was, consequently, that of the World Bank.

A week later, on the 26th with British troops at last out of the country, Nasser, during a three-hour-long speech in Alexandria, announced to a cheering crowd the nationalisation of the Suez Canal Company whose fees would help fund the construction of the Aswan High Dam. This announcement of *Operation Dignity and Glory* was the signal for a team of officials to move into the Canal Company Building and take over.

To appease the British and the French stockholders and their governments full compensation for shareholders, at the price listed on the Paris Stock Exchange at the moment just before the nationalisation announcement, was promised as was the free right of passage through the canal to ships of all nations. But on that very same day the Egyptians, contrary to the Canal Charter, actually prevented Israeli shipping from accessing the canal, the Straits of Tiran, and the Gulf of Aqaba.

Nasser tried to justify the nationalisation of the canal at that time by giving the date of the 1856 edict as the beginning of the Suez Canal Company's 100 years ownership which clearly made no sense at all. Payouts to shareholders of the company would not have begun until the canal was in operation and earning revenue. The 100 years actually began following the opening of the canal which was in 1869. The Canal Company's ownership of the canal was terminated then 13 years before the end of the agreed concession period stipulated by Viceroy Said.

However, even though this was the case, and despite most of the Suez Canal Company shareholders being British and French, it was, nevertheless, an Egyptian company since it had been registered in Alexandria. The fact that the company's headquarters building from where the share issue had been floated was in Paris had no bearing on the nationality of the company. Consequently, according to international law, the Egyptian government, in this case dictator Nasser, actually had the legal right to nationalise it. (See: Muddle in the Middle East, by Nikshoy Chatterji. Pub. Envoy Press, April 1987). When Eden was shown his advisors' report confirming that this was the case he shouted 'This is no f...ing good' and hurled it away from him.

So far as the Prime Minister was concerned, this seizure of the canal by Nasser, whom he absolutely loathed, was totally unacceptable. He had experienced first hand the consequences of the appeasement of Hitler in 1938, and saw Nasser's action as a threat to Britain's lifeline to Middle Eastern oil. On the 28th he retaliated by freezing all Egyptian assets in British banks.

British Prime Minister Sir Anthony Eden.

Instructions immediately went out to the War Office, Admiralty, and Air Ministry to prepare for an invasion of Egypt and by 2 August time-served regulars on reserve and ex-national service conscripts on AER were being recalled to the colours. General Sir Charles Keightley was put in charge of the whole operation but left planning to Lt-General Sir Hugh Stockwell, Task Force Commander of the Army. When Sir Dermot Boyle, Chief of the Air Staff, was given the news he was reported as saying to one of his colleagues that 'The Prime Minister's gone bananas: he wants us to invade Egypt.' (An Act of Folly, Jonathan Steele and Ian Black, The *Guardian*, Saturday 8 July, 2006.)

By as early as 8 August two alternative invasion plans had already been prepared. One was for the troops to occupy the twin towns of Port Said and Port Fuad at the northern end of the canal and the other was to have them land at Alexandria, make a rapid advance to Cairo where, hopefully, Nasser could be dealt with, and then cut across to the canal.

The Port Said plan was chosen first, then dropped in favour of the Alexandria assault, codenamed Hamilcar, which led to the letter H being stencilled onto British military vehicles. When it was found that the French spelt the word, Amilcar, it was replaced by the term Musketeer but with the H being left on all the equipment. Finally the planning staff reverted to the Port Said invasion.

In 1956 Port Said, was a town (city in British terms since it has a cathedral) whose built-up area, as seen on a street plan, gave roughly the appearance of a truncated right-angled triangle in which the short side formed the canal frontage and the beach served as its hypotenuse. With the base of this triangle on the south-west of the town measuring about one-and-three-quarters of a mile in length and the right-hand short side on the canal measuring just over a mile-and-a-quarter, the total built-up area of Port Said at that time, apart from various outlying commercial and industrial properties, sports grounds, utilities, and the prison, constituted a fraction over a square mile. El Gamel airfield is situated just off the map to the west of the cemeteries.

According to Dr Yahia Al Shaer the population of Port Said in 1956 was roughly 200,000 with about 75,000 of these being Europeans belonging to a range of ethnic groups from around the Mediterranean basin as well as the English and other northern Europeans. 'Port Said's life was orientated to the west with the influence of the French, Italian and Greek cultures being particularly strong and reflected several ways in the city life.

This relationship had in turn coloured the Port Said citizen, which made him differ from the rest of Egypt. Most Port Said citizens were Egyptian in a town that was not fully Egyptian as we lived with foreigners in our country. The Suez Canal Company owned all Port Fuad and its utilities including water and electricity and a substantial part of Port Said.

A Port Said citizen differed from the rest of Egypt as he spoke several European languages. Apart from [Arabic], English and Italian, he spoke French and Greek and maybe a couple of other languages. He never wore a Gallabiya, the national dress of Egyptians, unless he was a non-citizen of the city, mainly from the Fellahin or south Egypt… A higher standard of living than the rest of Egypt was due to the many foreign employees such as the British Army and Navy,

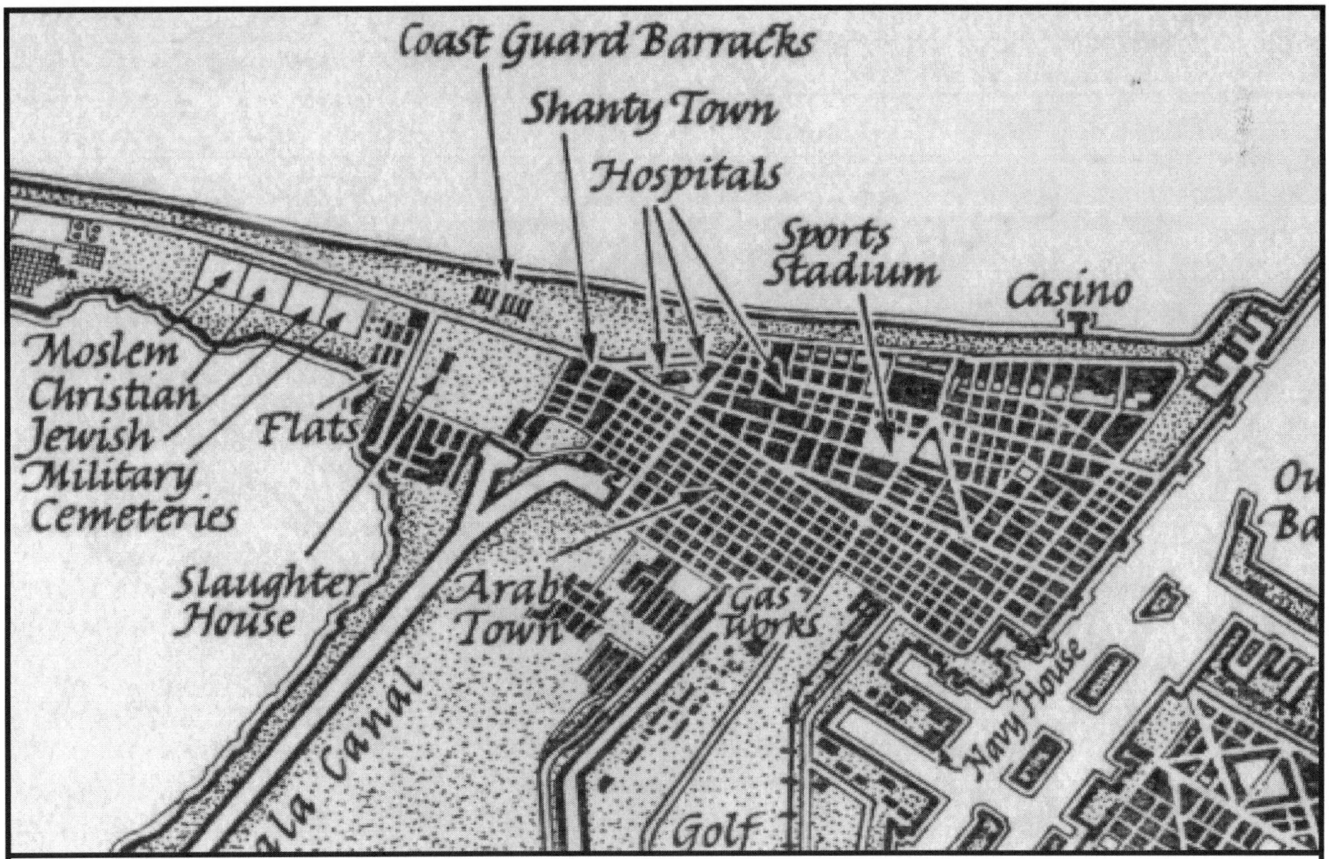

The map of Port Said in 1956 by kind permission of Roy Fullick and Geoffrey Powell from their book, *Suez The Double War* published in 1979 by Hamish Hamilton Ltd.

whose camps [had] dominated the southern half of the city.'

Meanwhile the British invasion build-up of men and arms continued throughout August. Large numbers of troops and equipment were soon pouring out from the UK to Malta and Cyprus. Other troops waited in holding camps in the UK for weeks on end shovelling coke and emptying dustbins.

Before the end of the month a small farm of kitset aviation fuel tanks was already being assembled at the tip of the Akrotiri Peninsula near Limassol in Cyprus, each one by a squadron of 37 Field Engineer Regiment, to increase the fuel capacity at the RAF base there. The fuel would be pumped to the tanks through a flexible pipeline from tankers anchored offshore. The tanks were completed by mid-September.

The fuel tanks at the Akrotiri Peninsula.

One member of the Cabinet not happy about the way things were going was, ironically, the Minister of Defence Sir Walter Monckton. On 24 September he sent a letter to Eden explaining that at the age of 65 he found the burden of his post too much to cope with and wanted relieving of this before Parliament reconvened in a month's time. 'I must frankly add that both in Policy Review and over Suez I have felt myself out of sympathy with many of my colleagues. It is this more than anything else which has lately made the work too much of an anxiety and coming on top of the rest has made this letter inevitable.' Monckton remained in the Cabinet so as not to embarrass or bring down the government but was shunted sideways to become Postmaster-General.

In his memoirs the British Minister for State Affairs Harold Anthony Nutting writing about Eden at this period, explained that: 'All the time here he was with this personal declaration of war against Nasser, but no means of putting it into effect. Although Nasser had nationalised the Suez Canal Company he hadn't given us any *casus belli*, he hadn't actually stopped a ship, or arrested a British subject, or shot anybody, or done anything which would give us the opportunity to go in and invade.'

The Manchester Guardian newspaper reported that the Suez Canal appeared to be operating as usual under nationalisation except for Israeli shipping not being allowed to use it. This at least gave the Israelis an absolutely understandable *casus belli* for invading Egypt if not the British and the French.

Eventually, however, it was the French who found a solution to the problem of finding a justifiable reason for attacking Egypt. They came up with a plan which they presented to their two partners in crime.

On 14 October two French diplomats arrived at Chequers, the Prime Minister's country retreat in Buckinghamshire. They brought with them a proposal that if the Israelis could be persuaded to attack Egypt from the east with the excuse that this was simply to gain their rightful access to the Canal under international law, then Britain and France could justifiably send troops into Sinai to keep the two warring sides apart. Britain could then occupy the Canal Zone in order to safeguard its security for world shipping. Eden loved the idea. He believed that this would so humiliate the Egyptians that Nasser would be driven from power. Nutting was present at the meeting at which, under Eden's instructions, no notes were to be taken.

Nutting found this collusion, of which only a chosen few in the cabinet were aware, quite unacceptable and suggested other ways of bringing Nasser down. Eden later rang Nutting and wanted to know, 'What's all this poppycock you've sent me about isolating and quarantining Nasser. Can't you understand - and if you can't understand it will you come to the Cabinet and explain why - that I want Nasser murdered? Much later in his diary Eden wrote that '... I had failed to remove Nasser from power like I had promised Nutting I would. I remember telling him how badly I wanted him destroyed, murdered, I didn't give a damn if there was anarchy and chaos in Egypt. Nasser needed to be knocked off his perch and I'll regret that I was not the one to do it until the day I die.' (Internet: Prime Minister Eden - Cold War Scrapbook).

Three years earlier in April 1953 while Eden was undergoing a gallstone operation a knife had apparently slipped and his bile duct cut. The surgeons were unable to repair the damage satisfactorily and from then on his health was never the same again. He began suffering recurrent infections and considerable pain, a condition which three further operations failed to rectify.

Eden's physician prescribed the drug Benzedrine to give him some relief without possessing a full knowledge of its side effects among which are 'insomnia, restlessness and mood swings.' It was later discovered that the Prime Minister had also been taking the barbiturate drinamyl which '...can impair judgement, cause paranoia and even make the person taking them **lose contact with reality.**' (Author's bold font). (Internet; Wikipedia, Anthony Eden, Health Issues.)

On 21 October the leaders of Israel, France and Britain, Ben-Gurion, Mollet and Eden, met in Secret to discuss the French proposal and decided this was the way forward. Three days later at Sevres on the outskirts of Paris the Foreign Ministers of France and Britain, Christian Pineau and John Selwyn Lloyd, met with Ben-Gurion to expand on the subterfuge. The Israeli Prime Minister agreed to the deception providing that the Egyptian Air Force was put out of action. The British agreed.

A few days later, on the 28th in Operation Kadesh, Israeli troops carried out the first phase of the plan and attacked Egypt across the Sinai Desert. On the 30th, after allowing the Israelis to advance well into Egyptian territory, Eden played the next part in the charade when he explained to Parliament that an ultimatum had been issued to the Israelis and the Egyptians that they must move back from the Suez Canal otherwise Britain and France would intervene to protect the waterway. The Israelis were ready to comply of course but Nasser, ordered to pull back his troops ten miles from the canal on his own soil naturally refused which of course was what he was expected to do otherwise the excuse to invade Egypt would be lost.

This invasion of Egypt by Israel led to Nasser ordering the arrest of some 1,000 Egyptian citizens who followed the Jewish faith, and the seizure of 500 businesses owned by Jews. He labelled them 'Zionists and enemies of the state'. In a move that brought back memories of Hitler's 1930's Germany Nasser ordered that 'Jewish bank accounts were confiscated and many Jews lost their jobs. Lawyers, engineers, doctors and teachers were not allowed to work in their professions. Thousands of Jews were ordered to leave the country. They were allowed to take only one suitcase and a small sum of cash, and forced to sign declarations "donating" their property to the Egyptian government. Foreign observers reported that members of Jewish families were taken hostage, apparently to insure that those forced to leave did not speak out against the Egyptian government. Some 25,000 Jews, almost half of the Jewish community left, mainly for Europe, the United States and South America, and Israel, after being forced to sign declarations that they were leaving voluntarily and agreed with the confiscation of their assets. Similar measures were enacted against British and French nationals in retaliation for the invasion.' (Wikipedia: Expulsion of Egyptian Jews, 1956).

In Britain, meanwhile, Nutting was unable to accept this corruption at the highest level in the government and on 31 October, despite Chancellor of the Exchequer Harold MacMillan trying to convince him that '... you will lead the party one day ...' he resigned without being able to explain to the Commons why, since this would have brought the Government down. And so a brilliant mind, and a person with the courage to tell the Prime Minister he was wrong, was lost to British politics.

On the same day the United States President, Dwight Eisenhower, talking about the Israeli invasion of Egypt, announced on television that '...We believe these actions to have been taken in error, for we do not accept the use of force as a wise or proper instrument for the settlement of international disputes....'

Eisenhower was not really averse to interfering in the politics of another country if it suited the United States but he was running for a second term in office in November and couldn't afford to get involved at that time. It was the Eisenhower administration that had been in power in 1953 when the CIA and MI6 between them orchestrated the 1953 coup-d'état in Iran. Less than two years after Suez, American troops were sent to Lebanon.

On the evening of the 31st the first RAF bomber, a Canberra from Cyprus, began the bombing of Egyptian air bases as the Israelis had been promised. Further bombing was carried out by Venoms from Akrotiri in Cyprus and Valiant bombers based in Malta. By 1 November the RAF was joined by Fleet Air Arm aircraft flying off aircraft carriers cruising some miles off the Port Said coastline. The Egyptian Air Force, whose pilots were not the best-trained and who never flew at night or in inclement weather, was soon no longer a threat.

Nasser retaliated to this further attack on the country by getting in touch with his Arab allies in Syria who then destroyed the oil pipeline belonging to the Iraq Petroleum Company which led to a terminal on the Mediterranean coast. All countries of Western Europe would now have to receive their reduced oil supplies via the long sea route around the tip of South Africa.

'On November 2, 1956 the First Sea Lord Admiral Mountbatten sent a letter to Prime Minister Eden telling him to stop the invasion before troops landed in the Canal Zone as the operation had already proved to be too costly politically. The next day Mountbatten made a desperate phone call to Eden asking for permission to stop the invasion before it began, only to be refused.' (Internet: Wikipedia, Suez Crisis).

In Europe on 4 November, with the world busy focussing on the Anglo-French-Israeli attack on Egypt, troops of the Soviet Union attacked Hungary with its Air Force and artillery pounding the city of Budapest its capital. The country would remain occupied for the next 35 years.

In a letter published in the *Times* newspaper, Lady Violet Bonham Carter, a member of the Liberal Party, wrote that 'I am one of the millions who watched the martyrdom of Hungary and listening to the transmission of her agonizing appeals of help (immediately followed by our "successful bombings" of Egyptian "targets") who have felt a humiliation, shame and anger which are beyond expression… We cannot order Soviet Russia to obey the edict of the United Nations which we ourselves have defied, nor to withdraw her tanks and guns from Hungary while we are bombing and invading Egypt. Today we are standing in the dock with Russia… Never in my lifetime has our name stood so low in the eyes of the world. Never have we stood so ingloriously alone.' (Internet: Wikipedia, Suez Crisis). She apparently voiced the feeling of the majority of the British population.

Even if Eisenhower hadn't had an election to think about, condemnation of the Russian attack on the people of Hungary on the one hand would have made it impossible for him to have supported the Anglo-British invasion of Egypt on the other. It was fortunate for him that he hadn't been made to do an about turn on this decision.

The British Government attempted to gag the BBC over the crisis with the Foreign Office trying to censor its Arabic Service broadcasts and Eden claiming that these were 'giving comfort to the enemy.' The Corporation refused to back down despite a threat that there would be future funding cuts to its budget.

As British troops were about to attack Egypt Eden made a broadcast in which he tried to justify the invasion. He feigned a conciliatory tone for the benefit of his BBC listeners but in reality his hate of Nasser was so great and his judgement so impaired, presumably by the medication he was taking, that he intended to make what in effect amounted to personal use of Britain's armed forces to topple him from power whatever the cost in lives - British, French, Israeli or Egyptian.

Opposition leader Hugh Gaitskell replied with the opposition point of view. Both broadcasts could be picked up on the transistor radios of confused squaddies in Cyprus and Malta and sailors aboard their ships as they waited to go into action.

Early on the morning of the 5th, Guy Fawkes Day, men of No.3 Parachute Regiment flying from Nicosia in Cyprus dropped on El Gamel Airfield on the western outskirts of Port Said to initiate the ground attack on Egyptian soil. At 13.45 hours a second wave of No.3 Para landed on the airfield together with more vehicles and supplies.

An hour-and-a-quarter later it seemed that the fighting might come to an end. At 3pm General Mogay, apparently the leader of the local Egyptian forces, contacted the French Paras and then Brigadier Butler, Commander of 16 Parachute Brigade, about negotiating a surrender. A ceasefire came into effect while talks took place and by the end of the afternoon terms had been agreed. However, it was already too late for three members of No.3 Para; Privates T A Barnett, T M Bates, and R W Sumners would not be returning to their parents. Unfortunately, for others in the Battalion and those who were to follow, Mogay claimed that he had notified Cairo of his decision to accept ceasefire terms but had been ordered to continue the defence of Port Said. The fighting resumed.

However, according to the late Keith Kyle in his book *Suez: Britain's End of Empire in the Middle East*, General Mogay had simply pretended he wanted a ceasefire in order to give his troops time to regroup. It was during this lull that the Russian Consul got involved and with a loudspeaker van had toured the Port Said streets encouraging civilians, including children, to take up arms against the invaders with the large stocks of Communist Block firearms that had just been released from a warehouse. He also gave encouragement by telling them that London and Paris

This was just one of the many piles of confiscated Russian/Egyptian arms and munitions that were later transferred in a fleet of trucks to the quay and taken out to sea where they were dumped. (Photograph Ronnie Hulton).

had been bombed by the Soviets. Once this re-arming had been achieved Mogay came back to explain to Brigadier Butler that Nasser had vetoed his ceasefire request, a request never made.

The following day the Marines landed on the beaches at the western side of the canal entrance. Chancellor of the Exchequer Harold MacMillan in a cabinet meeting had to report that there was a run on sterling which could lead to devaluation of the pound. Apparently the Secretary of the US Treasury, George Magoffin Humphrey, had just informed him that 'You ain't going to get another dime from us until you've gotten out of Suez.' (The Telegraph, 1 Nov 2006).

This, together with the fear of an Arab oil embargo and the pressure of world opinion, forced the cabinet and Eden to agree to a ceasefire, which came into effect at midnight on that day by which time a further dozen British troops had lost their lives.

The ceasefire failed to be observed by the Egyptians who kept up sporadic sniper attacks for the following six-and-a-half weeks until the Allies departed, the last ship, HMS *Duchess*, leaving the canal in the early hours of 23 November after waiting to see if the missing Lt Moorhouse was released and brought to the quayside. He wasn't; he was dead.

This was the day the ailing Anthony Eden and his wife left the UK for Jamaica and the holiday home of Ian Fleming, the creator of James Bond, to take a break from the pressures of office.

* * *

Ben Williams, RAF.

I was born at Preston, Lancashire, in January 1933, the last of three children. My father was what was known as a 'tackler' or loom overlooker in the cotton industry.

Shortly after I was born the family moved to Borrowash near Derby where Dad had taken a job with British Celanese at nearby Spondon which was experimenting with artificial fibres. Not long afterwards we moved to Macclesfield, the home of the silk industry, where I started school.

Shortly after the Second World War began in 1939 we moved again, this time to Middleton near Manchester where my father returned to the cotton industry. I went to Middleton Parish Church Primary School.

I remember the Manchester Blitz taking place and then my brother Stanley volunteering for service in the RAF. After training he was posted to a French Canadian Squadron at Middleton St George, an airfield just outside Darlington in County Durham which is now the Durham Tees Valley Airport. Here he became a flight engineer on Halifax bombers and commenced operations in June 1943. Two months later on his 13th operation during the night of 17-18 of August while on a raid on the Peenemunde rocket development site where the V1s and V2s were being built and tested, Stanley's aircraft was shot down and he was killed together with the pilot. The rest of the crew parachuted to safety and spent the rest of the war in a POW camp. Stanley was just 20-years-old when he died and Mum never got over his death.

In September 1943 while still only ten I joined my sister at Middleton Grammar School which was where, after joining the Train Spotters Club, I gained my first experience of chairing a committee. At 14, in pursuit of 'interesting' locomotives, I started cycling, which led on to youth hostelling and eventually to visiting places as far away as Lands End and Inverness. At 16 I became a racing cyclist, belonging to an 'illegal' organisation of mass-start racers frowned upon by the National Cyclists' Union.

I left school in the summer of 1949 when I was 16 and in August began work as an apprentice with Lancashire Dynamo and Crypto at Old Trafford, Manchester, one of the oldest Electrical Engineering firms in the world, and situated just across the road from Manchester United's football ground. While I was there Dad changed jobs again and we went to live in Swinton. At work, the management of LDC. decided that the apprentices should have their own organisation and I became its chairman for the rest of my apprenticeship. I also joined two youth clubs and ended up as leader of the one operated by the local authority. I also played league table tennis which I did for 57 years and also chaired one of the leagues I played in.

In September 1954, a month after the completion of my five-year apprenticeship I was called up for National Service and joined the RAF. After square-bashing at West Kirkby, a basic training camp on the Wirral, I was posted to Melksham in Wiltshire for electrical trade training. While here I purchased a 197cc Francis Barnett motorcycle which proved very useful for going home on leave and getting about generally.

By now I was also playing the trumpet so I joined the camp band. From this developed an interest in jazz, and with Danny a fellow band member from Bristol, I started going to jazz clubs. Fortuitously Danny knew the scene in Bristol and took me to an Ella Fitzgerald-Oscar Peterson concert at Colston Hall. Afterwards we went to the bar for a drink, thinking it likely that they would too. We were right. We spent the rest of the evening chatting to them since there were only two or three other people in there. Wearing a band badge on your uniform certainly helped to meet well known musicians.

At the end of my trade training at Melksham I was posted to RAF Binbrook in Lincolnshire which was a Canberra bomber base seven miles north-east of Market Rasen. From here I was sent on a Canberra bomber air electricians' course at English Electric's Samlesbury airfield, which is situated between Preston and Blackburn, and discovered that the instructor was a cousin. While I was there I saw Roly Beaumont, the company's chief test pilot, fly the then secret P1 Lightning aircraft at low level between the hangers.

Back at Binbrook I joined the Air Servicing flight until the 1st of September 1955 when I was attached to No.12 Canberra Squadron as a senior aircraftsman (SAC) and posted to Butterworth on the west coast of Malaya where our aircraft were used against the Communist insurgents. I took advantage of the many opportunities I was given to fly in the Canberra which I thoroughly enjoyed until the time when the bomb doors were opened and what had been a beautifully smooth flying experience became a rattling bumpy ride due the turbulence. We worked long hours but during any time off we were able to visit Penang Island just off the coast from Butterworth which was safe from the terrorists.

Ben's Squadron at Butterworth.

The squadron returned to Lincolnshire in March 1956 and not long afterwards the squadron received the freedom of Grimsby for our efforts in Malaya. For a while at Binbrook I did a bit of disk jockeying over the camp radio. Then, after Nasser's seizure of the Suez Canal in July we began preparing for the Suez crisis with the Canberras being loaded up with bombs to be flown out to Malta for stockpiling, a process which went on with increasing intensity. There was obviously no secrecy about what this was for so far as we were concerned. Being an electrician I was involved in servicing the aircraft on their return before they reloaded and flew out again.

Ben Williams.

Eventually, at about the end of August, we were put on standby for flying out to Cyprus, a time reduced to six hours by the middle of September. I was due for demob on the 20th and for a while I wondered if I was going to make it home since there was the possibility of a service extension. However on the 17th I received a letter from my parents indicating the imminent death of a relative. I showed the letter to my C.O. and he released me from service three days early.

A few weeks later the Canberras went into action bombing Egyptian airfields from bases in Cyprus. The only loss of a Canberra was that of a Mark 7 photo-reconnaissance aircraft on 6 November, the last day of hostilities. It was brought down by a Syrian Gloster Meteor.

The English Electric Canberra.

Back in Civvy Street I went back to Lancashire Dynamo and also met my late first wife Connie at a wedding. We married and went on to have our children Dave and Elizabeth. After a while I left LDC, went into industrial engineering with Colgate-Palmolive, then Lancashire Steel, later British Steel, and finally to local government with the city of Salford.

Running in tandem with all this was my involvement with youth work, the Lancashire Youth Club Association for which I was chairman of its Leaders Council, and a member of its executive Committee. I was involved in youth work for over 40 years.

In 1974, after the family developed an interest in canal cruising, we began fitting out a 40-foot-long steel narrow boat in which we were to travel virtually the whole of the canal system.

In 1981 I became a justice of the peace and sat for 22 years until I reached the age of 70, my sell-by date for this job. During this period, 1998, I lost my wife Connie and eventually remarried, to Jean, a widow who I'd known previously while we were organising youth activities.

We now give slide presentations to raise funds for charity, the main one being CRY, (Cardiac Risk in the Young) since my 11-year-old granddaughter died in her sleep. We are still using the 31-years-old narrow boat although not as extensively these days.

* * *

Geoffrey Baker, RAF.

I was born in Wallasey on the Wirral on September 6, 1933 and went to school there, first to Poulton Primary and then to Wallasey Secondary Technical School until I was 16.

Following the completion of my apprenticeship as an electrician I was called up by the Royal Air Force for my National Service in January 1955. After two or three days of the six weeks basic training at RAF Hednesford in Staffordshire I decided to sign on as a regular for three years since this would allow me to go on a course of my choice which was ground radar. I was also led to believe that after my training I would be given a posting where day-release to attend a technical college would be possible. This would enable me to qualify for a Higher National Certificate while in the forces and, of course, there was also the pay which was about twice that of a national service entrant.

At the end of the six-month ground radar course at RAF Yatesbury in Wiltshire I was posted to Fighter Command and immediately sent on a further three-month Nav (C) radar course, this time at RAF Locking near Weston-Super-Mare where I learned about state-of-the-art American-designed ground controlled approach radar equipment, This was pretty much the last of the sets using thermionic valves.

My first posting, in January 1956, was to RAF Linton-on-Ouse, some ten miles north-west of York where we had squadrons of Hunters and Canberras. In August I was posted to RAF Middleton St George near Darlington which was just in time for me to enrol for the start of classes at Middlesbrough Technical College so that I could continue with my studies.

RAF Middleton St George control tower.

However, this happened to be just at the time when the Government's preparations for Suez got serious. I'd hardly attended three or four weeks of classes and was on a short leave at home when a call came for all personnel to report to their nearest military base. The Fazakerly Army Barracks at Liverpool was mine so that was where I went. However, as soon as I saw the chaos there I just turned around and went home, making my way back to camp from there.

Shortly afterwards I was given a posting to Cyprus and sent to No. 5PDU (Personnel Dispersal Unit) at RAF Innsworth near Gloucester for the extra kit and inoculations I would need for the Middle East. On 17 October 1956 I flew out to Nicosia via Malta in what I think was a DC6. Here I was introduced to my new colleagues and a brand new MPN11a GCA mobile radar unit.

The MPN1a GCA mobile radar unit at Nicosia Airport.

Our function was to provide navigation assistance to aircraft, usually in the case of poor visibility, when the controller would give instructions to guide the pilot onto the runway.

Our mobile radar unit trailer was sited alongside the airfield's main runway in what was really quite open country. We felt that any danger the unit faced was not from the Egyptians but rather from George Grivas and his EOKA resistance organisation which was very active at that time.

On 4 November we watched quite a lot of activity on the airfield as quite a number of Valetta and Hastings transport aircraft were lined up alongside the length of the runway.

The invasion aircraft lined up by the Nicosia Airport runway.

The following morning they'd all gone. We quickly learned that they'd taken the Paras to drop on Port Said's El Gamil airfield. Following this I recall very little taking place that was out of the ordinary and I am not aware that our services were ever needed for real. I managed only two trips out of camp in my time at Nicosia since there was a problem; a gun was needed in order to leave camp and they wouldn't let you have one.

I flew back to the UK for personal reasons on 10 January 1957 and then continued my three-year service until I was demobbed from RAF Thornaby near Stockton-on-Tees in early 1958. My service with the RAF was an experience I'm glad I didn't miss. In fact it almost got me a job on the American early-warning DEWLINE project in Alaska but I decided to marry instead. It was 1960 before I obtained my HNC. Incidentally, I never did get my Suez medal.

I continued life in Civvy Street as an engineering draughtsman and then as an electrical distribution engineer with the South Eastern Electricity Board, from where I retired in 1993.

* * *

Keith Dagwell, RAF.

Keith was born in 1938 at Tunbridge Wells and brought up there. In 1954, after leaving school and knowing that National Service would soon be coming up, he signed on for four years with the RAF to learn a trade rather than risk being conscripted into the army. Four years was the minimum time needed for his requested option of an instrument technician's course.

After training Keith was assigned to the Joint Experimental Helicopter Unit (JEHU) based at RAF Middle Wallop in Hampshire. It was while he was here that the Suez crisis blew up and as early as 25th August the unit was instructed to make itself ready for 'overseas service'.

The Whirlwind S55 helicopters initially practised landing on a taped-out aircraft carrier deck on the Middle Wallop airfield then on the aircraft carrier HMS *Ocean* off Plymouth Sound from 29th September until 12th October.

On 27th October the *Ocean* sailed with the unit and its helicopters for Malta where it arrived on the 31st of the month. It was at this time the word experimental was dropped from the name of the unit and it became the JHU. On 3 November the carrier, with 45 Commando and 215 RAF Wing now aboard, sailed from Malta for the eastern Mediterranean.

By the morning of the 6th the vessel was lying a few miles off Port Said from where the ship's fleet of helicopters airlifted the men of 45 Commando ashore.

Soon afterwards, Keith's ground radar unit was ferried to the quayside and then trucked through the town to the captured airfield, running the gauntlet of sniper fire on the way. The JHU helicopters also ferried men and stores directly to the airfield from HMS *Ocean*.

Initially the men of the unit found themselves accommodated in the airfield's control tower buildings while they got on with the job of servicing the helicopters. Soon, however, they were re-

HMS *Ocean* approaching Port Said. Smoke from a Standard Oil storage tank hit by a rocket from a French jet.

Preparation of the helicopters.

The El Gamil airfield control tower buildings.

Servicing on the El Gamil airfield.

luctantly housed in rows of tents pitched close to the control tower building by a troop of army squaddies,

View of the tents from the control tower facing eastwards towards Port Said. The lighthouse seen in the distance.

View westwards from the back of the control tower; the Mediterranean on the right and the lagoon on the left.

When the unit was eventually withdrawn back to the UK Keith was one of those who sailed back on the LCT HMS *Ravager* with a number of their RAF helicopters as deck cargo. Some of these had had to be grounded since the body rivets were corroding rather badly under the marine conditions and were unfit for further flying until repaired. With one of the ship's engine not operating the journey though the Bay of Biscay in this flat-bottomed boat was a nightmare.

Immediately after his demob Keith joined Silver City Airways and by 1968 was working at Gatwick on the Vickers VC10. He later became an instructor in aircrew training on flight simulators until his retirement in 1997. However for a further twelve years he served as a consultant.

*   *   *

Terry Light, 3 Paratroop Battalion.

I'm a proud Bathonian of the green county of Somerset, born on Christmas Eve 1932, the same date, coincidentally, as my wife Olga although she arrived two years later.

For the first twenty years of my life I lived at home with my parents. My father was a clerk of works and also taught woodwork at one of the city's many public schools.

Mother kept the household running smoothly throughout the war even with the four young lady evacuees from London working for the Admiralty, part of which had been evacuated to Bath.

My primary school days at St Stephen's were happy ones although the main memory I have of this period was the Bath Blitz of April 1942 when nearly 500 citizens were killed during a series of moonlight German bomber raids when we slept in a Morrison shelter set up in the cellar.

With Father's school premises having been requisitioned for the duration the staff and pupils were moved lock, stock and barrel to Uppingham School in Rutland. Consequently we only saw him about one weekend a month during the war years.

In 1944 I started at the city's Grammar School which was the dominant academic and sports school throughout the mid-west country. The school during the four decades up to 1970 produced many famous old boys (called *Old Sulians*): Sir Roger Bannister the sub-four minute miler and neurosurgeon; Sir John Sawyers, diplomat and Head of M16; Sir Richard Roberts, scientist and Nobel Prize winner; and the Rt. Rev. C Morgan, Bishop of Colchester, to name just a few of those that excelled.

From grammar school I transferred to Monkton Combe School as a day boy and working pupil in the school gardens and farm with the ambition to make a career in agriculture or horticulture. We were taught the basics of animal husbandry and market gardening as well as the more traditional sixth form subjects.

From here I obtained a place at the Royal Agricultural College at Cirencester where it was play, sport and studying, although before I started here I went on a British Council Exchange Scheme to work and live at the Danish Red Cattle Breeding Centre based near Copenhagen, Denmark. This was real slave labour.

I completed my NDA in 1955 with thoughts of doing a tour with the Crown Agents as a livestock officer in East Africa. Farm Management in the UK did not look appealing since I considered employers such as farmers, land owners, and estate owners as a poor option in terms of job satisfaction and security. However the decision was taken out my hands with a sudden cultural and financial shock.

Back home the OHMS brown envelope had arrived. It enclosed a warrant for a one-way rail trip to York - do not pass go - and report, in July, to the Light Infantry Brigade HQ and Training Depot for potential officers at Camp Strensall. Shock! horror!

I wasn't interested in wearing the Queen's uniform and objected to this interruption in my planned career but there was nothing I could do about it. I suppose with my surname it had to be the Light Infantry.

At Strenshall I was put in a platoon of 16 from all parts of the country who were shouted at and seemingly chased about from dawn to dusk by moronic drill instructors. We were marched and countermarched at light infantry pace, 140 per minute, which is not easy for someone 6 feet 2 inches tall.

While here I passed the Unit Selection Board (USB) with the next step being the War Office Selection Board course (WOSB) at Barton Stacey in Hampshire. Four of us, over a period of days, were tested on initiative, leadership, military attitudes, etc., and went before the board. Of the four of us I was one of the two who failed. When I asked at the final board interview about my results the answer was something like ‘You have an unmilitary approach, you are not suitable yet as officer material but good luck!’

Back at Strensall my thoughts were that I didn’t want to be posted to a light infantry regiment on a boring UK or German posting so I applied for parachute duties – the parachute pay of two guineas per week would be useful – but without really knowing what I was letting myself in for. My father always warned me, ‘While in the Army do not volunteer for anything.’

I was accepted for the Pre-Para Course at Aldershot and later realised that the light infantry training had turned out to be a big asset.

I was physically and mentally fit otherwise I don't think I would have lasted the distance at Airborne Forces Depot to pass and thus proceed to No.1 Parachute School at RAF Abingdon. Without going into too much detail the training for me was a holiday camp but very professional, so I easily completed the mandatory eight jumps plus three more to fill in time while others on the course were catching up due to bad weather conditions.

Those of us who succeeded were awarded our wings and then, with no leave which we had expected, we were posted en-bloc to 3 Para at Aldershot.

We found Corunna Barracks in turmoil, with the Battalion on 72 hour’s notice to fly to the Middle East. Those of us ex-Abingdon were formed into a holding unit and tagged on to the companies consisting of regular troops. As I remember it I had no idea what was going on except it was the start of ‘an amateur serving amongst professionals.’

The Parachute Regiment was unique amongst regiments in that it did not openly recruit NS men since it was considered that by the time they become operationally useful the time for their demob was approaching. To my knowledge only some two to five percent of national servicemen served in operational units of 16 Independent Brigade. In my parachute training course at RAF Abingdon there was only one other infantry NS man and he was from the Royal Norfolk Regiment.

On completion of my parachute training I was posted with the rest of the regular army men on that course to 3 Para and then within 48 hours sailed to Cyprus. My papers only caught up with me later otherwise I think if they’d realised I was a national serviceman I may have been posted to a backwater unit in the UK.

This amateur soldier was trucked to Blackbushe Airfield where, with the rest, I was crammed into an RAF Coastal Command Shackleton, an aircraft designed for long range anti-submarine patrols. Usual story, the RAF couldn't cope with the requirements of the politicians so it was necessary to call upon aircraft outside Transport Command. On the flight to Cyprus we stopped for refuelling in Malta.

When we arrived at Nicosia it was not a sunny Cyprus but a wet and windy island. Soon after our arrival I was allocated to HQ Company, Intelligence Section, of the 3 Para Group, the Parachute Regiment. Our living accommodation was under canvas and on duck boards. This was to be our temporary camp for some months to come and consisted of mud and water everywhere, camp beds and kerosene lamps.

I can't remember the precise date but fairly soon after the nationalisation of the Suez Canal Company on the 26 July, we were taken off EOKA duties to start preparing for an operational drop. This included flying the full battalion back to the UK for intensive training which included a mass drop on Salisbury Plain. Then it was back to Cyprus for further field training including forced marches.

Meanwhile plans, maps and aerial photographic

prints came to the Intelligence Section from Brigade, the 16th Independent Parachute Brigade, for processing and briefings to be passed to the CO and the OCs commanding the assault companies. Changes to the original plan seemed to be taking place all the time. What I didn't know at the time was that RAF Transport Command were struggling to provide sufficient serviceable aircraft, Hastings and Valettas, to carry the required number of paratroops and their heavy equipment such as Jeeps and the 105mm anti tank guns, etc. Nothing seems to have changed even today. The lads in Afghanistan aren't provided with all the equipment they need to fight their war.

As soon as preparations began for the invasion drop itself we were confined to Camp Pegasus with the Royal Military Police guarding the exit from the outside and the Regimental Provost's lads on the inside. The Int, Sec. Tent, which contained a display of maps and aerial photographs being processed by the staff of seven, was deemed out of bounds except for those with a pass showing their 'need to know '.

In addition to this a censorship of all homeward bound mail was imposed in case someone belonging to HQ inadvertently disclosed our airborne destination.

As well as being involved in all this frenetic activity we had to prepare our personal kit which included weapons, ammo, field rations and, for us, additional maps and photos, all to be included in our canvas containers which were attached to each of us at the drop. However our personal equipment was lightweight compared to the weight in some containers such as those carried by the men in the mortar section of Support Company.

During the days and hours before the 5 November there was much speculation of where and when the mass drop would take place. There was also considerable discussion about a likely casualty rate but realistically each individual had his own private thoughts and fears. My recollections were: would the aircraft develop in-flight mechanical problems with me being trapped and unable to exit; once my parachute was open would I drift away from the DZ and land in the Mediterranean sea with my weapons container still strapped to my leg; would the aircraft be crippled by enemy fire

Aerial reconnaissance photograph, taken from the west, of El Gamil Aerodrome, the large rectangular area with the control tower buildings near the small dog-leg in the nearby road. Port Said in the distance. Photo 2 November 1956.

Aerial reconnaissance photograph of Port Said and Port Fuad. Note the fish dock at the top of the photograph, and the two canals coming in off the Suez canal to 'inland' wharves. Photograph taken on 2 November 1956.

with me trapped inside; would I land in an Egyptian minefield?

The night of 4/5 November was a bit of a blur and which I spent writing last letters to loved ones, killing time, and rechecking personal equipment until, during the early hours of the morning, we boarded the trucks to take us the short distance to RAF Nicosia. The aircraft I was to be on was the reliable four-engined Hastings, the workhorse of Transport Command. My bucket seat was No.13 on the port side and we flew out in the dark.

The four-engined Handley Page Hastings aircraft.

We jumped onto El Gamil airfield sometime about dawn with my exit to landing being seemingly over in seconds. Was I frightened? Yes of course I was. I can always remember being told in parachute training that the RAF would never expect jumps to take place from below 800 feet. The rumour mill at the time maintained that we exited from our aircraft over El Gamil at 600 feet. We later learned that this was indeed the case. This gave us barely time to check the parachute opening, release the personal weapons container, which was strapped to the leg, as we approached the ground, and still achieve an injury-free landing.

We were initially set up in the airport control tower. In addition to our Int Section the space seemed to be overflowing with senior officers such as the 2 IC, the Adjutant, the IO, the RSM plus other senior warrant officers and NCOs.

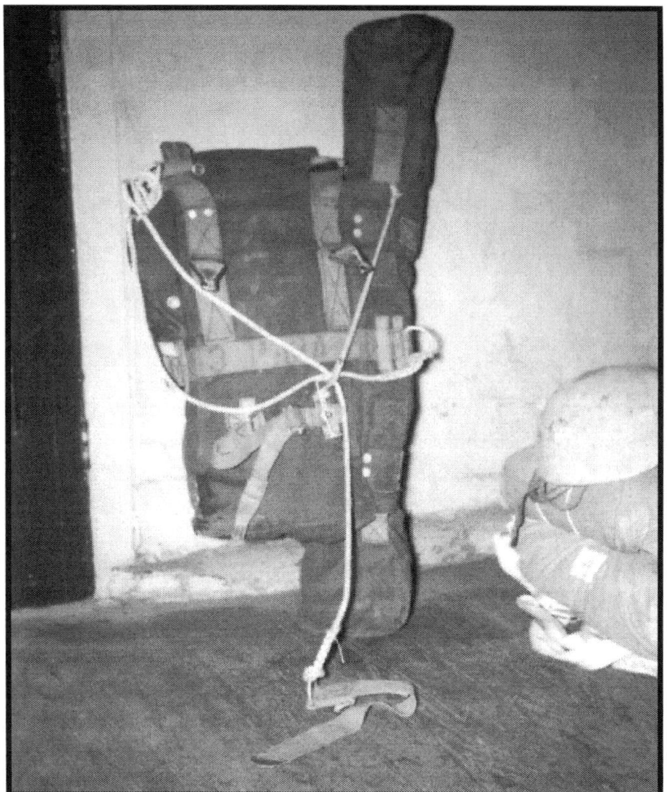

A personal weapons container. (Sandy Cavenagh photo).

The El Gamel Airfield control tower.

The sound of small arms fire and mortar bomb explosions continued all around the control tower and sometimes the thump of heavy ordinance. However I didn't feel particularly concerned since I knew that the assault companies were doing what they were best at which, at the moment, was securing the perimeter of the airfield then fighting their way towards the suburbs of Port Said through the sewage farm and the cemeteries

During the afternoon we received reinforcements when the members of D Company were dropped onto the airfield. They were followed later by the drop of heavy weapon containers and jeeps which floated down under canopies of parachutes.

When our assault lads were making their way into Port Said proper I led some members of the

A supply drop over the El Gamil airfield.

section to inspect houses and flats on the outskirts of the town for possible billets.

Towards the end of the first full day on Egyptian soil we established ourselves in a three to four storey building close to the edge of Shanty Town. There we always seemed to be held on standby expecting an Egyptian counter attack but which never materialised. The following morning, the 6th of November, HQ followed the continued advance of the troops through Shanty Town to the business and port areas.

When we eventually entered the built-up area of Port Said we found that other forces had come ashore from the seaborne landing and there were now Centurion tanks of the Tank Regiment positioned at strategic road junctions. From a lightly armed unit's point of view they were impressive metal monsters.

My enduring memory of being on Egyptian soil is twofold. The smell of rotting vegetation, sewage, burning material and other detritus, and the flies – the big black ugly brutes were everywhere. Being November the daytime temperatures were cool and the nights chilly so the flies were slow and easy to swat. But it didn't seem to make much difference since there were always more of them moving in.

Another distinct memory is of the activities of the Fleet Air Arm. The ground attack fighter-bombers, the Wyverns, were flying from HMS *Eagle.* These contra-rotating propeller driven dive bombers were impressive to watch as they circled in what I believe was called taxi rank formation up to 2000 feet above Port Said. A ground spotter would call up one of them to obliterate a troublesome Egyptian blockhouse or SU 100 self-propelled gun. The Wyvern would dive almost vertically towards its target, contra rotating blades emitting a distinctive scream, release its 1000 lb bomb onto the target and then, when I thought it would not pull out of its dive, it would flatten out and scream seawards. Very impressive! It was the equivalent of the German Stuka dive bombers of World War II.

Terry inspecting the remains of a Russian-built Egyptian SU 100 self-propelled gun near the flats.

Captured rocket launcher, arms and ammunition.

In my limited military world I was only vaguely aware of what was going on in the rest of the Port Said area. I remember seeing, during that first full day, the French paratroopers jumping from their Nord Atlas troop carriers although at dawn on the 6th I hadn't been particularly aware of the seaborne and helicopter assault by the other parachute battalions and the 3rd Commando Brigade.

Three Para Group's involvement, and therefore mine, in the Suez incident came to an end when we sailed back to Cyprus and Camp Pegasus to continue anti-terrorist operations against EOKA. Our return on what I think was the troopship *New Australia* was uneventful but when we docked at Famagusta in the hours of darkness the port area was floodlit with the quayside swarming with Military Police. As we disembarked we were searched to ensure that we were not concealing any 'liberated' souvenirs such as small arms which could have been sold or stolen to become part of the Island's terrorist arsenal. Before I disembarked I wondered why on the seaward side of the troopship I was hearing a series of splashes. It must have been our 3 Para lads offloading their souvenir weapons when they noticed the presence of the Military Police.

I think I can claim to be one of the few national servicemen to parachute into action as part of a mass drop. The El Gamil operation is still the largest mass drop by the British Army since World War II.

Those of us who'd been in the holding unit on our initial arrival from the UK were now allocated to various companies with me joining HQ Intelligence Section. The space in its marquee was devoted to maps and aerial photographs of the Island so that in a fairly short time I knew more about the topography of Cyprus than of the UK. The Section was ruled by a benevolent senior sergeant who had seen service throughout North Africa, Italy, Greece and then Palestine during the months before the birth of Israel.

The original Intelligence officer had left soon after I joined with his replacement being Lt J Burke. From my observations as a relative outsider 3 Para seemed to be 'managed' by the old sweats of the WO & Sergeants' Mess. The personnel of the Commissioned Officers' Mess were constantly changing as individuals completed their tour and returned to their parent unit. During the 1950s it was not possible to obtain a commission directly into the Parachute Regiment, officers were seconded from their parent unit.

In my little world I was made a junior NCO and therefore became involved in organizing the issue of operational maps and instructing new arrivals on the basics of map reading. I was even sent on an Aerial Photographic Interpretation course at nearby RAF Akrotiri.

All the 3 Para companies were heavily committed to anti-terrorist EOKA operations together with the occasional guard duty at Camp K where captured and therefore suspected local terrorists were interrogated.

During these operations there were successes, disappointments and accidental fatalities. A tragic series of fatalities was caused by the forest fires in the Troodos Mountains in which men from 3 Para died from smoke and fire.

My final months of service in mid-1957 based at Aldershot consisted of dull routine garrison duties but for the visits of two dignitaries. Bull with the Paras had always been practically non-existent since we had to be prepared to go anywhere and anytime at short notice. Therefore preparing for high profile parades with drilling and equipment-cleaning proved a painful experience.

One pleasing memory is of an initiative exercise in which we had to make our way, self-contained, from Aldershot to Dartmoor without spending any money. To prove that we had passed through various points we had to obtain the signature of the Postmaster at Shaftesbury, the signature of the Mayor of Honiton, and post a picture postcard of Dartmoor from the Cranmere Pool post box on the moors.

During July 1957 I was demobilised from mandatory full-time military service and posted to 10 Para, Army Emergency Reserve.

I commenced my career in the Agricultural Division of Pfizer Ltd, a multi-national US Pharmaceutical Company. Although this was not hands on farming it was the next best well-paid opportunity.

A big plus to come out of my short time in uniform was meeting a young lady from Newcastle upon Tyne. I met this lovely girl called Olga Thompson and corresponded with her over the next two years which culminated in our eventual marriage in January 1958. That was over 53 years ago so something very positive came out of compulsory military service.

After our marriage we lived in a flat in the Northern Ireland seaside resort of Bangor after which there were frequent moves around the UK following either promotion or changes of Employer. Among my various appointments were Technical & Training Manager, General Sales Manager, Marketing Manager, and Marketing Co-ordinator. Later we moved back to my home city of Bath where I joined a new employment culture by becoming a civil servant for my final years of employment.

During our retirement we are busy with our six grandchildren, three great-grandchildren and I also spend my time beekeeping, exam invigilating at local schools and on committee work with the Old Sulians.

* * *

Roger (Ginger) Clare, 3 Parachute Battalion.

We left the UK for Cyprus on 13 January 1956 in what I think was either a Shackleton or Hermes aircraft from Blackbushe Airport in Hampshire which various charter operators used for their trooping runs under contract to the government.

On our arrival at Nicosia Airport we were trucked to Tunisia Camp where we were installed in tented accommodation. After a while though, with January being the middle of winter, it became very wet underfoot so that we were soon up to our necks in thick yellow-brown mud. After a few weeks we moved to another tented camp situated to the rear of RAF Nicosia. From here we spent a lot of time on exercises or on patrols in the Troodos Mountains searching for EOKA terrorists.

After dark on 24 October we went out on Operation Foxhunter, yet another search of the Troodos area, which included the notorious pro-EOKA Kambos village and other small settlements. On the 29th Israel invaded Egypt and immediately a flurry of rumours started to circulate around the battalion regarding our next move. It soon seemed apparent that the British would become involved and towards the end of the afternoon we set off back to Nicosia. The following day we began our preparations, checking our gear, being issued with extra ammunition, magazines for the Bren gun, and ration packs, etc. It was obvious that something was up.

On Saturday the 3rd of November, Colonel Crook addressed all the other ranks in a large Nissen hut and announced that we were going to 'jump' into Port Said. Our task, he told us, was to capture El Gamil airfield on the western outskirts of the town.

As we continued with all the preparation that was necessary we could hear the howl of the RAF jets at the nearby airfield. These were the Hawker Hunters taking off to patrol the Cyprus sky and the Canberras departing to bomb the runways of the various Egyptian airfields to prevent their air force from interfering with the invasion.

On Sunday, 4th November we were driven the short distance to the airfield for a final rehearsal, each stick of paratroopers in its own truck matching its own aircraft. All our gear was laid out for inspection by the stick sergeant and our parachutes individually adjusted before being placed back on the correct seat in the aircraft.

After breakfast in the very early hours of the 5th we returned to the airfield, this time for the real thing, and boarded our Valetta aircraft, 20 to a stick. Also being used to transport some of the 600 men of 3 Battalion's A, B, and C Companies, plus small attachments of other units such as the sappers, were a number of Hastings aircraft, each able to carry sticks of 30. There were 26 aircraft in all. Just before we took off at about 5.15 the captain came through and told us that we would be flying at 800 feet and that the flight would take us about two hours.

We jumped at about 7.15 am and took some cas-

Sgt Major Chippy Robinson helping with preparations before boarding the aircraft.

ualties during the drop and then on the ground during the hour or so it took us to secure the airfield perimeter and take a few prisoners.

Exiting a Vickers Valetta aircraft from a static line.

Fierce fighting then continued eastwards as we made our way towards the town, clearing the Egyptian soldiers who were facing us, first in the sewerage works and then in the various ethnic cemeteries. Eventually we reached the blocks of flats at the western edge of Port Said.

Drop zone. El Gamil Airfield with control tower buildings on the left. Beyond are the sewerage farm, the cemeteries, the group of apartment blocks (the flats), and then, at the edge of the built-up area of Port Said, Shanty Town.

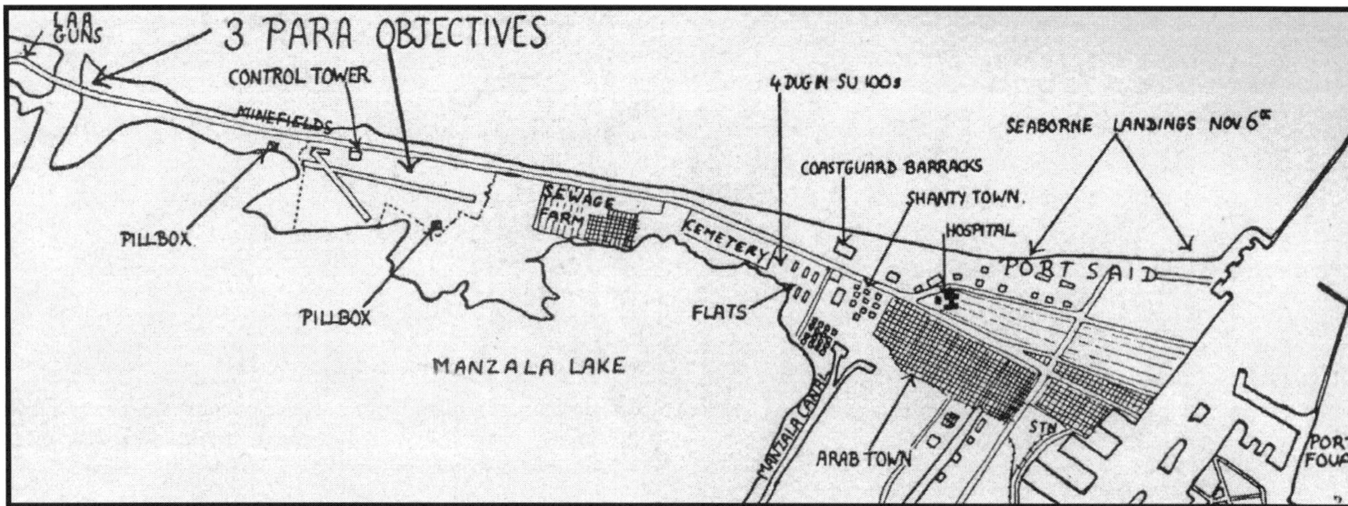

Map of the 3 Parachute Battalion objectives, El Gamil Airfield and beyond. (Map Sandy Cavenagh).

* * *

Brian Wilson, 2 Parachute Battalion.

No.2 Parachute Battalion sailed to Cyprus for security duties against EOKA in July 1956 on the troopship *Empire Ken*.

Some of the lads in the camp in Cyprus.

Lads of 2 Para waiting to board ship at Famagusta.

The Cyprus invasion fleet sailing for Port Said.

Entering the Suez Canal between the breakwaters. Smoke on the right rising from El Gamil Airfield.

Waiting for orders at Port Said quay. Brian at the front.

By the ceasefire 2 Para had advanced down the canal to El Cap where they dug in.

View south along the Suez and Sweetwater canals from the El Cap signal box.

View north from El Cap in the Port Said direction.

No.2 Parachute Battalion returned to Cyprus on 14 November to continue its security duties against Eoka.

* * *

Roger Alma, Royal Artillery, 33 Para Regiment

I was born in Edmonton, North London, in 1937, lived as a child in World's End Lane between Winchmore Hill and Enfield, and was educated at Enfield Grammar School.

After leaving school at 18 my National Service began in February 1956 with basic training in the Royal Artillery at Oswestry, Shropshire. For a grammar school boy coming from a working class background it was something of a culture shock to meet people from all over the British Isles and from all walks of life.

I had been warned never to volunteer for anything in the army. I did the opposite and had a wonderful time. Towards the end of basic training I volunteered for the Airborne Brigade and spent a tough and exhilarating month in Aldershot, firstly with the Artillery selection unit and secondly, in June with the Airborne Forces Depot Training Company, to qualify for parachute training. I found that my time at Abingdon was like a month at Alton Towers, and being awarded my 'wings' was one of the proudest moments of my life.

At the end of my training I joined 56 Battery of the 33rd Parachute Field Regiment, Royal Artillery, and had only just settled down into regimental life at Lille Barracks on North Camp at Aldershot when the Suez crisis suddenly changed the face of politics in the Middle East.

In August the regiment, under the command of Lt Col Guy Fawkes DSO MC, embarked on the aircraft carrier HMS *Theseus* at Portsmouth and, as part of the 16th Independent Parachute Brigade, sailed for Cyprus, stopping briefly at Malta on the way.

HMS *Theseus* at Malta.

We landed in Famagusta from where we were trucked to our base in Nicosia. The next couple of months were spent in training and on anti-terrorist operations, mainly in the north-east of the island, until we were brought back to camp to prepare for the invasion of Egypt. We were disappointed not to be among the units parachuted into Port Said, sailing instead on the LST *Charles McLeod* which was currently serving as a troop carrier.

As an assistant to Major Oldham the 56 Battery Commander I attended an 'O' or order group meeting at which the military situation was discussed. The information about the dispositions of the Israeli and Egyptian armies released at the meeting seemed to me at the time, and has proved to be the case since, firm evidence of the collusion that took place between the British, French and Israeli governments.

The approach by sea to Port Said was quite dramatic with columns of smoke rising above the city from burning oil installations and buildings damaged earlier in the day during the street fighting. By the time we arrived in the entrance to the Suez Canal on November 6 the town had already been secured. Consequently we were able to land unopposed near the statue of Ferdinand de Lesseps from where we were driven straight through Port Said, together with 2 Para and 6 Royal Tank Regiment, and southwards to El Cap where, to our frustration, we were brought to a halt at midnight by a ceasefire agreement coming into effect.

We settled down in the El Cap railway station, which became the Battery HQ. The view southwards was towards the Egyptian defensive positions in the distance at El Qantara.

The view south from the signal box.

The canal station mast was built somewhat like that on a ship with a crow's nest half way up which served as a useful observation post. We renamed the signal box Newcastle Central.

The renamed signal box at El Cap with Geordie Carr.

Not far from us across the canal, soldiers of the French Foreign Legion had also dug themselves in. Initially they kept mainly to themselves until someone arranged an 'international' football match which was then followed by a concert.

To further help pass the time some more entertainment was improvised. We held a regimental cross-country race in which the major obstacle was the Suez Canal. Being a poor swimmer I had to kick off my plimsolls to save myself from drowning and was forced to run the last five miles in bare feet. I decided not to take part in the regimental swimming gala.

While here I also managed to receive some driving lessons but these came to an abrupt end when I nearly ran over several officers of the Royal West Kent Regiment who had just arrived at the station. I made the mistake of laughing when they scattered and was lucky to avoid being put on a charge.

The arrival on the opposite canal bank of some Egyptian survivors of the fighting in the Sinai Desert, enlivened proceedings one day. Having retreated from the Israeli forces across the desert it must have been a shock to them when almost home to have our sentries let off a few warning shots. Fortunately none of them was hurt.

The only Egyptian I met while at El Cap was the young, shy and lonely assistant station master who had remained behind at his post when all the other villagers fled their ramshackle village before we arrived. No one at the time seemed to think he was a danger but looking back I wonder if he was a very clever spy.

The El Cap assistant station master.

With the arrival of the UN Force we returned to Port Said where we embarked on the RMS *Ascania* and sailed for home.

When we arrived in England the whole regiment was paraded in a cavernous customs hall. The customs officers were very kind. Not one of the kitbags and packs stuffed with contraband was inspected. The next solders to arrive home a week after Christmas were not so lucky.

Following home leave, during which I discovered much to my astonishment that there had been considerable political controversy about the Suez invasion, I rejoined the regiment in Aldershot. Here we were re-equipped with 4.2 inch mortars, sent off for training manoeuvres on Salisbury Plain, and given a new name – the 33rd Parachute Light Regiment, Royal Artillery. Shortly after this I was promoted to acting lance bombardier and also successful in being selected for officer training at Mons Barracks after which I left my friends in the airborne artillery for a new phase of my military career.

Roger Alma, second from left, passing out at Mons.

After passing out at Mons I had only three months left to serve and spent this time agreeably at the Royal Artillery depot at Woolwich as a fairly useless second lieutenant. I experienced some interesting encounters as orderly officer which included collecting a group of my old friends of 33 Parachute Field Regiment from the local police station. They had been arrested for disorderly conduct in town after a few beers but in transit back to camp they were no bother at all. 'It's funny calling you sir,' one of them chuckled. I don't think the local policemen would have found it so easy to take them into custody had the lads put their minds to being awkward.

There was a final twist to my service when, in the last two weeks, I was transferred to the short-lived Mobile Defence Corps, a unit set up to give assistance to civil defence in the event of nuclear warfare. After lectures on the devastating power of hydrogen bombs we were taught how to bandage a broken arm and given stirrup-pump drill. It was all rather surreal.

I declined to join a Mobile Defence Corps TA when I returned to civilian life in February 1958 to pick up an academic career at Queens' College, Cambridge, reading English. My army boot however continued their service for years.

* * *

Sandy Cavenagh, RAMC.

I was born in 1929 in the village of Kempsey near Worcester where my father was an ears, nose and throat surgeon. He had qualified as a doctor in 1915 and gone straight into the Army just in time for the battle of the Somme followed by Ypres. He finished the war with an MC and bar.

Our firmest friends in Kempsey were Hugh and Betty Jefferies and their son Acton who lived in Napleton Grange, an imposing black and white house going back to 1440, which had previously been occupied by Elgar for a few years during the mid-nineteen twenties.

Our first introduction to grief was when Acton was killed on 19 May 1940 while tackling a group of German parachutists near Lille during the invasion of France.

At the age of nine I was sent to the Downs School in Colwall which was just some six miles away on the other side of Malvern. This was a Quaker establishment – strong on music and art which became a lifelong joy – but with a pacifist and moral slant which could be oppressive. Eventually it was almost a relief to go on to Winchester where misbehaviour was dealt with by a beating if necessary.

I was a very weak performer in ball games, the river and rowing being my chief joy. Later, during medical school at Oxford, I went on to lose two boat races which inured me to failure.

St Thomas's Hospital in London followed since I had unquestioningly pursued the same training programme as my father 40 years previously. I spent a year there until my time as a house surgeon was drawing to a close with National Service looming.

I wondered whether to sign on for three years in the Royal Army Medical Corps instead of the compulsory two. I was tempted since Barbara and I were about to get married. Pay and married quarters favoured those on a three-year engagement. So, a week later, I went to the War Office and chose the option of a three-year short-service commission as a medical officer, and the possibility of specialisation.

At Waterloo Station on the day I reported for service early in 1956 I happened to meet David Hartley, a friend and contemporary from St Thomas's who was being called up in the same intake. 'Bet we spend the whole blooming time in Aldershot,' he had said as the train whirled us away. So we passed the whole of the journey devising means of escape from this humdrum fate.

At that time the Army attempted the heroic and impossible task of converting newly recruited doctors into officers and gentlemen in the space of a fortnight. At the Royal Army Medical Corps depot at Crookham a whirlwind series of lectures covered, in theory, every aspect of military administration. Meanwhile patient instructors taught us the elements of drill, saluting and even a little weapon training.

Quite early in our time here we received a lecture from John Kilgour, the charismatic OC of 23 Parachute Field Ambulance who attempted to persuade us that our 'humdrum fate' could be avoided by joining his unit. Consequently David and I ended our first week of training at Crookham by volunteering for airborne training together.

Three weeks later I was handed a telegram, 'report Maida Barracks Aldershot Monday April 23rd for airborne training.' This was for the Parachute Selection or 'P' course. The 'P' course was designed not so much to test fitness as mental stamina or determination. The technique was simple. Make everyone tired then get them to do something they dislike or are normally afraid of. Repeat this daily for ten days, and soon the potential parachutists can be picked out fairly easily.

To get tired we ran along the endless straight avenues of Aldershot and the tank tracks in Long Valley then uphill back to the barracks. A few minutes pause, and into the huge Maida gymnasium for PT and 'milling'. During milling two men of equal weight and wearing boxing gloves were put into a ring and left to knock hell out of each other for two minutes. You had to show that you could take it even if you couldn't give it. Following this we doubled down the road to the swimming baths where even non-swimmers jumped from the 15-foot board and then again, somersaulting in backwards.

After lunch, which we were almost too tired to eat, we went to the 'Trainasium' in the beech woods to take the course along high platforms, scrambling nets, scaffolding, cables and ropes, etc., among the branches. The instructor said 'Go!' and you jumped. Simple, applied Pavlov; the conditioned reflex! On an assault course I dropped a 12-foot log onto my toe. The nail separated and had to be removed by the depot Medical Officer. It looked like the end of 'P' course for me. However, two days later we were informed that about half the course had passed and I was among them.

The survivors of 'P' course reassembled at Abingdon three days later for the parachute course. However, I had begun to feel ill during my last few days at Aldershot and now I was feeling iller. I reported sick and was quickly diagnosed as having contracted glandular fever.

There was a shortage of parachute-trained doctors when I fell sick at Abingdon. My friend David Hartley who had passed the 'P' course with me was summoned from a hygiene course he was on and leap-frogged into my place. He completed his parachute training in a fortnight and flew out to Cyprus shortly afterwards to join '1 Para' the first battalion, proudly wearing his wings.

After convalescing for a month I joined the 23rd Field Ambulance in Aldershot under Lt Col Kilgour, who had encouraged me to join his unit in the first place, and continued routine training with his medical unit. Then, at the end of July, Nasser nationalised the Suez Canal.

A great tide of reservists returned to the Parachute Brigade and four days after the Canal had been seized we set sail for Cyprus aboard HMS *Theseus*. Before leaving Portsmouth we had been assembled on the flight deck for an address by the Brigadier, M A H Butler DSO MC, about what to expect in Cyprus. The deck itself was covered with 3-ton lorries, ambulances, and Champs and their trailers lashed into position in neat rows. A mere five days after leaving Portsmouth HMS *Theseus* had anchored off Famagusta on the east coast of Cyprus.

We went ashore and drove in open lorries through the blazing morning heat to Nicosia. John Kilgour took me on one side. 'I've just been on the telephone to the 3rd Battalion adjutant. You're to join them tomorrow. They've not had a medical officer now for a month.'

But only four days after arriving in Cyprus I flew home with 3 Para. The battalion was being taken off EOKA duties to brush up its airborne training in preparation for an operational drop. Its Medical Officer did not know how to jump at all and I went off to Abingdon while the rest of the battalion took part in a mass drop on Salisbury Plain.

At Abingdon regular soldiers spent a month over their eight descents. The Territorials compressed them into a fortnight. I found myself being directed from squad to squad in order to get it all over in time to return to Cyprus with 3 para.

After Abingdon there had been a few days of exquisite leave. Then a rainy afternoon found me on an open lorry driving to Blackbushe airfield near Aldershot. The battalion was returning to Cyprus and we flew through the night aboard a Hermes airliner.

Early in the year the 1st and 3rd Battalions had flown out to Cyprus to be held ready for a drop in Jordon where 'British lives and property' were once more in jeopardy. But the Jordon alarm had fizzled out. We should have flown home but the Governor of Cyprus, General Sir John Harding, asked for the Parachute Battalions to stay to combat Eoka. And so, from time to time, we would all depart on internal security operations to combat this ever-present threat..

On 29th October 1956, for her own ends, Israel launched an all-out attack on the Egyptian forces in the Sinai Desert and reached the Suez Canal in four days' fighting.

Then Britain and France issued an ultimatum to Israel and Egypt. Their forces were to withdraw ten miles to east and west of the Canal or the Anglo-French forces would intervene. Israel agreed, but Egypt had not yet acknowledged the ultimatum. If the objectives of recovering the Canal for its owners and deposing Nasser were to be achieved there would have to be recourse to arms.

On Tuesday 30th of October the officers were summoned to a Company Commander's conference. Major Lawrence Scragg told us that we were going to load for an Airborne Exercise. It's just like any other loading exercise,' said Lawrence, 'but it's got to be right this time.'

The fiction that this was a loading exercise was short-lived. By the middle of the week two additions to the battalion suggested something more urgent. The first of these was a section of the 23rd Parachute Field Ambulance with three medical officers. The other major addition to the battalion was the sappers. A troop of them were attached to us from 9 Squadron, the Independent Field Squadron of Royal Engineers with the Parachute Brigade.

On Thursday, 1st November, the night that the extra troops arrived, the officers of what was now '3 Para Battalion Group' were bidden to an 'O' Group by the Colonel.

'If this show is on,' Colonel Crook began, 'and it's by no means yet certain that it is, this is the 3 Para role. We are going to Port Said.' We were going to jump onto El Gamil airfield just to the west of Port Said where, according to Intelligence, we would be outnumbered five to one. In forty minutes the disposition of the battalion and the battle we were to fight was all made clear. Not until Saturday, 3rd November, did the soldiers know the details of what was planned.

The twenty-seven strong 'armada' of transport aircraft being prepared to take us to Port Said was made up of part-worn Valettas, each carrying twenty men, and Hastings each carrying thirty. It represented the entire available transport force of RAF Transport Command. Then one of the Valettas went u/s.

When our personal packing was almost finished we did a furious session of 'synthetic' training. We practised rolls on some very hard mats and exits from a makeshift dummy fuselage. Then it was over to the airfield where we performed aircraft drill under the vigilant eye of a Royal Air Force sergeant instructor. The Valetta, sitting on the tarmac in the midday sun on Nicosia airfield, was like an oven. The stick of parachutists emplanes in reverse order to that of jumping and this led to some confusion and the sergeant becoming somewhat exasperated. Then we received the news that the operation had been brought forward 24 hours to Monday the 5th November.

The exasperated RAF sergeant.

On Sunday the 4th the battalion held a drumhead service and the afternoon was devoted to a rehearsal. Each stick of parachutists was driven over to the airfield in a chalk-numbered truck to the corresponding chalk-numbered aircraft waiting on the perimeter track where we hauled our absurdly heavy personal containers out of the truck and laid them in neat lines on the dusty ground. Then we collected the parachute packs off our seats in the aircraft and fitted them on outside, adjusting the buckles of the harness to a snug fit. After that the parachutes were replaced on our seats. The weapons containers were stacked in the aisle down the centre of the aircraft. Everything was ready.

The Sims weapon container being demonstrated.

We were up for breakfast on Monday the 5th at 0115 hours. Then 'Chalk 7' reassembled by the truck and we were taken to the airfield where we prepared to emplane. We checked our helmets under Sergeant Crompton's gruff supervision. Then the sergeant called the nominal roll and finished off with the words, 'Before we emplane I have to warn you that the green light constitutes an order to jump.' Then we went aboard.

Once in our seats the captain of the aircraft came

Some of the lads aboard one of the aircraft.

aft to address us. 'We shall fly at 800 feet over the sea and come down to 600 to drop you. I'll cut the slipstream down as much as possible over the dropping zone.' We settled back in our seats for the two hour flight.

'Prepare for action!' The shouted instruction brought us all to our feet as the dispatchers lifted off the door. The webbing strops were run along the cable and we hooked our static lines to them. Then we hitched on the ponderous weapons containers and finally we 'told off'. 'Twenty okay.' 'Nineteen okay.' And so on down the stick.

'Red on. Stand in the door.' The red light shone for ages before the green light flashed. Sergeant Crompton and the next two men had jumped before I realised it. I shuffled after the corporal towards the doorway. Then my turn. Left hand round the edge of the door. Right! Into the slipstream and falling away.

There came a sag of deceleration as the parachute opened. No one near me! Rat-tat-tat from below and the sound of firing from all directions. Never heard so much shooting. I thought we must be giving them hell but in fact the first sticks had barely landed and all the firing was at us.

SMACK! A great whiplash in the right eye and my container fell away. I raised my hand to the eye. No blood but a white fog. Then the ground was coming towards me. I remembered to keep feet and knees together, made a light landing, and rolled. I looked around and found my equipment container had landed only 30 yards away.

The defenders were dug in and had several machine-guns sited to cover the airfield. The only cover of any sort was provided by rows of empty 40-gallon oil drums placed to stop aircraft landing. With thanks I thought of the 'B' Company boys who were between me and the enemy as I ran over to collect my container. I retrieved my battered perforated Bergen rucksack from the container which had fallen free for 500 feet. A small hole penetrated the bottom and there was a larger one in the flap at the top. The suspension cord of the container was severed and molten at the end. It had fallen free through enemy action, not my own incompetence.

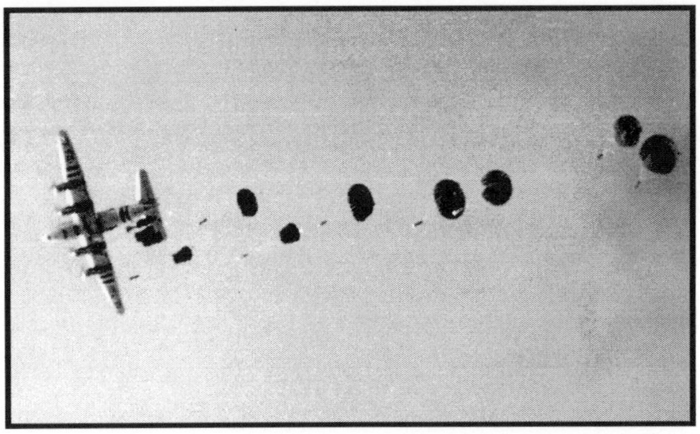

As I sat on the ground and elbowed my way into the rucksack straps I looked up to where the Hastings, flying in pairs, were coming in to drop their loads amidst more or less accurate ack-ack fire. That must have been what hit me. I lumbered off westwards towards the control tower buildings.

The first men landing at the airfield

Men of 3 Para taking cover behind oil drums

Behind me 'B' Company was battling at close quarters with the Egyptians. For what seemed an age they could only unpack their containers and be shot at. Everyone was keeping low to the ground, all except for Private Castelnuovo who was taking photographs.

Some of the boys were hit and two of them were killed as they returned the fire lying there in the open. Then mortar bombs began to fall. A series of sharp cracks close to my head made me flop down behind an oil drum. Behind the next one was Corporal Dunbavin. Stray bullets cracked and spattered around us. I asked him to take a look at my eye. 'Swollen, but doesn't look too bad.'

Heavy drop of seven old Jeeps.

'Unpacking' one of the jeeps.

We headed once more for the control tower, first running, then jogging, then walking, Innumerable figures were strolling across the scene, each carrying too much weight to move any faster.

By the control tower.

The control tower on the right and one of the Jeeps by the adjacent garage buildings.

'A' Company had cleared the buildings by the time we reached them and we were met by Company Commander Major Lawrence Scragg. 'Regimental Aid Post in the garage at the back over there Doc. What happened to your eye?'

Shortly afterwards Colonel Crooks and Brigadier Butler appeared at the control tower with bullets still flying about and mortar bombs exploding

The main garage, a building open at the front, was close to the control tower and served as the casualty station. An office built against one of the end walls was to act as the theatre.

Casualties in the control tower garage.

The first casualties came in within minutes. There was a penetrating chest wound, several compound fractures, a shattered knee joint, and an innocent-looking little wound above the right elbow but underneath which the artery was divided. The arm would have to be amputated. Soon the place was half full. Outside there was the crash of a close detonation and Major Dick Stevens, the OC of 'B' Company, was lying on the ground with his leg shattered below the knee.

Meanwhile his company had knocked out a pillbox without loss while advancing towards the sewerage farm beyond the eastern end of the airfield. Here they were mistaken for the enemy by two French Mystéres jet fighters but managed to take

At the bottom of photograph is the eastern end of the airfield runway. Beyond is the large rectangular area of the sewage farm complex followed by the group of cemeteries. On the far part of the paler ground are a number of blocks of flats.

cover behind buildings, again without loss. Apart from this the regular ground support aircraft had been faultless and very accurate. Within fifteen minutes of the drop it had been possible to call down air strikes on selected targets which saved time and lives. As the day wore on it became an accepted routine that whenever the troops were held up by Egyptian defensive positions an air strike was called down to pulverise them.

In the garage the surgical team had begun to operate on a severe chest wound. Closing the chest wound was the first of six major operations they performed that day and soon evacuation was needed to make more room. A request was put in for helicopter evacuation. Half an hour later in a great swirling shower of dust a naval helicopter landed thirty yards away from the garage.

The pilot threw out a pile of stretchers and cans of water. With shouts and signs he indicated he could take two stretcher cases and three sitting. We sorted out five of the worst cases and strapped them in. In another dust storm, they were off.

Meanwhile 'C' Company, after the sewage farm, was preparing to attack the Egyptian position in the cemetery. After a mortar bombardment and air strike on the cemetery wall at 10.28 they went forward at 10.30. The aircraft had done their job well and the men were able to reach the cemetery wall without encountering serious opposition.

The company battled cautiously forward as sudden bursts of fire would come from behind tombstones. Eventually, at the far end of the cemetery, the 'C' Company soldiers watched angrily as many of their enemies made for the wharves of the inland Manzala Canal and escaped southwards in any small boats they could find.

Meanwhile, the sappers of No. 9 Squadron had cleared the runway of the drums and a circling French Dakota was able to land regardless of the occasional mortar bombs still bursting on the airfield. A colonel was on board and with signs and my limited French I was able to understand that he was returning to Cyprus and had room for eight casualties on board. I went back to the garage to select the cases. The orderlies carried them carefully to the plane. One of the boys died just as the preparations were complete. His body was replaced with one in more urgent need of attention.

It was then that the Brigade Major looked dubiously at my eye and murmured something about 'getting another doctor'. Norman Kirkby the surgeon settled it. 'Take this bottle' he said, 'and make sure that drip keeps running on the plane. … And I want someone to look at that eye.' The transfusion of the wounded man had to be kept going at all costs and in my monocular state I was the most expendable member of the medical staff.

I climbed into the Dakota with the precious bottle of plasma and one or two items of personal kit. The pilot had no need to warm his engines and we were quickly away, a mere five hours after I'd arrived on the end of a parachute.

Meanwhile, back on the ground, 'C' Company had fought on beyond the far end of the cemetery until coming under fire from the large blocks of flats on the western fringe of Port Said itself. The open ground in front of the flats contained three or four dug-in Russian S.U. 100 self-propelled guns. Thanks to the air strikes these were soon overrun and abandoned.

One of the 3 Para lads inspecting an abandoned dug-in SU 100 anti-tank gun by the blocks of flats.

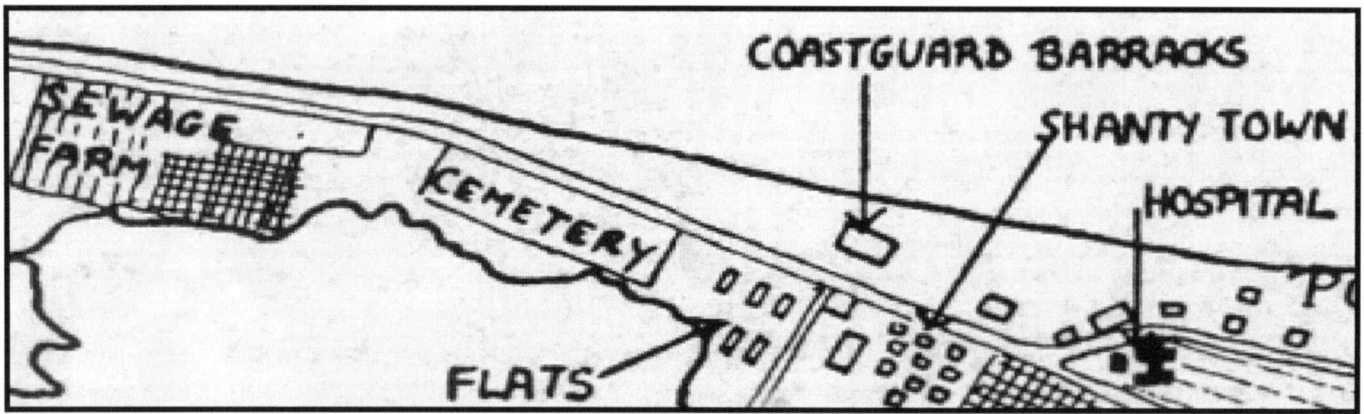

Sketch map of the relative positions of the 3 Para objectives.

Major Lawrence Scragg, OC of HQ Company on the left and some of his men inspecting one of the Egyptian Russian-built SU 100 self-propelled anti-tank guns on the road outside the Coastguard Barracks.

At the bottom left of this aerial view are the three-storey Coastguard Barracks seen in the previous photograph. On the right hand side of the road that forks right in the centre of the photograph is the large area of flattened Shanty Town.

After resistance from snipers in the flats was subdued the company went on to clear the coastguard barracks further along on the opposite side of the road before continuing into the town.

As those of us returning to Cyprus flew on we passed over the invasion fleet gathering for the sea assault on Port Said the next morning. And somewhere in the sky to the west of us the second 3 Para lift flew towards El Gamil airfield.

Back in Nicosia in the British Military Hospital the staff set about the task of repairing the damage to our own wounded. I was transferred to the care of the ophthalmologist. He gave my eye a most comprehensive overall, picked a fragment of metal off the cornea and pronounced the internal damage to be comparatively trivial.

The following day in Port Said a ceasefire was signed which came into effect that midnight. Later, during the day of 11 November, Remembrance Sunday, orders were issued for embarkation on the 12th when 3 Para boarded the *New Australia* for their return to Cyprus and Tunisia Camp. Five days later I was allowed out of hospital to join them there.

The Dome Hotel on the waterfront in Kyrenia, Cyprus.

One evening soon afterwards, at the Dome Hotel in Kyrenia on the north coast of Cyprus, the Officers' and Sergeants' messes entertained the RAF crews who had flown us to Port Said in the early hours of the fifth..

Upon demob in early 1959 I knew that to be a competent GP I must be able to do most emergency treatment, and acquire a working knowledge of obstetrics to complete the experience gained in medicine, surgery, paediatrics, and the sketchy general practice which 3 Para and its families involved.

I then entered a training practice in Worcester for six months until I rashly accepted an invitation from the climber Wilfred Noyes to act as MO for the grandly named 'Anglo-American Karakoram Expedition' to K2 in 1960.

Don Williams, one of the party, was seized with probable polio at 23,000 feet; I'd carelessly fallen 100 feet just before examining him, and one of the Nagar porters suffered a severe head injury. But we all came home to tell the tale. But high-altitude mountaineering cannot be justified for the family man.

By great good fortune I was taken on by the very good group practice at Brecon which I much enjoyed from 1960 until 1994. Despite cardiac failure and possessed of a pacemaker I'm still, quite undeservedly ticking at eighty-two.

* * *

Malcolm Elliott, RAMC.

I was born in Worcester on 21 January 1931 and

went on to attend Sunnyside School there until I was eight when I went to Worcester Royal Grammar School where I was a keen member of the Army Cadet Corps, running the signals section, and twice being awarded the Junior NCO Prize. I little realised the skills learned then would be so useful nearly ten years later.

I entered the Birmingham Medical School in 1949 and graduated M.B.,Ch.B. in July 1954. Dorothy and I were married the same year. After my two compulsory 'house' jobs at Birmingham Children's Hospital and the Queen Elizabeth Hospital I was called for National Service.

I didn't want to be a soldier and so when I went for my National Service medical I overdosed on amphetamine to raise my blood pressure. Amphetamine at that time was a freely available unrestricted drug used as a legitimate treatment for depression. Later known as 'speed' it became popular among drug users as an 'upper' and had to be banned. However, since it is pharmacologically similar to adrenaline, it elevates blood pressure. Nobody took my BP so all I got was a thumping headache, couldn't sleep for 36 hours, and still got called up.

I reported to Crookham Barracks of the RAMC in Aldershot in August 1955. Following two weeks basic training I was posted to Chester Military Hospital. After a few days I received a phone call telling me that Dorothy had been delivered of a son who was now two days old. The hospital switchboard had not bothered to pass on the original telegram telling me the good news when it first happened.

During basic training I had decided that since I was stuck in the Army – against my will for two years – I would get out of it what excitement I could and volunteered to join the Paras. After three weeks in Chester I was recalled to Aldershot to Para Brigade HQ. Somehow I managed to pass the very hard physical P course and was sent off to Abingdon for parachute training. After eight jumps I got my wings and was almost as elated and excited as when I graduated.

Then it was back to Aldershot to lead a platoon of 11 men to form one of three Medical Reception Centres in 23 Field Ambulance under the command of Lieutenant Colonel John Kilgour. We spent the next six months on training exercises familiarising ourselves with our equipment.

In June 1956 the whole 16th Independent Parachute Brigade was despatched to Cyprus aboard HMS *Albion,* a light aircraft carrier that had been converted into a troop ship. The trip was uneventful until three days out from Cyprus when there was a monumental storm. Most of the troops, including yours truly, were being seasick over the rails when suddenly there was a cry of 'Man overboard'. One soldier had been washed off the flight deck and fallen some 30 or 40 feet into the Med. The ship was doing about 20 knots at the time but incredibly it was brought to a halt in around a quarter of a mile. A launch was lowered and the soldier recovered.

Muggins was duty doctor for the army contingent for the day. My mal de mer disappeared instantly and I met the semi-conscious half-drowned casualty in the sick bay. The sick bay was superbly equipped and included X-ray facilities. The plate showed that the casualty had several fractured ribs and lungs half full of water. With appropriate therapy he improved and on arrival at Famagusta I went ashore with him and then by ambulance to BMH at Nicosia where he made a full recovery.

The brigade established a tented camp just outside Nicosia and from here we soon started anti-terrorist operations. I was certainly getting the excitement I had hoped for and there was more to come. After a 15-mile training march from the camp over the Kyrenia mountains to a 'safe beach' we were all lying somewhat exhausted on the sand when there was a series of explosions and I was covered in debris. Eoka had planted mines under the sand and remotely detonated them. One of them had been only 10 yards from where I was lying and sadly an RAF corporal was half on top of it. He lost an arm and a leg and was obviously desperately ill. The platoon had all the necessary kit to render first aid and we took him first to the Cottage Hospital in Kyrenia and then back to BMH Nicosia. Although our initial resuscitation had been successful we later learned that he succumbed to his injuries a few days later.

While there I learned that the only parachute-trained anaesthetist in the entire British Army had just finished his term and had been discharged. This was a month before Suez so I volunteered to be trained as a replacement at BMH Nicosia spending each day in the operating theatre..

With Major 'Rip' Norman Kirby (later Major-General Sir Norman) as my CO, we formed No. 9 Field Surgical Team, together with S/Sgt Neal, Cpl Worral, and Private Docherty as my anaesthetic assistant.

In the early hours of 5 November we were trucked to Nicosia airfield and went aboard our allocated aircraft of the Hastings and Valettas lined up along the side of the runway.

Cpl Worrall, Major (later Maj Gen Sir) Norman Kirby, Pte Docherty, and S/Sgt Neale. Preparing for the flight.

After dropping into El Gamil Airfield on the 5th of November, the first day of the assault on Port Said, we set up a medical facility in the control tower buildings with a resuscitation area and operating theatre where Norman performed some wonderful life-saving surgery with me having only the most incredibly basic anaesthetic equipment to work with.

Captain Elliott, in steel helmet, in the MRS.

We then received a message from the front line in Port Said to say a hospital had been captured and any supplies we might need were there for the asking. Taking the only serviceable Jeep, Docherty and I drove to the sharp end only to come under fire well before reaching the hospital. Several members of the leading platoon had been injured and were pinned down by an Egyptian Bren gunner. I managed to get the injured back into comparative safety and then saw them evacuated back to the airfield. I next radioed a situation report to the Company Commander who replied that 'You seem to have things under control Doc, carry on.' So I did.

Assuming command of the remnants of the platoon I removed my Red Cross armband and ordered a 105mm gun to be fired into the house where the Bren gunner was shooting from an upstairs window. The firing stopped. I stayed in charge at the front until a ceasefire was called 24 hours later. We then moved into the centre of Port Said and set up an operating theatre in the fruit market where we spent several days working on civilian casualties before being recalled to the UK. Where I was allowed to continue with my anaesthetic training at the Cambridge Military Hospital in Aldershot.

The Cambridge Military Hospital.

One morning, I was summoned before the Hospital Adjutant and reprimanded for failing to return a sergeant major's salute properly. Having been told only a short while earlier that I had been awarded a Military Cross for my exploits in Port Said I found it very difficult to maintain my self control in front of the pompous predecessor to the later television character Captain Mainwaring.

Captain Elliott with his wife and mother at the investiture.

The investiture by her Majesty the Queen at Buckingham Palace with my wife and mother present was obviously the high point of my short military career. As a national serviceman I did not possess a dress uniform but all my fellow officers at Brigade HQ were keen to have some piece of their kit worn by me at the Palace on the day. The only items of clothing of my own which I wore for the ceremony in front of Her Majesty were my boots and red beret.

National Service made a man of me. I made good friends and learned disciplines which have stood me in good stead for the rest of my life. Although I hadn't wanted to be a soldier I am now glad that I was. Returning to civilian life I became a general practitioner for about 10 years and then returned to hospital life and trained to become a consultant radiologist, working in several North Worcestershire hospitals until I retired in May 1992.

* * *

Robert Campbell, RAMC.

I was born in Liverpool on 29 May 1937. During the Blitz, which took place almost continuously through the autumn and December of 1940, we were bombed out of our house and moved to Huyton which is about seven miles away in the eastern suburbs of the city to live with my grandmother. Dad was away in the Army.

I attended St Columbus Primary School until I was about eight when we made another move, this time to Huyton Quarry. The school, which had classes of infants, juniors and seniors separated by just a curtain, was surrounded by farms and fields and I spent much of my time watching the steam trains pass by. My education suffered.

I left school in the summer of 1952 and, after one or two false starts, finally got a job in a timber yard where I worked for W H Todd until called up for National Service on 10 November 1955. I reported for training with the Royal Army Medical Corps at Crookham Camp near Fleet in Hampshire.

This was my first time away from home, and my first time in a pub with some of the lads. I was so small at the time that I had to show the barman my call-up papers before he was willing to serve me.

The first night there were some tears from one or two of the lads, but me, I was okay. I was just so pleased to have a bed to myself instead of having to share with my brother. At the end of training after a freezing cold winter I'd hoped to get sent to Singapore to see some of the world. Another Liverpool lad wanted to be posted to Chester because he was married with a baby. I got Chester, he went to Singapore. He was so desperate to stay in England that he went around asking the lads to break his arm.

At Chester I served as a dining room orderly. I wasn't qualified to nurse as I only passed grade 3 for bed making and bandaging. This suited me because I didn't like blood and needles. Later, while on leave, I was called back to camp where I was told to pack then sent down to Swindon in Wiltshire where I was attached to 36 Field Ambulance.

At this camp they frequently had night-time IRA alerts. One of the officers when on night duty used to drive around the camp in his sports car shouting 'IRA alert'. This meant that everyone had to get out of bed. One night however someone threw a bin at his car which brought to a rapid end this waking us up all the time..

Another of the officer had a rather funny salute with his hand not touching the side of his head. One group of lads decided to copy him on the next pay parade. The first few got away with it until the officer cottoned on and got his own back by saying 'Half a salute, half pay.' It wasn't funny any more.

A few days later we were on our way to Southampton and sailing on the *Empire Ken* to Malta. We slept below decks in hammocks with everywhere smelling of BO and sweaty feet. Shortly after our arrival we were transferred to the aircraft carrier HMS *Theseus* which, on 31 October, sailed for Port Said.

By early on the morning of the 6th of November, together with HMS *Ocean*, we had dropped anchor some miles offshore from the Suez Canal entrance while we waited to send off the Commandos in their helicopters. The Paratroopers had gone in the previous day to take El Gamil airfield. As well as carrying helicopters the ship had also been set up to take on board and treat the casualties that could be expected from the fighting. At sometime after 7am the Whirlwind helicopters began ferrying the marine commandos ashore and the ship started making its way towards the coast. By the late afternoon we were anchored within the entrance to the Suez Canal together with a great number of other ships.

We were only at Port Said for a short time. The next day we sailed out to sea to carry out the burial of a marine belonging to 45 Commando who had been killed in action during the assault.

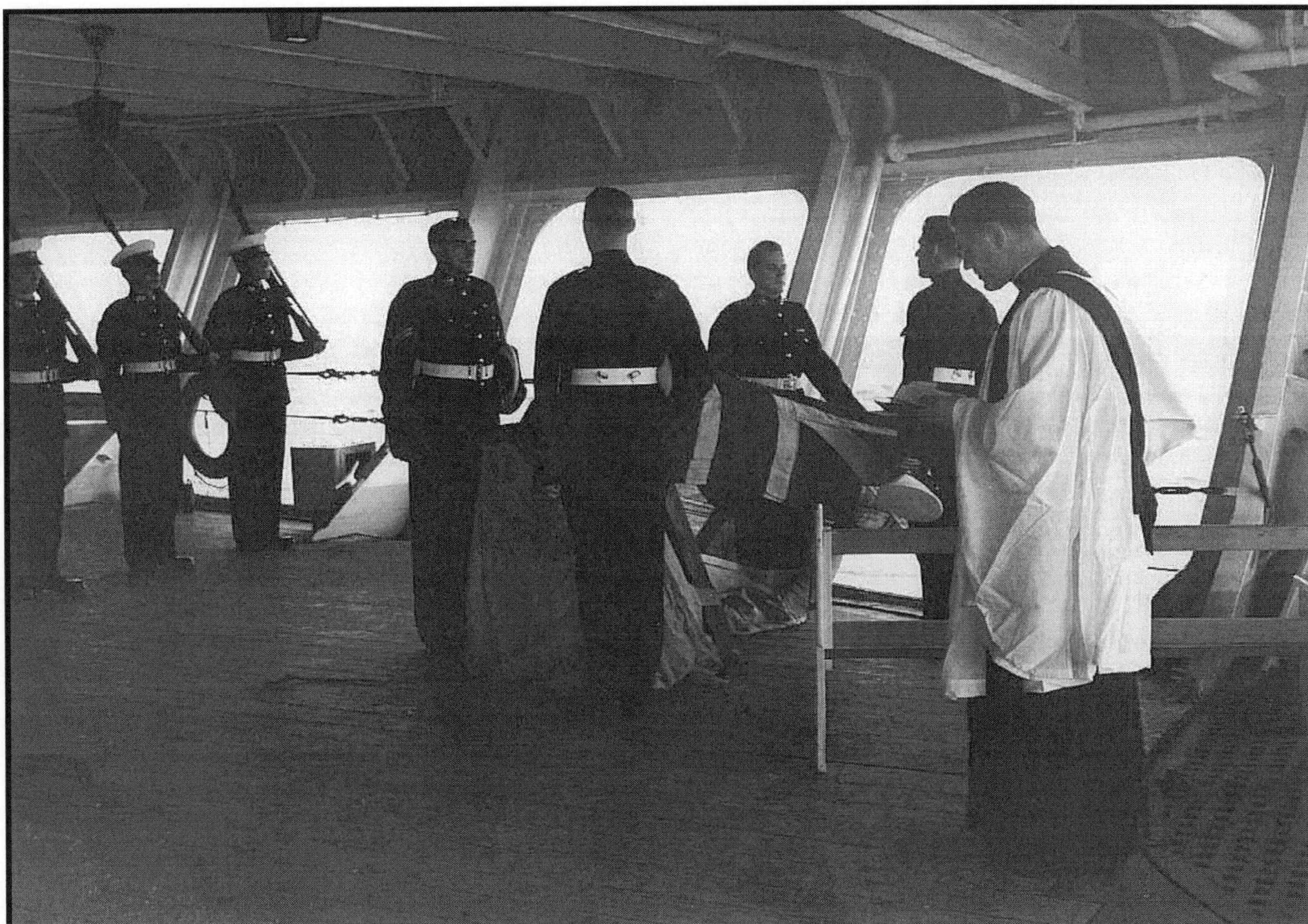

The burial service at sea for Marine Michael John Fowler of 45 Commando aboard the aircraft carrier *HMS Theseus.* With thanks to Tony Davie and the Royal Marines Association for permission to use this photograph.

We returned to Port Said briefly before setting off back to Malta with lots of our wounded and even some of the French wounded even though they had their own great white hospital ship anchored in the canal. Ambulances were waiting at the quayside to take the wounded to hospital. In Malta it became a holiday. I was made a regimental cook for A Company of my RAMC unit.

Robert in his new job in Malta.

After a few months we were posted to Cyprus where we spent a lot of time searching for terrorists in the Troodos Mountains while attached to the Duke of Wellington Regiment, 42 Commandos, the Artillery Brigade HQ, and later the Kings Regiment.

Robert sat on the front of the left hand vehicle.

While in the mountains we were based on the outskirts of a village for a while so we got to know the people quite well, especially when they realised we were medics. There was always someone in these places who could speak English. The MO would treat any of the villagers if he could. In return they would bring fruit, eggs, and chickens – sometimes live ones. One old man even offered us a donkey after the MO had given him a penicillin injection. They had heard about penicillin on the radio and thought it would cure everything.

On another occasion in the mountains the local schoolteacher brought an elderly lady to see the MO because she was stone deaf. When the doc checked he found that her ears were blocked solid with wax. He told her to come back the next day which she did, with some of the villagers. He syringed her ears with warm soapy water which cleared them. She thought it was a miracle and couldn't thank him enough. All her friends clapped him. I was able to do my bit by sometimes giving the children biscuits and chocolates out of the emergency rations.

After my demob in November 1957 I found that the timber yard where I had worked before my National Service had closed down so I got employment with the National Coal Board who had their own brickyard.

I married in 1960 and we went on to have a boy and a girl and now have four grandchildren – two boys and two girls. I worked for the NCB until 1968 when they closed the brickyard down so I went to work for BIP Chemicals who produced the powder to make plastics. I was a colour matcher for 14 years until they closed down too and I was made redundant again. I then found work with a shirt factory that supplied Marks and Spencer stores. When I was made redundant again I retired.

* * *

Jack (Tex) Halliday, RAMC.

At the time the Suez crisis came up I was a twenty-two-year-old married corporal in the RAMC serving my National Service at Catterick Camp in North Yorkshire working as an operating theatre technician in the military hospital there. Life was good, my posting was reasonably near home, and I enjoyed working in the operating theatre. Then, sometime in September, I was sent down to Mytchett in Surrey to take part in a training exercise. While I was there a lot of RAMC reservists were being called up to join us. Some of them objected to the army discipline again, especially those with long hair.

After a while, by which time it was October, my friend Geordie Edmundson and I were given a 48-hour pass and returned home, after which, since there was no immediate concern at that time for us over the Suez situation, we were to report back to Catterick. On a Sunday I said goodbye to my wife as usual and returned to camp. Monday was a normal working day in the theatre with several operations.

At about 24.00 hrs that night as I was about to get into bed the orderly sergeant burst in to the room and said, 'Corporal, get your kit together, you have to be on a train to London at 03.00 hrs.' I joined the rest of the theatre team comprising the surgeon Major Cowan, an anaesthetist – Captain Thompson I think it was, Sergeant Les Runecles, Geordie, and another private and we were soon on our way to the depot at Mytchett. From here we were whisked to Lyneham air base in Wiltshire, where, after a meal and some sleep we were put aboard a prop plane to an unknown destination which turned out to be Malta. The flight was slow and nearly everyone was sick due to turbulence.

Transport was awaiting us at Malta Airport to take us to the docks where we found ourselves at the side of this huge ship which turned out to be the aircraft carrier *Theseus*. Limping from a sprained ankle I had acquired I hobbled up the steep gangplank of the ship when I heard this voice shouting, 'Come on Tex, Where have you been?' Other personnel from Mytchett were already on board and looking down on us. I saw that 45 Commando were also on the ship.

By a stroke of luck I was able to leave the ship that evening and get to the NAAFI on the other side of the harbour where I bought a letter card to send to my wife to let her know that I was on my way to an unknown destination but that this would soon become apparent. We were expecting a child very soon. I found that Malta was heaving with all three military services

The next morning the *Theseus* and the *Ocean* slipped slowly out of the harbour. Lots of the personnel aboard the ships were lined up around the perimeter of the flight decks as we left for the open sea which is where we discovered that our destination was Port Said.

I found life on board *Theseus* to be an interesting experience. My sleeping quarters were in part of the helicopter hanger which would later be filled with the returning casualties. Everyone was speculating and discussing what the outcome would be and wondering if it would be the start of a third world war. You could sense the tension in the air. It was a very frightening experience, especially as we were all so young.

Theseus came to a halt in the early hours' darkness of the 5th of November. The sky was lit up with fires burning ashore and smoke everywhere. The smell in the air was like on the 5th November back home, which it was.

The next day at dawn I went up on deck to take a look around and was absolutely amazed to see the huge number of ships of different types as far as the eye could see.

Ships as far as the eye could see.

Shortly afterwards an announcement came over the Tannoy system with the news that Port Said would be shelled in five minutes time and this would continue for forty-five minutes. Big guns opened up from ships further out to sea and we could feel the vibration from the sea throughout the ship. After approximately ten minutes a further announcement stated that the shelling would have to cease as shells were bouncing on to the French who were occupying Port Fuad.

After the shelling stopped the order was given for the Commandos to prepare for an airborne assault of the beaches by helicopter. The Tannoy was continually repeating the message, 'Strictly no naked lights, handling av gas, av gas, av gas, no naked lights.' A massive elevator was bringing helicopters up onto the deck from the hangars below, with each one being fuelled and made ready for the assault. The Commandos then climbed aboard and, with a deafening roar, one after another took off.

Within about twenty minutes of them having left, the helicopters were returning with casualties and an order was given that we were needed below. This was the point where I witnessed my first real life war wounds. The first patient was one who had lost a lower leg. He was covered in sand so I didn't know what nationality he was, although I thought he may have been French. As he lay on the hangar bunk with forceps hanging from his arteries, he motioned that he would like a cigarette which someone kindly gave him. As time went by there were so many casualties that our sleeping quarters had to be used as a hospital ward. Some of them had terrible injuries and after some time treating them it was alarming to discover that our dressings were running in short supply. We wondered how this could be in a modern war situation and were forced into removing the dressings from some minor wounds, sterilising them, and applying them again wet.

Later that day, the sixth, under the cover of darkness, we scrambled down the side of the *Theseus* precariously holding on to some kind of webbing ladder and into a landing craft which had pulled up alongside. There were about thirty medics in the craft and an order was shouted, 'Keep your heads down and wait for the next order.' We were all silent as the craft pulled away, heaving up and down and rocking from side to side. The front end blocked our vision as to where we were heading and each one of was left with his own private thoughts. I remember vividly the red glow in the sky, the noise of aircraft and helicopters flying to and fro, the rat-a-tat of gunfire, and the choking foul smell of smoke all around us. Then suddenly we were at the quay.

As the ramp was lowered we were told to run across the road and make our way into the damaged building opposite. Keeping low, struggling with our kit, stomachs churning, and hearts pounding we crossed the quay into what we found was the Casino Palace Hotel.

We entered the building very cautiously following orders from someone we couldn't see carrying a torch. Port Said was without power at this time. I remember ascending a very wide wooden staircase to a long corridor with very wide wooden floorboards which were covered in broken glass and debris. Rooms were situated along each side of the corridor. The next order was, 'Put your kit down where you are, put your head on it, and try to get some sleep until the morning. During the night I was wakened by a door opening behind me and a figure appeared in a long white gown. I thought, am I dreaming or seeing a ghost? Then a female voice said, 'I want to go the bathroom.' I realised then that civilians caught up in the war were still in the hotel. In the morning however further investigation revealed dead people lying in some of the rooms. (It was assumed that these people were murdered by Egyptian soldiers who broke into their rooms to use the windows as vantage points for setting up their weapons). Beds had been urinated on by the soldiers to prevent them being used again.

The night seemed endless and sleep was virtually impossible with intermittent gunfire echoing around us for most of the night. When morning finally arrived I took a look outside and to my horror saw several dead Egyptian soldiers scattered about. They had been fully armed and each wore a flat bag which contained what appeared to be a large oatmeal cake.

The hotel seen from the quay. Note the shell hole at the top right hand corner of the building.

Our first job that morning was to find a place where we could operate on the wounded. The bar area was quickly adapted to become an operating theatre although the conditions were very bad. The windows were broken and covered in muslin and we were short of water, light and medical supplies so had to improvise the best way that we could. Our lighting amounted to some bulbs hanging from two pieces of crossed wood suspended from the ceiling and powered by a generator.

The water boiler for tea and coffer on the bar top we found useful as this was used to sterilise the instruments. The water was brought ashore in jerry cans and was very limited. And so it was that under these conditions we operated day and night treating both our own casualties as well as Egyptians including women and children. Nationality did not matter and casualties were treated in order of condition, all on an equal basis. The surgeon, Major Cowan, was brilliant; whatever the casualty he handled it quickly and efficiently. Sergeant Runeckles and myself alternated between sterilising the instruments and assisting the major to carry out his work.

All of the wounded who were still awaiting treatment were accommodated in a large room to the left hand side of the bar. Most were lying on the floor but others were on stretchers. The dead bodies from the rooms upstairs were taken outside to the large garden to await burial. I remember seeing about four dead Commandos on stretchers with their green berets placed over their faces in a separate corner of the garden. I don't know where they were taken but they were certainly not buried by us.

A large deep trench had been dug out of the lawn and a few bodies had been placed into it. The most traumatic part of my service in Port Said was carrying a beautiful woman outside on a stretcher to be buried. She was one of those murdered in their rooms upstairs. A small red and white flatdeck Coca Cola truck carried several of these rigor mortised bodies to the trench. Since we could not walk into the trench we had to roll the bodies into it and the sight and sound of the bodies hitting each other brought tears to my eyes. It is a memory that has stayed with me ever since. One of the bodies, whose hand was missing, had a nice gold watch on the forearm. One of the persons nearby said, 'I'm having that watch!' I quickly intervened and told him that all removable jewellery had to go into a special box for deceased' effects.

Towards the end of my stay in the hotel one of the reservists came up to me and said, 'Hey Tex, I've just been across the road to the water bowser and while I was there some bugger took a couple of pot shots at me from this direction.' On investigation we discovered an Egyptian sniper hiding in the cellar. We disarmed him and brought him upstairs. He was tired and hungry and looked relieved to be out of it. He must have been there for a few days.

After a short while we moved out of the Casino Palace Hotel and set up hospital in a beautiful big building with marble floors which were being cleaned by a number of squatting tall men wearing long robes tucked beneath their legs. We discovered they were Sudanese. The building became No.2 CCS (casualty clearing station) and was situated on the coast road heading westwards towards El Gamil airfield.

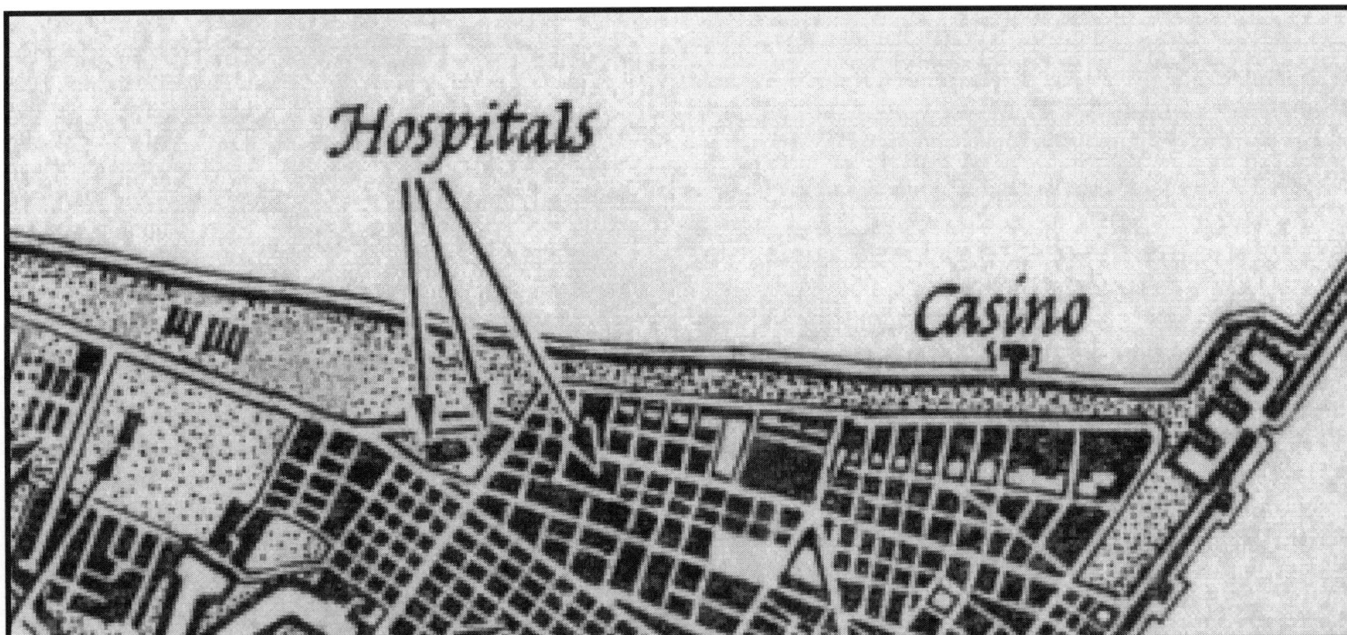

The Casino Palace Hotel formed the block shown on the canal waterfront with a white dot at its centre on the bottom right of the built-up area of the street plan. The second location for 2CCS, according to Jack's description, would appear to be one of the premises shown backing on to the beach just to the right of the group of hospitals.

The building backed on to the beach and had much spare land surrounding it within a high perimeter wall. There was sufficient space to accommodate latrines out at the back which consisted simply of a large pit with a plank across it on which we sat side by side. If you were not careful you were in the shit. On one side of the building the Catering Corp lads had set up a small kitchen with a dining area under canvas. It was good to be provided with hot food despite the problem of having to eat it before the flies did.

We found a large room containing a stainless steel sink which gave us the ideal place to make an operating theatre. However we needed an operating table and a washing machine for the laundry. We visited a small local hospital nearby which was partly demolished but were able to find an operating table in good condition so we took it with us. Sergeant Runeckles and I were then given permission, with an armed escort to prevent looting, to enter any unoccupied house to find a good washing machine. We quickly found one in the second house we entered. We now had a good set-up to carry out our operations.

Casualties of one form or another came in every day and one I remember particularly was a fairly high ranking officer whose name I can't remember who had been sprayed with bullets from an automatic weapon from his lower legs to the upper part of his body. Amputated limbs were taken outside to be buried deep in the sand within the perimeter walls.

Unfortunately, due to our location which was away from Port Said centre, we didn't get the chance to visit any shops or meet the locals. We stayed mostly within the grounds of the property while we were there but towards the end we were able to take a dip in the sea which was very nice.

I remember the time when two of the army reservists were wheeling and dealing through the bars of the locked iron gates in the perimeter wall. We had a surplus supply of green army blankets which were found to be in demand by the Egyptian locals. These were passed out through the gates in exchange for English money. This was a good racket for the two guys until an attempted stabbing of one of them by a local. This stopped the illegal trading.

A nice surprise for me was to receive an army telegram telling me that my son, Christopher John, had been born on the 22nd of November. I celebrated with two mates and we had some chocolate, hard tack biscuits and a bottle of beer each which we had saved. One happy day!

We continued to live and work at 2 CCS until we left Port Said aboard the troopship *Dunera* on 22nd of December. Before our departure we witnessed the French loading their looted cars, motorcycles, bicycles, and anything else they could get on their ships which they were obviously being able to do. We weren't! From the beginning we had been instructed to behave properly and nothing was to be looted. I saw a beautiful Citroen and a Mercedes being hoisted onto the deck of this French ship and thought how nice it would be to have a car like these but at the same time thinking that I wouldn't want a foreigner coming along and stealing my car.

Christmas and New Year were spent aboard the *Dunera* together with some of the West Yorkshire Regiment and the Royal Scots. Needless to say the Yorkies celebrated Christmas and the Scots New Year. This resulted in our being occupied over these two periods stitching up scalp wounds and other minor injuries caused by bottles and fists.

On arriving in Southampton all our kit was checked for arms and ammunition. Any found were naturally confiscated and then we were transported to Mytchett Barracks prior to returning to our respective units, in my case Catterick Military Hospital. Before leaving Mytchett everyone attended a parade to be inspected by base personnel who hadn't been to Port Said. One sergeant said to me, 'You are in shit order, you are a mess; get your uniform cleaned up corporal.' What this idiot didn't realise was that I had worn the uniform continuously for most of my time at Port Said since we had no operating theatre clothing and consequently it was bloodstained.

Back at Catterick life carried on as before and I stayed there until the end of my service.

* * *

Alan Brown, 40 Royal Marine Commandos

I joined the Royal Marines in June 1953 when I was 20 and spent 26 weeks training which covered infantry, commando and seamanship courses after which I got married.

In June 1954 I was drafted to 40 Commando which since May the year before had been based in the Canal Zone. Just two months later Britain and Egypt signed the Anglo-Egyptian agreement in which Britain was to pull its troops out of the Canal Zone Not too long afterwards we returned to Malta.

When the troubles began in Cyprus in 1955 we were sent there as part of the force required to combat the activities of EOKA. We remained on the island until the summer of 1956 when the Suez Crisis began and we returned to Malta to begin training for what turned out to be the invasion of Port Said.

During the evening of 30 October the brigade embarked on a number of ships in the Grand Harbour to go out on what we believed to be an exercise. About a half of 40 Commando, including me, was allocated the LST *Reggio* and the other half to another landing craft.

The LST *Reggio* in the Grand Harbour at Malta.

View from the *Reggio* upon leaving the Grand harbour to join the convoy. Fleet of Bedford RL 3-tonner lorries lined up on quayside.

We set sail at about midnight and after about half an hour were informed over the Tannoy system that we were on our way to 'Suez'.

HMS *Reggio* seen from another ship in the convoy making its way towards Egyptian waters at about 6 knots.

View from HMS *Reggio* of other LCTs nearing Port Said.

Some two-and-a-half miles or so from the Egyptian shoreline the LST's began launching their Royal Tank Regiment Buffalo amphibians. Each of them, with about thirty Commandos aboard and lying low in the water, set off for the final run to the beach.

The first wave of 40 Commando which was made up of 'A' Troop led by Captain R Grant, and 'X' Troop, which was my troop led by Major A P Willasey-Wilnsey, landed on the Port Said beach to the left of the Casino jetty at 0447 hours.

The casino in much happier times.

The Buffaloes ran the men up onto the sand and between the blazing beach huts from where 'A' Troop cleared a large block of flats 200 yards ahead. 'X' Troop cleared a building to its right.

The Casino Palace Hotel at the beginning of the waterfront was soon captured by 40 Commando which then began working its way along the canal side and the adjacent parallel streets towards firstly the Commerce Basin and then the larger Arsenal and Shérif Basins.

Buffalo and dead Egyptian combatant.

After initial objectives were achieved X Troop regrouped for the next phase of the battle. Alan on the far right.

The waterfront Quay Soltan Hussein in pre-world War II days. The building showing at the far end of the street is the Suez Canal Company offices.

The Suez Canal Company Building between Commerce Basin on the right and Arsenal Basin on the left.

Arsenal Basin seen from the north.. Smoke from the Standard Oil storage tank fire a little further down the

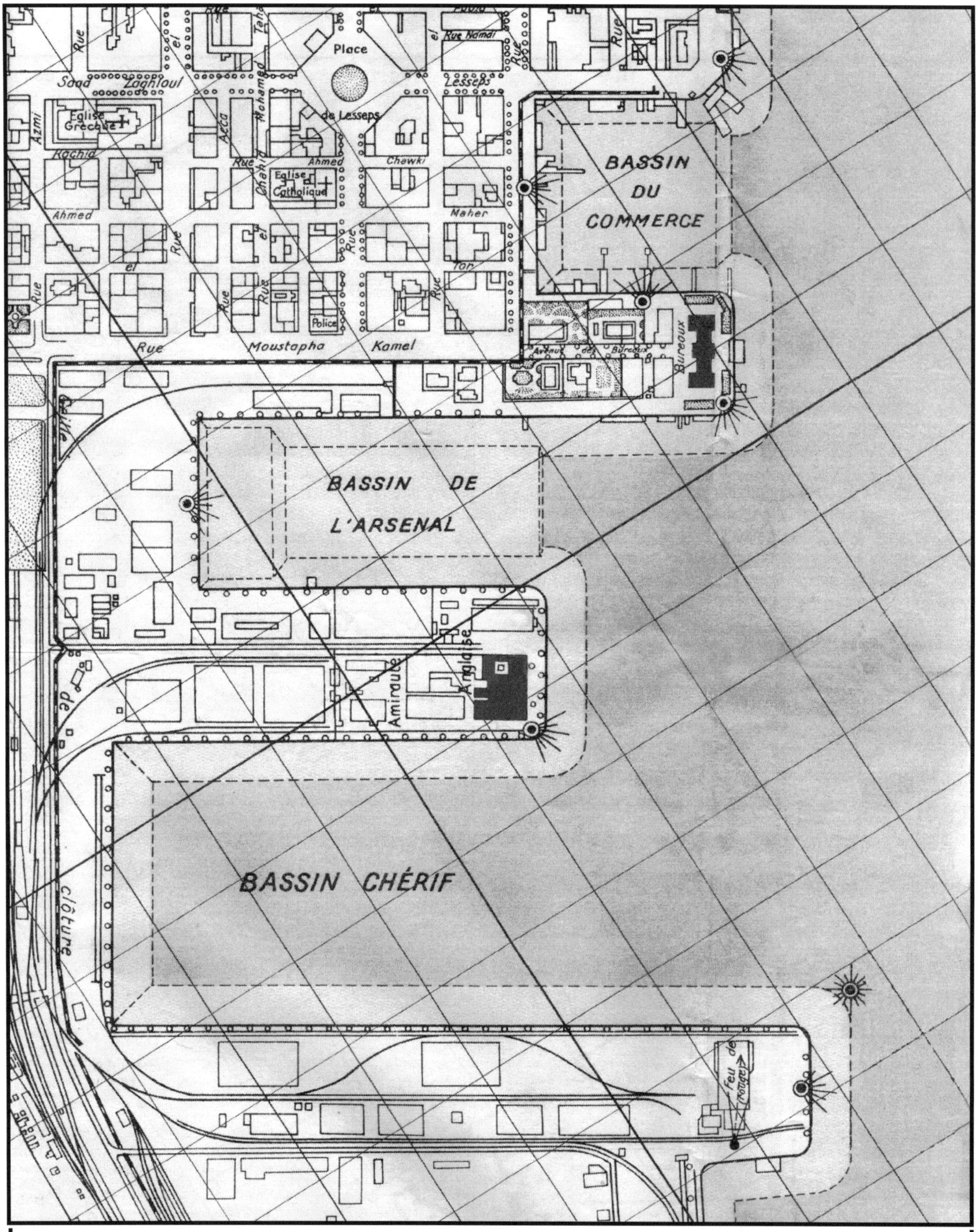

The building shown in black between the Commerce and L'Arsenal basins is the Suez Canal Company offices, seized by Colonel Nasser on the 28th of July. The other building shown in black situated on South Quay between the La' Arsenal and Chérif basins was Navy House which belonged the British Admiralty until the British withdrawal in 1954.

The Egyptian troops holed up in Navy House provided tough opposition for 40 Commando who, towards the end of the afternoon, were forced to call up for an airstrike. By this time it was close to dusk but there was just enough time for Sea Hawks from the carriers out at sea to blast the building with rockets which killed some thirty of the defending troops. By then it was too dark to continue the fighting on the ground and it was decided to pull back until the following morning. By then however the ceasefire had taken place and it just remained, later in the morning, for the survivors to be taken prisoners and the dead recovered.

A number of 40 Commando marines on the edge of South Quay facing Navy House on the left out of the picture. On the right across the mouth of L'Arsenal Basin is the three-dome Suez Canal Company building.

Burnt-out ruins of Navy House following the air attack by Fleet air Arm fighters.

The next day Navy House was taken with the assistance of tanks. The Egyptian survivors of the battle the previous day were taken prisoner and the dead recovered.

40 Commando Marines and the raising of the white ensign outside Navy House.

The warehouse where 'X' Troop spent the rest of its time in Port Said after the ceasefire.

My Troop and the rest of 40 Commando remained in Port Said until the 14th of November when, with 45 Commando, we returned to Malta.

After my return from Suez I went on to serve on the aircraft carrier HMS *Victorious* for two years before returning to 40 Commando and postings to Malta, Singapore and Malaya. I was demobbed in 1965.

* * *

John Clowes, 40 Commando.

John, a signaller with 'B' Troop of 40 Commando, was 19 at the time of the Port Said invasion. He had spent some time in Malta following the announcement of the 'Suez' emergency. When 'B' Troop went aboard their LCT in the Grand Harbour on the 30th of October they thought it was for just another exercise. Only after they had set sail did they learn the truth.

Photograph of some of John's signals mates in Malta prior to leaving for Egypt. Back: Don Burst, 'Chalky' Romilly. Front: ?, 'Dutch' Holland, 'Jesse' James.

Part of the convoy on its way to Egyptian waters.

A landing craft making for the shore.

As they approached the Port Said coastline the Commandos could see that shelling from the Daring class destroyers behind them had pounded the beach huts and set many of them on fire. A number of explosions then erupted from some of the huts, possible from abandoned ammunition.

The beach huts after being shelled by the destroyers.

A beach hut managed to survive the shelling.

Only minutes after the shelling and just before the first wave of LVTs carrying A and X Troops hit the beach to the left of the Casino jetty at 0447 hours, aircraft of the fleet Air Arm carried out the final strike and strafed the length of the beach.

The beach huts in more peaceful times.

John's B Troop came ashore three minutes later in the second wave, which also included P and Y Troops, and crossed the road to the large open area on the south side of the Fish Dock by the De Lesseps Statue.

An aircraft on its way to strafe the Egyptian defences.

On the bare ground between the fish Dock and the Casino Palace hotel. Smoke from the Standard Oil storage tank.

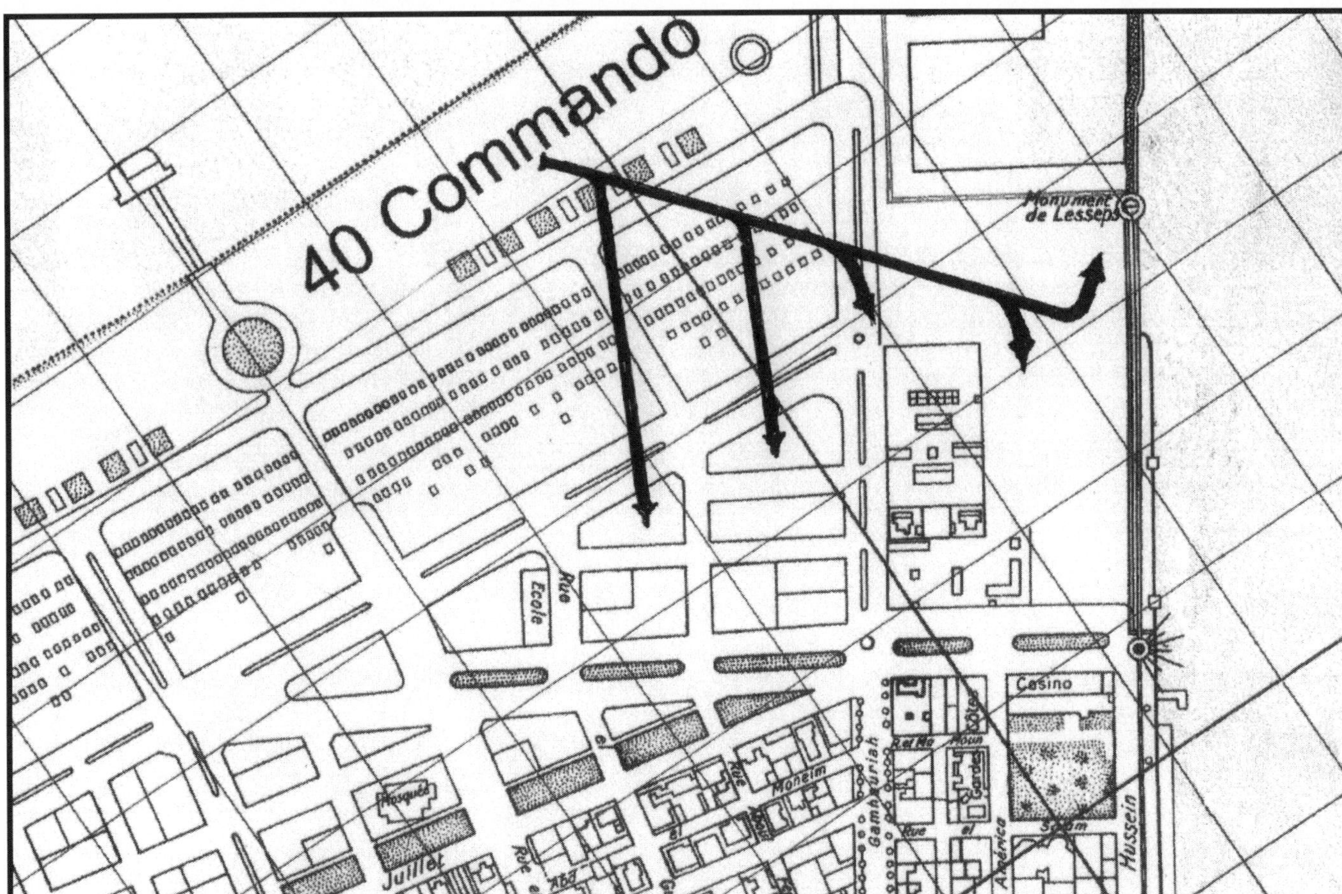

Directions taken by the various troops of 40 Commando as they fought their way from the beachhead down the eastern side of Port Said to eventually meet up with 42 Commando on the south of the built-up area of the city.

Soon after the previous photograph was taken 'B' Troop secured the Fish Dock and the open area of land south of the De Lesseps statue as far as the Casino Palace Hotel which, with the capture of Port Fuad by the French, effectively secured the entrance to the canal as far as this point.

45 Commando helicopters arriving at the open ground by the De Lesseps statue from the aircraft carriers.

More 45 Commandos coming ashore by the statue.

One of the locals being questioned by the Commandos on the forecourt of the Casino Palace Hotel.

The length of the Casino Palace Hotel with its verandah-covered open-fronted lean-to lounge area fronts onto what was called in the 1930s Shari Kitchener and may possibly still have been in 1956. The next block but one along from the hotel was the Artillery barracks, certainly it was in the 1930s, and the next photo is possibly of this building although John can't recall if it was.

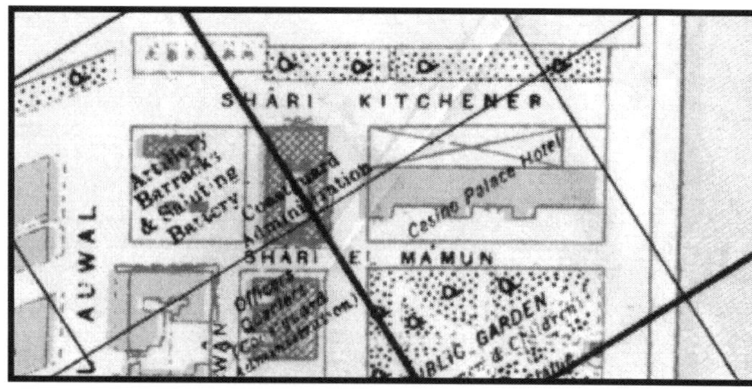

Possibly the barracks.

Centurion tank and a Ferret car in unknown place.

The 40 Commando Marines regrouped along the Casino Palace Hotel side street then, in phase II, began fighting their way south along the Quai Sultan Hussein waterfront, the parallel Rue America, and the other adjacent streets. They were fired upon by snipers from windows and doorways everywhere as they made their way to the first objective, the Port Police Station on the north-western corner of the Commerce Basin. Fortunately, by this time, the armour of the Royal Tank Regiment had come ashore and was able to lend its much needed support to the Commandos.

The waterfront— Quai Sultan Hussein.

One of the Centurion tanks mounting a watch on the doorways and windows of nearby buildings.

View south along the Rue de America or possibly the next street over. The Lighthouse is outlined against the smoke rising from the Standard Oil Company fire down the canal.

The Commandos fought their way down the waterfront to the mouth of the Commerce Basin, making quite rapid progress considering the fierce opposition from snipers. They took only about 15 minutes to reach and capture the Port Police Station on the north-eastern corner of the basin where they took twelve policemen prisoner.

The Port Police Station in more peaceful times.

A marine on one of the amphibious Buffaloes.

B Troop then led the way round the corner onto the quay on the northern side of the larger L'Arsenal Basin where they quickly found themselves coming under accurate fire from soldiers in the customs buildings. Marine Fudge was killed and John was hit and took no further part in the action.

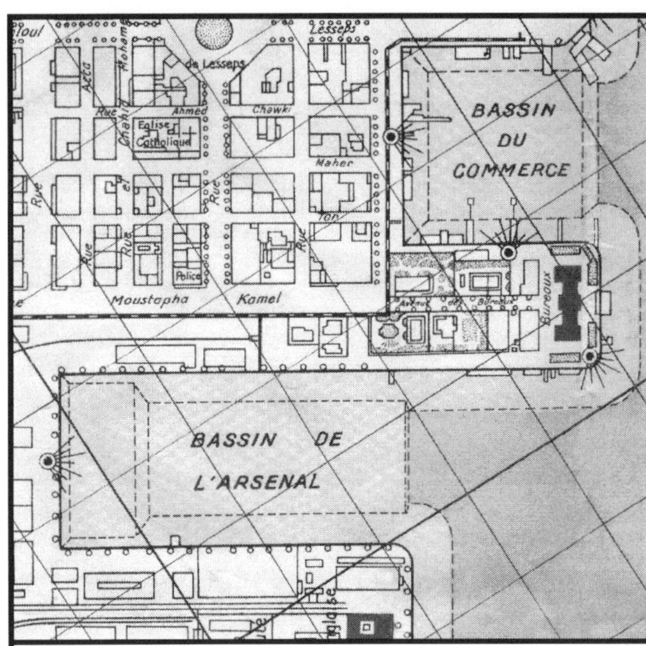

The customs offices are the two long buildings on the northern side of the Arsenal Basin.

Two more marines were hit and fell wounded as they ran forward to enter one of the buildings. Before this battle had ended two more marines were wounded and Lieutenants McCarthy and Upton killed.

The bodies of the dead marines were interred temporarily but later recovered and taken back to the UK. The two Lieutenants were laid to rest in the Haslar Military Cemetery at Gosport.

* * *

John (Joss) Mee, 42 Commando.

I was born on 9 December 1936 and lived at Grange Cottages, Papplewick, a small country village near Hucknall in Nottinghamshire where my dad was a farm worker. When five I began at the Hucknall National School which was a very good school.

In March 1945 we went to live on a farm three miles east of Mansfield and I attended school at Forest Town. I was handed a black board and some chalk to write with. I couldn't believe what I had come to. My mother said, 'They must think we are retarded or something.'

Most of the children came from mining families living around the local colliery. I made some good friends while I was there, a few who are still friends today.

In April 1947 when I was ten we moved to another farm, this one close to Mansfield Colliery where I attended Carter Lane School. As soon as the headmaster interviewed me I knew that I was back at a hard school. In September when I moved to the Ravensdale Secondary Modern School where all those who had failed the 11+ exam ended up I was either top or second in the A stream for the two years I was there.

In 1949 my dad left the farm and went to work at Mansfield Colliery. We moved back to live in Forest Town Village where, of course, it was back to the old school. The teachers there were very good with me. I think I was classed as an alternative pupil because, now age thirteen, I was entered for an exam, the 13+, which I passed and gained entry to Mansfield Secondary Technical School. This school was a converted POW camp comprised of Nissen huts linked by a covered way but it was a very good school.

When I was fourteen-and-a-half I started working for a concrete manufacturer. He paid me one shilling and sixpence per hour. It was very hard work but he gave me employment on a part-time basis for years.

I left school when I was fifteen-and-a-half in the summer of 1951 and started work for British Rail as a 'number taker' based in the weighbridge office at Clipstone Colliery where I recorded the weight of wagons in and out.

When I was seventeen-and-a-half I tried to join the Marines as a regular but the recruiting sergeant told me that I was too small. However he did tell me that in six months' time when I was called for National Service I might have grown a bit more and that I should apply to join the Navy or the RAF. This, he said, would ensure that I got my medical at Nottingham rather than Mansfield. It seemed that if you took your medical at Mansfield you were unlikely to get in the Navy.

Towards the end of 1954 it came time for me to register for National Service. I decided to have a go at either the hardest or the easiest option, nothing in-between, so when I registered I requested the Royal Navy or the RAF as I had been advised. I duly attended premises in Canal Street Nottingham where I took an exam and a medical. I was informed that the only vacancies in the Royal Navy were for Marines, stokers and cooks. I think four of us put down for the Marines.

My name was called out together with one of the others and we had to go back to see the doctors again. The other chap, although he was a big lad, was failed almost immediately for a patch of eczema on his arm. I was asked to pull myself up on a shower curtain rail then hold my legs out straight them part them while the doctor shone a light around my nether regions. You are okay he said. You'll have no problems physically. He was right, all that digging and general hard work had given me a body to be proud of although I was only five feet five inches tall.

On 19 January 1955 I reported to Lympstone Infantry Training Centre Royal Marines. What a shock! I got off the train at Exeter together with a few other lads and went outside where there was a lorry with a canvas-covered back waiting for us together with a bull-necked sergeant running around like a ball of steam shouting and barking orders.

The intake I was in was 871 Squad NS with lads from all walks of life including public schoolboys and university graduates all sharing the same hut, same food, same clothing, same bedding, same haircut and the same discipline. I couldn't believe how anyone so posh could be as hard as me; it just didn't happen where I came from. I still respect those public school lads to this day. Many of them moved after a while to go on the WOSB, the War Office Selection Board, where they would be assessed as officer material.

I took a bit of stick to start with being so small but I soon realised that at 18-years-of- age a lot of the bigger lads were a bit gangly and not that good physically. After training however those that made it became what they were supposed to be, Royal Marines.

In the summer of 1955, with the intake now only about half its original size, we were trucked to somewhere remote on Dartmoor then dropped off to march the rest of the way, in full fighting order and with rifle, to a camp called Bickleigh Commando School which was the home of 42 Commando just north of Plymouth. The sergeants and corporals here we called platoon weapons instructors but they also took us on speed marches, scramble courses and all the other things that constitute a commando course.

I was determined to make a good impression on my instructors because, being so small, I could see that scornful look they had regarding national servicemen in a regular regiment where the minimum length of service at that time was seven years in the colours and five on reserve. The instructors took us around the scramble course which was hard enough just walking. They showed us where to cross the river and where to rope up the cliff. You couldn't take short cuts because they could see you all the way from the hill they started you from. It was two miles on the double from the camp to the start point. All equipment was checked and if you lightened your pack they would put a building brick in it. They started us off in threes and I went for it. I caught up with Bartrop, the first man of the group before ours, on the two mile double going back to camp but couldn't pass him. He was a good lad. On arrival back at camp we immediately went to the rifle range where we were given five rounds and had to put all of them in the bull at 25 yards.

The next day on parade the sergeant didn't yet know many of our names but, looking at his clipboard, he shouted out, 'Who's Mee?' On the rear rank I clicked up and shouted 'Me Sergeant.' He moved his position so that he could see me. I don't think he could believe his eyes when he saw who it was. 'Well done,' he said, 'You've broken the course record.'

I really enjoyed my commando course with the only event I found hard being the 30-miler. I was put with the two tallest lads in the squad, 'Lofty' Hobbs and Bill Lowe. After about 26 miles my short legs just wouldn't open far enough and I had to keep doubling to catch up but they wouldn't wait for me. They knew I would finish with them and I did. I really hurt the next day but the day after that I was okay.

After getting my Green Beret I was disappointed not to be sent to 3 Commando Brigade in Cyprus. Instead I was posted to HQ Commando which was just a matter of changing huts. I wouldn't have minded being in a fighting troop but HQ Company with its 'old sweats', cooks, storekeepers, and me being the Adjutant's attendant, didn't impress me one little bit. However, it turned out to be the best thing that could have happened.

The Adjutant took to me when he understood what my hopes had been. Consequently anywhere the unit went he got me included and any course I fancied I got on it. During this period I went to Scotland, Denmark, Norway and Germany, not as a commando but dressed in blues and blue beret.

When the unit was made operational for the Suez crisis I shouldn't really have gone because I didn't have long enough left to serve but again, he got me on it. I think it was sometime in August that we went aboard the cruiser HMS *Cumberland* at Plymouth and sailed for Malta. When we were well inside the Med the instruction was piped for all hands to go over the side to bathe. I couldn't believe how warm it was.

On our arrival in Malta I was billeted in the M'tarfa Barracks where I was given a job in the Officers' Mess as well as continuing to be the Adjutant's attendant. He assured me that soon some square pegs in round holes would emerge and that I would get into a fighting troop. Sure enough after about a week or so an old three-badger found the training too hard and a swap was arranged and I moved into 25 Section Y Troop of 42 Commando.

My speciality was to be the Energa (grenade) man. I practised in my own time on the football field with nets in the goal to catch the dummy grenade. When I asked the lieutenant for permission to have a go with a live grenade he said, 'Don't be daft lad, they cost ten bob a piece.' I later carried a primed grenade in Port Said but didn't use it so never saw one explode.

Using old derelict buildings we trained day and night on clearing them and covering each other's back. We did a lot of landings on rocky shores and scaling cliffs. We also did whole unit exercises out at sea with aircraft overhead from carriers.

Sometime late in September a buzz went round that there was some leave available in which we could go to Sicily or the Italian mainland on a minesweeper currently anchored in Valetta harbour. Together with an old sergeant who had been to Bari during the Second World War I went first to Catania in Sicily and then to Brindisi. From here we went about by bus, guests of the Italian Navy. I enjoyed that trip very much. We returned to Malta in a force 6 gale and I was very sick, catching a cold at the same time. I reported sick back in Malta and was excused duties for about three days

It was then that we got orders to pack all our kit for a loading exercise and we even kidded ourselves that it was the real thing. When a group of matelots chucked two crates of Hop Leaf beer in the back of the lorry with their best wishes I think we realised it was. At the waterfront I went aboard the LST *Anzio* and we sailed on 30 October. During the journey to Port Said we were shown some aerial photographs of where we were going to land and our objectives. I was surprised that the buildings looked so big; they were nothing like I had imagined Egypt to be. I kept thinking about my parents since I was worried about them; they didn't know where I was and what I was doing. I had this worry until I was able to write a letter home.

As we sailed closer to Egypt I noticed a change in the mood of the men and the officers. By now 25 Section was a very close group, something that only servicemen can understand and I felt that we marines seemed to bond like glue. A sort of determination developed. I think we were reassuring ourselves that we were not going to let each other down. I remember that the day before landing I asked 'Artie' Short to lend me his scissors to cut my finger nails. Artie was a stretcher bearer and carried a small first aid kit. When I'd finished I thanked him and gave them back to him. I never saw him again after that. He was killed the following morning.

Relaxing aboard the Anzio on the way to Port Said. Rear: Hugh 'Lofty' Leader. Middle: Harry Diaper, 'Jacko' Jackson. Front: John 'Joss' Mee, 'Leo' Lees.

Aboard the *Anzio*. Facing the sea: Bert Ford, Johnny Borwell. Against the rails: Sgt 'Sticks' Norris, 'Leo' Lees, Harry Diaper. Four Squatting: 'Jacko' Jackson, L/Cpl 'Danny' Daniels, 'Joss' Mee, Hugh 'Lofty' Leader.

I landed in Port Said on 6 November with 25 Section, Y Troop. We must have been to the extreme right of the assault beach since I can't remember any landing craft to our right. When the front of the landing craft dropped down I jumped into the water up to my chest. We were carrying more weaponry and ammo than I had ever carried in training and I moved as fast as I could until I the water was shallow enough for me to get my legs to swing clear in a hurdling motion. I ran up the beach like lightning to get behind a small wall. I had a strain in both sides of my groin for a week.

When the sergeant collected us together we started on our task of clearing the sea front buildings. After clearing two blocks we finished up in a school. It was there that Sgt 'Sticks' Norris told us that we had lost Howard and Short. Sgt Dennis of S Troop had also caught a bullet and was dead. A very sad moment. Our troop took no further part in the fighting. By now 45 Commando had landed by helicopter assault in the area behind the De Lesseps statue and was proceeding to the front.

View from the roof of the building taken over by John's Troop. This was situated behind the area where they came ashore two streets back from the beach huts west of what had been the Casino jetty before the invasion.

The same view taken from an upstairs side window.

Sgt 'Sticks' Norris in the 'requisitioned' building with borrowed fez. Note he is keeping his feet off the bed.

The rest of my time in Port Said was spent on internal security duties which consisted of the prevention of looting, guarding food outlets, bakeries, the power station, and the distribution of paraffin.

'Lofty' Leader with Bren Gun guarding the grain store.

'Leo' Lees with a barricade formed with bags of grain.

When we were guarding the grain store and bake house we befriended the children and gave them sweets and chocolates. We got to know all their names and I can still remember some of them. I used to sing pop songs to them and they would sing school songs back to me. It was all good fun.

Smiling local faces despite everything.

'Lofty' Leader with a new trusting young friend.

'Lofty' Leader and Harry Diaper. Early patrol in Port Said.

When the fuel bowser first came round it was like hell let loose. I was on duty at the time and am sorry to say that I was forced to use my rifle butt to gain some sort of order. After a while we mastered the routine. We turned the men away and only served the women, looking after the younger ones first. After a couple of days only the women turned up and these were mostly the younger ones who seemed to enjoy the flirting in spite of their Moslem strictness. However we always treated them with respect.

While we were guarding the power station we came across two Alsation dogs living in some concrete pipes. After a couple of days I managed to coax them out and after winning their confidence they wouldn't leave my side. I got the impression that they had been military trained. The 2IC liked me to accompany him in his Austin Champ with the dogs. I think he thought it looked good to the army bods.

At the power Station. 'Joss' Mee, 'Jacko' Jackson, 'Leo' Lees, 'Lofty' Leader.

Relaxation time. Mucky book among the palms?

Temporary graves of Marines B Short and D Howard.

United Nations troops marching into Port Said.

We left Port Said on the aircraft carrier HMS *Ocean* sailing for Malta where we stayed for a couple of days before returning to Plymouth by sea. We passed Gibraltar on my 20th birthday. Back in the UK I took a couple of week's leave then returned to the Royal Marine Barracks for release.

Two years! It seemed a lot longer. I can't imagine someone from a little pit village doing what I did in those two years; the mates I made and the comradeship. Most of my mates from home didn't do National Service because they worked down the pit and were exempted. At this time they were earning £8 per week. I was mostly paid 28 shillings although for the last six months of my service I think I got £3. I think I know who got the best deal.

After my discharge I went back to working on the railway. I got married in 1962 and built a bungalow next to my parents where I live today. I am still with my wife; we have three children who are all okay; and four grandchildren all okay. We are both in good health and I am on no medication at all. I did have two knee replacements about three years ago and they made me a new man after all the pain I had suffered for more than three years.

* * *

Ken Applegate, 42 Commando.

I was born in Gorleston-on-Sea in May 1934 and among my earliest memories is that of my father playing the cornet in the Salvation Army Band while my younger brother John and I were little sunbeams singing in the choir. Another memory takes me back to the Second World War and standing at my bedroom window watching German aircraft strafing the South Denes fishing net drying frames belonging to the herring drifters. God only knows what they expected to hit.

Because of the escalation of the war John and I were evacuated to a little village called Warnford in Hampshire. We had not been there long before we realised we were getting more bombs there than back in Gorleston. The reason for this soon became apparent; not only did we have a searchlight battery just two fields away from our cottage, but we were also on the German bomber flight path to Southampton docks.

When my father returned home from North Africa with the RASC and heard we were not too happy down south he managed to get a posting to Norwich and we returned to Gorleson. After a while I managed to get a place at the City of Norwich School for some serious studying.

After the war Dad finished in the Army and started up a driving school. I transferred to Great Yarmouth Grammar School. By the time I was 16 I felt unsettled and unfulfilled and realised I needed to make some positive decisions about my future.

At school I'd been in the Army Cadets and now I joined No.4 ACF at Gorleston. I'd always had a hankering to make a career in the service with a specific desire to join the best and the hardest. I decided to join the Marines. My parents disapproved violently and thought I was too young at 17 and that I was wasting all that they had kept me at grammar school for. My father eventually agreed and signed the consent form. I joined up at the Royal Marine Recruiting Office in Norwich, took and passed my medical in London in June 1951, then fulfilled my attestation and swore my allegiance at 0900 hours on 14 August 1951, before continuing on to Deal in Kent to start my induction and joining routine.

A body of untrained, untidy, scruffy, ignorant, useless, hopeless non-beings is what we were told we were on our arrival at Deal Royal Marines Barracks. My new identification number was RM11000 of 585 Squad. At the passing out parade I was honoured with the Silver Whistle for best all round recruit. Deal brought us together as a unit and as comrades. Tommy Dodds and I became inseparable and he turned out to be the closest friend of my life.

On 26 October we moved to the Royal Marines Barracks at Eastney, Portsmouth, where the bull eased and we were taught seamanship. It was damned hard work humping 4-inch and 6-inch shells around and the favourite punishment for a misdemeanour was to stand with the breach of a 4-inch gun in your arms. We also spent many an hour rowing a naval whaler around Portsmouth harbour. I think we all enjoyed our time here since we all did well in the exams and passing out parade.

Our next port of call in December was the Infantry Training Centre at Lympstone on the River Exe estuary where we began our initiation into field activities. We started to work with a full range of weapons including grenades and took classes in map and compass reading. ITC was a taster for what was to come next at the Commando School at Bickleigh which was to be the culmination of all that had gone before. We underwent weeks of horror, heartbreak, stress, pain, mental and physical abuse, as we were pushed to the limit. I hadn't realised there were so many ways of using rope to cross a river.

The training just got harder and harder and we got faster and fitter as we started to do 3-mile speed marches then 6-milers and 9-milers. Then we were dropped off in pairs in various areas of Dartmoor with Very pistol, compass and a couple of cheese sandwiches and told to find our way the 30 miles back through bogs and sudden fog banks.

We went on to carry out many raids across Plymouth Sound in high-speed Doreys carrying out ambushes to kidnap various personnel and capture items of warfare from the 'enemy', sometimes with a capsize. There were also the cliff face descents with ropes. Those of us fortunate enough to pass the course were delighted and honoured to achieve our main objective, the coveted Green Beret.

We eventually returned to Plymouth Barracks to prepare for the pass out parade. This all culminated in 585 Intake marching past as King's Squad, with the Major General Royal Marines taking the salute. It was a very proud moment for us all.

Those of the squad who elected to go for Commando Brigade as opposed to Big Ships were sent back to Bickleigh for further extended training. I chose to train as a member of Support Troop where I learned the ins and outs of 3-inch mortars and the Vickers Medium Machine Gun. It was here that I first met Sergeant Don Dennis our weapons instructor who was to become a good friend. Also coming into my life at this time as another oppo to go with Tommy was Johnny Higgs. The trio stood together for the next few years. The course involved lots of activity on the moors again but this time with the added 120lbs weight of the Vickers.

On 30 August 1952 we went back to Royal Marines Barracks at Plymouth to await our postings. Ours was Malta. We were equipped with tropical clothes, had our jabs and went on a short embarkation leave. Within six weeks we were heading up to Liverpool and on to the troopship HT *Lancashire*. With training over what could be better than a Mediterranean cruise?

We set sail on 18 October and after some steering problems in the Bay of Biscay passed through the Straits of Gibraltar and on to Malta. Three Commando Brigade spent the next two years moving around to any trouble spots and fulfilling serious training requirements in the Middle East. There was also plenty of time to take in the sites with my mates. After arriving back at Plymouth on 22 October 1954 we went off on three months leave to see our families.

Our return was to the Infantry Training Centre where we had to wait for the home posting of our choice. My choice was HMS *Ganges* the shore establishment situated at Shotley in Suffolk which was not far from home. The wait turned out to be for a year but what an eventful twelve months it was. Food becomes important when time stands still so I spent quite some time in the NAAFI, or was it because of the little blond girl who worked there? Her name was Audrey and we were married in the little town of Alton all within three months of meeting. We found a flat in Exmouth from which I commuted each day to camp where I had got myself an administrative job. I was over the moon with the birth of our son Ken.

In January 1956 my request for a posting to HMS *Ganges* was finally ratified. My duties there were policing the training base from where the young ratings who couldn't stand the pace used to do a bunk. It was our job to bring them back.

To begin with Audrey and I lived at Gorleston

with my parents and I commuted to Shotley. However, after a few months we were given a new Admiralty house at the base. It was a super place and we soon settled in.

The euphoria didn't last long though. Early in August there was a dreaded knock at the front door. I was to report immediately to No.42 Commando Unit at Bickleigh. Things had blown up in the Middle East. While I went down to Devon Audrey and Ken returned to my parents' home.

I was feeling down having to leave my family but my spirits were soon lifted when I met up with all the old gang from the Support Group, many of whom had also left family behind. Within a couple of weeks we were completely re-equipped with tropical gear and fighting kit including the very latest in weapons. In a further two weeks we were on our way yet again to Malta. Once there we spent a few weeks training and honing up our fitness until, after a couple of false alarms, we finally got the word it was a GO!

The armada of British assault ships left Malta late on 30 October with 42 Commando being carried aboard the LSTs *Suvla* and *Anzio*. It was a fine sight as we ploughed steadily through a fairly calm sea at 4 to 5 knots. Standing on the deck on 2 November taking in some fresh air I had never seen such a mass of ships at any one time except on film showing the D-Day landings. Suddenly there was a massive hissing of air and water just off our port bow and there right in the middle of the convoy was the huge black form of an American submarine surfacing. Just as quickly it disappeared again. The next night there was another sighting which caused some action. The lead ship in front of us started signalling with her lamp at a strange silhouette which appeared in our midst. The intruder refused to reply or identify herself. With patience exhausted a couple of well placed star shells soon brought results. Again it was identified as American, this time a frigate.

Early on the morning of 6 November we were on deck waiting. Wow! What a sight! Looking forward I could see the French fleet lying off Port Fuad on the left of the canal mouth. There in all its glory was the French battleship *Jean Bart*, one of the most enormous battleships I had ever seen. The pungent smell of cordite was in the air with crashing explosions from the naval shelling and dive bombing of the beaches.

Time for a final check of my gear: Vickers Machine Gun, tripod, two liners of ammunition and tripod across my shoulder, 9mm pistol, four hand grenades, first aid kit and a few salt tablets. Our LCA (assault landing craft) had already been lowered into position when I reached her and I climbed over the side into position. At about 0400 we were launched on our way towards the right-hand beach. Then there was an almighty crash. Well that didn't last long I thought, thinking that a shell had hit us. But no, it was another LCA that had hurtled into us on the port side.

As we approached the beach which was now about half a mile away the temptation to have a peep over the bow ramp was so overpowering I just had to. There was a British high speed launch at anchor just offshore with a marine standing up in the bows, legs apart, arms behind his back, staring at the beach ahead. I'd have known that stance anywhere, it was my old buddy Colin Bendall who had joined up with me; I'd been best man at his wedding. As we sped past him making for Green Beach Colin yelled, 'Give them hell Appy.'

I wondered if my senses were getting more acute, the noises getting louder, and the smells stronger. My heart and the adrenaline were pumping. I was asking myself if I would be able to handle myself and would I let anyone down? At about 200 yards from the beach the bow doors started to open and then the landing ramps went down. Looking ahead to the beach it looked just like the film I'd seen of the D-Day landings. Then there was a thud and we had bloody grounded and were still 100 yards from the beach.

The water was cold and reached up to my chest. I felt more like a pack horse than a fighting machine with the MMG tripod on my back. As I waded forward I glanced right and left. My mates were in the same situation so I didn't feel alone as we hit the beach. A constant cracking greeted us as bullets parted the air around us. Fire was also coming from our right. There was a shout from the lieutenant to walk lively but not to run or we'd fall over with the weight. 'Sod this,' said either my number two or number three, 'I'm getting under those beach huts.' The fact that they were on fire didn't hinder our progress to them; other silhouetted figures had the same idea.

Up on the esplanade behind the blazing huts we formed up keeping our heads down as much as we could. In a casual manner the lieutenant stood on the road in front of us, bullet spurts hitting the ground around him, as he coolly explained that a couple of the lads have stopped bullets and are pinned down in the main square off the sea front. They needed support and this could be given from the apartments opposite.

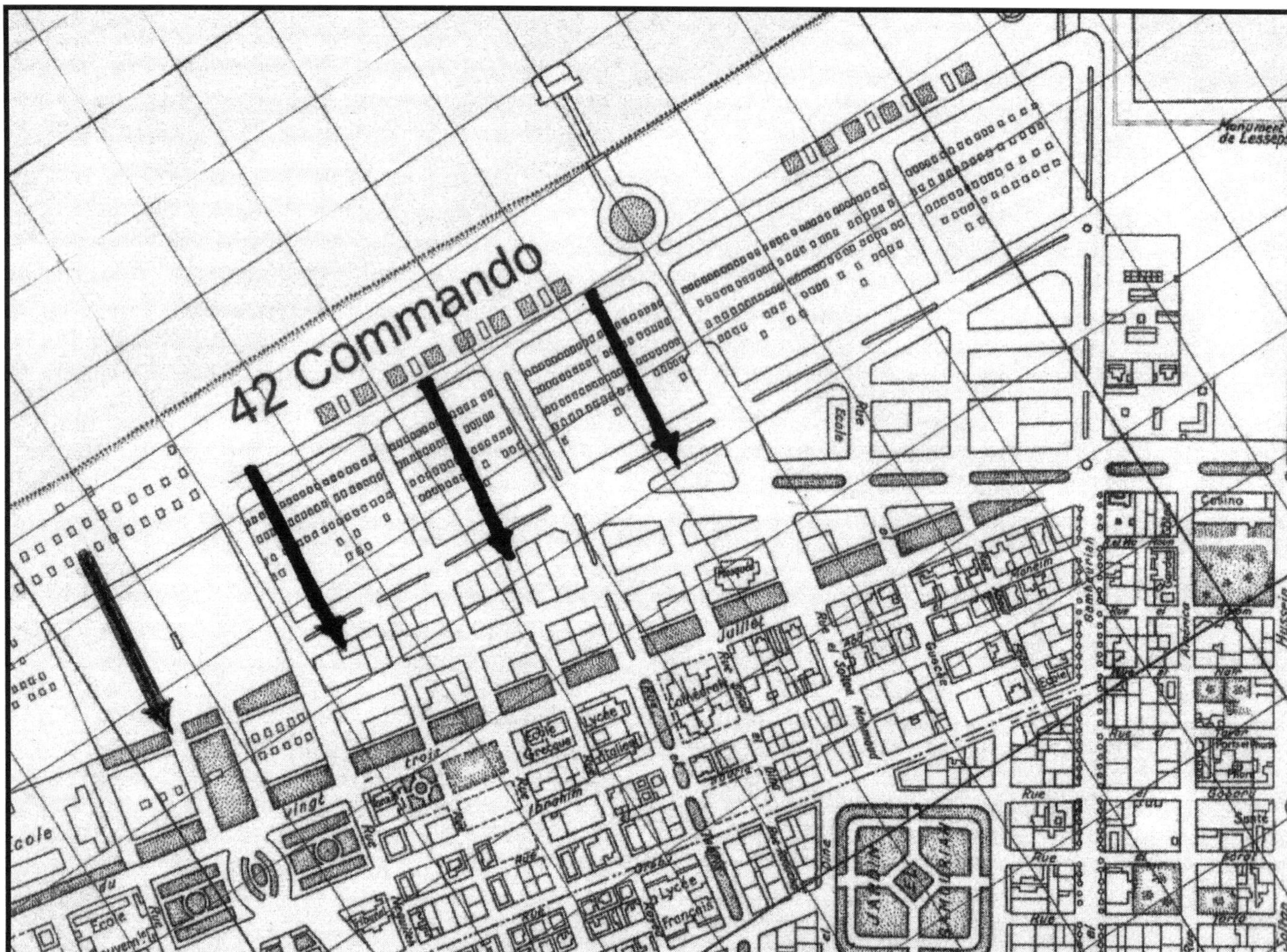

This is where 42 Commando came ashore to begin making its way south on the western side of the town.

My team quickly made its way across the road and into the large apartment block, along a corridor, and into a main bedroom facing the square in question. One swipe of the arm and the dressing table in front of the window was cleared and the machine gun set up and loaded with a liner of 250 rounds of .303 bullets. On pulling back the curtains and opening the windows a tremendous din of gunfire greeted us.

As if on cue the sergeant burst through the door. 'Have you a target?' I hadn't and he thrust a pair of binoculars into my hand. Enemy targets on the balconies above our pinned down troops were picked out and I concentrated my fire on the target. A sudden burst of small arms fire brought my attention back into the room. The side window of the room had been shattered by one of my mates neutralising a member of the opposition who was about to take a pot shot at me from a building in that direction. We soon relieved the balconies of their occupants and our wounded lads were reached. While all this was taking place, so one of my mates told me, another of the chaps had entered the room looking for 'goods' and found £60 in British notes under a pillow before making a quick exit.

An order was given to muster outside the apartment and to prepare for a fast breakout to the south. By this time the Royal Tank Regiment's Centurion tanks had come ashore and were lining up alternatively with our amphibious tracked Buffalos carrying the troops in what was supposed to be a rush through to the open south side of town. What a bloody hope! The maximum speed of a Buffalo was 15 miles an hour; how can anyone rush in one of them?

The convoy had been assembled on the sea front by the time we reached it and consisted of 12 to 15 vehicles. Ours and another team were ordered to set up the Vickers Guns on the lowered rear ramp of the lead Buffalo so that we could shoot up both sides of the street.

We moved off and turned into Rue el Mahraussa, the main through route south in Port Said. Hellfire, what a welcome! The opposition were up in the buildings flanking both sides of the road and greeted us by hurling grenades and shooting into our vehicles from the windows and balconies as we slowly drove through. The screams of wounded men could be heard coming from inside the Buffalos. The armour had been removed from the vehi-

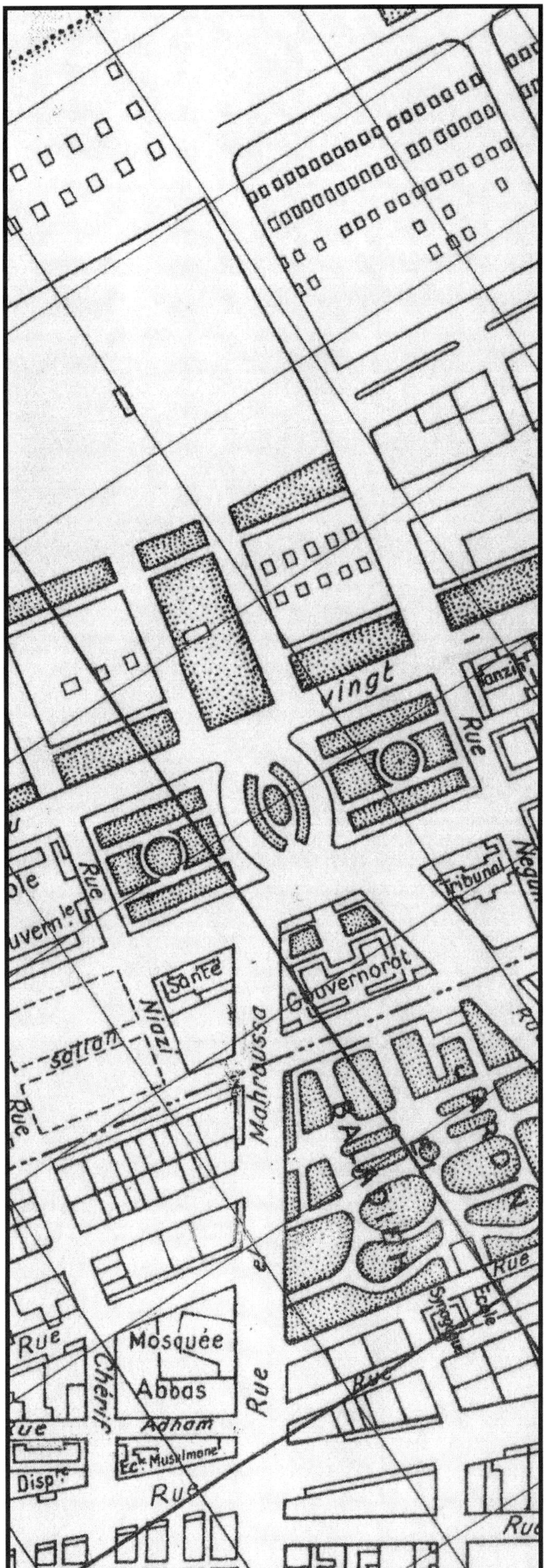

Rue el Mahroussa, the route south.

cles to make them lighter for landing so there was nothing to stop the bullets. My number two had been hit and a few choice words from Frank Stanley on the other Vickers told me that he and his number two had also been hit. The lack of speed was killing us.

The Rue el Mahroussa became the Rue Mohamed and then we were through and into the more open suburbs. What a relief! Shortly, to our right, we came to the Port Said Prison.

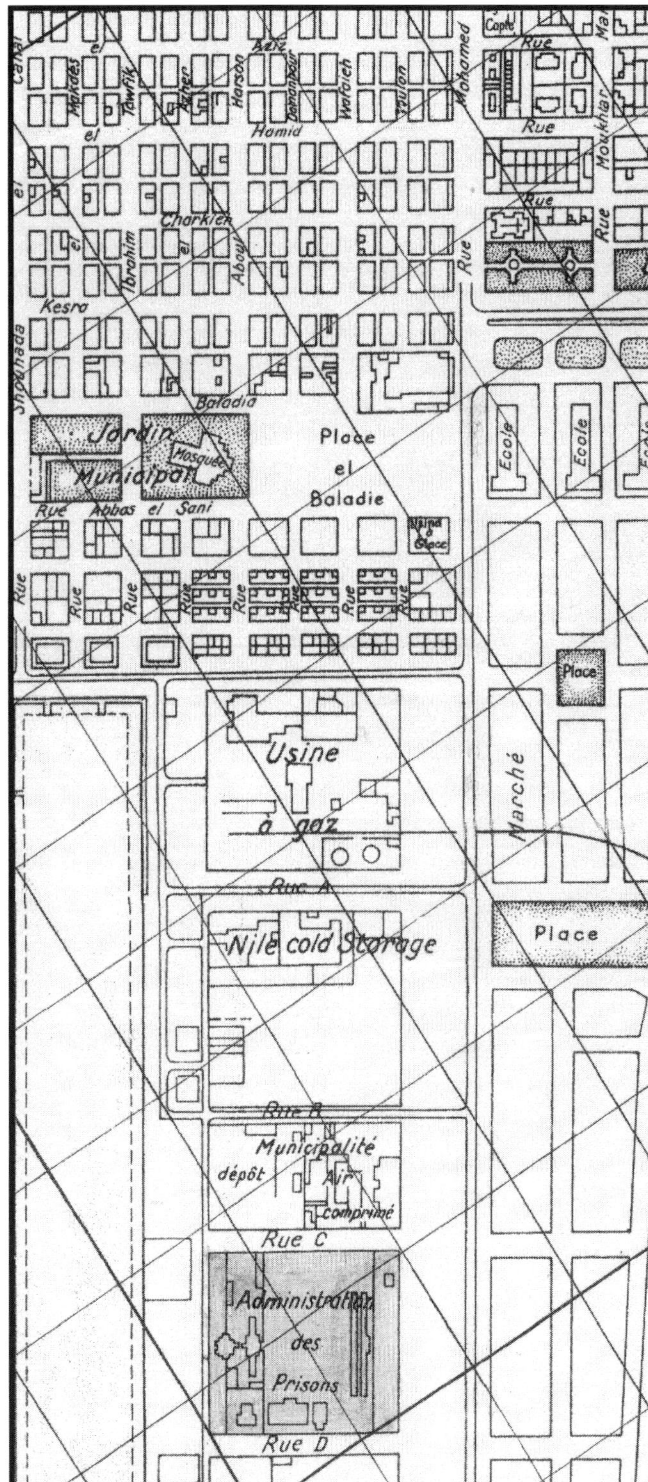

South of the built-up area along the Rue Mohamed: gas works, storage depot, municipal building, and the prison.

We stopped and the lieutenant shouted 'debus'. I whipped off my beret with my left hand to support the red hot barrel of the MMG and jumped off the ramp. I began setting up to face the prison when we were ordered back aboard. We'd stopped because our driver had been killed and someone else had taken his place. The Buffalo set off and I ran while throwing everything aboard, all 130 pounds of it, and myself after it, glad now that it was going at only 15 miles an hour.

The Port Said Prison.

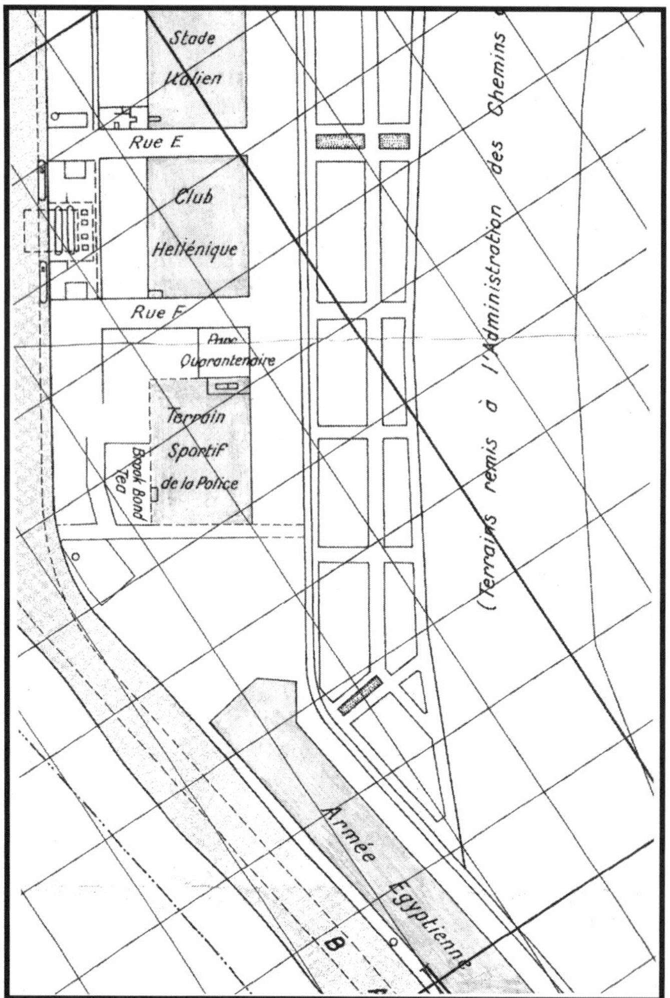

The Italian, Greek and Police sports grounds, and the Egyptian Army Barracks.

With the atmosphere full of bullets again cracking around us we passed beyond the prison. To the left I noticed a small copse of trees with vehicles under camouflage nets and what appeared to be the muzzle of a field gun aiming right at 'me'. Bloody hell! I fired at least two belts of ammunition (500 rounds) in as many minutes and peppered everything in sight under the trees.

We continued for a few minutes more, passing two or three sports grounds on the right, until we came to the Egyptian army camp which had been abandoned so we entered and debussed.

I quickly set up my gun at the entrance to the guard room as by now the enemy was giving us a lot of flak from a boat yard across the other side of the road. One of my guys was hit so I gave him a morphine tablet. By now the helicopters had been called in to take out the wounded so using his own blood I put an 'M' on his forehead.

There was now time to take in the situation and I saw that the Egyptian flag was still flying at the entrance to the camp. That's not bloody on, I thought, we hold the camp now. Without thinking I ran to the flagpole to take the flag down but found that there was no rope. It was just nailed on. This wasn't going to stop me though and despite the flak still cracking the air I shinned up the pole and pulled the flag down. A brilliant souvenir to take home! Then I thought about it. Why the hell did I do that just for a flag?

By now it was getting quite late in the day but the lieutenant had just received orders to go back to the copse area and take the power station. By now things had quietened down and the power station was easy to take and hold. For the first time in the day we could sit down and have our first food and a smoke while the lieutenant sorted out the guard duties for the night. With darkness there was total silence.

Tom and I took the first watch and part way through a piercing scream filled the night. Tom and I ran towards its source to find that one of the lads was running amuck. Either the tension of the day had got to him or he'd run out of rations for he'd bitten right through the lieutenant's hand.

It was about this time that the news came through that a ceasefire had just come into effect at midnight. It came too late for some of the lads though. We learned the names of those who did not make it. One of them was Sergeant Dennis who had taught me all I knew about the Vickers MMG. I'd been to his home and had tea with his wife and children. Another was Brian Short who had died under a beach hut just after we came ashore. Quite a few of the lads had been wounded and were to spend some time in hospital.

After dawn we moved out to occupy the prison with orders to search for snipers, who were still operating in defiance of the ceasefire, and enemy deserters. The sights and the stench in the building were indescribable. Dead bodies had to be checked out. Some had been prisoners but others were civilians which I found very upsetting. It was a relief to be out in the open air again.

Our next duty was to check out that little copse I'd fired on yesterday to see what was there. We found plenty of arms and ammunition but also an army Austin Champ vehicle with a Rolls Royce engine. I'd always wanted to drive a Rolls so in my enthusiasm I said, 'Let's get it started and drive it back to the power station.' However this wasn't going to happen. Some idiot had sprayed the area with bullets and wrecked what had once been a delightful little vehicle.

Our next duty left a bad taste. A riot had broken out at a food store just outside the city where women and children were stealing sacks of flour. They had not eaten properly for weeks it seemed which was well before we landed. Breaking up the crowd was difficult so we had to fire over their heads. It is not something I remember with pride. Over the following period looting among the Egyptians became a way of life and they tried it on at every opportunity. While helping to curb one of these riots I was interviewed by BBC News for a radio broadcast.

Gradually the British units pulled out and as usual we were among the last. The locals begged us to stay and not to leave until the French had gone. Enough said! We returned to Blighty on HMS *Ocean*, offloaded the transport and equipment at Plymouth docks, had our personal gear moved to the RM barracks, and then went on leave. I was one of the lucky ones who would be seeing my family again.

Returning to Plymouth didn't seem so bad now that I was close to home again with not long to serve. I was able to get on an NCOs' course where I gained a pass and certificate, with stripe to lance corporal. The course ended on 9 August 1957 and I was finally released from the Marines to start life again as Ken Applegate in Civvy Street on 19 October.

My mate Tom Dodds told me of a job going at a chicken farm in Hampshire. We moved there but it didn't work out. Then the American company Standard Telephone and Cable gave me a chance. I wound coil formers for the Scotland to Belgium cross-channel telephone cable within their air-conditioned plant in Southampton. While there we had our daughter Lesley and moved into a new council house. I was also promoted to foreman at the plant. The kids loved their holidays back home at Gorleston Beach so after two years I thought it was time to move back home to Gorleston with my family.

My liking for food took me to the Birds Eye's door at their Lowestoft factory where I worked for 32 years and finished as a departmental manager before taking early retirement.

* * *

Tom Dando, Somerset Light Infantry attached to 42 Commando.

I was born on 19 of April 1937 and bred and buttered in Somerset at Paulton near Midsomer Norton. For my education I went on to attend the old-established King's School which is situated at Bruton, a lovely town towards the southern end of the county.

I left school when I was 18 and soon afterwards was called up for my National Service. After a medical at Wincanton I joined the Somerset Light Infantry. During training I was sent to Strensall near York on a Pom's (potential officer material) course. On the final assessment of the WOSB (War Office Selection Board) I was asked by one of the officers what I wished to get out of my time in the Army. After I replied 'Me' I was immediately returned to unit.

In about December 1955 I was posted to Crownhill Plymouth where I was attached to 42 Commando where I was put in command of No. 5 Detachment Anti-Tank Section under section commander Lt Tim Beath. At that that the Marine Commandos didn't have their own anti-tank sections.

We were using BAT 105mm recoilless anti-tank guns. However, it was found that the 'squash head' ammunition was apparently unstable in hot climates so we then rapidly retrained at Bahar-ic-Caghag Bay in Malta using the 'old' 17-pounder weapons towed by Stuart guntowers which were Stuart tanks without a carapace or turret.

17-pounder gun exercise in Malta.

Later, after the nationalisation of the Suez Canal Company by Nasser, we went out to Malta again for more training exercises.

A practice landing from the LST HMS *Suvla* (L3518) at Mellieha Bay, Malta.

Tank Landing Craft exercise in the Grand harbour, Malta. HMS *Counterguard* (4043) and HMS *Buttress* (4043).

At the end of October we went aboard the LST HMS *Suvla* for an exercise that turned out to be the real thing and we continued the voyage to Egypt.

One day a couple of us where enjoying a quiet cigarette in the dark on the stern of the LTC when the Oerlikon gun above our heads opened up. You can imagine our consternation. We learned later that it was a false alarm caused by a submarine from the US 6th Fleet that was tracking us.

The invasion itself, which took place at dawn, went well. We had the ships firing over our heads

Relaxing on the way to Port Said.

'Here we go!'

so it was very noisy and I have suffered a ringing in my left ear ever since.

A naval observer in one of the first wave of craft making for shore earlier had called on naval gunners to silence the fire coming from the Casino Jetty. It was now burning furiously.

42 Commandos wading ashore near what use to be the Casino Jetty.

There was relatively low level resistance, just some sporadic fire as we waded ashore on the right hand side of the blazing Casino and up the beach to take cover under those of the beach huts that were not on fire. It was under one of these, I later learned, that our mate Brian Short had been killed instantly by machine gun fire that had opened up from across the road while he was lying down taking cover.

The remains of many of the beach huts after the fire started by Navy shelling.

Once we had secured our length of the beachhead and the blocks of flats across the road, which were then taken over as Brigade HQ, we started to advance towards the power station and other utility buildings at the southern end of town. It was then that things really started to warm up and get quite hairy as we passed between the high buildings which harboured snipers and grenadiers. I remember Lt Westwood kicking a grenade that had been thrown down at us out of one of the 'DUKW's as we were travelling along.

View from a Champ/Land Rover along the length of Rue el Mahroussa towards its continuation Rue Mohamed Aly.

By about this time 45 Commando had started to come ashore in a fleet of helicopters to the area behind the De Lesseps statue on the canal side to link up with 40 and 42 Commando and between them to begin controlling the town.

Shell holes in a building, generally by a window, marked the place where a very brave sniper had met his end.

After the ball was over. Tom taking a well-earned smoke.

During the evening, by which time we learned that a ceasefire was to come into effect by midnight, we had taken refuge in a block of flats for the night. The lavatories were fitted with integral bidets within the bowls and one or two of the lads were very wary of sitting on them fearing that they may have been booby trapped. You could understand their caution.

No.6 detachment anti-tank gun crew. With 42 Commando. 8 November 1956. Keith Fuller. 'Butch' Bramley, Rob 'Brum' Willis, L/Cpl Gill, Brian Keays.

The building that became our 'hotel' for the rest of our stay in Port Said.

View down on local children outside the flats scrambling for sweets thrown down by the lads.

Buffalos parked up outside the flats near the beach. Surviving beach huts seen at the end of the street.

Following the ceasefire we began to carry out extensive patrols and searches throughout the town. After eight days 40 and 45 Commando returned to Malta while we remained in the town until about the 27th November after the UN peacekeeping force had taken over.

View from the flats down on what was being used as a POW compound across the street.

View from the flat of UN troops arriving to take over.

Two more of those who paid the price. One temporary grave is of Sergeant Dennis and the other of Corporal Crawford of the Somerset Light Infantry detachment.

I expected to remain with 42 Commando for its return to the UK on HMS *Ocean* and then rejoin my regiment, the Somerset Light Infantry. However I discovered that the latter had recently been posted to Limassol in Cyprus and this is where I rejoined the regiment to serve the remainder of my National Service on patrols and searches involving Eoka. I was demobbed in October 1957.

* * *

Chris Pickering, 45 Commando

I was born on 26 January 1937 in Newcastle upon Tyne where, when I was five, I went to St Catherine's Primary School in Jesmond Road. I passed the 11+ examination which took me to St Cuthbert's Grammar School in West Road.

At 16 I joined the Royal Marines Forces Voluntary Reserve and subsequently went on two of their one-week-long courses at the Royal Marines Barracks at Eastney on the coast at Southsea. I left school in July 1955 with A-levels in chemistry, physics and biology and was accepted by King's College Newcastle for a BSc course. However, as I was now 18, I decided to do my National Service first and get it out of the way. Since I was a member of the RMFVR, when I was called up on 1 October 1955 they sent me to the ITC (Infantry Training Command) of the Royal Marines at Lympstone on the River Exe near Exeter.

I spent 14 weeks there during which I attended a four-day WOSB (War Office Selection Board) at Andover in Hampshire. I failed it, for which, in hindsight, I thank the Lord since I would have missed so much fun if I'd spent all those months at an officer training school. We, the 884 Squad, passed out on 12 January 1956. The following day we arrived at Commando School, Bickleigh, just outside Plymouth and just over a month later, on 15 February, received our green berets and joined 42 Commando, also based at Bickleigh.

From the 27 February until 6 March I attended a snow warfare course at Aviemore in the Scottish Highlands after which I returned to Bickleigh until mid-April when I went to HMS *Seahawk*, the Culdrose Royal Naval Air Station at Helston for abseiling and climbing practice. I am possibly the only national serviceman to have completed a CL3 Cliff Leaders' Course which was during that glorious three weeks on the sea cliffs around Cornwall.

This was all in preparation for 6 of May when a team of us left for Nodes Bay near Sandown in the Isle of Wight where we took part in *Operation Runaround*, and gave a demonstration of cliff climbing for NATO top brass. *Runaround* was interesting in that it included trials in which members of 42 Commando were delivered to their attack area by helicopter rather than by sea craft, the first time this had ever been tried

On the 31st I left for a cliff assault course at Sennen Cove in Cornwall for seven weeks of climbing the sea cliffs at Land's End which lasted until 24 June when I returned to Bickleigh. On the 5th of July we embarked at Plymouth on the Daring class destroyer, HMS *Delight*, and sailed to Norway for a NATO exercise named *Midnight Sun*. We arrived back at Bickleigh on 25 July and spent the next six weeks undergoing more intensive training.

On 6 September two of us were posted to Malta. We travelled up to Paddington by rail then made our way to Blackbushe Airport where we boarded a Viscount aircraft. The flight flew via a refuelling stop at Nice in the south of France. On arrival in Malta we were taken to a tented camp at Ghian Tuffea and joined 45 Commando, swapping our white lanyards for red ones. I remember it was a scorching day and I got sunburned on the beach. While I was here I joined in some fairly routine training and was given the job of troop clerk for a while.

Earlier 45 Commando had been serving in Cyprus together with 40 Commando as part of the force dealing with EOKA but in early August it had sailed for Malta to undergo special assault training. We also received training in street fighting among some old empty buildings.

On 29th October we embarked on the aircraft carrier HMS *Theseus* supposedly to take part in what was called *Exercise Boathook*, involving communications practice with Allied Forces Headquarters in Cyprus. This was the day I wrote a letter home:

R.M.V. 202566. Mne. Pickering
'X' Troop
45 Commando RM
BFPO.
29.10.1956 [Monday]

Dear Dad and Mum

As I am writing this in office hours I may be very brief in order to get finished before the sergeant major returns. .....

I nearly wrote to you a week ago to tell you we were moving somewhere. Then they decided it was only an exercise and we weren't going anywhere. They've changed backwards and forwards so often even the CO doesn't know. It was an operation at first (the real thing) then only an exercise. Eventually it all fell through until this morning when we were told to be ready to move by 4pm today. We are going away for 10 or 12 days (the whole 45). We may come back to Malta, we may not.

The idea is, with the authorities, that we will be aboard the test convoy going through the Suez [Canal] next week. That's almost positive. We are taking all the weapons and ammo we can lay our hands on. We embark on the aircraft carrier Ocean on Tuesday or Wednesday and if Nasser tries anything funny we jump in the helicopters, of which there are dozens aboard, and deal with it.

If you hear of fun and games in the Suez area next week, then you can enviously think of me getting free trips around Egypt in a helicopter. JUST THE JOB. I'll bring you a sphinx back for Xmas. If Nasser's bluffing and we get there and back, we'll be working our guts out painting the ships etc.

For the time being then you'd better not send me any parcels, shirts, pedigrees or anything; they'll only be something else to carry. Also use the same address minus Malta. The BFPO will find us.

While I am writing this I can see through the door 2 helicopters landing on the parade ground about 50 yards away. Probably a couple of field marshals in for a cup of tea. By the way, we trooped the colours for the Corps birthday yesterday. It went off quite well. Admiral Sir Guy Grantham, GCB, CBE, C in C Mediterranean Fleet was reviewing officer. He gave us a very big build up and cut the birthday cake for us at dinner time in our dining room. I have enclosed a programme. Ah well, the Sgt. Major is back so I'll close here. I'll have plenty to write about on board. Don't worry whatever you do. It will probably end up by being a damned good holiday. All my love to you.

Chris.

Ps. I'll keep you informed.

Pps. I've never tried typing in a helicopter.

Late Monday evening. Ppps

Dear Mum again,

I wrote the first 4 pages of this letter this morning. Since then I've had half an hour off for lunch and worked in the office till 7pm. I just caught up supper and have finished packing.

Those helicopters I mentioned were to carry ammo and stores down to the carriers in Grand Harbour, Valletta. There are rumours now that the move is nothing to do with the test convoy, also most of our troops are definitely going on the HMS Theseus not the Ocean, me among them. Some of the crew off the Theseus said last night that they were going to Cyprus next. We might then go to

Cyprus and train there in case anything happens in Suez.

Tomorrow, no doubt, there will be a lot more rumours, changes of detail and other alterations. However, a few points are positive as I've written them this afternoon.

We've packed away every item of gear and are carrying enough for 12/14 days in rucksacks.

We are going on HMS Theseus so you may hear where that's going before you hear from me.

We are training or fighting from helicopters – luxury!

Well, I'll leave it at that. You realise of course that none of this is public. I had to sign the 'Official Secrets Act' on front of two witnesses when I got this job. Ah well, I'll post this and probably write tomorrow.

Lots of love again,

Chris.

Packing stores in Malta.

About half of us finally embarked aboard the *Theseus* and the other half of 45 Commando on the *Ocean* on Friday the 2nd of November and sailed the following day at 5 o'clock in the afternoon. Also aboard the *Theseus* was No.845 Helicopter Squadron which would be ferrying us ashore. After 24 hours at sea we learned that we were going to invade Port Said.

On the morning of the 6th just before 7am 40 and 42 Commandos went ashore from their landing craft along the beach at each side of the Casino Jetty, some of them soon meeting up with the paratroops who had taken El Gamil Airfield, the sewage farm, the cemetery and the Coastguard Barracks the day before. Not long after this we were brought up to assemble on deck to board the Whirlwind helicopters and then we lifted off, about five men at a time, and flew the short distance to

Preparing to fly off the *Theseus.*

Port Said where we landed on the area next to the De Lesseps statue.

Three helicopters flying in to land close to the De Lesseps Statue.

Landing behind the De Lesseps Statue.

Then the helicopters returned to the *Theseus* to collect the second wave and the third until all 450 men of 45 Commando were ashore preparing to link up with 3 Para as well as 40 and 42 Commando. As soon as it was safe to do so we reassembled and began cleaning our weapons. When landing we had had to pass through the dust storm thrown up by rotor downwash.

The 45 Marine Commandos approaching the buildings on the south-west corner of the 'De Lesseps' landing area.

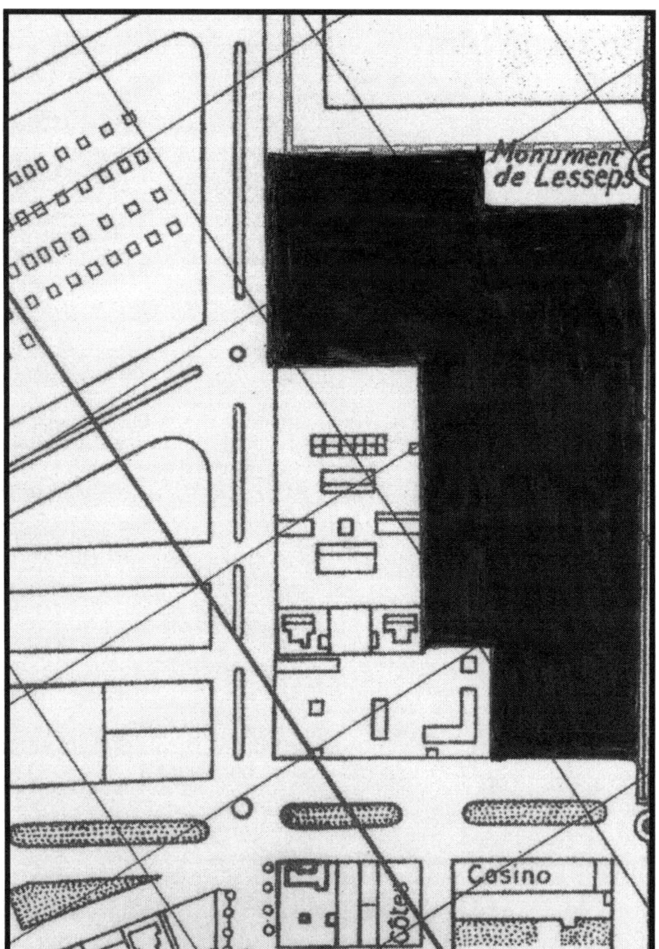

The 45 Commando helicopter landing area by the De Lesseps statue at the canal edge. The Casino is the Casino Palace Hotel, used as a casualty clearing station immediately the Egyptian defenders had been chased out.

The De Lesseps Statue landing ground soon after the landing. First of the trucks now ashore.

We were just about to move off into the town when we were strafed by what I learned later was a Fleet Air Arm Wyvern from the aircraft carrier *Eagle.* The pilot had apparently been issued with incorrect co-ordinates for an enemy gun believed to be firing on one of our destroyers out to sea. There were about 16 casualties of varying degrees in all including the CO Lt Col N H Tailyour and Major Long his Intelligence Officer. One soldier was killed and two marines, 'Bomber' Clark and Colin Ireland, had to have legs amputated. This is what has become known as the 'Friendly Fire' incident.

Eventually we made our way into the town and were involved in ten to twelve hours of house-to-house, room-to-room fighting. What more could a young chap ask for? It nearly became my career.

That first evening as we were settling down for the night in a commandeered apartment block someone tripped over his mates webbing and pulled the pin out of a phosphorus grenade. Time for sharp exit! A lot of the collateral damage to this particular building was due to this accident.

Our new accommodation.

After having burnt out our accommodation we moved to a very nice apartment block in the suburbs with a roof garden.

During our time in Port Said we went out on a number of security patrols as well as mounting guard on our pad of course. Some of also learned how to ride a commandeered motor bike.

X Troop on patrol in some of the ruins of Port Said.

Photograph of gun taken in Port Said

Chris aboard the *Empire Fowey* on the return to Malta.

After about a week or so we returned to Malta aboard the *Empire Fowey* and moved into M'tarfa Barracks close to the centre of the island. Superb!

The M'tarfa Barracks in Malta.

In February we went by TLC to Tripoli in Libya then into the wilderness near Tarhuna for six weeks of desert warfare training. We returned to Malta for a couple of weeks then sailed by TLCs to Cyprus for duties against EOKA. We went on stake-outs and searches, and I was involved in supervising the blasting at the Amiondos asbestos quarries so that EOKA couldn't get its hands on explosives from here. We were also caught up in fighting the tragic forest fires that broke out in the area at that time. I flew home from Nicosia on the 6th of August 1957.

After National Service I decided against university. I had always wanted to farm and hoped for a job eventually as a farm manager so I decided on a more direct approach and enrolled as a student at Kirkley Hall, the Northumberland County Agricultural College at Ponteland not far from Newcastle. I was still officially on disembarkation leave when I started there in September 1957. During that first year back I also joined up again with the RMFVR and was lucky enough to get onto a CL2 course. The next year I won my parachute wings at Abingdon as well as winning the Rose Bowl at Kirkley as top student.

In November 1963 my father and I acquired a small farm of 170 acres next to RAF Acklington in Northumberland. I farmed there for 40 years and was farming 1,000 acres when I retired in 2003. I sold up and retired to the lovely coastal village of Warkworth close by. I am married to Louise and we have three children.

To this day I have much to thank for my time in the Royal Marines. It was possibly the most enjoyable two years of my life. All this reminiscing made me think of Captain Hamish Brian Emslie,

MC, MD, who was my troop commander through most of my National Service. He was a man we all worshipped and who we would have, and often did, follow to the ends of the earth. Last week I 'Googled' him and discovered he had been killed in action on 13 March 1966 while serving with the Sultan of Oman's armed forces. I cried my heart out.

* * *

Edgar Gordon Coleborn, 45 Commando. (Story supplied by Edgar's son Jim.)

My Dad, Edgar Gordon Coleborn, was born on 19 September 1915 at Fareham in Hampshire. At the age of 11 he was awarded a Foundation Scholarship to Price's Grammar School in Fareham. In 1930, when 14, he left school and obtained a job as a junior clerk with Austin and Wyatt, a local firm of auctioneers and estate agents.

At the age of seventeen-and-a-half in the early spring of 1933 Dad enlisted in the Royal Marines and carried out his initial training at the Marine Depot at Deal in Kent before undergoing further instruction at Stonehouse Barracks, Plymouth.

On the completion of his training he was posted to the battleship HMS *Nelson*, flagship of the home fleet, and followed this with a spell under the Quartermaster at Eastney Barracks Portsmouth. In 1938 he married Phyllis May Long. My sister Anne was born a year or so later. Soon afterwards Dad was promoted to the rank of corporal and drafted to HMS *St Angelo*, Malta, a shore establishment situated in a coastal fort at Birgu in the Grand harbour.

Mum and Anne followed Dad soon afterwards just before the Second World War broke out but when Italy entered the war on the side of Germany on 10 June 1940 Mum and Anne returned to the UK just as the bombing and siege of Malta began.

Dad was posted to HMS *Nile*, the shore station at Alexandria in Egypt, at that time the headquarters of the Mediterranean Fleet, where he was promoted to sergeant. Soon afterwards he returned to the UK via the Suez Canal and round the cape to rejoin the Quartermaster's department at Eastney Barracks. It was while Dad was stationed here that I was born, at Liphook in Hampshire on 25 March 1944.

After a spell in the Admiralty during this latter part of the war, during which Dad was promoted to the rank of Colour Sergeant, he returned in 1945 to Eastney where he became a Quartermaster Sergeant, the youngest QMS in the Marine Corps at that time.

On 31 March 1949 Dad was promoted twice on the same day to both Superintendent Clerk, with the non-commissioned rank of Warrant Officer, and to a Commissioned Sergeant Major. He was the last Royal Marine to hold the rank of Superintending Clerk. Following this promotion he was posted to the Royal Marine Reserve (RMR) at Govan, Glasgow. Here he found accommodation for the family in the Ibrox area and so became a keen Ranger supporter.

Dad's next move was to the Pay and Records Office at Melville Barracks, Chatham, where he gained experience in the Corps' Paymaster Department. In about 1954 my father was promoted again, this time to lieutenant, and posted to Malta where he became the Pay and Records Officer of 3 Commando Brigade, the amphibious arm of the Royal Navy. This was at the time when the British forces were withdrawing from the Canal Zone where life for the troops had become quite difficult and it led to the headquarters of MELF being transferred to Cyprus. With the Greek community now realising that the Brits intended to stay in Cyprus for a considerable time to come their unrest triggered the EOKA terror campaign a year later which led to the Marines HQ together with 40 and 45 Commandos being sent to the island where they set up their headquarters at Limassol.

In late July the following year the Suez crisis suddenly erupted and shortly afterwards the Brigade in Cyprus was pulled out of the island and returned to Malta on the aircraft carrier HMS *Ocean* for intensive training including street fighting. No. 42 Commando, then operating in the UK as a training unit, was despatched to Malta on the cruiser HMS *Cumberland.*

I was 12 at the time, living with my family in Malta, and saw the build-up of troops and equipment myself. I attended the excellent Tal-Handaq Secondary School which was run by the Navy with naval and English civilian instructors for the children of service families. Each morning my school bus passed the Marsa Club and gradually I saw its hockey, football, rugby and cricket pitches becoming submerged under a sea of armoured and soft-skinned vehicles. Even the ubiquitous Maltese goats had been thrown off their scrubland to provide somewhere to pitch the hundreds of tents that were needed to accommodate the ever growing numbers of troops arriving for the coming offensive.

It is perhaps not widely known that the original intention of the military planners was to attack Egypt at Alexandria and with this in mind during the run up to the invasion discreet enquiries had been made throughout Malta to identify the whereabouts of any aluminium ladders capable of extending to 12 feet or over in length. This in itself would not have caused comment unless, like my father who had served in the Mediterranean Fleet Headquarters in 1942 during the Second World War, you knew that it was just such ladders that would be needed to get onto the breakwater at Alexandria from the sea.

On the evening of Tuesday 30 October we were having a meal in a restaurant in Sliema when it was interrupted by an announcement on the radio giving a long list of units and ships' companies that were required to return to their bases and ships at once. That put a dampener on proceedings. The brigadier of the Brigade, Brigadier R W Madoc, OBE ADC, had made it his mission to bring the entire brigade to a state of 12 hours' notice which was an amazing piece of administration. His efforts were rewarded when the main force of 40 and 42 Commando was able to depart just before dawn the following day, Wednesday the thirty-first.

At 5pm on the evening of Saturday the 3rd of November the aircraft carriers *Theseus* and *Ocean* sailed eastwards each carrying half of 45 Commando including my father. Over the next day or so a lot of time was spent in rehearsing loading and exiting the helicopters.

On the morning of 5 November, just before 7am, 40 and 42 Commando carried out the seaborne assault by landing craft on the beach of Port Said. Less than an hour later the men of 45 Commando, including Dad, were ferried ashore by helicopters, landing on the large expanse of open ground by the De Lesseps' statue. This was a very high tech operation at the time.

The active service role of my father, the Brigade Imprest Officer (paymaster), was as the OIC HQ Troop. His lot made their way to a block of flats nearby where I believe his job was to collate information coming in from the front line units for the use of the brigadier and his staff. The entrance to the block of flats they chose to occupy was locked and Dad said it was the only opportunity he would ever have to shoot the lock off a door with his pistol just like in the films. Unfortunately a young marine got there first and kicked the door in. It was from here that some nice little ornaments found their way into our family's possession.

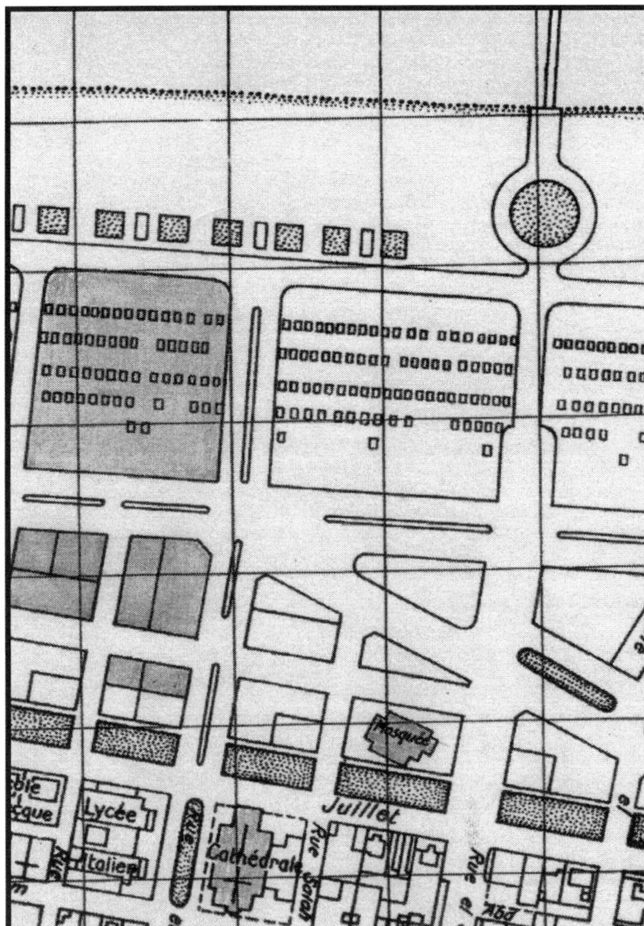

The two blocks of flats (shaded) taken over as Marines HQ, and the beach huts in front of them.

Marines HQ. View from right-hand block of flats (shown on the map) down to the front of the left-hand block.

View out over the beach huts to the shore from the front of the left-hand block of the Marine HQ flats.

A closer view of the damage to the area of the sea front beach huts.

View of shell damage to the building behind the right-hand block of the HQ flats taken diagonally from the left-hand block as seen on the map. Note the Catholic Cathedral to the left and its position on the map.

View of the Catholic Cathedral from the seaward direction, and the nearby mosque; both shaded in on the map.

Over the next week following the ceasefire and the arrival of the first UN peacekeeping personnel in Port Said the first British troops began a gradual withdrawal and the Paras embarked for Cyprus on the 12th of November.

During the late fifties the numbers in the armed forces were being gradually reduced and many redundancy payments were being offered. Dad decided to apply for this option and it was granted. He left the services on 24 November 1960, retiring with the rank of captain after almost 28 years service with the Marines.

On returning to Civvy Street Dad took employment with the Westminster Bank in Portsmouth with the family settling in the nearby town of Portchester. He finally retired in 1980 at the age of sixty-five.

* * *

Hubert (Huw) Walters, 45 Commando.

Huw has provided a number of photographs that he took during the time of the Suez Canal crisis.

The boats going in. The smoke to the right centre is from the beach huts and Shanty Town, that on the left from the shattered storage tank of the Standard Oil Depot.

View from the sea. 45 Commando going in by helicopter.

View from the block of flats serving as Commando HQ.

View to the right from one of the HQ block of flats.

Somewhere in the built-up town. The lighthouse can be seen through a gap in the skyline towards the left.

View from in front of the Marine HQ flats by the wreckage of the beach huts looking eastwards towards the Suez Canal. The De Lesseps statue can be seen on the right-hand skyline.

View westwards from the 'De Lesseps' landing ground towards the blocks of flats and what remained of the beach huts in that area.

A military meeting being held in a 'stadium' in Port Said. This is possibly where the first 45 Commando helicopter landed before having to fly off quickly under a hail of gunfire to find an area less hostile, by the de Lesseps statue.

Marines at the rear of the school.

An abandoned enemy gun.

Members of the Assault Engineer platoon all tidied up and ready for their departure from Port Said on 14 November aboard the *Empire Fowey* bound for Malta.

Photo taken from by the side of the railway station of one of the three adjacent secondary schools used as billets for some of the Marines and Royal Engineers. The 'boulevard' runs through on the left to the Rue Mohamed Aly.

Some of the lads relaxing while waiting to embark on the *Empire Fowey.*

Brian Stidwell, 45 Commando.

The following photographs are from Brian's personal collection.

Centurion tank in one of the main thoroughfares.

An Alleyway across the street.

Some sort of stores facility being guarded by 45 Marines.

A similar view from the roof of a building being used as a vantage point by 45 Marines.

Group of marines and Bedford RL 3-tonner truck on security duty in a run-down part of Port Said.

The Marines sorting through a captured arms cache.

And more.

And even more.

Brian's troop spent a day at one of the mosques.

Note the damaged building on the left and the tower of the Catholic Cathedral on the skyline.

Pretty Egyptian Girl. How can she smile so brightly?

Life is not easy for some, war or no war.

45 Commando Marines waiting to embark on the *Empire Fowey* on 14 November 1956.

Good-bye Port Said.

The troopship *Empire Fowey*

Viewing De Lesseps for the last time; next stop Malta.

Guy Smith, Royal Navy, HMS *Eagle*.

Guy Smith was born in 1932 and from the age of eight to seventeen was educated at Oakham School in Rutland. On leaving school he went to train as an apprentice fitter at Morgan Fairest, Sheffield, a firm making plant and machinery for the brewing trade. During his apprenticeship Guy became a member of the Royal Naval Volunteer Reserve which meant obtaining time off to go to sea every so often, mainly in destroyers. This experience gave weight to his request to join the Royal Navy when interviewed for National Service.

Guy's initial training took place at Devonport after which he managed to be selected for Field Gun Crew training which was very tough, despite being fed steak for breakfast, with morning runs in boots on a shingle beach. Although not making it into the first team he enjoyed the whole experience. After training Guy was drafted to the aircraft carrier HMS *Eagle* on the radar side of things.

The aircraft carrier *HMS Eagle.*

From the 7th of April 1956 until the 16th HMS *Eagle*, under the command of Captain H C D MacClean, carried out trials in the English Channel and took aboard its aircraft squadrons.

On 20 April the *Eagle* sailed for the Mediterranean and on the 24th, during passage through the Bay of Biscay, undertook power trials during

HMS Eagle being refuelled in the English Channel by the Royal Fleet Auxiliary ship *Tidereach.*

which it achieved speeds of up to 34 knots. The ship arrived in Gibraltar on the 23rd, remaining their for two days before continuing on to Malta where, after a few days, it went off to show the

The aircraft carrier HMS Eagle creating plenty of foam.

flag for the next five months in Italy, Turkey, Lebanon and France as well as returning for spells in Malta and taking part in exercises. On 15 May, the

The *Eagle* leaving Gibraltar.

Eagle became the Mediterranean carrier fleet flagship for Rear-Admiral M L Power. In September the ship briefly spent time in Cyprus waters.

The *Eagle* and the *Bulwark* lying off the Shallow water port of Limassol in southern Cyprus.

During the week from 13 until 20 October the *Eagle* was anchored at Gibraltar undergoing a short refit when an urgent message was received to return to Malta. The ship was back in Grand Harbour by the 25th of the month to join the *Albion* and the *Bulwark*. By this time the invasion of Egypt was definitely on although so far as the lads were suppose to know, the urgent return was for an exercise

Guy kept a diary of his time aboard the *Eagle* during the Suez crisis and the following passages are direct extracts.

'The fleet started to leave Grand Harbour, Malta, at 0830 Monday the 29th of October 1956. The carriers *Albion* and *Bulwark* went out first leaving all available tugs to manoeuvre *Eagle* past the breakwater in the face of a strong crosswind. The two other carriers steamed east immediately to the area of the proposed signal exercise around Cyprus. *Eagle*, carrying the flag of Vice-Admiral Power, Flag Officer Aircraft Carriers, decided to spend the forenoon with flying practice off Malta knowing that with her superior speed *Eagle* could catch the rest of the force before dark.

Launch of a Sea Venom from the starboard catapult.

One of Eagle's Sea Venoms practising 'touch and go', the Navy's equivalent of 'the RAF's circuits and bumps'.

Launch of a Westland Wyvern, a turboprop aircraft with contra-rotating propellers, from the port catapult.

A Sea Hawk taking off from the Eagle's Port catapult. Note the catapult strop falling away.

A Sea Hawk landing on with its arrester hook extended.

Disaster struck the flagship during the flying period Monday forenoon. During a launch with a Sea Hawk on the starboard catapult the wire from the ram room to the flight deck parted whilst taking the initial tension. The aircraft was gently pulled over the bow of the ship and sank immediately it hit the water amidst a cloud of steam from a white hot engine.

The pilot clambered out of the cockpit and swam to the hook of the helicopter waiting to pick him up. He was in the water for less than a minute. This was Lt Middleton's thirteenth 'ditching', the fourth in *Eagle*. The disaster was the wrecking of the starboard catapult, not too much the loss of the aircraft.

After the Sea Hawk had been pulled over the bows by the broken wire having gone 'berserk' the piston in the catapult ram room 'caught up with itself' and, being under no load, its final recorded speed was over 240 knots. This caused the rod of the ram, some 30 feet long, 18 inches in diameter, and made of a special steel, to break clean in two. Plates in the ship's side below the water line will have to be removed in order to replace the ram, obviously a task to be undertaken during a dockyard refit and not to be even attempted by the ship's own engineers.

The Captain, whilst addressing the ship's company that evening said that although the ship had lost one of its catapults, which was a tragedy and such a bitter disappointment after all the hard work put in during the previous months to bring the ship up to her unequalled height of efficiency he did not think it would affect the fighting power of the ship provided the other catapult remained serviceable. Israel, he said, had mobilised and that explained why the ships were steaming eastwards at 26 knots.

Tuesday morning two practice aircraft strikes were launched, one before dawn and one after dawn, normal high speed cruising being resumed at eight o'clock. During the forenoon, whilst the force was off Crete, the captain announced that Israel had attacked Egypt and that her troops were within 70 miles of the Suez Canal. The Navy, he said, must be prepared to act at a moment's notice.

Wednesday morning, one pre-dawn practice strike was launched. All aircraft were recovered before 0700 and normal high speed cruising resumed, this time to an area well north of Cyprus to take part in the great 'Signals Operation. During the forenoon the Captain announced that it was his '... great honour to inform the ship's company that the United Kingdom was about to come to arms with Egypt.' The Anglo-French governments had issued an ultimatum stating that unless Egyptian and Israeli forces withdrew ten miles either side of the canal, force would be used. Under the 1950 Agreement with Egypt one of the clauses stated that if the safety of British personnel and possessions was imperilled the UK retained the right to re-occupy the Canal Zone until the trouble was settled. Britain intended to re-occupy the area and would do so by force if the stated withdrawal did not take place. Twelve hours was allotted for the withdrawal, expiring in the early hours of Thursday morning.

Wednesday evening *Eagle* refuelled from the RFA tanker *Wave Ruler* [missed from many lists of RFA vessels taking part in the Suez crisis] and joined up with the remainder of the force around midnight.

The *Eagle* and another vessel refuelling.

A closer view.

During the hours of darkness the ships steamed south east and by dawn had arrived some seventy miles or so north west of Port Said lying at the entrance to [the] Suez [Canal]. During that day reconnaissance air patrols were sent off to search for and photograph all ships, movements and fortifications as a double check against intelligence reports.

Three Sea Hawks on patrol from the *Eagle*.

View of the coastline to the west of Port Said showing the road coming in from Alexandria at the bottom of the photograph, crossing the El Gamil Bridge and passing along the side of the El Gamil Airfield. Port Said in the distance.

El Gamil Airfield and the eastern end of its main runway at the bottom left. Beyond it lies the sewerage farm, the cemeteries, blocks of flats, and the beginning of the built-up area of Port Said. To the right is the Manzala lagoon.

It was announced that the carrier squadron would launch its first sortie at dawn on the morrow. During the early evening Valiant and Canberra bombers of the RAF flew over in large numbers on their way from Cyprus to start the hostilities in Egypt. Within a matter of minutes it was announced on the overseas Service of the BBC that Sir Anthony Eden had informed the Commons of the air strike.

Dekheila airfield being bombed.

Two o'clock Thursday morning, one Sky Raider, a search aircraft equipped with powerful radar, was launched from *Eagle* to keep a good watch on the area. At half past four a combat air patrol was launched consisting of four Sea Venoms to provide overhead cover for the force.

Four Sea Venoms in formation.

Action Stations was sounded off at 0500 and the first strike was launched at 0520. This strike consisted of forty-three aircraft from all three carriers and their task was to destroy as many enemy aircraft as possible either in the air or on the ground.

It was continually impressed on all pilots that military objects only were to be attacked and these were to be left alone if it was considered that civilian life would be endangered by their destruction. Unluckily, RAF bombing had been pretty inaccu-

Sea Venoms lined up on deck ready to start their engines.

Sea Venoms warming up their engines.

The deck crowded with Sea Venoms, Sea Hawks, and Wyverns towards the stern prior to take-off.

Smoke from the starter cartridges of two Sea Hawks.

Eagle and Hawk.

The El Gamel road bridge being attacked. Two near misses but a direct hit on the bridge approach. The bridge was hit on a subsequent raid.

rate on Wednesday evening and considerable damage had been done to the Arab quarter of Port Said.

Other results were good. Many enemy aircraft were either set on fire or damaged and other strategic targets dealt with. All our aircraft returned safely from these raids.

During the early morning of 1 November a French force had arrived in the area including the carrier *Arromanches* (ex-*Collossus*, RN) and *Lafayette* (ex-US Navy), the battleship *Jean Bart* and the heavy cruiser *Georges Leygues*.

Carrier-borne air strikes continued against airfields and military installations throughout the day. A Sea Hawk pilot noticed a tug towing an old landing craft topped up with concrete out of a basin towards the canal. He dived to attack and saw the whole crew of the landing craft jump over the side and swim for it before he was anywhere near them. These antics made the pilot laugh so much that he could not direct his aircraft onto the target with sufficient accuracy to release his bombs so that he had to climb and make a second attack, scoring a direct hit on the landing craft. His guns camera proved the pilot's story that he hit the landing craft before it reached the main channel of the canal. Photographic evidence the next day indicated that the master of the tug had towed the rapidly sinking block ship to the centre of the canal before slipping his charge and therefore completed his mission of blocking the canal.

Fact and figures of the day's operations were given by the captain during his nightly talk. 138 sorties out of a possible 147 had been launched by the *Eagle*. Out of 78 enemy aircraft destroyed by the force she had taken 42. Out of the 92 damaged her share was 59. Eagle's aircraft had dropped 18 of 1,000lb bombs, 28 of 500lb bombs, [fired] 148 rockets, and [used] 30,000 rounds of 20mm shells. The main galley had supplied 8,457 action meals, 175 large loaves of bread had been distributed to ships in the company by helicopter. Three bags of mail had been flown in from Cyprus by one of Bulwark's Avengers, and the ship had steamed 370 miles during the day's operations

During Thursday evening just after half past seven when everyone was hoping for at least an hour or twos' sleep Action Stations was sounded off. The two duty Venoms were placed at a moment's notice and the duty Sky Raider was similarly placed for radar search. About half a dozen small but definite contacts had been picked up on the close range radar steaming between 25 and 35 knots around the force. Just after 8.15 fifteen two contacts slipped between two destroyers of the screen and made towards the carriers in the centre. The nearest echo was at a range of three-quarters of a mile, a very alarming situation indeed considering that the movements of these contacts corresponded favourably with a daring but efficient method of MTB attack. The contacts disappeared frequently but reappeared on the same course or pattern shortly afterwards. The carriers were rather late in turning north away from the enemy coast but leaving an extremely able screen to deal with the intruders. Eagle fled at thirty two knots leaving the other two carriers to follow as best they could. Two of the Daring Class ships, by far the deadliest for their size in the world steamed flat out fifty yards apart at one of the contacts but nothing was seen. *Duchess* and *Diamond* employed the same action with the other contacts but with the same result. Finally, one of the destroyers fired a star shell over the affected area but the water was clear of any craft whatsoever.

The captains made a very exhaustive inquiry into the cause of these 'false' contacts. One of the ships in company reported that while off Cyprus at about the same time last year she had similar contacts on her radar. During a discussion of these effects in Famagusta a few days later a Cypriot ornithologist said that in late October and early November the Eastern Pelican, the Dalmation Pelican, and the Caspian tern migrate to the swamps and the lakes of the Nile Delta. Large numbers of these birds had been observed flying over Cyprus at the time in question and they were accepted as the cause of the trouble. The captain assumed that the birds had been attracted by the heat of the boilers (all the ships having been darkened completely) had circled the force, then continued on their way southwards. It was the only feasible explanation he could offer.

Action Stations was sounded off at 0500 Friday morning. First launch was at 0520 by all available aircraft. Airfields and supply dumps were again the targets, results again being very commendable. On one of the early Sea Venom strikes one of the aircraft was hit by what must have been a rifle bullet and about a square foot of the perspex canopy above the pilot's head was blown off. Apart from the pilot and observer being nearly frozen to death the aircraft landed safely.

During the forenoon it was announced that the first phase of Operation Musketeer was over. The Egyptian Air Force for all intents and purposes had been destroyed. Action Stations were released into Defence Stations. Just after 10.00 action stations was sounded off again. About four aircraft were moving at high speed closing in on the force and behaving in a highly suspicious manner as shown on radar. These aircraft were assumed to be MIG 15s one of the latest Soviet fighters. Luckily the aircraft were identified by radar as friendly. Four very unpopular pilots landed their Sea Hawks a few minutes later.

Strike and covering aircraft continued to be active all the afternoon. Just after three o'clock two divisions of Venoms were launched to attack military targets quite a way inland. Soon after half past three very faint transmissions were heard in radiotelephony, presumably from one of the Venoms. The signals were too faint to be understood and very soon ceased. Shortly after this a Venom pilot came through saying that one of the aircraft had been hit by flak and had suffered severe damage. The pilot was instructed to fly alongside the crippled aircraft and guide it home as best he could. Although out of touch with each other by radio the pilots and observers managed to converse by sign language. Lt Commander Wilcox, the pilot of the damaged Venom, intimated that a Bofors (40 mm) shell had exploded on contact with underside of the cockpit, made a hole about two feet in diameter, severed the hydraulic and electric main supplies, punctured a fuel tank, and injured the observer in the legs. Neither could he use his radio or lower his undercarriage. Not a very happy predicament! He then reported that his fuel was far too low for comfort. The other aircraft passed this vital information back to the ship where the flight deck was prepared for a crash landing. All other aircraft aloft were ordered back to the ship where they all landed and were struck down below in the hangar leaving the crippled Venom and its guide a 'free deck'.

At a quarter past four two aircraft appeared overhead, leader landed on, and then the 'lame duck' made a practice run before actually landing .

Lt Wilcox landing the crippled Sea Venom wheels up.

Arrester wire tightening.

Wilcox brought his crippled aircraft in at dead the correct height and line, caught the first arrester wire without even dragging the hook along the deck, opened the throttle very slightly in order to keep the 'belly' of the aircraft off the deck. When the arrester wire was drawn to its full extent the aircraft just dropped less than a foot to the deck. Elaborate fire fighting gear was not even used.

Dropped just a foot onto the deck.

The fire-fighting team approaching the aircraft.

The pilot helped to lift his injured observer, Pilot Officer Olding, RAF, out of the cockpit and onto a stretcher. The ship's doctors set a fractured leg and cleaned up flesh wounds. Olding was transported to the Military Hospital in Cyprus where gas gangrene set in and amputation became necessary. (Olding, seconded from the RAF, remained in the RAF and retired with the rank of group captain. He died 19 October 2012 aged 79.)

Lifting the Sea Venom clear.

That evening the Captain again gave facts and figures of the day's proceedings.

Saturday morning the dawn strike went in as usual at 0520. Due to heavy cloud the targets were not fully illuminated and took some finding. However, fairly good results were achieved. A Wyvern strike on the bridge crossing the Sweetwater canal was only partially successful, the bridge being damaged but no actual direct hits scored. A strike of 13 Sea Hawks was then sent in to complete the mission. Two direct hits were scored and the embankments carrying the road on either side of the bridge were demolished. Two Wyvern pilots then insisted on going in and completing the mission. Two further direct hits were scored leaving the eastern span of the bridge completely demolished. .

Over the entrance to the canal Lt McCarthy's aircraft was hit by flack. He managed to bring the aircraft some 4,000 yards off shore before ejecting. As soon as McCarthy gained his dinghy two Egyptian shore batteries, one on either side of the canal entrance, opened up on him. These positions were quickly eliminated by covering aircraft.

Immediately it was known that the Wyvern had ditched *Decoy* was despatched at high speed to rescue the pilot but as soon as it was learnt that McCarthy's life was in danger a helicopter with heavy fighter escort was sent in. McCarty was fished out of the water unharmed and happy. The fleet was at that time seventy miles offshore. *Decoy* would have taken two hours to reach Port Said whereas the helicopter took only 35 minutes.

Sunday was Eagle's day with the replenishment force. During the forenoon the ship ammunitioned from RFA *Retainer* taking on some 90 of 1,000 lb and 120 of 500 lb bombs, 49,000 rounds of 20 mm, numerous rocket mortars rocket heads, etc.

HMS *Eagle* coupled up with RFA *Tiderange* for refuelling.

During the early afternoon *Retainer* slipped and five replacement aircraft were recovered from Bel Adem in Libya. At four o'clock the ship coupled up to RFA *Tiderange* for fuel. This evolution was completed soon after eight, when four Sky Raiders were recovered, again from Bel Adem.

Soon after dawn on Monday the paratroopers went in. They touched down on the narrow neck of the Port Said peninsular. Carrier-borne aircraft covered the landing as pre-arranged to provide close support for the ground troops.

Port Said over the horizon. A misdirected French Corsair rocket hit a Standard Oil Company storage tank next to the canal at the south end of town and set it on fire.

After a few anxious hours one of the pilots managed to make faint radio contact with the ground forces who informed him that they had lost the batteries to their main transmitters and were also desperately short of medical supplies. A helicopter was soon sent inshore with all the 12 volt batteries that could be spared from the fleet together with large medical supplies, especially morphia. The helicopter landed at Gamil Airfield near Port Said under heavy but wild enemy fire, delivered his load, and took on five badly wounded men. This pioneer flight was heavily escorted at one time by five Wyverns, 4 Hawks and 4 Venoms.

Wounded paratroopers being lifted from the helicopters for treatment below deck.

It was soon decided to run a ferry service with the fleet's four Whirlwind helicopters, two each from *Eagle* and *Albion*. Further medical supplies were taken inshore but the troops' most urgent need turned out to be fresh water, and ingoing Whirlwinds were loaded with empty Bofor's ammunition boxes or rather aluminium containers topped up with water.

During the afternoon, as a Wyvern strike was crossing the coast on its way home the leader's engine faltered. He tried to limp back to the ship but had to eject when the engine finally petered out. Hardly had he hit the water when a helicopter full of wounded dropped its hook and fished him out of the sea.

About a quarter to five the Egyptian commander of the Port Said garrison asked for a cease fire in order to parley for surrender terms. This was naturally granted but less than a quarter of an hour later enemy mortars opened up on the paratroops. Venom aircraft flying overhead were not allowed to shoot up the offending troops so one of the aircraft flew over the Egyptian lines as low and as fast as possible therefore creating a terrific noise. This was just as effective as any amount of bombs or mortars. The mortars were not heard again.

Just before dusk a helicopter went inshore on a final mercy mission. The Whirlwind's maximum load is normally six people, four passengers and a crew of two. The pilot found eight remaining casualties so contrary to all warnings and instructions the helicopter struggled back to the ship carrying ten people, quite a remarkable feat.

Tuesday morning, just before seven local time, the seaborne troops touched down. French storm troops landed on the beaches at Port Fuad and troops of No.3 Brigade RM on the beaches at Port Said. Although the Egyptians had not accepted the surrender terms of the previous evening the British troops landed with very little opposition, ships of the Allied fleet having bombarded the area prior to the landing. During the day many sorties were flown at the request of the ground troops who were meeting isolated pockets of stiff resistance, usually centred round a Russian-built tank. During the afternoon intelligence reported that six MIG aircraft had landed at Cairo West Airport. A division of Sea Hawks was despatched to eliminate these fighters. During the first attack four MIGs were destroyed and while the aircraft were circling for the second attack they flew down the main street of Cairo so low that one pilot on his return to the ship swore that he was window gazing. Needless to say the remaining MIGs were destroyed in the second attack. On the return journey the pilots espied tanks at El Qantara and during the ensuing attack Lt Mills had his engine shot up by flack. When it became apparent that he could not control his aircraft any longer he ejected and landed in the desert. Almost immediately a wagon closed in on him but a burst of machine gun fire across his bows from one of the covering aircraft put paid to its advance. Lt Commander Bailey piloted a helicopter many miles behind enemy lines to add another rescue to his already considerable total.

Tuesday evening a general ceasefire was ordered to come into force at midnight GMT. This news was received by most people as a blessing but some of the professionals regarded it as an end to their frivolity.

The Standard Oil Depot fire at the southern end of the Abbas Hilmi Basin

View of the oil storage fire from an *Eagle* aircraft.

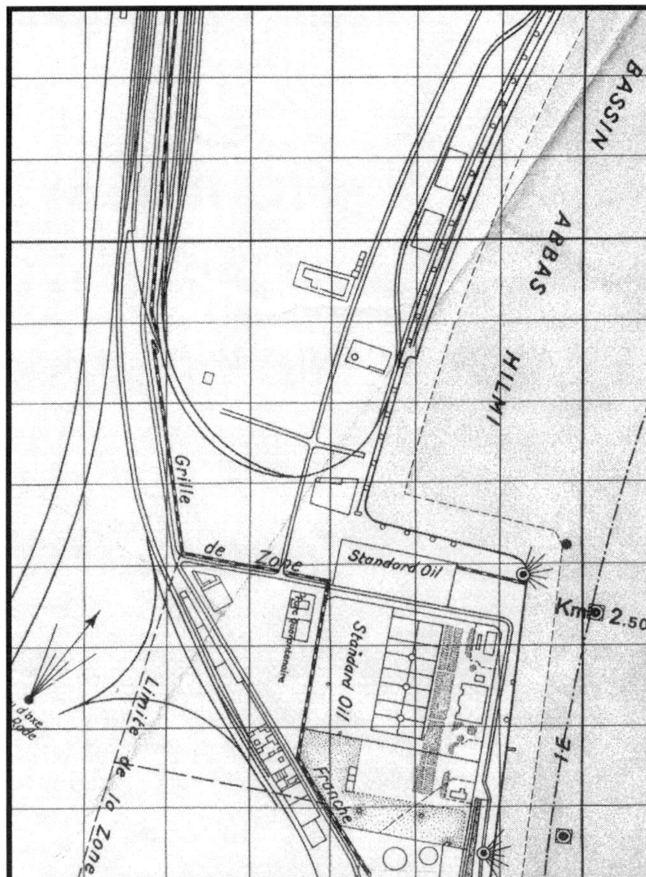

The Standard oil terminal on the southern quay of Abbas Hilmi Basin.

The fire at the coastguard Barracks on the coast road between Port Said and the El Gamil airfield.

Another view, from over the Manzala lagoon, of the Coastguard Barracks on fire.

The Suez Canal Company building with the Commerce Basin to the right of the photo and the Basin L'Arsenal to the left. The road running along the Arsenal Basin quayside at the side of the building runs on to the Rue Mustapha Kamel which in turn becomes a wide boulevard with the white railway station tower on its left followed by the three white schools.

Navy House on the South Quay between Arsenal Basin out of the picture on the right and Shérif Basin seen on the left. Prior to the British forces withdrawal in 1954 this was the home of the Royal Navy in the canal Zone. The building was the scene of fierce fighting involving 40 Commando and was severely damaged in an aerial attack.

During the early hours of Wednesday morning *Eagle* steamed to within seven miles of Port Said in order to make the transfer of the wounded to *Ocean* and *Theseus* as short as possible. The two light fleet carriers were being used as troop transports and hospital ships, and each was equipped with a squadron of helicopters.

Relaxing at last. A game of hockey.

Eagle rejoined the carrier force in the early afternoon and the Admiral and staff were transferred to *Bulwark* by helicopter. *Eagle* was soon making her way west through heavy seas at 26 knots towards Malta some thousand miles away where she arrived early Friday morning. The reason for the return to Malta was a complete overall of the remaining catapult. Since the start of the operation it had launched some 620 aircraft without as much as a murmur in five days flying. The makers guarantee 2,000 launches per catapult but the actual number launched runs into tens of thousands since installation.

During Operation Musketeer a tragic accident took place aboard the *Eagle*. Owing to the present emergency the guns of all aircraft are permanently loaded. Whilst a Sea Venom was being manoeuvred in the lower hangar a cannon shell dropped into the breach despite safety catches being on. The shell ignited a 90 gallon tank in a Wyvern which set everything off. Asbestos pre-curtains and armoured doors were dropped and everyone evacuated at top speed. Just as the deck was sealed the fireworks began in earnest. More fuel tanks and thousands of rounds went off. Water sprays were turned on and water poured on the decks above turned to steam. Four Wyverns and two Venoms were lost as well as all the spares and stores in that area. The two inches of armoured steel doors in the hangars saved the day.' [Clive Naylor killed].

Guy was demobbed about March 1957 and on his return to civilian life entered the quarry industry based mainly in Matlock, Derbyshire. He Married Nina in 1968 and during their leisure time they became heavily involved in vintage cars, races and touring. Guy retired in 1995 and died of cancer in 1996.

(Many thanks to Nina for the use of Guy's photos and diaries, and also for her personnel memories.)

* * *

David Brian Manning, Royal Navy, HMS *Eagle*.

David was born on 25 June 1936 in Beckenham, Kent. His family moved to Leeds in 1939 and in September 1947, having passed his 11+ examination, David went to Roundhay Grammar School where he joined the naval section of the school's combined cadet force.

After taking his A-Levels in the summer of 1954 he went to Leeds University and passed the first year of the B.Sc (Hons) Electrical Engineering course. At this stage, in the summer of 1955, he decided to do his National Service without further deferment and joined the Navy, doing his training at Devonport and going on to serve on the aircraft carrier HMS *Eagle* at Port Said.

View from *Eagle* on leaving Gibraltar for Malta.

HMS *Surprise,* Dolmobahçe Palace, Istanbul, 6-11 June.

The *Eagle* crew on deck.

HMS *Eagle* with the frigate HMS *Surprise* and the cruiser HMS *Birmingham* 15-19 June 1956 at Beirut, Lebanon.

Fifteen degrees tilt. *Operation Thunderhead* with the American Navy. 25-28 June 1956.

Forklift truck rolling to the edge of the deck, 25-28 June.

And over the side it goes.

US Navy Grumman Couger touch-and-go cross-decking on *Eagle* during *Exercise Thunderhead*, 25-28 June 1956.

Wyvern landing on.

The mess kitten on dog watch.

Stirring the ship's Christmas pudding.

After his service on HMS *Eagle* David spent some time on the aircraft carrier HMS *Ocean*.

On his return to Civvy Street David got a job at Lancashire Dynamo and Crypto Ltd in Manchester as a test engineer and it was while he was here, in 1959, that he married Patricia who he had known from his schooldays. They went on to have a son in 1962 and a daughter in 1964. This was the first of many posts in industry that took David around the country and around the world. He also wrote two sections on Rotating Machines for the Handbook of Electrical Installation Practice published by Blackwell Scientific Publications.

David died in his home at Hankerton, Malmesbury, Wiltshire, of a heart attack on 20 May 2000 when he was sixty-three.

(Thanks to David's widow Patricia for the photographs and information about his life.)

* * *

Bill Bowes, Royal Navy, HMS *Eagle*.

Bill was born on the 3rd of October 1935 in Layton, Blackpool. In September 1940 he began his primary education at Sacred Heart School and from the age of 11, after having passed the 11+ examination, went on to St Joseph's College. He found that he hated it there and would have much preferred to have gone with his mates to St John Vianney, the secondary modern school.

Bill left school at Christmas 1950 when he was 16 without bothering to take the GCE examinations and got a job learning to be a typewriter mechanic at Bernard Hopes in Birley Street. As soon as he was 17 in October 1952 he signed on for 12 years with the Royal Navy and after a brief induction and some basic training at Portsmouth was sent to HMS *Ceres*, the shore establishment at Wetherby in Yorkshire, the Navy's Supply and Secretariat Training School.

From here he went back south for further training, this time at Devonport where he was involved with the 15-inch gun HMS *Vanguard*, the largest British battleship ever built and, alongside it, the rather unusual-looking shallow draft monitor class vessel HMS *Roberts* which at that time was being used as an accommodation ship.

HMS *Roberts*. (Photo, Captain Rex Cooper).

During 1954 Bill was posted to HMS *Drake*, the Navy Barracks at Devonport, Plymouth. At the end of May he passed the LSA (Leading Stores Assistant) examination and in July, while still only 18, married his fiancée Audrey Bury while home on leave in Blackpool.

Following their honeymoon Audrey returned with Bill to Plymouth where they found a flat together. Bill then underwent some further training at HMS *Raleigh*, the shore base at Torpoint opposite Devonport on the Cornish side of the River Tamar. Also in 1954 Bill was posted for a while to South Shields at the mouth of the River Tyne where he assisted with the dehumidification and preservation of the corvette HMS *Oakham Castle* prior to its being mothballed.

Back at Torpoint Bill was assigned to the aircraft carrier HMS *Eagle* which had just completed five months of repairs in the Devonport dockyard. In April 1956 the ship sailed for the Mediterranean to show the flag, starting at Gibraltar.

The *Eagle* at Gibraltar.

From Gibraltar the ship then went on to Pozzalo, Sicily, for a two-day visit on the 6th and 7th of May before heading down to Malta for a fortnight during which she joined up with the carriers HMS *Albion* and HMS *Centaur* for a grand fly past of Carrier Squadron aircraft.

The *Eagle* floodlit at Malta in May.

Four Skyraiders in Grand Fly Past of carrier squadron aircraft in Malta.

Early in June the *Eagle* began its 'showing the flag' summer cruise programme with the first port of call being Istanbul and the Sea of Marmara in Turkey which took place between the 6th to the 11th of the month.

HMS *Birmingham* leading the *Eagle* into Istanbul harbour.

HMS *Eagle* lying off Istanbul.

The frigate HMS *Surprise* lying off the Dolmabahce Palace.

The *Eagle* and ships in line astern in the Sea of Marmara.

Pincher and Bill on the Sea of Marmara.

From 15th to 19th June the ship was at Beirut.

In mid-July the ship took part in 'Maltex' the annual inter-Allied joint services defence of Malta exercise, designed to test Malta's air defences. It then sailed for a visit to Naples from the 24th to the 30th of the month.

The *Eagle* and the County-Class heavy cruiser *Cumberland* in Naples harbour.

Photo taken of the actor Gary Cooper and his wife Veronica after visiting the Blue Mosque in Istanbul.

Gracie Fields entertaining the Navy on the deck of HMS *Eagle* on 30th July 1956.

Exercise Thunderhead with the US 6th Fleet, 25th–28th June 1956, Fifteen degrees list to starboard at speed.

The lads crowding round.

Gracie Fields, a closer view.

Bill at Syracusa, Sicily, after fleet exercises in September.

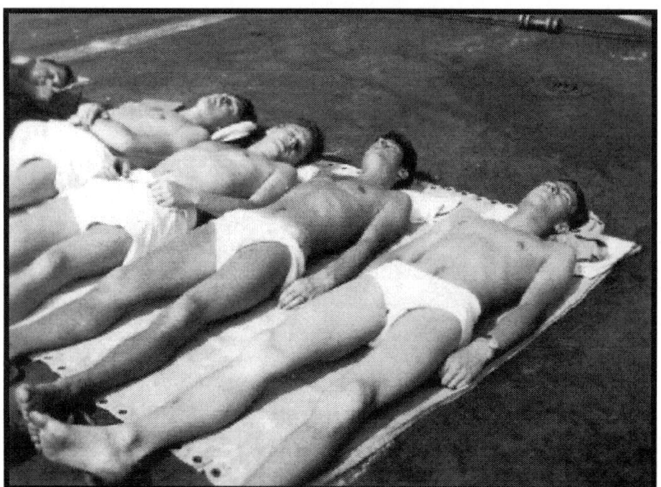

Shiner, Pincher, Tony, Bill and Wally enjoying the Mediterranean sun on the deck of the *Eagle.*

Towards the end of the summer *Eagle* was due to end its commission and return to the UK. Bill was particularly keen to get back home to see his new baby daughter Carol who had just been born in May. However, at the end of July, the Suez crisis blew up and the ship received orders to remain in the area.

On the 28th of September the *Eagle* arrived in Toulon in the south of France on a four-day visit.

HMS *Eagle* entering Toulon harbour.

Part of the harbour and naval base city of Toulon in the south of France.

After a short spell in Malta the *Eagle* sailed to Gibraltar and spent a week there from the 13th of October until she was urgently recalled to Malta because of the Suez Canal crisis, arriving there on about the twenty-sixth.

On the 29th, together with the carriers *Bulwark*, *Albion*, and the French *Arromanches*, the *Eagle* sailed eastwards from Valetta and after dark on the 31st took up station some 50 miles off the mouth of the Suez Canal to await further orders.

Earlier, at 1615 hours that afternoon, the attack on Egypt had already begun with Canberra bombers from Cyprus and Valiants from Malta having dropped bombs on Egyptian airfields to minimise any possible interference by the Egyptian Air Force on the invasion fleet.

The following morning from just after 0500 hours Eagle's Seahawks and Sea Venoms started to take off, also to bomb airfields and destroy aircraft on the ground including Mig fighters that had been supplied by Russia. These attacks continued over the next two days until the 4th when the carrier had to be re-supplied with fuel from the RFA ship *Tiderace* and with ammunition for her aircraft from the *RFA Retainer*.

Refuelling from *Tiderace* in a 'drop of roughers'.

Refuelling from *Tiderace*.

The following day, the 5th, *Eagle* was back on duty and before dawn launched eight Sea Venoms to protect the skies above El Gamil airfield while the drop by 3 Para took place.

On the same day after dark there was nearly a tragic accident when two aircraft, one whose pilot was making his first deck landing in the dark, both came into land at the same time. A collision was avoided in the last second or so when one of the pilots saw the danger and banked out of the way to go round again.

Wyverns ready to warm up for launch on a sortie.

Wyverns lining up for the catapult.

The sea assault and helicopter landings by the Marines took place early on the 6th and throughout the day *Eagle* launched hundreds of aircraft sorties in support of the troops until late in the day when the starboard catapult broke down under the pressure of use. However, by this time it no loner mattered since by then a ceasefire had been agreed upon and came into effect a minute before midnight.

Throughout all this activity on deck and in the hangars Bill and his colleagues behind the scenes had been kept equally busy by the demands made

Further supplies from the RFA vessel *Wave Sovereign*.

on the ship's stores and secretarial staff generated by the battle and the need to keep records. Consequently they had been unable to see much of what had been going on above their heads although they were able to hear it and feel the charged atmosphere.

The following day, the 7th, after Vice Admiral Power the Flag Officer aboard the *Eagle* had transferred across to the *Bulwark*, and after the wounded who had been brought aboard for treatment during the fighting had been moved to the *Theseus*, the *Eagle* set out for Malta to undergo repairs and arrived at Grand Harbour on the 9th two days later.

Repairs were made in only four days and the ship set out eastwards on the 13th and arrived off Port Said on the 15th when Lt General Stockwell came aboard to thank the ship's company for their valuable service in the recent fighting.

On the 19th, while servicing was taking place, one of the guns of a Sea Venom below deck was fired accidentally killing Clive A Naylor, a young airman, and writing off one aircraft and damaging others. Bill was one of those detailed to help clean up what was quite a mess in the hangar where the accident had taken place. The *Eagle* stayed on station until the 22nd of December when, after dark, the final convoy of ships carrying the last of the troops sailed from Port Said. For the initial part of the return journey both *Eagle* and the *Albion* were kept on high alert to provide air cover if this became necessary.

The written-off Wyvern brought up on deck.

The *Eagle* sailed into Malta on Christmas Day and spent just a few hours there before continuing on to Gibraltar. She arriving there on the 28th and departed on New Year's Day. The ship arrived back in Plymouth on the 4th of January. Bill was at last able to see his eight-month-old baby girl Carol for the first time.

In a letter addressed to Captain Maclean and the ship's company Earl Mountbatten praised the part they had played at Port Said, telling them that the success of *Operation Musketeer* had revolved particularly around the presence of the *Eagle*.

After leave Bill returned to HMS *Raleigh* and went on to take the examination for petty officer ready for when his name reached the top of the list. After some time spent here Bill was posted to HMS *Bulwark* – once on carriers always on carriers, he used to tell Audrey. During his subsequent service he and Audrey had a second child, Colin, born in February 1958 and then Alison in November 1962

Gradually the time spent apart from Audrey and their growing family began to affect Bill and when the end of his 12 years' service approached he decided to leave the Navy rather than sign on for a further spell. A careers officer advised him that his qualifications and experience in the Navy would well suit him to a job in the Civil Service and on leaving the Navy in October 1966 with eight weeks terminal leave he took the civil service examination and obtained an appointment in Blackpool.

Bill's last job was with National Savings from which he retired after a heart attack. He died on the 3rd of January 2006 aged 70 with cause of death being given as an abdominal aneurism.

(With thanks to Audrey for the photos and information about her late husband Bill.)

* * *

Brian Adams, HMS *Eagle*, Royal Navy.

Like many, Brian acquired a set of photos taken or processed by the ship's 'official' photographer.

The captured El Gamil Airfield on the western side of the control tower buildings. An enlarged view of this photograph shows that there are ships along the whole of the horizon. Tent lines can be seen on the eastern side of the control tower.

The view looking south from just inside the canal entrance on the 6th of November, the day when it was deemed reasonably safe for the ships to enter although sniper bullets were still flying about.

View of the blockships and Allied ships anchored within the harbour entrance against the eastern mole. The large white vessel is the French hospital ship La Marseillaise.

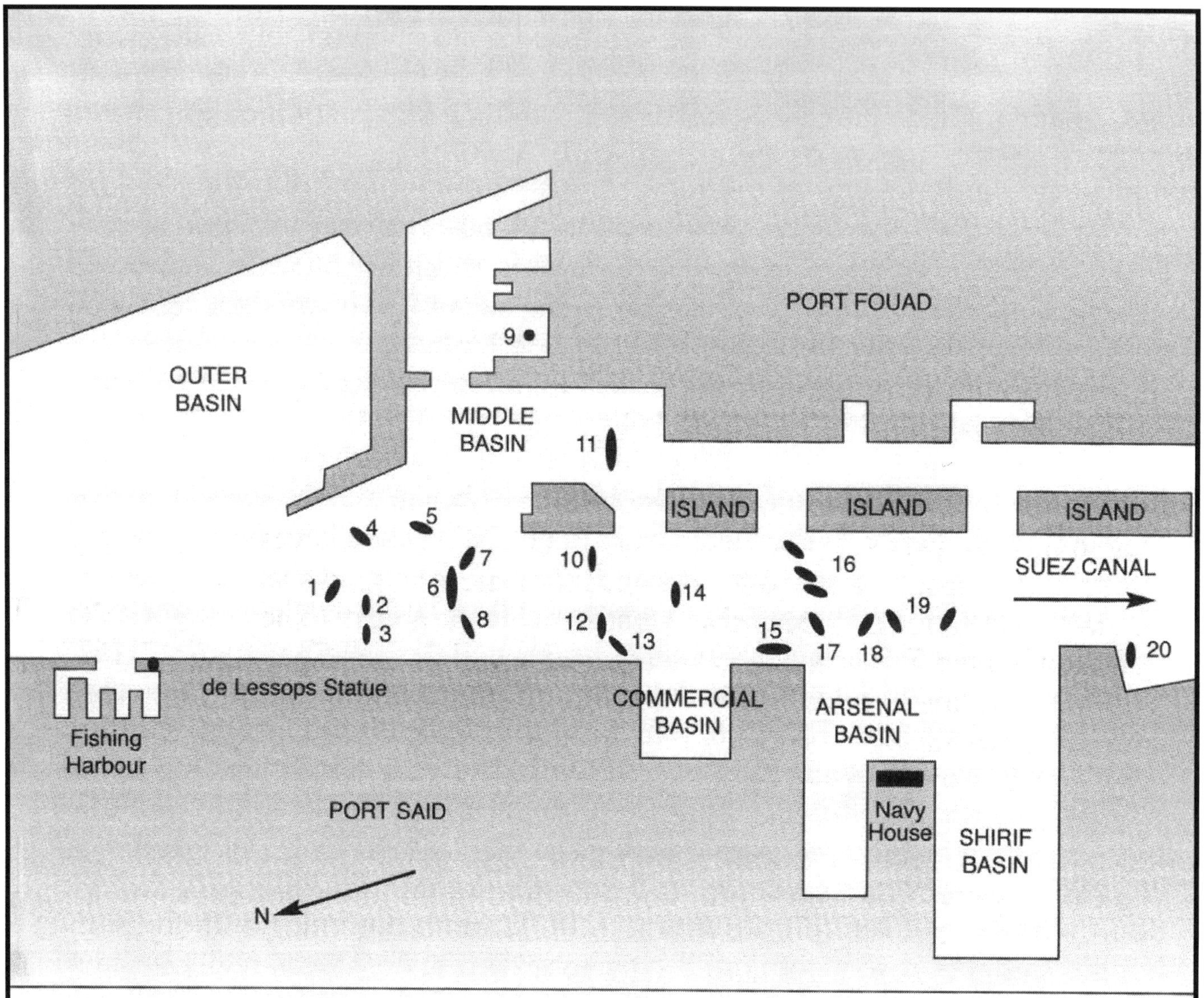

No	Type	No	Type
1. *No 823*	150 ton crane	13. *No 6*	dredger
2. *No 827*	80 ton crane	14. *No 19*	bucket dredger
3. *No 839*	15 ton crane	15. *Ardent*	tug
4. *Pollux*	salvage craft		
5. *Peleuse*	bucket dredger	16. *Agile*	tug
6. *Paul Solente*	suction dredger	*Cheddid*	tug
7. *Neptune*	hopper	*Quircg*	tug
8. *Triton*	hopper	17. *Hercule*	tug
9.	floating dock	18. *Le Hardi*	pilot boat
Bassel	tug	19. *Garii*	tug
10. *No 37*	hopper 1	*Barq*	tug
11. *Iacovos*	merchant ship	20. *Actif*	tug
12. *No 44*	hopper		

Diagram of Blockship positions in the Suez Canal at Port Said in November 1956. With the kind permission of Geoffrey Carter from his Book 'crises Do Happen' and of his publisher Maritime books, Liskeard Cornwall.

The blockship in the foreground was the salvage vessel *Pollux*, listed as 4 in the diagram.

A closer view of the *Paul Solente* between its two salvage ships and the bucket dredger *Peleuse*, listed 5.

The suction Dredger *Paul Solente,* listed as 6, is resting on the canal bottom. The Canal Company building can be seen further along the quay.

The French hospital ship *La Marseillaise* lying close to the eastern mole.

Close to the quay is the *Paul Solente* again, now with a salvage vessel on either side and partially raised. In the foreground is the bucket dredger *Peleuse*, listed 5.

The maintenance ship HMS *Forth* and the LST *Lofoten* lying inboard against her. The entrance to the Fish Harbour at the upper left.

Gamourian Gardens which measure 170 yards square, have been referred to in the literature on the 'Suez conflict' as Consulate Square. The British Consul was held captive here and had to be rescued by the Commandos. In the top left of the photograph is the Fish Dock with the De Lesseps statue on its corner. The large flat area by the statue is where 45 Commando was brought ashore by helicopters. Lying off the De Lesseps promenade are HMS *Forth* and the LST *Lofoten.* The French hospital ship *La Marseillaise* lies at the top right in the outer harbour on the Port Fuad side of the canal. One landing craft is tied up at the quay by the Casino Palace Hotel and the other by the public gardens, occupied on the night of the sixth by 3 Field Squadron of the Royal Engineers. Some 170 yards south of these gardens is the Lighthouse.

Troops assembled on the helicopter landing ground. The Casino Palace Hotel is off the photograph to the left.

Further along the landing area by the De Lesseps Statue. Behind it is the Fish Dock with French landing craft.

Some of the Egyptian wounded

Egyptian POWs at Port Said railway station awaiting repatriation to the Egyptian lines beyond El Cap.

Egyptian railway carriage and locomotive being operated by the Royal Engineers for the repatriation of prisoners and no doubt for 'rides' as well

Egyptian gun on the beach destroyed by aircraft attack

Collection post of Egyptian arms captured by the British near the Casino Palace Hotel. These were taken out to sea and dumped.

Another view of the arms collection

Three Egyptian craft commandeered by the Navy. What seems to be a houseboat in the middle has become her Majesty's ship *RN1234*. HMS *Forth* and HMS *Lofoten* are seen behind.

* * *

Brian Hodkinson, Leading seaman, HMS *Eagle*.

I was born in November 1932 in Doncaster and joined the Navy in September 1948 as a 15-year-old at HMS *Ganges*, the shore training establishment for boys at Shotley Point in Suffolk.

In 1955, my seventh year of service, I joined the aircraft carrier HMS *Eagle* and remember the time (17 May) when those of us not on duty were on the island structure in our 'goofing positions' watching the flying programme and flight deck activities which was always a magnificent sight to say the least. The funnel casing was the warmest place to be in cold and windy weather. Then over the Tannoy system came the instruction to 'Clear goofing positions.' A Wyvern was having problems landing and had to go round again. The aircraft finished up embedded in the funnel where some of us had recently been. The engine stayed there and the rest of the aircraft dropped onto the deck below. A close call, and for Lt Jarrett who survived.

The wreckage of the Wyvern and a bed of foam.

Inspecting the damage.

On another occasion, April 1956 I think, a pilot was not so fortunate. I was duty sea boat coxwain when we were called out to go out to a downed Skyraider. We were lowered to the point of slipping 'fore and aft' and held there as the *Eagle* raced

Waiting to be lowered.

to the location. At the crash site we could see the tailplane sticking out of the glassy sea. We were lowered into the sea and began to search for the pilot.

We cruised around until the forward lookout spotted a parachute beneath the water. With the aid of our long boathook we brought it to the surface and retrieved the pilot's body. We returned to the ship and on being hoisted back aboard sadly handed over our charge together with the parachute which was immediately cut up there and then by the CPO Safety Equipment.

By October 1956, having just completed our two-year commission, we were in Gibraltar Harbour undergoing repairs on our refrigeration system before continuing home to Devonport. One sunny morning I was on the after boat deck when I heard the voice of our captain over the Tannoy speaker. He announced that instead of preparing for our final leg home we would be returning to Malta.

In Malta's Grand Harbour we took stores aboard and were allowed time ashore when our duties permitted. While preparing for what was to come we saw that there was an ex-Royal Navy Egyptian destroyer in the harbour which had been receiving dockyard maintenance. Owing to the political tension at the time it was having to leave Malta and return to Egypt. On its way out of the harbour it would be passing several Royal Navy ships including the *Eagle*. I recall that, just as a precaution, our port side secondary armament was manned and a row of dumb barges from the docks had been placed against the side of the ship to fend off any attempt at ramming. I watched as the destroyer sailed past peacefully and off to the east.

When we sailed for the Suez crisis action I was involved in the usual sea duties. Watch on, watch off, day and night throughout the whole episode except for an escort duty ashore in Cyprus during one visit and occasional assistance duties handling armaments under the supervision of the flight deck crew. When the battle began and we were called to action stations I was one of a team operating a radar-controlled gun from safely below the waterline in the gunnery transmitting station behind numerous closed armoured hatches. However the surface threat from the Egyptian Navy was short lived.

During off duty times we watched the flying and flight deck activities as usual from the island superstructure 'goofing positions'. After one of the air attacks ashore I witnessed the return of a Wyvern pilot who had had to eject some miles off the coast of Egypt after carrying out a mission. We had been told of his plight sitting in his inflatable dinghy while being fired at from a coastal battery. However he was soon well protected by his fellow pilots flying overhead and was eventually scooped up by a helicopter and safely returned to the *Eagle*. I distinctly recall his enormous grin of relief as he alighted from the rescue helicopter and met his fellow pilots on the flight deck.

A further incident involved one of our Sea Venoms that had received flack damage whilst on a sortie. The pilot managed to return and made a successful wheels-up landing on the flight deck. The observer however had received severe leg injuries and later had to have his lower leg amputated.

One day, a week or more after the fighting had ceased, a serious incident occurred in the lower hanger as I was passing through the port upper hangar access. A series of explosions there caused compression to egress via the two steel doors giving access to the upper forward lift well. These doors burst open and black smoke billowed out under pressure. I made a hasty retreat out of the way. Fire broke out causing a tremendous amount of damage to electrical cabling along the bulkheads in both hangars which required jury cabling to be rigged. Fortunately the fire curtains and sprinklers put out the fires. Those of the ship's company not required for damage control activities were sent to emergency stations in case we needed to abandon ship. Mine was the port after gangway. We had a destroyer standing off but it was not needed. Planes were damaged in the incident which involved the accidental firing of a shell by one of the aircraft parked below. Aircraft damaged beyond repair were later jettisoned off the bow end of the flight deck as the ship slowly went astern. At least one chap was killed and another I knew received severe damage to his hand as he attempted to beat the closing of an armoured hatch.

My last recollection of the Suez Crisis was the withdrawal out to sea of about 100 ships of various shapes and sizes as we escorted them westwards and away from Egypt. My sympathies went out to those in the flotilla of flat bottomed landing craft as they ploughed through a heavy swell homeward bound for Blighty.

We arrived back in Devonport early in the New Year. The national servicemen who had completed their time went off on demob and the regulars enjoyed some well-deserved leave. I went on to serve for another two-and-a-half years before returning to civilian life, although I had a short spell in the Royal New Zealand Naval Reserve.

Brian by one of the aircraft.

Brian, in the middle, with two of his mates.

In September 2010 my wife and I celebrated our 50th wedding anniversary. We are both in good health and enjoying our retirement. And I trust that all those old shipmates of mine have been similarly blessed.

* * *

Stan Alty, Fleet Air Arm, HMS *Eagle.*

I was born 30 December 1932 in Liverpool. When war broke out in September 1939 I was evacuated to Southport with my sister. When we were taken back home I saw that many of the houses around us had been hit by bombs, all intended for the nearby docks.

At the end of my primary education in 1944 I passed the 11+ examination and in the September started to attend Bootle Grammar School for Boys. I was very keen on sport at this time and went on to represent the school at soccer.

I left school when I was 16 to take an electrical engineering apprenticeship which I could have continued until I was 21 but when I was 18 at the end of 1950 and saw all my mates being called up for National Service I decided to join the Fleet Air Arm of the Royal Navy. Because of my electrical background I was given the choice of an air/radio or air/electrical course. I chose the first one and on its completion was posted to naval air stations and carriers. In 1955 I got married during one of my leaves.

In April 1956 my squadron joined the aircraft carrier HMS *Eagle* for what was intended to be a six-months-long cruise in the Mediterranean after which we were to be relieved by the *Ark Royal.* In July, however, Colonel Nasser the Egyptian leader decided to nationalise the Suez Canal Company and so set in motion a strong reaction from Britain and France. At this time the *Ark Royal* was in dock at Devonport being given a major refit and was not ready to take our place as planned. So our tour was extended and we were retained in the Mediterranean.

By now I had passed the necessary examinations and was promoted to the rank of petty officer. HMS *Eagle* was made the flagship of the invasion fleet and our aircraft together with those of the carriers *Bulwark* and *Albion* made many of the strikes on Egyptian targets before the troops went in and during the invasion. Land-based bombers from Malta and Cyprus also carried out some of these attacks which were mainly on airfields to immobilise the Egyptian Air Force The *Eagle* eventually sailed for home at the end of the year, docking in Devonport on about 6th January 1957. A year later I left the Navy and started a new career. I retired when I was 65 and enjoyed a happy retirement until my dear wife passed away in April 2011 leaving me with some happy memories and some sad. I have three children and eight grandchildren.

899 Squadron of the Fleet Air Arm enjoying a tot of rum in the mess. Stan beneath the right arm of the chap at back right.

The *Eagle*, *Albion* and *Bulwark* making for Egypt.

Aircraft being brought up on deck.

The squadron being prepared for flight.

* * *

Richard Essam, HMS *Theseus.*

I was born in Coventry on 12 February 1937 and received my secondary schooling at the City of Coventry Boarding School at Cleobury Mortimer in Shropshire until I was 15 in 1952 when I started an electrical apprenticeship with Coventry Corporation. This was also the year I first saw Rachel who I was then introduced to the following year.

When I was 18 and it was time for National Service I requested the Royal Navy since my father had been accepted for the service in World War II but hadn't actually served because of his involvement with Rolls Royce on the Merlin and Griffin engines. My godfather had served with the Coldstream Guards so I chose them as an alternative but I would only be accepted with them if I signed on for five years. Ultimately I was given the Navy and was conscripted on 1 June 1955.

I began my service at HMS *Raleigh* at Torpoint doing square bashing and basic training along with QR's and AI's (Queen's Regulations and Admiralty Instructions) and then training in high temperature and high pressure steam propulsion after which I qualified as a mechanic engineer ME2 and then ME1 six months later. From here I was transferred to HMS *Drake*, HMNB. (Her Majesty's Naval Base) Devonport.

In about mid-August I was posted to HMS *Theseus,* (Captain A A C Miers VC DSO RN) anchored at Portland harbour. The same day the ship sailed for Portsmouth to undergo its annual maintenance, much of it in the dry dock.

We returned to Portland on 20 September but were there for only about a month before we were again back in Portsmouth preparing to take aboard a contingent of troops, transport and equipment for a voyage to Cyprus where reinforcements were needed to deal with a rise in EOKA activity. We sailed out of Portsmouth on 27 October bound for Famagusta. From there we returned to Malta where we teamed up with our sister carrier HMS *Ocean.* We set out for home on 8 November, returning via Gibraltar and Tangier in Morocco to Portland where we arrived on 1 December. At the end of the month Captain Myers left the ship and Captain E F Pizey DSO RN took his place.

We went out into the Channel on 20 January 1956 for Home Fleet exercises at the end of which we spent almost a week visiting El Ferrol, the Spanish naval base on the north-western tip of Spain. On 2 February we arrived back in Portsmouth where the ship began an extensive refit part of which was to make her suitable for carrying helicopters. Early in May the *Theseus* was made the flagship of Rear Admiral Sayers, the officer in charge of the Training Squadron.

On 11 June, with the changes made, we sailed to the waters of the Cromarty Firth on the east coast of Scotland. On the 19th, while anchored at Invergordon with our sister ship *Ocean*, each carrier took aboard four whirlwind helicopters of 845 Squadron and together over the next few days we carried out working-up exercises.

In the last week of June both ships set out across the North Sea until, after a couple of days, we parted company, the *Ocean* continuing on to Hamburg while we went to show the flag at Kristiansand in Norway. After a week, on 3 July, we sailed back out to sea and joined a number of other ships to take part in exercise *Fairwind* which included anti-submarine drill. On our way home we managed to fit in a visit to Tynemouth before finally arriving back at Portland on July 24 when the helicopters departed.

Two days later Colonel Nasser the Egyptian leader seized the Suez Canal Company which immediately led to the British and French Governments making preparations to invade Egypt in order to return the canal to its shareholders.

All leave was pretty much cancelled right away and ten days later on 5 August, after taking aboard elements of the 16th Parachute Brigade, their stores, ammunition and transport, we set out on a trooping voyage to Cyprus. By the 11th we had arrived at Famagusta where we offloaded the troops and cargo and took aboard in their place members of the Commando brigade who were returning to Malta for advanced training. After dropping them off we left Malta on the 18th and were docking at Portsmouth by the twenty-second.

During this time it had been decided that in the coming conflict against Egypt best use of the *Theseus* and the *Ocean* would be as floating bases for troop-carrying helicopter squadrons. So during September yet another conversion took place which also included the provision of facilities in the hangars for the treatment of wounded when brought back to the ship. This gave members of the ship's crew the chance to take the summer leave that had been cancelled earlier.

The upgrading was completed towards the end of September and at the beginning of October we went out to Spithead between the Isle of Wight and Portsmouth where the Joint Helicopter Unit, which had been practising landings on a marked out aircraft carrier deck at RAF Middle Wallop, came aboard to try out the real thing. On the same day the *Ocean* had taken 845 Naval Air Squadron aboard at Devonport for exercises in Plymouth Sound. On the 9th she joined us at Spithead for joint exercises.

With this working up concluded we duly began loading ammunition, fuel, victuals, etc., and together, like the *Ocean*, embarked the Royal Marine contingent and their equipment. Between the 12th and 14th the two ships swapped over their helicopter squadrons for some reason with 845 Squadron coming to us.

Just prior to setting off from Portsmouth on 22 October.

Vehicles stored at the aft of the deck prior to leaving.

Ships in the convoy to Port Said.

On the 22nd of October we set off down the English Channel making for Malta where we arrived on the 26th soon after which men of 45 Commando began practising going aboard the helicopters in full battle kit. We set sail for Egypt on 3 November.

On the 5th, after having completed the morning watch (0000 to 0400 hours) I returned to my mess ready to sleep when I was instructed to report to my ABCD (atomic, biological, chemical destruction) damage control station as soon as possible. The chief stoker in charge of the section went through our expected details which took place when we felt the way came off the ship and the flight deck starting to become active.

The chief sent me to observe which other vessels were nearby. It was the morning the Paras went in. The day continued in the usual routine.

Approaching the Egyptian coastline. Smoke rising from the Standard Oil refinery blaze on the canal side.

We arrived in Egyptian waters very early on the morning of the 6th November, dropping anchor some miles offshore where we waited until it was time for the Commandos to go ashore.

Waiting offshore for zero hour.

Preparing the helicopters.

The Commandos coming up on deck to assemble and prepare for boarding the helicopters.

The Commandos lining up to board the helicopters.

A helicopter setting off for the shore.

Just after 0800 hours the helicopters began ferrying the Commandos to the area behind the De Lesseps statue then coming back for more until all were ashore less than two hours later. They were then able to start bringing the casualties back to the carrier for treatment.

A wounded marine being put on a stretcher from one of the returned helicopters.

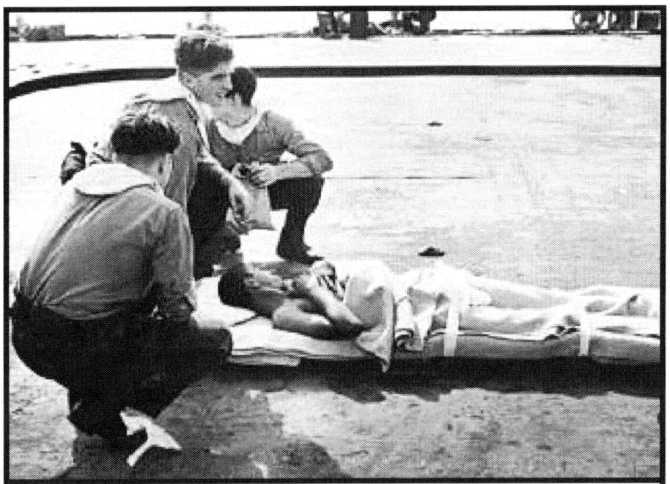

An Egyptian casualty waiting to go below for treatment.

By the late afternoon the waterfront area of Port Said was sufficiently secure for the captain to take the *Theseus* into the outer harbour where we found ourselves anchored close to HMS *Ocean*.

View from HMS *Theseus* anchored in the canal entrance.

During the night one of the wounded, a 19-year-old Marine caught up in the so-called friendly fire incident the previous day, died and in the morning we sailed out to sea for his ceremonial burial.

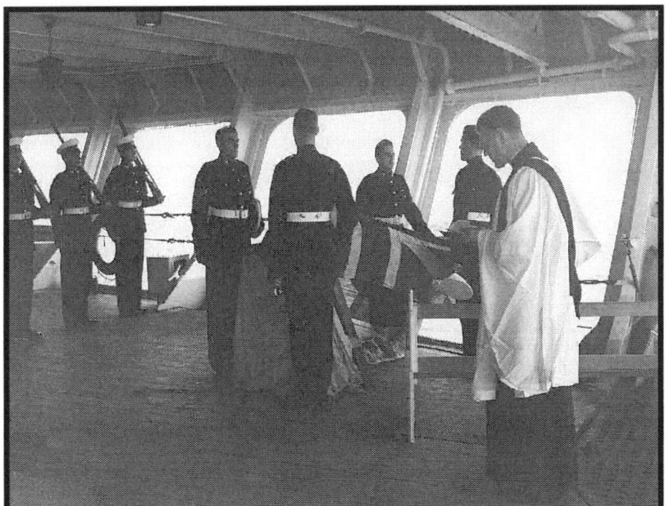

Marine John Fowler burial. (Photograph Tony Davie)

On our return we took the last of the wounded aboard then later in the day, the 7th, sailed for Malta where ambulances were waiting to take them ashore.

Troops belonging to the Duke of Wellington Regiment were immediately taken on board and before the day was ended we were setting off to sea again, this time to Cyprus where the regiment was disembarked at Famagusta to help in the fight against the EOKA insurgents. We arrived back in Malta on the 17th of November and remained in the Grand Harbour until the morning of the 5th December when our helicopters were flown off the ship and we steamed back to Port Said to begin evacuating our troops, vehicles and equipment now that the United Nations had taken over in the town.

We were back in Malta by the 10th and after unloading was complete returned for our second evacuation of troops and transport. We set out on the 15th of December, this time for home, at last. I remember when we were approaching Blighty the English Channel was not exciting – wet snow and rain. By the 21st we were moored at the Portsmouth Railway Jetty. The following day Captain Pizey made a farewell speech to the ship's company at the end of his service in the Navy. I got home for Christmas.

HMS *Theseus* was decommissioned in January and I was posted to HMS *St Vincent*, an officers' shore-based training ship in Gosport, and remained there until my demob in May 1957.

After the Navy I helped my father run a business supplying tractor cabins and got married to Rachel in 1961. We went on to have a son and daughter and twin sons. The firm ran through until 1971 when we closed owing to Health and Safety Regulations following the introduction of safety cabins. I then joined a company in Birmingham which supplied threading tools.

In 1981 Rachel and I moved to Looe in Cornwall where we ran a B/B for almost twenty years before giving up in 2000.

* * *

Norman Wild, HMS *Theseus*

Norman was born in Battle Hospital, Reading, Berkshire on 29 October 1935 then taken home to Medmenham near Maidenhead. The family later moved to East Garston near Newbury which is where Norman went to school. He left school at the age of fifteen and went to work on a farm until he was called for National Service by which time he was living at Marsh Benham near Newbury. It was at this time that he saw a Navy advert in a Sunday newspaper which said 'Let us pay you to see the world.' He signed on as a regular.

Soon after his interview and medical he was instructed to report to Victoria Barracks at Southsea to begin his training. After this he spent some time on HMS *Cleopatra*, flagship for the Reserve Fleet at Portsmouth, followed by spells at the shore establishment HMS *Dryad* close to Portsmouth Harbour, the carrier HMS *Centaur*, the carrier HMS *Eagle*, and HMS *Ceres*, the shore base at Wetherby in Yorkshire which was the Supply and Secretariat training establishment. Eventually he was posted to HMS *Theseus*.

Early in August 1956, just after the Egyptian leader Colonel Nasser had nationalised the Suez Canal, the *Theseus* sailed for Cyprus with the Parachute Regiment which was to replace the Commandos in security duties there. Norman remembers that while at Famagusta they had to keep throwing hand grenades over the side to deter any ideas Eoka might have had to fasten limpet mines to the side of the ship.

With the Paras ashore the Commandos came aboard to be taken to Malta for further training in preparation for the invasion of Egypt. *Theseus* then continued on to the UK to collect members of 45 Commando and their equipment before turning around to take them to Malta to join up with the rest of the brigade.

HMS *Theseus* entering Grand Harbour, Malta.

A conjuror keeping the lads entertained at Malta.

On about 2 November the *Theseus* set out for Port Said and made history, together with HMS *Ocean* when its Commandos went ashore in helicopters rather than in conventional assault craft.

Helicopters ready to receive the Commandos from below.

Norman never saw any of the action at Port Said since, being one of the cooks, his action station was always below deck near to where he worked in the galley so that the cooks could take turns in preparing the meals. However, once the ceasefire was signed and the *Theseus* had anchored in the mouth of the Suez Canal he was able to come up on deck when off duty and take in the sights around him.

On his return to Civvy Street Norman became a postman and served 30 years until retirement.

The view of Port Said from *HMS Theseus* as it noses between the breakwaters at the entrance to the Suez Canal.

The view from the Outer Basin. The blockship *Paul Solente* with the central dome of the Suez Canal building behind it. To the left are the flames and smoke of the Standard Oil Company storage tank fire.

Smoke still drifting across from the airfield fire and from the beach huts. The fishing docks entrance.

Commandos returning to re-embark on the *Theseus*.

* * *

Jim Hunt, HMS *Theseus*.

Life for me began in Derby on 1 April 1935 and I could be described as anchor-faced because I just loved everything Navy. When I was 13 while at secondary school I joined the Sea Cadets and 'served' on TS *Malaya*, a stone-class training ship in Derby where I finished up as a 3-badge petty officer.

I left school when 15 in 1950 and began an apprenticeship as a painter and signwriter. On reaching the age of 17 I enlisted in the RNVR (Royal Navy Voluntary Reserve) based at the Mersey Division with the Number MD 4616. This was to en-

Jim at 17 in 1952 on a course , Whale Island, Portsmouth.

sure that when I had to do my National Service I got into the Navy. My ship, the sloop HMS *Eaglet*, previously HMS *Bevis*, was permanently moored at Salthouse Dock in Liverpool. This service involved one weekend per month as well as two weeks annually spent on a ship. Over the next four years I served on HMS *Dido*, HMS *Carisbrooke Castle*, HMS *Teazer*, as well as HMS *Eaglet*.

When I was 21 in 1956 I came to the end of my apprenticeship and National Service deferment and, naturally enough, was called up into the Navy. In April I started at Victoria Barracks, Southsea where, as would be expected, the training came fairly easy for me.

After the barracks my training continued on the aircraft carrier HMS *Ocean* of the Home Fleet Training Squadron based at Portland Harbour. While I was with the ship we went on a European tour together with HMS *Maidstone*, the submarine depot ship, in which we visited Rotterdam, Hamburg, Oslo, and Stockholm as well as Rosyth on the Firth of Forth in Scotland.

On about 1 July joined the carrier HMS *Theseus* and in early August we made a trooping trip to Cyprus carrying reinforcements for the Parachute Brigade, initially to combat EOKA but which later became part of the build-up of numbers for the planned *Operation Musketeer*, the action intended to return the Suez Canal to its owners following its recent nationalization by Egypt's Colonel Nasser. We arrived just six days later and disembarked the troops and their equipment and soon afterwards we took aboard members of the Royal Marine 45 Commando for passage to Malta for intensive training.

HMS *Theseus* at Malta.

We then returned to the UK where we arrived on the 2nd of the month at Portsmouth. Throughout September we managed to take some leave while the ship was in dock.

For most of the first half of October we carried out training close to the Isle of Wight with a helicopter squadron. We thought it was just a routine exercise but it turned out that we were preparing for *Musketeer*. On the 22nd, after embarking troops and a squadron of helicopters, we sailed for Malta where we took aboard about half of 45 Commando, the other half going aboard the *Ocean*. On 3rd November we set sail for Egypt.

The convoy approaching Egyptian waters.

Captain Griffiths inspecting member of 45 Commando on their departure for the Port Said waterfront by helicopter.

Commandos boarding helicopter to be taken ashore.

We arrived a few miles off Port Said during the early hours of the 6th where the Marines made ready to be ferried ashore by the helicopters.

Helicopter taking the first *Theseus* commandos ashore.

Returning helicopters.

Wounded being taken below on the aircraft lift.

The first departure was soon after 8am. Casualties were brought back by the returning aircraft.

Later in the day when most of the fighting was over and almost all of Port Said, especially along the waterfront, had been secured, we were given permission to make our way inshore and then enter the canal and to anchor against the eastern breakwater that formed the mouth of the canal.

We now carried out the usual routines as well as other jobs such as dock security. That very same day it was announced that a ceasefire was due to come into effect at midnight. The following morning the *Theseus* began taking aboard the last of the wounded and later in the day we returned to Malta where they could receive treatment.

We then took members of the Duke of Wellington Regiment aboard and transported them to Cyprus for a tour of duty. Over the next few weeks we sailed backwards and forwards between Malta and the eastern Mediterranean until the 15th of December when we collected our last batch of troops for evacuation from Port Said and sailed for the UK. We arrived at Portsmouth on the 21st for Christmas at home. This was the end of the line for the *Theseus* which was decommissioned and remained in the harbour for the next four years before eventually being scrapped.

I hadn't really taken to big ships so for my next posting I volunteered for submarine service and was accepted. For a while I became a member of the 'spare crew' for HMS *Maidstone*, before joining one of its submarines, HMS *Scorcher*, for some sea time to complete my two years National Service in April 1958.

Soon after my demob I returned to Portsmouth to marry my girlfriend Ann at St Mark's Church, North End on 24th May. We had met while I was stationed there. Back in Derby I returned to my old job in the painting trade for ten years or so before joining the Nuclear Department of Rolls Royce Marine. During my time with the firm I worked on 28 submarine reactors and visited nearly every submarine being built which kept me in touch with the Navy. I eventually became Assistant Production Controller before retiring in 1994.

I keep busy as an active member of the Royal Naval Association, the Submarine Association, and am on the Unit Management Committee of the Derby Sea Cadets unit, now the TS *Kenya* after a name change some years ago from TS *Malaya*.

In 2008 my wife and I celebrated 50 years of marriage.

* * *

Peter Croot, HMS *Bulwark*.

I was born in June 1932 at Bridlington, a seaside resort on the Yorkshire coast. We were still living there when the war started and when the town took in great numbers of evacuee children from the port of Hull which was expected to be a target of the Luftwaffe. But the Luftwaffe attacked Bridlington too and I experienced a number of the raids. We always went under the stairs since this was supposed to be the safest place and so it proved to be because in 1941 we were bombed out and none of the family was hurt, thank God! Two bombs had dropped close together but only one exploded otherwise I might not have been here to tell the tale. Soon after this raid we moved to Norton, a small town close to Malton 25 miles away where Dad, who was a policeman, was transferred.

I left school in the summer of 1946 just after the war at the age of 14 and got a job in an engineering factory, staying there for three-and-a-half years until my friend and I decided to join the Navy, he as an electrician and me as a stoker. We signed on at the end of 1949 for seven years with five in the reserve.

During training I served aboard various ships for short periods of time one being the last of our battleships, HMS *Vanguard.* On the completion of training I was posted to my first ship, the frigate HMS *Loch Tralaig* stationed at Londonderry in Northern Ireland. While I was with the ship we took part in anti-submarine exercises out in the Atlantic which included a Sunderland flying boat.

The Sunderland Flying Boat viewed from HMS *Tralaig.*

After 12 months with the *Trallaig* I was transferred to HMS *Dolphin*, the submarine base at Portsmouth where I worked in the Trials and Refit Office as a general helper. It was while I was there, on the 16th of April 1951, that the submarine HMS *Affray* sailed out of the harbour and disappeared, lost with all 75 aboard.

My next draft was to HMS *Albion*, an aircraft carrier undergoing the final stages of its construction at Swan Hunter on the Tyne. The ship was quite close to completion when it was decided to install the new angle-deck arrangement. It was the first time this British design had been tried on one of our ships. Also installed on the *Albion* at this time was the mirror-sight landing device which helped pilots of the new fast jets to make safer landings on a carrier's deck.

The *Albion* and her angled deck.

There were about 24 of us with the ship at Swan Hunter and we spent 12 months standing by the ship assisting with the trials and testing of the machinery and equipment. While here we lived in digs among the locals at Tyneside which is where I met Stella who I married on 13 March. When the rest of the carrier's 1,000 plus crew eventually came on board it was our job to show them where everything was. The ship was finally completed on 26 May 1954 and commissioned.

On taking over the ship from the builders we sailed south to our base in Portsmouth and began the working up trials in the English Channel. Stella moved down to Southsea for the rest of my time in the Navy and got a job working in the offices of the Southdown Motor Company.

One evening in June our helicopters were called on to help in the search for possible survivors from a Swissair Convair jet that had run out of fuel and ditched in the sea off Folkestone. Also in the Channel, off the coast near Weymouth in Dorset, we carried out working up exercises with the aircraft that would be landing and taking off from our new angled deck. Early in September we also took part in 'touch and go' exercises with the De Havilland 110 third prototype WG240, forerunner of the naval version Sea Vixen.

The WG240 was the aircraft that the De Havilland test pilot John Derry and his observer Tony Richards had flown for the first five days of the Farnborough Air Show exactly two years earlier.

The De Havilland 110 taking off from a carrier for the first time ever on 25 September 1954.

On the sixth day it had developed an engine problem and they had taken up prototype WG 236 instead. During one particular manoeuvre a design fault weakness at the end of one of the wings manifest itself and the plane disintegrated killing the crew and 29 spectators. By the time the aircraft was trialing with us this fault had been rectified

Later in the month, now with our 813 Squadron of single-seater Westland Wyvern aircraft aboard, we sailed to join the Mediterranean Fleet calling at Marseilles on the way. We carried out further exercises in the Mediterranean and also became the flagship of the fleet aircraft carriers. The following month Lt Bruce Macfarlane, one of the pilots of 813 Squadron flying a Wyvern, suffered an engine failure as he was catapulted off the front of the deck. The aircraft fell into the sea and reportedly was cut in half by the Albion's stem. The lieutenant in his cockpit is believed to have sunk to a depth of 80 feet before being able to activate his ejector seat and reach the surface where he was eventually plucked to safety by the standby helicopter. It was eventually discovered that with the sudden acceleration involved in the catapult launch of these first operational Wyverns there was a momentary starvation of fuel to the engine.

If I remember rightly four aircraft were lost in this way although I think all the pilots managed to get out. As a consequence of these flameouts as they were called the aircraft were put ashore on the southern coast of Malta at HMS *Falcon* the Fleet Air Arm shore base at Hal Far and didn't return to service until the problem was solved.

While on the *Albion* at Malta, March 1955, we had a visit from the Duke of Edinburgh who made a 'breeches buoy' transfer over to the ship from the

The Duke of Edinburgh transferring to the *Albion.*

Duke of Edinburgh aboard HMS *Albion* in March 1955.

Royal Yacht *Britannia*. The Duke's uncle, Lord Louis Mountbatten, Commander-in-chief of the Mediterranean Fleet as well as being Supreme Allied Commander of the NATO Mediterranean Command, also came aboard while I was there.

The Royal Yacht *Britannia* viewed from the *Albion.*

Towards the end of the year we returned to Portsmouth where the *Albion* began preparations for its next commission. I left the ship at this time and during 1955 went on an engineering course at Portsmouth which I passed on 30th September. Those newly-qualified at this level were called stokers. On 1st November I sat and passed a Fleet Board examination which qualified me to become a petty officer (Engineering Mechanic).

My next move was on 5 November 1955 to another aircraft carrier, this time HMS *Bulwark* which I joined at Portsmouth. The ship had been built by Harland and Wolf in Belfast and commis-

HMS *Bulwark.*

sioned in October 1954. Since then she had been operating as a trials and training carrier in British coastal waters to give pilots of the Fleet Air Arm 'touch and go' practice on her angled deck, as well as carrying out courtesy visits. Earlier in the year, in February, Avenger aircraft of 703 Naval Air Squadron based at HMS *Peregrine* at Ford in Sussex had made the first arrester hook landings on the ship in the English Channel.

Early in 1956 as part of our schedule we paid a courtesy visit to Copenhagen before continuing on to various ports around the British Isles as a break from our routine training with aircraft of the Fleet Air Arm. Late in July, while about to spend a few days visiting the waters of the Scilly Isles, we received a message curtailing our trials and training programme and instructing us to return to Portsmouth. The Egyptian President Colonel Nasser had just nationalised the Suez Canal Company and with the mounting tension this created we were quickly brought up to a state of readiness.

While taking aboard great quantities of stores of all kinds and de-mothballing our Bofor guns we were joined by large numbers of reservists needed to bring the ship up towards its wartime complement. We set sail for the Mediterranean on the 4th of August with three squadrons of Sea Hawks, 804, 810, and 895, coming aboard. We made very quick time to Malta where we joined the Mediterranean Fleet.

HMS *Bulwark* in Grand Harbour, Malta.

Over most of the next ten weeks we were involved in numerous exercises to prepare us and our three squadrons for the invasion of Egypt, not that we were officially told this was what it was all for. We also managed a visit to the French Port of Marseilles during this period.

HMS *Bulwark* visiting Marseilles in September 1956.

We finally arrived back in Malta with the other carriers on 24 October and five days later sailed out with the fleet apparently on yet another exercise, this one called *Boathook*. However, on this occasion it was the real thing. There were French ships alongside us and together with all the escort ships involved it was quite a sight to see. The American Sixth Fleet followed us at a distance; the US Government didn't agree with Premier Eden's decision to attack Egypt and they were monitoring what took place. From now on, since we still didn't have a complete wartime crew, we had to work four hours on and four hours off continuously night and day for the next two months.

By this time I was a petty officer in charge of the ship's hydraulic steering machinery. When not on duty I still had to be available to supervise one of the damage control centres in case of an attack on the ship.

The *Bulwark* heading into the wind at speed preparing to launch its aircraft.

Bulwark's aircraft ready for take-off. Destroyer escort.

A Sea Hawk over Egyptian territory.

On the 1st of November our aircraft began attacking targets in Egypt and this continued each day through until the ceasefire came into effect on the 6th by which time, so I learned later, our aircraft had carried out over 600 sorties against the enemy. The 6th was also the day that Vice Admiral Power joined us from the *Eagle* which had had to return to Malta for repairs on its catapult.

Our job done we eventually left Port Said for Malta on the 16th of December, arriving there two days later.

Bulwark entering the Grand Harbour, Malta.

We then continued on to Portsmouth. By the time we arrived back in the UK I had been kept back a little over my seven years and after two weeks leave I was demobbed from Portsmouth Barracks after receiving a demob suit from a depot nearby.

My wife and I then moved back to Tyneside and bought our first home. I began work with Post Office Telephones which after privatisation became BT of course. I was with them for 34 years and retired as an external plant manager.

Many years after my demob I discovered that the Navy should have offered me a period of training to further my skills in preparation for civilian life but none was given. The five years reserve service was stopped two years after I left the Navy.

* * *

Peter Ainscow, HMS *Bulwark*.

Peter was born in 1931 at Prestwich, Manchester. He passed the examination to go to Grammar School at 11, passed School Certificate in 1947 and Higher School Certificate in 1949. In 1950 he was taken on for a one-year probationary college apprentice with Metropolitan Vickers of Manchester followed by a three-year electrical engineering degree at Manchester University then back to the final year of his college apprenticeship at Metrovicks which he completed in 1955. As part of his university course Peter had taken a vacation job at a power station near Manchester, one with the Underwater Countermeasures and Weapons Establishment at Havant near Portsmouth, and for eight weeks in France at the plants of Alsthom Electricité le France in Paris and Belfort near Basle. He had taken French as a subsidiary subject for Higher School Certificate.

After a long deferment Peter now had to carry out his National Service. Wanting to use his electrical knowledge as a B.Sc graduate in electrical engineering and as a member of the Institute of Electrical Engineers, he was loath to waste two years doing any job in the services and applied to join the Royal Navy. He was interviewed at the Admiralty Arch offices in London where he was offered a special two-year term in the electrical branch of the Royal Navy which he accepted.

Peter carried out his training at HMS *Collingwood* the shore base close to Fareham and was commissioned as a sub-lieutenant.

Peter, 2nd left, middle row, and his training group at HMS *Collingwood*, near Fareham on Portsmouth harbour.

Peter was posted to HMS *Aerial*, Worthy Down near Winchester and later to the RNAS Brawdy overlooking St Brides Bay in Pembrokeshire which was the base for the aircraft carrier HMS *Bulwark*. Here he was appointed Station Flight Air Electrical

Newly-promoted sub-lieutenants at HMS *Collingwood*. Peter 2nd left on the back row.

Officer looking after the SF aircraft which consisted of helicopters, Vampires, Gannets and others. When 895 Squadron was formed it was not intended as a front line unit with an allotment of sea time and it had no electrical officer. Peter managed to become that – he wasn't sure how he claims – but considered it a great opportunity. The *Bulwark* made a social visit to Copenhagen in early 1956 and that was supposed to be its sole sea time. However, in late July, Egypt's Colonel Nasser started being nasty and suddenly the squadron personnel were told that they would be boarding a carrier for definite sea exercises.

The squadron was given a long weekend break before going abroad except for Peter and a few others who were kept at Brawdy to organise the squadron's departure. Peter had to cancel a holiday with his girlfriend and could only tell family that he was going abroad – not to tell them where – and to just read the papers. The *Bulwark* sailed from Portsmouth on what Peter thinks was the 3rd of August, his girlfriend (now wife) Nora's birthday. It arrived in Malta on the seventh. The squadrons aboard were 804, 810, and 895.

Valetta, was the home of *Bulwark* for the next

View of Gibraltar from one of the aircraft.

HMS *Bulwark* entering the Grand harbour, Valetta, Malta on 7 August 1956.

thee months. Peter was enjoying his time in the Navy and the regulars in the service were the best bunch of colleagues he could have wished for.

Peter went from consuming grog – one part rum, two parts water – which gave one a great appetite after lectures, to supervising its issue as officer of the day. As a commissioned officer in the wardroom he enjoyed the G and Ts and in particular Horse Neck which was brandy and ginger. After eight weeks at sea, with supplies of such items getting quite low, a message appeared on the wardroom notice board to the effect that no more jugs of Horses Neck would be served. However, serviceability of aircraft was always the priority, mainly maintenance and servicing in the carrier hangar.

The Ship's side rigged for swimming.

During flying exercises one day a Sea Hawk upon landing had its arrestor hook pulled out or broken by one of the arrestor wires. There was insufficient length of deck left for the pilot to brake the aircraft and he slid off the bow into the sea, fortunately to the angled deck side of the bow. Although it was for such an eventuality that the an-

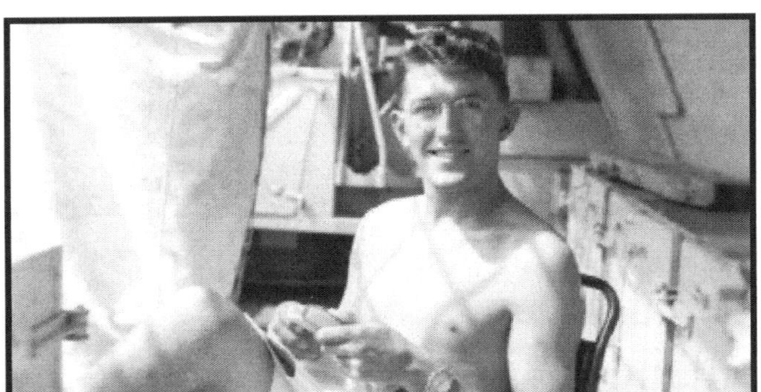

Peter enjoying the sun.

Sea Hawk sliding towards the end of the deck.

Oh My God!

Over she goes.

The *Bulwark* returns to the scene. The pilot was plucked to safety by the duty helicopter.

The pilot deposited safely on the flight deck.

gled deck had been introduced in the first place, on this occasion the aircraft had actually been nudged to one side by catching a parked aircraft which had spun it around and over to port. This had caused the aircraft to land flat rather than on its nose enabling the pilot to make an easier exit than he might otherwise have had.

On 4 October Sub-lieutenant Gordon J Meredith, a pilot of 810 Squadron while on a flying exercise in his Sea Hawk over Malta, had a warning light come on in his cockpit. After informing the ship of his problem by radio he decided he would have to eject. However, as he left the aircraft his seat failed to fall away and his parachute to release and open and he fell to his death. After a search his body was found near a cemetery still strapped into the seat.

When the attack on Egypt began aircraft from Cyprus and Malta delivered their bombs from an altitude of 30,000 feet on Cairo and other military air bases. The pinpoint accuracy of their bombing effectively damaged the runways so that when *Bulwark* arrived off the Egyptian coast its Sea hawks were able to fly into the Cairo area and shoot up most of the aircraft on the ground, including the Russian Migs which were most feared. These were unable to take off either because they were damaged or the runways were. There was no air retaliation, although some of the returning aircraft suffered anti-aircraft gun flak damage.

Looking down on *Bulwark* and her escorts.

A Sea Hawk over the Nile delta.

One of the Sea Hawk squadrons on the flight deck.

Rockets attached.

Sea Hawk ready to be launched.

Sea Hawk 239 landing back on the *Bulwark*.

Arriving back in Malta in mid-December.

Tied up at the quay in the Grand harbour.

As the men returned from the campaign they were aware of the feelings back at home. However as a military operation it was a great success and they knew that had they been allowed to proceed they would have captured the canal in days.

*   *   *

John French, HMS *Albion.*

I was born in 1934 and bred as a Bristolian and at eleven went to the local secondary modern school as it was called in those days. I left school at 15 and joined a printing firm. I was well over 21 when I started my National Service due to my being deferred to finish my apprenticeship in the printing industry. When I went for my first interview and was asked which service I wished to go in I said any service that would enable me to be a PTI since my first interest was sport, particularly rugby, cricket and gymnastics. So when I got my papers I was quite surprised to find myself going into the Navy, the one service in which I couldn't train to specialise as a PTI since it wasn't a navy 'trade'. (Navy PTIs were chosen from established seamen/ tradesmen.)

I started my service on 15 August 1955 at HMS *Daedalus*, a shore station at Lee-on-Solent, just two weeks after my father had died. Shortly afterwards I was sent to HMS *Gamecock*, the land-based establishment and one-time RAF Bramcote near Nuneaton, for six weeks of initial training. While I was there, following interviews concerning which trade or branch I would be assigned to, the decision was made to place me in the photographic branch. One of my hobbies was photography.

On 29 September I was drafted, together with eleven other new entrants, to HMS *Peregrine* another shore station, this one at Ford in Sussex (now an open prison) where the Photographic School was situated. It was a shortened crash course for national servicemen although I believe we were the only national servicemen to enter this branch of the Navy. It was a hard twenty weeks but enjoyable and I was able to get home at times for short or long weekends.

Following the course I was drafted, on 14 February 1956, to HMS *Excellent* at Whale Island in Portsmouth Harbour, yet another 'stone' frigate and home of the Portsmouth Command Photographic Unit. Here I spent three months learning my trade on a busy station alongside long-service personnel which gave me a good grounding for what was to follow. One leading hand about to leave the Navy after nine years was job hunting. He came back one day to tell us he had found a job with the BBC and was going to be a cameraman with a starting salary which to me sounded enormous for those days. This is an illustration of how well naval tradesmen were thought of.

On 26 June 1956 I joined HMS *Albion*, a 28,000 -ton aircraft carrier currently undergoing a refit at Portsmouth dockyard after its return from a commission in the far East.

I learned that some months earlier, on the 5th of January to be precise, a three-seater Fairy Gannet had crashed into the sea while operating off the ship but had landed flat and stayed afloat allowing the crew to be rescued by helicopter.

A Fairy Gannet on the starboard catapult.

A Gannet landing on.

A Gannet catapulted (with flaps up) into the sea. Gannets back on board after 'Suez'. Seventh of May 1957.

Helicopter landing. Deck crewman with wheel 'chocks'.

I was destined to stay on the carrier until my demob. It was my first chance to be a real sailor. After exercises in the English Channel off Portsmouth we visited Oslo, the cleanest city I have ever been to; even the cranes at the docks seem to have been painted and polished for our arrival.

On 15 September with the Suez Crisis upon us and our aircraft, belonging to 800, 802, and 849 squadrons, now aboard we left for the Mediterranean and Malta where we were to be based. En route we called at Gibraltar where we were joined by three carriers of the US Navy, all at least twice our size. Going ashore with all these sailors in the harbour was like being packed in a sardine can but the experience was something that will forever remain in my memory.

During exercises in the Med we visited Marseilles where we lost two sailors in a yachting accident just offshore, and also Messina in Sicily. From here we went on a trip to Mount Etna which we climbed in shorts not realizing that the summit lay in deep snow.

Early on 29 October, together with the *Eagle* and our sister ship *Bulwark*, we sailed for the eastern Mediterranean. We were the first ships to leave for the attack on Egypt and arrived in striking distance on the thirty-first.

The three aircraft carriers together on their way to Egypt.

On 1 November soon after dawn our aircraft began attacking Egyptian airfields. In particular our aircraft attacked Almaza airfield to the east of Cairo with 800 Squadron Sea Hawks firing rockets for the first time.

If my memory is correct we were flying off aircraft 18 hours a day. Being at action stations for

Sea Hawks being prepared for a sortie

A Sea Hawk being launched from the port catapult.

A Sea Hawk just Landed.

The *Albion* with its two lifts operating.

Pom-pom guns forward of the island.

Pilots being briefed for a sortie.

The *Albion* refuelling from an RFA ship.

The visiting task force officers.

most of this time was very hard. Every aircraft's take off and landing had to be filmed whether on active service or not. I don't know whether this was Admiralty policy or Captain's Smeeton's. Each aircraft also carried a G45 camera in its wings aligned with the guns. These had to be removed from the aircraft, taken to the darkroom, developed, and then shown to the pilots before their next sortie, all well within two hours. One aircraft in each squadron also carried an R24 reconnaissance camera.

One day I was on duty on the flight deck from 4am feeling that it seemed a longer spell than usual. Later, as I was coming off duty and making my way to the mess deck thinking it was very rough today, I suddenly went blind and collapsed. I woke up 36 hours later in sickbay and gradually recovered over the following week. I was never actually told what had been wrong but I have always been under the impression that I had a nervous breakdown.

In mid-November, about a week after the cease-fire came into effect, General Stockwell, Commander of the Land Task Force, was ferried out from Port Said by helicopter to the *Albion* with his entourage.

General Stockwell, on the left, and other senior officers of the task force arriving on the *Albion* by helicopter.

Geoffrey Carter on page 82 of his book *Crises Do Happen,* describes one incident during the visit: 'Members of the ship's company mounted a special Guard of Honour on the flight deck. They wore their uniforms and caps back to front and marched backwards to The Goons' chart success 'I'm Walking Backwards for Christmas'. On being invited to inspect the guard, General Stockwell obliged, entering into the spirit of the occasion by reversing his own cap.'

Walking backwards for Christmas.

General Stockwell making a night-time inspection.

On 22 December as the last of the ships and troops sailed away from Port Said the *Albion*, together with the *Eagle* remained just offshore to the very end ready to deal with any possible last minute interference by the Egyptians to the departure.

At the end of May 1957 HMS *Albion* was present off Invergordon on the east coast of Scotland for a three-day Fleet Review. The Queen was there in the Royal Yacht and came aboard to attend a fleet concert.

The fleet and the Royal Yacht.

Captain R M Smeeton MBE RN and the Queen.

I look back on my National Service with pride and as an experience I'm glad I didn't miss. The one thing I did miss was my sport – you can't play rugby or cricket on an aircraft carrier. The day the ship arrived back at Portsmouth just prior to my demob my friend John Thorne, who I learned to play rugby with at school and club, was hooking for England in Paris. His understudy at Bristol Rugby Club at that time was John Thorne who also went on to play for, and captain, England.

I left the Navy on 1 September 1957 at Lee-on-Solent and continued in the printing and packaging industry as an assistant works manager. Unfortunately I was unable to adapt my photographic skills in the printing industry because although the company I had been with were willing to employ me the union would not accept me as a 'still' photographer.

I then took a job as a sales representative working for a small London company, then a big national company for 15 years until its demise in 1982 when I went self-employed working as an agent for a Dutch Company covering the whole of the UK. I retired in 1994 partly due to my hearing.

Twenty-five years after leaving the Navy I went for an audio test where they informed me that at some time in the past I had been subject to very loud noises! I learned that the damage to my eardrums would have been the cause of my collapse. The photographic darkroom was situated right at the bottom of the ship next to the deck catapult machinery and while flying was in progress it was impossible to talk to anyone. No earmuffs in those days. I do get a war pension but I am now left with very poor hearing.

* * *

Alan Jacobs, Fleet Air Arm.

In 1956 I was a crew member of X Flight of 845 Squadron of the Fleet Air Arm flying the American Sikorsky S55 helicopter built under licence by Westland as the Whirlwind.

At the beginning of the year the squadron had been based at Eglington in Northern Ireland where it operated as an anti-submarine unit. During April we were involved in exercises in this capacity before being divided into two to go on overseas goodwill visits aboard the carriers *Ocean* and *Theseus*. We spent time in the Mediterranean particularly around Malta.

On 22 September, with the Suez Crisis getting more serious, the squadron was brought back to the Fleet Arm base at Lee on Solent to practise troop transportation exercises. At the end of the month the squadron flew onto the *Ocean* at Devonport to begin exercises with the Commandos who it was intended we would be carrying. Two days later the ship moved out into Plymouth Sound where landings were practised while the ship was at anchor before it moved to Spithead for advanced landing and take-off exercises with deck parties involved.

The Squadron then joined the *Theseus* and on 22 October, with a large contingent of Commandos aboard, we sailed for Malta where the helicopters flew into Hal Far for more lifting exercises with the commandos.

Then it was on! We were going to 'Suez' to sort out the crisis between Israel and the Arab combatants, or so we were led to believe. However, for me there was just one tiny problem. We knew where we were going but hadn't been told whose side we would be on. I am a Jew.

I had no intention of fighting against my own

people so went to see my Divisional Officer and told him that if Britain and France were to side with the Arabs, I would state 'conscientious objection'. The officer, in a panic, arranged for me to see the padre who wholeheartedly agreed with the way I felt. Luckily, as it turned out, we would be fighting the Arabs.

As the flotilla of warships belonging to Britain and France set out from Malta the training continued. We had 45 Commando under Lt Colonel N H Tailyour DSO aboard. As we got closer to the Egyptian coast we could see on the horizon a smudge of smoke. The following day it had become a strong pillar of smoke drifting on the wind and we were told it was the oil refinery at Port Said. As we got closer it was possible to smell it. Then we were flying 45 Commando ashore and bringing back the wounded. The hangar deck had been kitted out with bunks. Once the wounded had been taken off, we were able to take more Commandos aboard in no more than a minute while the ground crews could refuel us in under four. More wounded were brought back, not only British and French but also Egyptians.

Later, when *Theseus* entered Port Said harbour, we got a good view of the ships blocking the canal, vessels of all sorts, not from the Allied shelling but from the Egyptians deliberately blocking the waterway. The statue of Ferdinand De Lesseps was still intact but seemed to look quite forlorn by the canal entrance. The squadron lost one chopper. It ran out of fuel and had to ditch in the sea. I think all aboard were rescued.

Stories were soon abounding about how the Egyptian male population of Port Said was hurriedly conscripted to defend their town. Some told of being collected from their homes, given a rifle (no ammunition) and dropped off at the beach and told to fight to the death. Quite naturally they surrendered as soon as possible. This was my Suez adventure.

* * *

Robinson, Trevor John, HMS *Forth.*

I entered the mouth of the Suez Canal aboard HMS *Forth*, a submarine depot ship, on 6 November 1956. I was a petty officer shipwright on the vessel which was normally based in Malta. It had the ability to bake large quantities of bread, cook food, and provide washing facilities for the troops. We also acted as floating headquarters.

When it came time for the troops and Navy to withdraw, a salvage fleet was assembled under the auspices of the United Nations to lift the wrecks Nasser had used to block the canal. However when these vessels arrived a lot of their crews got cold feet and wanted home. Volunteers from the Royal Navy were asked for and, disregarding the old adage 'never volunteer', I was one who did.

I was assigned to LC (lifting craft) 10. These were barges which had no engines, operated in pairs, and were able to flood down four feet before passing cables under the wreck and then pump out which lifted the wreck four feet. A tug then towed the three vessels into shallower water until the wreck grounded upon which we repeated the process. These craft were designed to work in tidal waters for a lift of up to 15 feet. With virtually no Mediterranean tide we had numerous goes to move just one wreck out of the channel.

Just before the last marine commandos departed they climbed up a flagpole on the quay, fastened the Union Flag to the top, then cut away the halyards and greased the pole all the way down. It was their going away present to the Egyptians.

The last of the Allied ships left Port Said on 22nd December except HMS *Duchess* which remained at the quay until the early hours of the 23rd in case the abducted Lt Moorhouse was released for the final departure of the British. It didn't happen, the officer was already dead.

The statue of De Lesseps pointing to the Orient.

Shortly afterwards, at the end of the month, some of the locals decided take out their anger at the French being involved in the invasion of Port Said by blowing up the statue of De Lesseps, the Frenchman responsible for the construction of the Suez Canal. It took them three goes with each bang bigger than the one before.

Ferdinand unmoved by the puff of smoke.

Did he move?

The statue crashes to the causeway.

The seagulls scatter.

Finally De Lesseps shot up into the air and came crashing down off his plinth.

Being 'supposed' UN personnel we were each issued with a pair of blue overalls and a blue beret. We also had an occasional visit from a Swedish UN trooper and we were supplied by a UN supply ship (RN). As petty officers we were allowed a bottle of gin a week and all the beer we could beg, steal or borrow. It all came to an end in early March and we were collected by tank landing ship and returned to Malta.

* * *

K S Hett, officer aboard HMS *Manxman*. (Retired Lt Commander K S Hett MBE RN)

HMS *Manxman* was re-commissioned in early 1956 under the command of Captain D T Tibbits DSO, DSC, RN as the flagship of Flag Officer Flotillas, Mediterranean. She had been built as a fast minelayer during WWII with speeds in excess of 40 knots.

HMS *Manxman.*

During her refit in Malta *Manxman* had been fitted out with cabins and facilities to serve as a flagship capable of operating with the Mediterranean Destroyer Flotillas although she was not fitted with the extensive communications facilities needed for the control of war operations. The vessel was on a Local Foreign Service Commission which meant that the families of the ship's company were able to live in Malta.

After Nasser had nationalised the Suez Canal the British Government was faced with problems. The ships of the Mediterranean Fleet were not kept abreast of government plans but we could see the build up of naval forces, including amphibious units, in the Mediterranean around Malta.

During the late summer and autumn there was a series of naval amphibious exercises around Malta in which *Manxman* was involved. Clearly we were practising for an assault on Egypt to recover control of the canal.

I was aware that sealed operation orders had been issued. The operation planning team regularly visited Malta and the orders were recalled and reissued as the plan changed and was updated.

Eventually the order was given to mount the assault from Malta. The amphibious assault craft convoy was formed up and the *Manxman* was nominated as an escort and as the flagship of Rear Admiral D E Holland-Martin DSO DSC. Other escorts were destroyers, frigates, and the cruiser *Jamaica* leading.

The cruiser HMS *Jamaica*.

Late at night on Monday 30 October the convoy MES1 sailed for Egypt. Our sealed orders could now be opened. This was the first opportunity for the ship to learn the precise nature of the operation.

The passage east was relatively uneventful though the convoy speed was very slow for *Manxman* due to the presence of many small landing vessels. One evening a report suddenly came up to the bridge that we had a 'man overboard'. *Manxman* immediately closed the ship to carry out a search, but the next ship astern spotted the man in the water and picked him up. The man overboard had been at the stern of the ship where he had possibly lost his balance.

On 2 November *Manxman* was refueled from the RFA replenishment ship *Wave Laird.*

The RFA vessel *Wave Laird*.

Task force: a frigate, an aircraft carrier just beyond it, two helicopters, and three more vessels on the horizon.

On the morning of 4 November Rear Admiral Holland-Martin transferred from *Manxman* to the cruiser HMS *Jamaica*. Although we had the accommodation for a flag officer we didn't have the communications capabilities for this role.

In her role as a minelayer *Manxman* was fitted with taught wire measuring gear for precise navigation when laying mines. The gear comprised a large reel of piano wire which was dropped and anchored to the bottom of the sea. The wire was then paid out as the ship moved ahead and gave a very accurate measurement of distance steamed. The ship was instructed to use this equipment to lay the datum dan with great accuracy for the start of minesweeping operations ahead of the assault force. The ship had been warned that this task could be needed before the operation orders were opened and *Manxman* had practised the use of the equipment during the rehearsals in the autumn.

The ship was detached from the convoy and proceeded at high speed towards Cyprus. During this passage a darkened ship was encountered. After a challenge it was identified as the French Battleship

Jean Bart. We of course were not aware of the highly secret discussions and collusion between the British, French and Israelis over this operation but this encounter was kept secret.

Once off the coast of Cyprus the taut wire measuring gear was set to work, a very accurate position fix was made, and the ship set off for the entrance to the Suez Canal. Distance steamed was measured with great accuracy. The precise course steered depended on good steering by the quartermaster and the accuracy of the gyro compass. When the correct distance had been run off on the measuring gear the datum dan was laid and *Manxman* withdrew from the immediate approach to Port Said and joined the fleet lying to the north.

Members of the press had not joined the initial phase of the operation, presumably for security reasons but as soon as the landing operations had stabilised *Manxman* was ordered to Cyprus to collect the journalists. The ship embarked the party at Limassol during the early morning of 6 November then sailed at high speed for Port Said. The sea was rough and at high speed *Manxman* was tossed around by the sea in a very uncomfortable motion. The ship was too unsteady to lay tables and serve a proper meal so everyone, including the journalists, was given sandwiches though many were unable to eat anything.

By the time the *Manxman* reached Port Said the harbour had been secured and HMS *Forth* was anchored there as the base ship. *Manxman* berthed alongside her and the journalists left the ship. Captain Tibbets, well aware of the need to keep in with the press, personally spoke to each of the journalists and shook his hand as he left the ship.

Manxman remained in Port Said and the adja-

View to the right: De Lesseps statue and the fishing dock.

Manxman captain David Tibbits, and Denis Swithinbank.

The LST L3516 HMS *Striker* on the left.

The frigate HMS *Ursa* in the harbour.

View from HMS *Forth*. Pontoon walkway for easy access to the 'promenade'. The De Lesseps statue is just out of sight to the right. The dark building at the left end of the promenade is the Casino Palace Hotel. Slightly further down the canal is the lighthouse.

The French hospital ship *La Marseillaise* and an aircraft carrier anchored out of the way against the eastern mole.

The LST HMS *Reggio.*

View towards Port Fuad from the bow of the *Manxman* with the blockships *Pollux* on the left and *Peluese* on the right.

A closer view of the *Pollux* and the *Peleuse.*

cent sea for much of the time that the British operations continued. Mail and fresh provisions were important items in support of the military forces in the area. *Manxman*, because of her speed made several trips between Port Said and Cyprus to bring these in. Rear Admiral 'Crap' Meiers VC was the Flag Officer Middle East operating with a very small staff in Cyprus. He arranged with great efficiency all the items that *Manxman* collected from Cyprus. It is said that because of his small staff he humped some of the stores around personally. On arrival back in Port Said the stores were offloaded into a pontoon alongside HMS *Forth*. It is alleged that because of the distribution difficulties it had not always been possible to distribute the fresh items before *Manxman* arrived back with another load. Forth always arranged to sweep into the sea any items remaining on the pontoon before *Manxman* arrived back; they knew that Captain Tibbets would hit the roof if he thought that the results of our labours in obtaining stores was not properly appreciated.

Priority was given to clearing the sunken ships blocking the canal especially those in the main fairway. HMS *Manxman* was privileged to be the first ship to steam through the area after the part clearance to test that the canal could be reopened. The ship did not transit the area beyond but turned around once she had passed through the area of the blockages. Manxman's passage was filmed and shown on the newsreels.

Manxman at the oiling berth on the canal.

At the oiling berth.

Another view from *Manxman* at the oiling berth.

A French general visits HMS *Tyne* to farewell the Commander Task Force.

Manxman was in Port Said when British forces withdrew from Egypt. Her final task was to to take the Force commanders and other senior officers to Cyprus.

Our departure was delayed in the hope that Lt Moorhouse who had gone missing early in the campaign would turn up. Finally we had to leave.

Waiting to evacuate.

Manxman then embarked her passengers and sailed for Cyprus before making for Malta. It was just before Christmas.

Would it be possible to get husbands back in time to join their families on Christmas Day? There was no chance that the slower ships leaving Port Said would get back by Christmas but *Manxman*, with her high speed, might just be able to make it if the weather did not slow her down. *Manxman* steamed into her flagship berth in Malta during the forenoon of Christmas Day.

* * *

Michael J Salts, HMS *Manxman*.

I was born in April 1937 in Lowestoft in Suffolk. The Second World War started before I was three-years-old and we had to become accustomed to the sound of anti-aircraft guns and bomb explosions as well as spending nights in the air-raid shelter in our garden. During one of these raids a whole row of houses not far from our home was demolished. I was almost six before I could start school as there was a shortage of teachers due to the war. I remember we had to carry a gas mask wherever we went and that I was evacuated to a 'safer' place on three occasions.

After the war we went to live in Cheshire nearer to my father's relatives. When coming up to the age of eleven I won a scholarship to attend Birkenhead School but was there for only two terms before we moved again, this time to North Wales where I attended Abergele Grammar School. A further move took us back to Lowestoft where I became a pupil at the Secondary Grammar School. One of my recreations was to sail on Oulton Broad near my home.

I left school at 16 in the summer of 1953 and joined the Metropolitan Police Cadet Force working in south-east London. On approaching 18 years of age I had the option to remain in the police or accept call up. I had seen an advertisement in a recruiting office stating that if one joined the Royal Navy one might become a midshipman and learn the Russian language. That sounded good to me so I made an application and was accepted. However, after joining I was never offered a midshipman's role nor given a chance to learn Russian.

I began my two weeks initial training in late 1955 at HMS *Victory*, the shore base at Portsmouth. In January 1956, after training, I was flown out to join the crew of HMS *Manxman* as an ordinary seaman. She was lying in the dockyard at Valetta, Malta, and we, the new additions to her crew, were temporarily housed in the shore base HMS *Ricasoli* overlooking the harbour. Manxman had just undergone a refit and it was our job to prepare her for sea trials.

Life on board was a great eye-opener for the landlubbers like me. Accommodation was really cramped and it took some time for us to become accustomed to sleeping in hammocks over the mess-deck dining tables. The regulars must have viewed us as an imposition because we had to learn even the most basic features of shipboard life, traditions accumulated over hundreds of years. Looking back I can sympathise with the petty officers and leading hands who had to wet nurse us through those early days. They were not always patient with us but we learned the hard way and were gradually welded together into part of the team.

Our superiors had the job of selecting those suitable for the multitude of tasks vital to the efficient running of the ship. My first role was as a Main Signals Office messenger and I was chosen apparently because I had acquired some basic typewriter skills learned during my time as a police cadet. Apart from typing and duplicating messages I was required to distribute copies personally to the wardroom officers and CPOs. But many other tasks fell to my lot too, floor scrubbing and cleaning being the least of them. A large number of new signal flags had arrived and each had to be fitted with toggles and their rope-ends back-spliced, a job that was fitted in between other more pressing activities.

Michael on the flag deck.

During the sea trials off Malta we carried out some high speed runs to test the boilers., We were told that *Manxman* was possibly the fastest ship in the world with a maximum speed of about 42 knots and I certainly found that steaming at such high speed was a rare experience. Everyone was warned to stay below decks during these runs. The ship shuddered frighteningly from stem to stern and the bow spray came right over the superstructure. The actual maximum speed achieved during these trials was 38 knots.

Early in our tour we were given the chance to become familiar with the task of refuelling the ship while at sea. This usually entailed a rendezvous with one of the Royal Fleet Auxiliary (RFA) ships. We would steam alongside her at a steady speed, pass ropes or cables across the gap between us and convey a heavy fuel pipe from the RFA to our upper deck to commence the refuelling. At the same time we might also use a light jackstay to transfer food and other essentials.

I recollect one occasion when ‘Jimmy the One’, our First Lieutenant, was being transferred in such a fashion. By misfortune the two ships rolled inwards at the same moment causing the light jackstay to dip its passenger into the sea. Thoroughly soaked his dignity was further shattered when the crew yelled with delight and gave him a less than encouraging cheer.

The officer transferring via the light jack stay.

On another occasion I visited the heads, as toilets are called in common navy parlance, just as gunnery trails were about to start. These were close to the bows and consisted of about a dozen cubicles containing water closets each separated from the next by steel partitions about four feet high which gave a minimum of privacy. The forward 4-inch gun was located immediately above the heads and part of its support pillar and ammunition hoist actually passed through the heads compartment. Seated there I did not anticipate the consequences of a 4-inch shell being fired. The violence of the explosion can hardly be imagined unless personally experienced. Enclosed as I was in a virtual steel box I felt the blast in every fibre of my body and my ear drums felt shattered. I got out of there as fast as I could but my ears were ringing for quite some time afterwards.

In mid-April we took part in a massive NATO exercise called *Medflex Dragon*. A total of sixty-four ships and sixty-plus aircraft of the alliance took part with the main focus being convoy protection. We spent a lot of time at action or defence stations and when the exercise came to an end on the twentieth it was with a most impressive fly-past and steam-past close to the Grand Harbour at Malta.

After some months at sea I was selected to serve as bowman with the crew of the Fast Motor Boat. Evidently my previous boating experience had been noticed on some form I had filled in previously. This was regarded as a 'plum' job because when in harbour I would be relieved of some of the watch-keeping that my mess mates had to do. I was pleased to discover that the coxswain of the FMB was Leading Seaman Nobby Clark from my home town of Lowestoft.

By the late summer lots of rumours were beginning to circulate throughout the ship about the Suez Canal business. These gave rise to lots of uncertainty among the crew. Letters from home where there was better access to news led us to believe that we might get involved before long. Sure enough we soon found the frequency of our patrols to Cyprus waters increasing. The island was being used as a base for the build-up for the Port Said assault. Among our tasks was conveying war correspondents, stores, and army personnel to this trouble spot.

Eventually, in Malta, on the last Sunday of October, the 28th, we quickly began to provision the ship and two days later, with Flag Officer Rear Admiral D E Holland-Martin now aboard, joined Convoy MES1 assembling outside Grand Harbour where, late that evening, we set off for the rendezvous off Cyprus.

The journey east was one of the worst I can recall. The weather was very rough and progress slow because we were escorting a fleet of small landing craft. The soldiers we were carrying aboard *Manxman* were having a very bad time. There was a lot of seasickness which meant that much of the ship below decks was in a deeply unpleasant state.

Early on the morning of our approach to Cyprus one of the seamen was sent to uncover the FMB and prepare it for lowering ready to disembark a sizeable number of war correspondents who would be covering the invasion. It was dark at the time but we could just see a few lights on the shore several miles away. The seaman, who will remain nameless, must have missed his footing because he fell into the sea. Fortunately someone witnessed his fall and reported 'man overboard' to the officer on the bridge. By the time the ship was stopped Nameless must have been half a mile behind us.

Manxman turned round and steamed back on a reciprocal course with all hands alerted to watch for their hapless comrade. The large signalling lamp was used as a searchlight. The journalists were now at the ready with their cameras and notebooks. Thankfully Nameless was eventually spotted and lifted back on board safe and sound.

Thinking that his fall had not been noticed, he explained afterwards, he had cast off his Wellington service issue boots in order to swim to the shore. A wise precaution you might think. The Navy didn't think so. He was later charged with some offence against Naval Regulations for losing items of property.

On 2 November we had our fuel replenished from the Royal Fleet Auxiliary vessels *Wave Laird* and *Brown Ranger*.

RFA *Brown Ranger*.

During action stations and gunnery practice I had a role in the Transmitting Station where the equipment was housed for keeping the heavy guns on target. It was a fairly small compartment deep in the lowest bowels of the ship equipped with something akin to a computer, albeit an ancient one, operated by five or six men. Our task was to operate the various controls of this machine to ensure that the movement of the ship did not cause the guns to go off-aim. The TS was not a pleasant place to work especially when we were sailing through areas where it was thought mines had been laid. Escape from here would have been a forlorn hope.

In such a small space occupied by several sweating bodies the air was usually thick since the ventilation was considerable less than adequate. I recall one occasion when the Gunnery Officer came down to observe the men at work. He was smoking a foul-smelling pipe which poured clouds of blue smoke over us as we tried desperately to concentrate on the task in hand. During the Suez crisis we spent many hours in that airless rat hole relying on situation reports over the loudspeaker to let us know what was happening topside. On occasions the temperature reached 120 degrees.

The *Manxman* was engaged in the bombardment of the Port Said targets. I well remember the night of 5 November as being for us the biggest Guy Fawkes Night ever. Many ships were lying offshore and the air was filled with shell blasts.

The next morning we could see huge plumes of smoke rising from an oil terminal at the back of the town and other areas. The saddest moment for me was when I saw a fatal accident involving a helicopter which was loaded, so I understand, with wounded personnel. It was flying quite low and when a huge wave caught its undercarriage it was pulled straight down like a stone just a hundred and fifty yards from us. There were plenty of small boats scuttling round the area but nothing could be done so far as I could see apart from the rescue of one man who escaped in a life raft.

Following the cease-fire, which took place at midnight on the sixth, *Manxman* was directed into the port area just inside the entrance of the canal.

In the entrance to the Suez Canal. View of Fishing Dock and De Lesseps statue.

As it happened *Manxman* was the first ship to enter the head of the canal after a safe passage had been cleared. We negotiated a route between some of Colonel Nasser's block ships until we could berth. I was on duty in the admiral's barge at the time so had the opportunity to take a few camera shots of Manxman's progress through the mayhem.

View of the blockships.

More blockships.

Two-funnelled dredger No.6 blockship on front of the Canal Company Building.

Manxman threading its way between the blockships.

We then returned to Limassol in Cyprus conveying personnel and stores backwards and forwards. We returned to Malta for a while but in December

The *Manxman* at the south side of the blockships beyond the Abbas Hilmi Basin. The hip-roofed building on the left is in the grounds of the waterworks.

Another view of the building in the water works grounds

The Supply ship HMS *Ranpura.*

we were back to Port Said via Cyprus for more tasks. By mid-December we returned to Limassol again when I wrote a letter to my parents dated Sunday 16 December.

'As I write we are anchored in Limassol, having arrived here yesterday morning from Port Said. Our programme had been altered after we sailed from Malta so we went straight to Suez. On arrival there we dropped off some Christmas stores, including turkeys, cakes, biscuits, and decorations for HMS *Forth* and HMS *Tyne*. During that forenoon the ship's company was addressed by the First Lord of the Admiralty, Lord Hailsham, who had been out to Suez with C in C Med in order to take stock of the situation out here.

He told us he was agreeably surprised at what he found, having expected to find things in a much worse state. But he seemed worried that we were having to evacuate the canal so soon before we could remove more of the block ships. Apparently the U.N.O. has very inadequate equipment for lifting the sunken wrecks and it will be a long time before large vessels can pass through.

We sailed from Port Said that night at 11 p.m. with the First Lord and the C in C on board, arriving in Limassol yesterday morning as I told you. I was bowman of the barge (Nobby was cox'n) and we had to take the V.I.P.s and their staff ashore. The weather was very rough and we had a tough job on our hands. (There is no harbour, as such, at Limassol.) However, they both thanked us for what we did and of course we were rather proud to have been able to do this for them. Prayers and a Bible reading were read to the ship's company by the Captain, this morning being Sunday.

The latest news concerning our movements is that we return to Suez tomorrow, Monday, supposedly to cover the withdrawal of the troops. Later we will have to escort some of the slow-moving landing craft back to Malta and will probably be at sea on Christmas Day. However, as usual, everything is 'in the air' so to speak, and we can be certain of nothing. .....'

'..... In fact we arrived back in Malta at 0815 hours on Christmas day much to our relief and returned to our berth in Sliema Harbour.

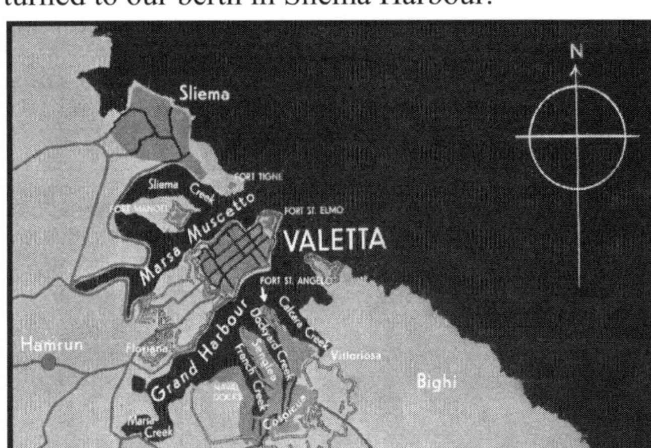

The harbours around Valetta in Malta.

We were, without exception, exceedingly weary after our experiences of the previous two months, but the Manxman's cooks prepared a splendid breakfast and lunch for us – at least as good as we might have expected at home. There was mail waiting for us – parcels, cards and letters – and we even had a few Christmas trimmings to decorate the mess.'

I was released form Malta in the summer of 1957. Rather than travel home by troopship with the rest of my shipmates I determined to make my

Christmas day in the mess. Mike at the left front.

way overland with a pal. We obtained permission to do so after a lengthy process. My official demob date was around September 1957. On leaving the Navy I joined the East Suffolk Police Force. I retired early due to ill health in 1985. Since then I have lived in Cumbria. I have a wife, four daughters and 12 grandchildren.

* * *

Gordon Eke, HMS *Tyne*.

I was born in September 1936 at Thames Ditton in Surrey. By the outbreak of war in 1939 the family was living at Tolworth nearby where my father was employed by a company engaged in road construction. By 1940 he was switched to airfield construction in Cornwall at St Evel and at St Mawgan. My mother was not too happy about having the family split up during hostilities so we followed Dad and took rented accommodation close to his construction sites.

In Cornwall I started my education at the small village school in Lanjeth near St Austell. Despite my parents thinking this area would be much safer than in London we were bombed even here with one bomb landing in the garden of the house opposite, fortunately failing to go off. Dad was also strafed a number of times while working out at the airfield.

In 1943 we moved back to Tolworth where I went into the junior school. Being in London we were bombed again and in 1944 we experienced both V1 and V2 attacks and consequently spent quite a bit of time in the shelter at school and in the Anderson Shelter out in the back garden. After the raids my friends and I would scour the streets for pieces of shrapnel.

In 1947 I moved to Surbiton Secondary School where it was hard to be late since it was just in the next street. The school leaving age was raised from 14 to 15 while I was there so instead of leaving at 14 as I had expected I was kept on until I was 15 in 1951. The school didn't seemed to be prepared for looking after all these 14-year-old boys and girls for a further year so we were very much left to our own devices and I spent a lot of time twiddling my thumbs.

When I left I joined a local printing firm on a seven-year apprenticeship. In 1954 the company went into liquidation and as I was almost 18 and National Service was still a requirement I decided to take a break in my training. I opted to join the Royal Navy as my first choice. As there were very few national service candidates accepted in the Royal Navy I was quite surprised when I received my call-up papers one day to find that I would be reporting to the Navy's Victoria Barracks Portsmouth on 24 January 1955.

On the completion of my initial training there I was transferred to HMS *Ocean* on the 7th February for further training as an ordinary seaman. Almost immediately we sailed for Gibraltar. I stayed on the *Ocean* until 22 April and on completion of my sea training was transferred back to the HMS *Victory* Barracks in Portsmouth to await a posting to an operational ship.

While at Victory Barracks I was seconded to HMS *Nightingale*, also in Portsmouth harbour, to help paint the ship. This was one of the last coal-burning ships in the Royal Navy and was well past her sell by date as far as facilities were concerned. I was on board for only a short time but it was an interesting experience although I was more than pleased when recalled to Victory Barracks for onward posting to HMS *Tyne* on 28 May.

HMS *Tyne*, a destroyer depot ship displacing 14,000 tons, was currently berthed in the dockyard at Rosyth when I joined her part way through a courtesy cruise around the British Isles and other nearby countries. This was part of her ongoing function as Flag Ship Home Fleet. During these cruises I managed to see France, Holland, Spain, Gibraltar, Malta and Cyprus and many ports in Britain. For an 18-year-old who had never been away from home before, other than for holidays and camping with the scouts but never outside the UK, this was a wonderful experience.

Being HQ ship Home Fleet we had all the top brass from the various divisions present on the ship. As far as I can remember we had three admirals, eight captains and thirteen commanders along with all their staff, as well as our own officers and crew. Our full complement was about eight hundred.

On commencing my service on HMS *Tyne* as an ordinary seaman I was initially assigned to the forecastle division and action station in B Gun Turret. All the ship's guns were in mothballs so the chance of them being fired was, to say the least, remote.

On 24 May 1956 I was promoted from ordinary seaman to able seaman and transferred from the forecastle division of the ship to the watch-keeping part of ship. I then became a bosun's mate. This entailed manning the wheelhouse with four others when at sea on a four hours on duty and four hours off duty watch for 24 hours and then 24 hours off. Whilst in harbour our duties were to man the officers' gangway on the quarter deck and vet all comings and goings of visitors and ships officers.

After spending about three months watchkeeping I volunteered to become a 'dhobi wallah' working in the ship's laundry. This was a much sought after position as it carried extra pay for working in extreme conditions. I assumed I would spend the rest of my national service in this very cushy number but a certain Egyptian decided to nationalise the Suez Canal and the rest is history.

My involvement in the Suez crisis began early in August while on leave. About a week after arriving home I received an official brown envelope containing orders to report back on board immediately. On returning to the ship we sailed for Devonport dockyard to ammunition the ship, take on stores, and re-commission all armaments.

When this was completed we sailed for Malta with a brief stop at Gibraltar to collect extra specialist crew members. While in Grand Harbour at Malta we took aboard Vice-Admiral Durnford-Slater the senior naval officer of the fleet as well as Lt General Sir Hugh Stockwell before sailing for Cyprus on 27 October on what we were told was *Boathook*, a communications exercise. On arriving off Limassol Air Marshall Bennett was brought out to the ship so that we had the leaders of all three services aboard. The reason for this, we then discovered, was that *Tyne* had been chosen as the Headquarters Ship for *Operation Musketeer* since it was extensively equipped with all the latest communications electronics. Because of this we also had signal specialists aboard from The RAF, the Royal Corps of Signals, and then French signallers.

We sailed south for Egypt on 4 November and while en route were given our first taste of firing our 4.5 guns with live ammunition at a target towed by one of our destroyers. All the gun crews were pleased we were on the firing end of the guns and not on the receiving end whose captain signalled that he thought he was supposed to be on our side.

On the fifth, anchored well out from the Egyptian coast, our communication teams made radio contact with 3 Para who were making their assault on El Gamil airfield. The following day with the airfield taken and the commandos having gone ashore just after the loosening up of the defences by naval gunfire, the *Tyne* closed in until we were lying just off Port Said.

General Stockwell viewing the results of the Navy bombardment of the Port Said coast.

One of the cooks and a mate viewing the results of the gunfire on Port Said.

View from the foredeck of HMS *Tyne* of the task force fleet lying off the coast of Port Said on 5 November 1956.

More of the fleet lying at anchor on 5 November.

A gun crew closed up off the coast of Egypt..

Helicopters taking off from HMS *Ocean* with commandos bound for Port Said on the morning of 6 November.

As far as I can remember the overall plan of *Musketeer* was for our forces to continue on down the length of the Suez Canal until it was secure and open it up to shipping again. This plan met with much opposition from the UN and in particular the USA. During the early evening we heard on the radio from the BBC in London that a ceasefire was to take place at 2359 hours local time that night. This was confirmed officially by the Government in London shortly afterwards.

On the seventh, with Port Said in allied hands,

although there was continuing sporadic sniper fire taking place despite the ceasefire, the *Tyne* entered the canal and anchored just inside the entrance along the western mole.

HMS *Tyne* entering Port Said harbour on 7 November.

Apart from being the HQ ship of the fleet we also had a large bakery on board and this was working 24 hours a day to meet demand. These supplies were delivered to numerous small groups in the town and as far south as El Cap. Consequently most of the Tyne's small boats were employed on the 'bread run'. We also had a laundry which was operating round the clock. In temperatures of over 100° F this turned out not to be the cushy number I had volunteered for.

Berthing in Port Said harbour. *La Marseillaise* and beyond it HMS *Ocean* with a helicopter taking off.

View of western mole and French trooper from flag deck.

View from stern of Tyne toward the Port Said waterfront and the lighthouse.

Another view of the ships anchored by the eastern mole.

A crane, one of the obstructions, being lifted.

The bucket dredger *Peleuse* sunk as a blockship.

The salvage vessel *Pollux*, No.4 in the diagram of wrecks.

Another view of *Pollux*.

Discussion at one of the basins. The vessel is the *Domiat*—not the one sunk by the *Newfoundland* on 1 November.

An army Austin Champ and the Canal Company building.

View westwards taken from the side of the Casino Palace Hotel. Tent erected on the central reservation.

Street scene in Port Said. Forces personnel to be armed and at least in twos.

Bedford QL three-tonner truck in Port Said.

Centurion tank parked by the surviving beach huts.

Together with the last of the remaining ships we finally withdrew from Port Said on 22 December after just over six weeks spent in the mouth of the canal, and made for Malta. We were still at sea at Christmas 1956 and this turned out to be a great experience with all traditional roles on board being reversed. This meant that the officers served the ratings and marines with a classic English Christmas dinner. Where the cooks managed to acquire all the ingredients from is a mystery. They even made an enormous Christmas cake. The final event was an inspection of every mess on the ship by the Captain who was in fact the youngest rating on board dressed in the Captain's best uniform. His assistant was the Captain in the junior rating's uniform.

Sailors ashore inspecting the Centurion tank.

Christmas at sea on the way back to Malta. Standing: Patsy, Jock, Kit, Pincher, Doug, Belly, CDR Forster, Knobby. Sitting: Belly-Ache, Gordon, Dizzy, Hooky, Fats.

Lord Hailsham and entourage departing from HMS *Tyne*.

Gordon and Geordie back in Malta.

The wheelhouse watch team, Gordon second from right.

We arrived back in Portsmouth around the middle of January 1957 and with my National service just about over I was transferred to the HMS *Victory* Barracks to be demobbed. On 26 January I finally left the Royal Navy to continue my apprenticeship as a printer with a company my old firm had found for me. This eventually led to me obtaining a first class City and Guilds Certificate. Two years later in 1959 I married June.

My printing career spanned over 60 years in numerous roles from machine operator to director of a publishing and printing company. June and I have spent 52 very happy years together and long may it continue. Along the way we gathered two sons, three grandsons and one granddaughter.

*   *   *

Roy Williams, HMS *Tyne*.

Roy has provided a number of photographs from his time with HMS *Tyne* during the Suez Crisis.

HMS *Tyne*.

The French cruiser *Georges Leygues*

The *Tyne* preparing to berth in Port Said harbour.

HMS *Tyne* anchored close to the western mole.

Remains of an Egyptian gun, and the bodies of its crew wrapped in blankets, after being hit by a shell.

HMS *Forth* from the *Tyne* the day before the withdrawal.

* * *

Neville James Willey, HMS *Dalrymple.*

Neville was born on 16 February 1934 at Greenwich, London. In 1938, together with his mother and twin sister Jean, he went to live in northern India where his father was serving as a regular in the Royal Artillery. By 1942 the family was living at Mhow in central India while the father was serving in North Africa and it was here that they learned that he had been posted as 'missing in action' at El Alamein.

At this time it was thought that the Japanese might invade India and as many families as possible were being repatriated to England. We went by sea to Cape Town in South Africa and spent three weeks there. At that time you sailed from Cape Town to Britain either in convoy or in a single fast ship. The family sailed by the latter, the *Otranto*, with other families and 4,000 Italian prisoners of war. Despite the risk of U-boat attack the ship stopped one day to pick up the survivors from a lifeboat of a torpedoed refrigeration ship of the White Star Line. Eventually the ship reached Liverpool from where the family went to Bristol to stay with the paternal grandparents. While living there Neville was educated at Fairfield Grammar School and also joined the Bristol Sea Cadet Corps. After a while it was discovered that Neville's father was a prisoner of war of the Germans and he was one of the last prisoners to be released at the end of the war.

Neville left school in 1950 and worked as an office boy at Bristol Aero Engines, Filton, for one year before joining the Royal Navy as a regular. After basic training he went for an electrical training course at HMS *Collinwood* near Fareham in Hampshire. The course lasted six or seven months. Neville's first posting was as an electrician to HMS *Tintagel Castle*, a castle class frigate/corvette based at Portland and used by the training squadrons. He was with the ship for two years.

Neville's next ship was HMS *Dalrymple* and he served on her for two years as a leading Electrical Mechanic. In mid April 1956 he wrote a letter to his mother in Bristol which his widow Margaret came across only as recently as late May 2012. The letter reads:

Sorry for not writing previously but there has not been much to say. We have been doing a survey of Malta as you know and it has been pretty monotonous work. Malta itself is not up to much and I think it is adequately described as 'the land of bells and smells'.

We had a 'rabbit' run to Sorrento and Capri lasting 5 days. I got a small sewing table for Jean and a cameo brooch and sewing box for you which I will bring home to you. When we went to Capri a party of us went into the Blue Grotto. The cave is nothing remarkable but the colour is a very remarkable blue. After that we went round the island which though very small is very mountainous. We got a small open car and piled in. As there was no more room for me I had to sit on the back which was quite hair-raising as most of the roads either overlook precipices or climb up them. I saw Gracie Field's villa which was very lovely but she was not home.

We are going to get home on the 29th May, refit until September, come out here to finish off our survey then back to the UK to recommission in January. But before we get home we are going as a representative of the British Med Fleet and the Survey Branch ... to Grace Kelly's wedding. We will be staying there for four days from 16th to 20th. (April).

In Monaco harbour. American destroyer USS *Heerman*, French destroyer *Kersaint*, HMS *Dalrymple* in white.

Overall view of the three representative vessels.

Monaco harbour at night.

Well that's the main news from me. My leave is not settled yet but I expect to get 28 days during June or July. I am hoping to get two weeks on the Broads this time. Thanks for the letters and mags. Love to all from Neville.

In another letter written towards the end of the year Neville wrote:

... Sorry I have not written before but we have been very busy. When we got into Gib we were caught by a gale alongside the wall and buckled a few plates. This work took two weeks to repair so we were late getting into Malta. In Malta we worked very hard preparing for C in Cs. We managed to get through that all right and were just getting started on surveying again when the Suez crisis came up. We were recalled to harbour and stayed there for four hours while we got sealed orders. Then we left Malta and sailed for Tobruk. We took two days to get there. We then killed time by doing a bit of surveying. This went on for a week until we received orders to sail at 2am on Saturday the 3rd [November]. We joined up in a series of convoys heading for Port Said. We heard on the 5th that the Paratroops had landed. We also were told what our job was. We were to enter the harbour, after the sweepers had swept it under the protection of a destroyer. We were then to anchor and send our boats away to survey the wrecks in the mouth of the canal. We did all this. It was not dangerous as the Commandos and Paratroopers held the harbour and all the commanding positions. We could hear firing going on in the town and see the fires. The Egyptians had too much on their hands to worry about us.

View from *Darlrymple* lying offshore from the beach to the west of Port Said.

Forty Commando in LCAs A7 and A1 making for the beach to the left of the blazing jetty Casino

Commandos in the LCAs A7 and A5 making for the beach.

Forty-two Commando in LCAs A6, A5 and U5 making for the beach to the right of the jetty Casino.

Tank landing craft in the Port Said outer harbour.

The Port Said waterfront on the left, blockships in the inner harbour, fleet ships anchored in the outer harbour.

View across the canal inner harbour to Port Said. *Pollux* in centre, Peleuse at the left, No. 823 crane being lifted at the right, *Paul Solente* being lifted at the back left.

The blockships in the main channel which were the first to receive attention.

We may be here until Christmas or we may be finished when UNO takes over. I took a few photos as we came in and will send them to you when they are developed. We are now on the job of clearing the wrecks.

The *Pollux*, and the *Peleuse* with smoke drifting from the Standard Oil Company ruptured storage tank to the

Another view of the above and the source of the smoke.

The *Paul Solente* with the *Peleuse* in the background.

Peleuse receiving attention.

The lifting craft LC11, based at Hartlepool, preparing to raise the *Peleuse* on the left.

The *Paul Solente*.

Three salvage vessels, the one in the left foreground being *Dispenser.*

The *Paul Solente* viewed from the bow.

The salvage ship *Dispenser*.

The large ship on left is L'Orient. Foreground centre and right are the LC11 and LC10 of Hartlepool

Suez Canal Company building at the front, the Navy House building on the left, and the long high grey building towards the top right of the photograph is the prison

I have just received your letter of the 6th saying that Gran Willey is dead. I am very sorry about it. That's about all for now.

Will write later when we know what is happening about UNO.

Love Neville.

In a third letter written after leaving Port Said Neville wrote:

We are now surveying off Malta again. We get back to the UK on April 8th and I go on 36 days leave on May 1st, also going on draft at the same time.

Until the Army left we carried on working normally in Port Said. When they left we put up the UN flag, took on UN guards, and became part of the United Nations Salvage Unit.

We saw de Lesseps statue being blown up and took pictures of it. The salvage fleet was not allowed to work until a couple of days before the New Year. Nobody knew from one hour to the next what we were going to do. Everyday there was a rumour that we were going to leave that day.

The Gypos wanted us to leave and made the UN officials give way. We were told to leave on New Year's Eve. We were to tow an army lighter to Cyprus that was part of the salvage fleet and had broken down. We steamed out of Port Said with the lighter and as we reached the three-mile limit hoisted the White Ensign to the masthead and hauled down the UN flag. Two hours after we left we had a signal from Admiralty telling us not to leave until the rest did but by this time it was too late. We dropped the lighter at Limassol and carried on back to Malta where we got our first mail for nearly three weeks and parcel mail for nearly five weeks. We also got our first run ashore for two months.

Then we did a couple of weeks sounding round Malta and then went to Palermo in Sicily, and Naples for a run ashore then back to Malta for some more sounding. We are hoping to finish the work at Malta before we leave and will be glad to see the last of it. We leave here on 20th March (1957) for Gib and then home.

I am trying to fix up a week on the Thames Estuary for 25th May to 1st June. I may also go on the Broads as well. Tell Father I now have £105 in the bank.

That's all for now,

Love Neville.

The last ship Neville served on was HMS *Roebuck* based at Dartmouth. This had previously been a destroyer but by this time had been converted to a type 15 frigate in 1952.

Neville left the Navy in 1959 and went to work for Sevalco, Avonmouth until 1998 as an instrument mechanic. He married Margaret in 1962 and their two sons were born in 1965 and 1969. His hobbies were boat model-making and for many years he kept a 29-foot Bermudan sloop in Poole Harbour and was at his happiest sailing the Solent. Neville died on 2 March 2,000 of asbestosis.

(Many thanks to Neville's widow Margaret for the photos and, together with Jean Bennett, nee Willey, for the information about Neville and his father Joseph.)

*   *   *

Mike Cross, *HMS Dalrymple.*

I was born on 8 October 1937 at Wells Road, Bath in Somerset although I suppose I am lucky to be still living and able to tell the tale of my service at Port Said. On the nights of the 25th and 26th of April 1942 the Germans bombed the city of Bath in one of their reprisal raids for the RAF having bombed the two medieval timber-built architectural gems of Rostock and Lubeck on the north German coast a month before. These were called Baedeker raids because the targets were chosen from the German Baedeker tourist Guide to Great Britain which listed them together with other similar towns for their beauty and heritage value.

We lived in the Holloway area of Bath and our house was one of those demolished in the raids. I was five at the time and survived with my mother and younger brother because we had gone down into the cellar when the sirens sounded. We were dug out by the rescue services the following day.

I went to school in the city and although I enjoyed it generally I was only really interested in sport. After leaving school at 15 in 1952 I began work as a butcher's lad but as soon as I was seventeen-and-a-half I signed on at Victoria Street in Bristol on 22nd February 1955 for 12 years in the Navy and on the 5th of March was assigned to HMS *Ocean*, an aircraft carrier training ship for the initial part of my service.

On 13 September, with my training over and having become an able seaman, I joined the survey ship HMS *Dalrymple* whose name came from the 18th century British hydrographer Alexander Dalrymple. We were on a Mediterranean commission captained by Commander J T K Paisley and based in the Grand Harbour at Malta where we were carrying out survey work.

HMS *Dalrymple* at Malta.

Early in April 1956 we visited Sorrento in Italy for R and R after which we sailed for Monaco where we were present on the 19th for the wedding of Prince Rainier to the American film actress Grace Kelly.

HMS *Dalrymple* entering Monaco harbour.

I was able to get ashore to watch the couple being driven through the streets from the church. The *Dalrymple*, which was floodlit in the evenings, provided a guard of honour for the couple as well as a marine band we carried on the ship. The band accordionist later led a conga line among the tables in the famous casino and nobody took any offence. We had a great time with lots of free beer flowing.

Grace Kelly and her father before the wedding ceremony.

Prince Rainier just before the wedding ceremony.

Prince Rainier, Princess Grace and the navy guard.

The *Dalrymple* guard of honour on a Monaco street.

Postcard acquired by Mike in Monaco.

In July we went back to the UK where the ship began a refit and took on a new commanding officer, Lt Cdr J D Winstanley RN. We returned to the Mediterranean in September and on our way swept the channel in Gibraltar harbour to check for possible obstructions after a storm. We then went on to Malta where we continued with the survey work in the Grand Harbour and the local coastline as well as being given our annual inspection.

Our next job was intended to be a survey of the waters at Tobruk in Libya but by this time the Suez Canal business, which had flared up in July, was getting serious and we found ourselves involved in preparations for whatever was going to happen. I think by this time it was about the 27th of October.

Later we discovered that our task would be to help in clearing any blockships the Egyptians could be expected to drop in the Port Said harbour if any attack was made on the country following its takeover of the canal. We had to fuel up, provision the ship, and head east in great haste as part of MES2, the second of the two large convoys that were to sail to the Egyptian coast. The only arms we carried were a few saluting guns and Bren guns. I think we set out on the 30th of the month.

We sailed into the entrance of the Suez Canal on the 6th of November soon after the minesweepers had checked that the channel into the harbour was free of mines. It was our job to plot the position of the sunken ships lying in the inner harbour which I found to be very interesting work. We also met a lot of the troops who were allowed to come aboard the *Dalrymple* to make use of the showers, have a decent meal, and partake of a glass of beer, or two.

By the 9th a partial passageway had been opened up so that smaller vessels with a narrow beam were able to pass through to berth in the inner harbour.

Close-up view of the blockship *Pollux.*

After a while we started to take part in the salvage operations, one of the twelve ships involved in trying to get the canal open for normal traffic. Sometime in the middle of December the First Lord of the Admiralty who at that time was Lord Hailsham, visited Port Said and came aboard the *Dalrymple* to inspect the salvage work taking place.

We continued with this task even after the United Nations' peacekeeping force took over in Port Said and the last of our troops left on 22 December. With their departure we had to fly the UN flag and exchange our naval uniforms for overalls and berets. The photo of the ship's company was taken by a naval photographer who came aboard for that purpose since, unlike some ships, we didn't carry our own.

All the time we were working in the harbour and with the British and French troops no longer there to protect us we were subjected to quite a bit of small arms and sniper fire and the UN troops didn't seem to do anything about it. We were still there to witness the attempts by locals to bring down the De Lesseps statue which they finally achieved.

By the end of the year the Egyptians were objecting to the continued presence at Port Said of the British vessels *Darymple* and the Royal Fleet Auxiliary *Fort Duquesne* even though we had been involved in lifting seven of their blockships. Consequently we were forced to leave and on New Year's Eve we sailed back out to sea towing a Z lighter to Famagusta in Cyprus. We were one of the last British ships to leave Port Said.

From Famagusta we returned to Malta and briefly continued our survey work for a few days until we made visits to the Italian ports of Naples, and Palermo in Sicily, as compensation for the eleven weeks we had gone without shore leave.

In the New Year we resumed our coastal survey of Malta, including that of the nearby island of Gozo. This kept us occupied until the end of March when we made passage to the UK via Gibraltar where we carried out some more work in the harbour. We arrived back in Devonport on 8 April 1957 and I left the ship on the 1st of May as it began a refit. I then spent about 20 months ashore on courses etc., until September 1957 when I was posted to HMS *Girdleness*, an ex-maintenance ship now full of white-coated boffins working on experimental guided weapons mostly in the North Sea. I remember half the ship's company going down with Asian flu which was rife at the time. I remained with the ship until 14 January 1958 after which I spent some more time at a shore base.

On the 27th June 1959 I joined the frigate HMS *Whitby* which, like the *Dalrymple*, also operated with the Mediterranean fleet. I served on the ship until February 1961. I then spent nearly two years ashore until posted to HMS *Gurkha*, yet another anti-submarine frigate, in January 1963. I served on her out in the Middle East in the area of Bahrain for a year. On the way out there we buckled a propeller in the Suez Canal and spent Christmas that year in a Karachi dry dock waiting for a replacement. The skipper survived a court martial over that. Whenever I was at home between ships I was a member of the Devonport Field Gun crew, and competed at Earl's Court in 1958, 1961, and 1964.

I left the Royal Navy in October 1967 after which I became a plant fitter working on the M4 Motorway, the Avonmouth Bridge, the Bristol West Dock, and various pipelines. I also worked 18 years abroad in Sudan, the Cameroons, Nigeria, Ghana and Iraq.

I am now happily retired with my very understanding wife Maureen, and have three children and four grandchildren. Recently I took up the tenor saxophone and have enrolled as a silver surfer on the Internet. I've also just finished rebuilding an old Mini so keep myself busy.

* * *

James (Danny) Irvine, HMS *Dalrymple*,

HMS *Dalrymple*, under the command of acting-Commander Jack Paisley RN, was recommissioned in Devonport in May 1955 to carry out a survey of Malta. The ship's company, with the exception of the senior and junior survey branch ratings, were from the Devonport Port Division.

We sailed in August 1955 and arrived on station in mid-October after carrying out small survey searches on passage. One of the highlights of the first part of the commission was representing the UK and Royal Navy at the wedding of Grace Kelly and Prince Rainier at Monaco. The *Dalrymple*, being a survey vessel, had been chosen because Monaco was the headquarters of the International Hydrographic Organisation. To carry out this task we embarked the Royal Marines Band of RO2 Med, which was based on HMS *Phoenicia*, the shore station on Manol Island, Malta. We returned to the UK on I May 1956 to give leave and to allow the writing up of the fair charts of the first part of the survey.

In August we returned to Malta with a new commanding officer, Commander Winstanley and first lieutenant, Lt Commander Lowis, both survey specialists, to carry out the second phase of the survey.

On 31 October we were ordered to join the fleet being assembled for the Suez campaign. The only armaments that we had onboard were 4 x 12-pounder saluting guns which were struck down. On 2 November we joined the slow convoy with the support vessels. During the passage to Port Said we were despatched to Tripoli on the North African coast to investigate the source of heavy radio signal traffic which, on our arrival, we found came from an American CIA yacht.

We were ordered to join up with the main fleet and continue to Port Said with the second convoy and to carry out a survey of the sunken ships there. As we had no armaments we were to be protected by a destroyer and instructed that on our arrival we were to moor in the holding basin on the Port Fuad side of the harbour.

45 Commando being flown ashore by helicopters from out-of-view aircraft carriers on the morning of the sixth.

Helicopters and their commandos coming in to land on the spare ground by the De Lesseps statue.

A 45 Commando helicopter making its way down the length of the western causeway to the De Lesseps Statue.

View from HMS *Dalrymple* off the Port Said coast.

View from HMS *Dalrymple* as it passes the end of the Port Fuad mole opposite the Casino Palace Hotel.

Immediately on anchoring on the 6th, the day of the sea invasion, we launched all survey boats and, with crew carrying small arms, commenced the survey of the canal as far as the troops had reached before the ceasefire took effect later that day.

One of the survey boats being lowered down the side of the Dalrymple

The boat gets away.

Motor launch with Bren gun mounted.

Lifting ships on either side of a wreck. HMS *Forth* iat the back. Bow of the tug *Careful* protruding on the left.

In addition we acted as a support vessel to the lifting craft and UK tugs, one of which was the Devonport based steam tug *Careful* which lay alongside us when not busy.

While our main task was to support the survey parties other members of the ship's company had different tasks to perform which included putting navigation lights on the buoys marking the surveyed channel. We came under small arms fire while doing this despite the ceasefire..

On 19 November the First Lord of the Admiralty Lord Hailsham boarded the ship from a motor launch and spoke to the officers and ships' companies of the *Darymple*, *Lofoten*, RN bar vessels, the tug *Careful*, and the lifting craft. He informed us that we were to remain at Port Said when the fleet withdrew and that RN personnel were to change into civilian clothes (overalls and berets). Officers were to use Merchant Navy cap badges and no badges of rank. *Dalrymple* was to be the senior ship with the landing ship HMS *Lofoten* acting as supply ship. The squadron became the first ever UK warships to show both the Red Ensign and the United Nations flag in lieu of the White Ensign.

The rest of the fleet withdrew at dusk on 22 December with the ship's company of the fast minelayer *Manxman* singing to those left behind, *Now is the hour* and the *Oggie* song. We now came under the command of the United Nations and armed Finnish soldiers were placed on board as protection. Work continued on salvaging the wrecks although it ceased briefly at Christmas to allow all ships' crews to celebrate the festival.

Lord Hailsham coming aboard the *Dalrymple*.

Overall view from HMS *Dalrymple* of the ship-raising work taking place in Port Said harbour.

An officer with the rank of captain and Lord Hailsham.

Aerial view of the Standard Oil Company site and burnt-out storage tanks. South side of the Abbas Hilmi Basin.

Lord Hailsham addressing some of the crew on *Dalrymple*.

The burnt-out oil storage tanks.

Buildings on the north side of the Bassin Chérif wrecked during rocket attacks. The large white building towards the top centre of the photo is the railway station. The three identical building on its left are secondary schools.

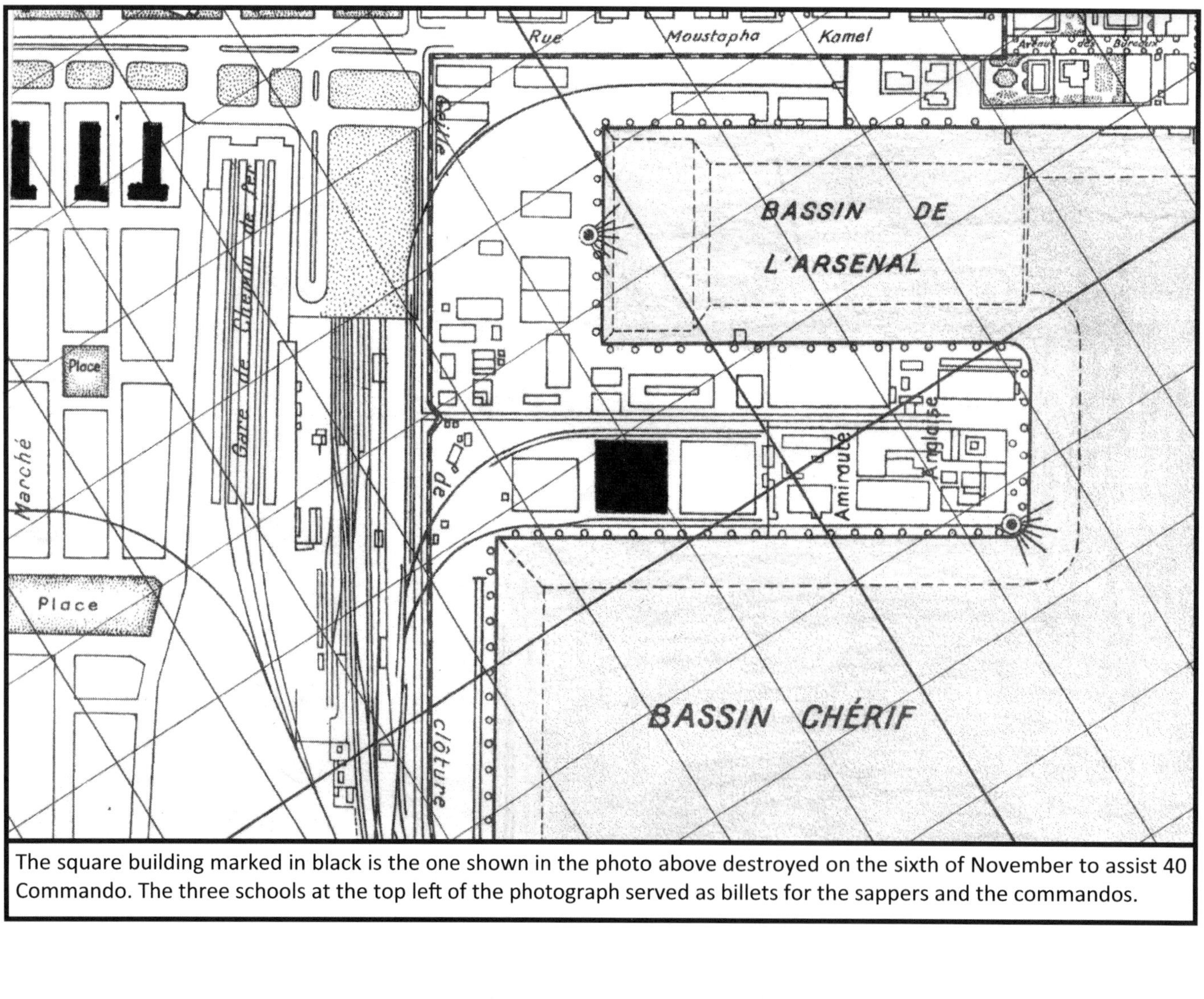

The square building marked in black is the one shown in the photo above destroyed on the sixth of November to assist 40 Commando. The three schools at the top left of the photograph served as billets for the sappers and the commandos.

On Boxing Day we enjoyed the traditional 'attempted boarding' of the ship which we repulsed in the old-fashioned way by hose pipes. We

also watched the locals trying to remove the Union Jack from the flag pole outside the Casino Palace Hotel where it had been nailed and then the pole greased by some of the departing lads.

We were also witness to the toppling of the statue of the Suez Canal builder de Lesseps. Some of the crowd of onlookers were standing too close to the monument during the final detonation and were killed.

Some of the lads dressed up for the 'attempted boarding'.

Salvage crew of the *Dalrymple* at Port Said harbour. Two helmeted United Nations soldiers at front left and front right.

By now, after pressure from the Egyptians, we had been given orders to leave and the following day, New Years Eve, at dusk, towing four of the lifting barges for delivery to Famagusta in Cyprus, we slipped anchor and started to move. We then saw that the Egyptians had brought a number of army field guns onto the Western Mole that we would have to pass on our way out of the canal. Just then four ships of the 6th Frigate Squadron came into view at speed off the entrance to the canal and formed a protective ring around us as we cleared the harbour. The White Ensign was broken out and the Red Ensign and UN flags lowered. The Frigate Squadron leader then came alongside and transferred a large backlog of mail which had piled up for us.

After towing the four barges to Cyprus we made passage to Malta where we continued the survey work. On its completion in May we returned to Devonport where we were met on arrival by HM tug *Careful* now back home. She escorted us to our birth in the dockyard to pay off.

Dalrymple crew families waiting at Devonport Naval Base.

John G Davis, HMS *Letterston.*

In 1941, aged 13, I went to Dartmouth Naval College in Devon. At the time of the Japanese surrender in Tokyo Bay I was in the flagship HMS *Duke of York*. The following year I saw the devastation in Hamburg and Berlin. 1948 took me to a destroyer, HMS *Chequers*, for two and a half years in the Mediterranean, the last year as first lieutenant with Prince Philip. We visited most countries round the Mediterranean as well as Sudan, Saudi Arabia, and Aqaba as a guardship.

In 1952 I qualified as a specialist in TAS (Underwater Warfare). I was a junior staff officer in the Med during 1954-55. By the time of the Suez Crisis I was Captain of the minesweeper HMS *Letterston.*

We sailed from Sheerness in a thunderstorm and joined the rest of the 104 Minesweeping Squadron in the Channel. Having got to Malta everything went quiet for a while.

HMS *Letterston* (M1160) arriving in Malta.

We did exercises, once with a platoon of soldiers who had difficulty firing their guns from a rolling ship. After a brief visit to Italy I was sent to join the anti-EOKA patrol around Cyprus.

Whilst at sea the signal came to open two fat envelopes, one being the amendments to the other. We went into Famagusta and spent much of the night putting in the amendments before reading the orders for the assault on Port Said. The next day the Army supplied us with diesel from jerry cans. They came in a succession of trucks and were poured into a drum then pumped by hand into our tanks. The smell was horrible.

The Flag Officer Cyprus, a submariner who had won the VC in the Dardanelles, said he would speak to the ship's company before we sailed. As the sun was setting over the mountains we mustered on the jetty. His stirring speech ended, 'I wish I were coming with you lads.' From the back the cook piped up, 'You can have my place sir.

We met the invasion fleet some distance from the Port Said coast. Great pains were taken to get the navigation right by running taut wire. The datum was to be marked by a giant dan buoy specially made in Malta and slung alongside HMS *Woodbridge Haven*, the minesweeping depot ship, for the journey from Malta. We watched as the buoy was launched. It wobbled several times then fell flat. Too much top weight!

With two other minesweepers we laid a line of dan buoys from about thirty miles off the Egyptian coast and were followed by the assault craft. As dawn broke on the sixth of November the minesweepers led the assault craft close to the shore then left them near the beachhead. We returned offshore to pick up the Clearance Diving Team and then the Port Control Party which we took into Port Said harbour as the helicopters were flying in with the commandos. For *Letterston* that was the end of the operation so we went to a berth in the harbour.

View from HMS *Letterston* of the 45 Commando assault by helicopter coming in along the western causeway.

Two 45 Commando helicopters coming in to land by the back of the De Lesseps Statue.

Over the next day or two all attention was on the news with the Russian invasion to put down the uprising in Hungary, the diplomatic turmoil in

London and Washington over the crisis with Egypt, and the order to withdraw.

The blockship *Paul Solente* with the waterfront behind.

HMS *Upton*, another of the minesweepers, had one engine out of action. She was the first coastal minelayer to have Deltic engines installed and they had teething troubles. As I was due for a new appointment in the UK I was told to exchange with her captain and take *Upton* home.

We sailed for Malta in company with two other minesweepers. The following day, as I was standing on the bridge, there was a roaring noise and the funnel looked like a Bunsen burner. I had been told that if this happened I should stop the engine and wait for it to go out – but it didn't. The fire was not only in the funnel but the aluminium in the engine room was burning. The engineers went below and put it out. The Chief was later given the BEM for his involvement in this. Another minesweeper took us in tow and three of four days later we arrived in Malta.

It took a month to fit two new engines after which I was told to sail to the UK at 13.5 knots; any slower and oil might pass into the exhaust, any faster and it might ignite. With a gale behind us we made a quick passage up the Channel. It was dark as we got to Portsmouth and home for Christmas.

1959-60 took me to the Pacific in a frigate. This included two months as guardship at Gan, Maldive Islands, and a visit to Japan where I saw the impressive war memorial at Kyoto dedicated to the fallen of all nations. A little later I took retirement for ordination – but that's another story.

* * *

Ronny Mayoh, HMS *Shavington*

On 1 May 1951 at barely 16 I joined the Navy's HMS *Ganges* the shore establishment at Shotley near Ipswich as a boy seaman. I regard the training there to have been pretty intensive. The programme consisted of Seamanship, Gunnery, and lots of Education which was a very good thing as it made a definite improvement in mine. There was also plenty of sport which I thoroughly enjoyed. I remember that any reading other than the seamanship manual was definitely frowned upon by the instructors. By the time we left for two weeks of sea training on the frigate HMS *Largo Bay* based at Rosyth on the Firth of Forth I think we were both confidant and competent to do the job.

From the *Largo Bay* I went as a boy seaman to HMS *Theseus*, a light fleet aircraft carrier, where I became an ordinary seaman. Next I went to HMS *Vernon* the Torpedo and Anti-submarine School shore base at Portsmouth on an underwater weapons course and qualified UW3.

My next posting, during 1953, was to HMS *Volage*, an anti-submarine frigate of the Dartmouth Training Squadron then generally based at Londonderry but with spells at Rosyth.

While I was there I attended and passed a shallow water diving course, held partly at Rosyth itself in the old destroyer pens but also close by at the old boom defence depot at the shore establishment of HMS *Safeguard* where there was a diving tank. I now became an Able Seaman.

During the spring of 1955, having just turned 20 and having passed the Fleet Board held at Rosyth as a leading seaman, I was drafted to HMS *Diligence*, a small shore base at Hythe on the west bank of Southampton Water. I teamed up with another leading hand and Lieutenant Campbell and together we formed the trials party for the ten ships of 108 Coastal Minesweeper Squadron. All were brand new vessels with brand new crews.

The work involved installing and rigging all the equipment on each ship. They carried sweeps for contact or moored magnetic and acoustic mines. We went to sea in each vessel in turn, streamed and calibrated each individual sweep, while at the same time teaching the rudiments of these operations to the crews. After the trials were over we were allocated to our ships. My mate went to Leverton, and Lt Campbell and I to *Floriston*, he as the commanding officer and myself in charge of the sweep under the direction of the first lieutenant. Eventually the squadron sailed to Malta then to Cyprus where we arrived on 5 November 1955. We worked in rotation with other ships of the squadron three months at a time on anti-gunrunning duties against EOKA in which we boarded and searched the odd caique we came across for arms.

Nearly a year later, in the early autumn of 1956, *Floriston* went into dry dock in Malta for a refit.

HMS *Floriston* at Malta.

Floriston commissioning service. Ronny Mayoh on the far right with the 'order of service' in his hand, Lt Campbell on the port side of the bow.

While this was taking place some of our lads went back to England to bring another sweeper out while the remainder of us went to St Angelo Barracks. A few weeks later Lt Campbell came to collect Jock Watson and myself and took us to the reserve ship HMS *Shavington*, Jock to check the electrics and me to see to the minesweeping gear.

A few days later, with a make up crew, we were on our way to Port Said, where, on the 5th of November, we swept a channel in the entrance of the Suez Canal. Eventually, with hostilities over we sailed back to Malta where I rejoined *Floriston* under a new commanding officer. Jock and I were allowed just two hours ashore before sailing back to Port Said. After a while we sailed north to Cyprus and something like another three-month spell there before returning to Malta for a break before returning for the next patrol. We were based offshore from Famagusta.

HMS *Shavington* (M1180).

Both Lieutenant Campbell and I were qualified shallow water divers although not approaching the standard of the clearance divers. We were only used twice. A cache of arms or explosives had been reported hidden on the underside of a middle ground buoy. We went down but found nothing. The second time was in the harbour. The terrorists had sunk the customs launch and I went down to secure the lifting ropes to salvage her.

We were hardly allowed ashore. The only exception was a Queen's Birthday Review. After the dress rehearsal the different contingents went back to their billets in the back of lorries. Before we had arrived back aboard the *Floriston* the RAF lads were dead. A group of terrorists had come out of an orange grove and lobbed explosives into their truck. I don't know if any of them survived.

When the commission was finished I was sent to HMS *Vernon* at Portsmouth for a further course after which I was posted to HMS *Dalswinton* another coastal minesweeper, based at South Queensferry on the Firth of Forth near Edinburgh. Whilst serving at *Dalswinton* I passed the Fleet Board for the rank of petty officer, a rank I was unable to achieve since I eventually left the service before reaching the top of the list.

My final year in the Navy was spent at Culdrose Naval Air Station at Helston in Cornwall. This was another trials job, this time on anti-submarine torpedoes dropped from aircraft which were Shackletons and helicopters. From here, on 28 March 1960 I left the Navy to return to a good and interesting civilian life. I had thought about staying on but an opportunity came along for me to earn a decent living as a civilian.

* * *

Brian Sims, HMS *Floriston.*

My National service began in November 1955 and was served in the Royal Navy as an engineering mechanic. After initial training in Cornwall I was drafted to the 108th Minesweeping Squadron based in the Mediterranean at Sliema Creek, Malta. Our nine ships, shallow-draft coastal minesweepers, were constructed of timber which made them immune from magnetic mines. They were being used at this time mainly for anti-smuggling and gun-running patrols against EOKA off the coast of Cyprus.

From September 1956 onwards, with the Suez Crisis build-up taking place, our squadron numbers were increased with the arrived of additional ships from the UK and exercises undertaken with minesweepers from the French Navy. I was part of the crew of HMS *Floriston* which had just completed a refit.

We left Malta at the end of October as part of the invasion task force that also included carriers, destroyers, frigates, landing craft and the various support groups.

Our minesweeping activity was centred on the approaches to Port Said around the canal entrance and the invasion beaches.

The Navy House with the White Ensign flying again.

Five minesweepers 'parked up' near the Fish Dock.

View of the De Lesseps Statue by the Fish docks.

View of the blockship *Pollux*.

The French hospital ship, *La Marseillaise*.

* * *

Michael Alan Clark, HMS *Ceylon.*

I was born on 7 October 1935 at Atherstone in Warwickshire. My father was a regular soldier serving in the Royal Engineers so we moved around a fair bit. When war was declared in September 1939 we were living in Sheerness on the Thames estuary. My father was away at the time so Mother, thinking that we lived too close to London for safety moved us to Rosyth on the Firth of Forth in Scotland not realising, I assume, that the town was a large naval base. The following month this was the target of the first German bombing raid of the war. When a stray bomb landed very close to our house a mile from the dockyard Mum had a further brainstorm and early in 1940 took us to Portsmouth, another prime target. In the September of that year when almost five I began school and completed my education at Portsmouth Grammar School in the summer of 1952 when I was sixteen.

Knowing that National service would be coming up in a couple of years time and not wanting to endure the discipline and drill of the Army I enlisted in the Royal Navy on 16 September just two months after leaving school.

After three weeks of basic training I was sent to HMS *Ceres*, the Navy's shore training establishment at Wetherby in Yorkshire for specialist training in bookkeeping and administration. This lasted until February 1953 when I joined HMS *Mercury*, the Royal Navy Signal School near Petersfield in Hampshire.

HMS *Ceres* at Wetherby in Yorkshire

For my next posting in February 1955 I moved to HMS *Daedalus*, the Royal Naval Air Station close to Lee on Solent, the headquarters of the Fleet Air Arm, where I worked in the office of the Flag Officer Air (Home) before joining HMS *Ceylon*, a six-inch gun cruiser, in August 1956 as a leading writer. The ship had just undergone an extensive refit. We commissioned on 11 September and sailed for Portland and our work-up trials on 8 October.

The cruiser HMS *Ceylon*.

On the twenty-sixth, without completing our work up, we suddenly set sail at full speed for Malta arriving there in just four days.

HMS *Ceylon* lying in the Grand Harbour, Malta.

HMS *Ceylon*.

We refueled and provisioned before leaving on 1 November for the assault on Port Said. While this was taking place we remained some distance offshore close to the French battleship *Jean Bart*. We saw plenty of smoke rising from the town but neither ship fired a shot. We had been ordered not to open up with our six-inch guns in support of the commando assault so as to avoid civilian casualties.

Smoke from the Standard Oil Company fire on the canal.

Ready for the action that never came.

We remained in the area until 23 November when we sailed for Malta where we stayed until 3 December when we sailed for Portsmouth. We arrived there on 14 December just in time for Christmas leave.

On 21 January 1957 we sailed for what was to be the best cruise anyone could expect to have. During the year we paid visits to ten ports in East and West Africa as well as Zanzibar, the Seychelles, Mauritius, Cochin in India, Ceylon, Aden, Bahrain, Kuwait, and finally transitting the Suez Canal and returning to Portsmouth on 5 December.

But the good times were not over yet. On 5 January 1958 we set out again, this time across the Atlantic arriving in Montego Bay in Jamaica then visiting Guantanamo Bay in Cuba, St Georges, Bequia, Bridgetown in Barbados, Plymouth in Monserrat, Bermuda, and Halifax in Nova Scotia after which we returned to Portsmouth on 31 March, remaining there until 14 April when we decommissioned. During that period we had sailed a total of 60,049.5 miles and spent 185 days at sea.

I married Nancy on 21 March 1961 while serving on the destroyer HMS *Battleaxe*. We had met while we were both members of an amateur drama group in Portsmouth. The rest of my naval career was fairly humdrum with only two highlights: a two-year tour in Paris with NATO followed by a two-year tour in Singapore, in both of which I was accompanied by my wife.

I finally retired from the Royal Navy in October 1975 and went into production control with an electronics company. I also joined the Royal British Legion at this time and am currently the treasurer at the Hayling Island Branch. Nan and I were happily married for 43 years until she passed away in August 2004.

* * *

Keith Smith, HMS *Jamaica*.

Keith, who joined the Navy at Chatham when he was seventeen-and-a-half, became a cook. During his service he spent two years aboard the light cruiser HMS *Jamaica* which included the period of the Suez Crisis.

Jamaica, was laid down in April 1939 at the Vickers Armstrong shipyard, Barrow-in-Furness, and completed at the end of June 1942. Apart from supporting the Allied landings in North Africa in November that year the ship spent the rest of the war involved in Arctic convoy duty. She went into reserve in 1951 until 1954 when recalled for service with the Mediterranean Fleet.

Keith has provided the following photographs.

HMS *Jamaica*.

The English, French, and Admirals's flags flying.

Helicopters delivering 45 Commando to Port Said from the carriers. Others bringing back the early wounded.

More guns that wouldn't be needed.

Battle flag flying. The lads observing aerial activity.

French hospital ship in the canal mouth outer harbour.

Burnt-out former Navy House.

Surviving oil storage tanks at the Standard Oil site.

* * *

Trevor Cook, HMS *Alamein.*

The destroyer was laid down 1 March 1944 on the Tyne and named to commemorate the Battle of Alamein in North Africa two years earlier. The vessel was launched on 12 May 1945, commissioned on 20 March 1946 and joined the 4th Destroyer Squadron. Trevor has provided the following photographs.

HMS *Alamein.*

General view across Port Said harbour towards Port Fuad and the bucket dredger blockship *Peleuse.* Photo taken from the waterfront by the Casino Palace Hotel.

View from the quay by the Casino Palace Hotel towards the outer harbour anchorage.

HMS *Alamein* and a French frigate lying against her.

* * *

Colin Evans, HMS *Diana.*

I was born in December 1932 at Rhosymedre in Denbighshire, a village between Wrexham and Oswestry, but brought up and educated in Oswestry. In January 1949, just turned 16 and straight from school, I joined the Royal Navy as a boy seaman. Like many others before me I suffered HMS *Ganges*, the boys' training establishment at Shotley in Suffolk, for a period of eleven months followed by three months with the training flotilla based at Rosyth on the Firth of Forth aboard HMS *Wilton*, a Hunt Class destroyer. From here I joined the frigate HMS *Burghead Bay* in the Devonport local flotilla at Plymouth.

In mid-1951 we were told we would be off to the West Indies for 12 months after exercises and trials at Portland. However, on our return to Devonport for a final week before sailing, we learned that about 20 of us were going ashore into HMS *Drake* for various courses. The following morning, carrying our kitbags and hammocks, we exchanged places with 20 or so ratings from the barracks who took our places aboard the *Burghead Bay*.

While going through our joining routine in the barracks we discovered that most of us weren't going on courses at all but would soon be on our way to the Far East. I spent some time at HMS *Tamar*, the shore |base at Hong Kong. When I returned to the UK it was 9 December 1954, exactly three years to the day since I had last walked through the gates of HMS *Drake*.

During 1955, which was the year I got married, I did a diving course and also a gunnery course. On completion of the latter at the end of the year I was instructed to report to the drafting office where I was told I would be joining the destroyer HMS *Diana*, currently in Devonport shipyard being prepared for its next commission, and how lucky I was since she was going to Australia.

Diana was now captained by John R Gower, uncle to David who would later become the England cricket captain. There was no mention at that time of an island called Monte Bello or atomic weapons tests but I soon found out after joining the ship in January when we had to attend lectures on Atomic Chemical Defence. We were supposedly going to observe two tests, G1 and G2, in what was called *Operation Mosaic*.

The *Diane* was recommissioned on 28 February and at the end of March we eventually set out from Devonport together with *Daring*, *Decoy* and *Diamond*, other Daring Class destroyers, first stop Gibraltar. When the mail came on board there those members of the crew with wives and girlfriends living in Devon and Cornwall, and there were many of them, began raising their voices. Apparently the Western Morning News or Evening News had reported the ship's departure and where we were going in great detail as well as stating that every man on the *Diane* was a volunteer. I don't think there was such an animal among the 300 of us on board. The rest of our journey to Malta was fairly uneventful.

Diane entering Valetta harbour at midday 9 April 1956

We stopped for three days at the island where we would normally have remained with our sister destroyers. But we were then detached for our journey to Monte Bello sailing on 12 April. We passed through the Suez Canal and made stops at Aden, Colombo in Ceylon, and Penang in Malaya where I don't recall shore leave being given in any of these places, and then on to Singapore.

I can't remember how long we stayed at Singapore although I know we were certainly given priority attention in the dockyard before we continued on through Indonesian waters and finally to the Monte Bello islands which lie about 80 miles off the north-western tip of Western Australia. For some reason there was a delay in the preparations for the first of the two tests so Captain Gower was given permission to take us the 1,200 miles or so south to Perth's port of Freemantle where I, and only I, was given three-days leave because I had an Auntie and an uncle living way out in the bush from there. They picked me up in Perth and drove me out to their home which was great.

After about a week in Freemantle we sailed back north up the west Australian coast to Monte Bello and Trimouille Island, arriving there on 14 May. G1, the first of the two experiments took place two days later. *Diane* was anchored about what I believe was 15 miles away from the island and just before the explosion was due we were assembled on the upper deck and told to turn our backs to the distant test tower and then, 20 seconds after the detonation, we could turn round and look. I swear I saw the flash in my eyes even though it must have come through the back of my head to get to my retina and this was accompanied by a strange feeling of warmth. Many others said the same. After a short time we were told to turn round to witness the mushroom cloud.

But this 'observation' wasn't the end of our involvement. We were then battened down below while the ship sailed into the fallout from the explosion. I don't know whether it was before or during our entry into the fallout that the engine room switched on what is called the pre-wetting system. In Diana's case lots of hose pipes had been connected to the fire hydrants all over the ship.

We had practised this several times on our passage to Australia and as far as I could tell it seemed to be very effective. When it was decided by the men in white suits, who nobody knew by the way, that it was safe to go up on deck, two decontamination teams were sent out, one forward with Dennis Buck in charge and one aft led by me.

A team consisted of a leading hand and three able seamen all clad in protective clothing of seaboots, waterproof trousers, what I think were World War One gas capes, gloves, and respirators. With the Geiger counter we had been given all I found were two small spots of radioactivity, one by the Squid mortars and the other by the torpedo tubes. However, a good scrub with brooms and water and they were gone.

After the first explosion we expected to go back to Freemantle since the second of the two nuclear experiments wasn't due to take place for another month. But because we had been involved in a nuclear test the Australian authorities decided that we were now unwelcome in any of their ports and instead we sailed back to Singapore where the crew managed some time ashore. We also picked up the mail for our troops on Christmas Island. This was not the Christmas Island in the Pacific which would also become a nuclear test site, but the one not far from Monte Bello in the Indian Ocean.

We arrived back at Monte Bello on 7 of June with the best part of two weeks still to go before G2. To keep us occupied the officers arranged lots of recreational activities until it was time to make our way to Alpha Island for the second of the nuclear tests. This took place on the 19th and again we were ordered on deck to see the mushroom cloud, a much bigger one this time. Then it was a repeat of being battened down, the pre-wetting and the rest of the routine.

Everything went more or less as before except that this time we found no contamination on the upper deck so that it seems the pre-wetting must have proved itself. These are my memories of the Monte Bello tests but it all took place more than 55 years ago so my recollections may not be completely accurate.

The 'mushroom' cloud of the *Mosaic* G2 test.

I learned many years later that this second device was far bigger than Prime Minister Eden had guaranteed the Australian premier it would be. The truth was not revealed by the British Government until a number of years after Australian Prime Minister Menzies had died.

We were now finished at Monte Bello and on our way back to join the fleet in the Mediterranean we picked up the outgoing mail from Christmas Island then returned to Singapore for a couple of weeks and on to the island of Penang. Our next port of call was supposed to be Rangoon in Burma but the visit was cancelled, probably due to the ongoing civil war there, so instead we made our way across the Bay of Bengal to Madras on the east coast of India. From there we went to the port of Trimcomalee in Ceylon before continuing west across the Arabian Sea to Aden prior to making for Malta through the Suez Canal. We arrived in Aden at about the end of July just as the Egyptians announced the takeover of the Canal. We were instructed to remain in the area so we pottered about the Red Sea for a while until eventually joined by HMS *Kenya*, and HMS *Modeste*.

In late September HMS *Newfoundland*, which had also been present at Monte Bello although not as a guinea pig ship like us, arrived at Aden from Trimcomalee to relieve HMS *Kenya* which then made her way home via the Cape. Some time during this period we were making our way to pay a courtesy visit to the Somali port of Mogadishu on the Indian Ocean when our orders were changed and we turned and headed northwards towards the Red Sea making for the southern entrance of the Suez Canal. On our way we sailed up the Gulf of Aqaba to see if any British nationals in the area wanted to leave. Apparently none of them did so we returned to the Red Sea and joined up with the *Newfoundland* to continue north to the Gulf of Suez where we waited for further orders..

We were joined later by the rest of Task Force 324 which was assembling at the southern end of the Suez Canal to protect British shipping interests in the area in what was called *Operation Toreador*. As well as ourselves and the *Newfoundland* there was also the frigates *Modeste* and *Crane*, the Royal Fleet Auxiliary vessel *Royal Sovereign*, two French frigates, *La Perouse*, and *Gazelle*, as well as the French coastal minesweeper *Jasmin*.

Late on the afternoon of 31 October *Operation Musketeer* began with the RAF attacking Egyptian airfields. An hour or so after midnight in the early hours of the following day an unidentified darkened ship was spotted lurking in the vicinity of a number of merchant ships sailing north in the Gulf of Suez. When we and the *Newfoundland* approached it was seen to be the Egyptian frigate *Domiat*, the ex-Royal Navy ship HMS *Nith*. She was signalled to stop and appeared to be slowing down but then switched off her navigation lights and speeded up while turning her guns towards the *Newfoundland. Newfoundland* opened up with both her six- and four-inch guns in a number of broadsides which hit the Egyptian vessel. We too opened fire with our forward A and B turret 4.5 guns. We in the A turret and gun bay heard captain of the turret Dennis Buck announcing 'hit, hit, hit!' This was followed by 'She's turning over,' then shortly afterwards by, 'She's going, she's gone!' Before she was disabled *Domiat* had managed to hit the *Newfoundland* with two shells one of which killed a crew member and injured four more.

We picked up nearly 70 survivors from the *Domiat* who we tried to land at Port Sudan on the Red Sea and at Aden but were refused in both places by the authorities because of local feelings. Eventually we managed to land them at Dijbouti into the non-too friendly arms of French colonial troops. There was a bit of wailing and gnashing of teeth and cries that they were British prisoners of war and not of the French.

They had been well looked after aboard the *Diana* with the many wounded all being treated well and with the surgeon from the *Newfoundland* amputating the leg of one of the badly injured survivors. They all seemed to be quite a cheerful lot and would have much preferred to have stayed on board with us despite the oppressive heat below deck. Only one officer on the *Domiat* was rescued and five years later in 1961 when sailing through the Suez Canal aboard HMS *Messina* I saw that he was the pilot taking us through.

I have heard it claimed that *Diana* finished off the *Domiat* with torpedoes. This is not so. I knew Leading Seaman Shearer who was in charge of the torpedoes very well and he never indicated afterwards that he had been involved in the sinking of the enemy ship.

On 24 November we left the Gulf of Suez and returned to Aden after four weeks of action readiness then went off to spend Christmas at Mombasa. We returned to the UK via the Cape, arriving back at Devonport in February in 1957. After a refit we joined the Home Fleet and operated in home waters until August when the ship reached the end of its current commission and the crew was dispersed. In 1980 I left the Navy as a Chief Ordnance Artificer after 30 years of service.

A few years ago I received two letters regarding my involvement in the Monte Bello nuclear bomb testing programme. The first was from a doctor enquiring about my health and that of any of my children born after my return to the UK. She was working on behalf of an organisation in New Zealand representing returned servicemen who had taken part in Britain's nuclear weapons programme and who were now suffering from all sort of health problems.

The second letter was from a film company planning to make a documentary about the Diana, the only ship to have sailed through two lots of radioactive fallout. As soon as they learned that my health was okay I didn't hear from them again. Captain Gower died in 2007 at the ripe old age of ninety-five.

* * *

Roy Cragg, HMS *Decoy*.

HMS *Decoy*, together with HMS Diana was one of the six Daring Class destroyers that took part in the Suez Crisis. Roy has provided a number of photos taken at that period of the ship's service.

HMS *Decoy* entering the Grand Harbour, Malta.

HMS *Decoy.*

Roy Cragg aboard HMS *Decoy*.

HMS *Decoy* steaming at speed.

Jack-stay prepared for the transfer of a Royal Artillery major from HMS *Ulysses to Decoy.* He would be in radio contact with a spotter plane calling the accuracy of the destroyer guns firing at the dug-in tanks along the beach.

The ship's cat Bitumastic.

Approaching the entrance to the Suez Canal

The French hospital ship *La Marseillaise* anchored in the outer harbour of the canal entrance.

Royal Navy ships anchored in the mouth of the Canal.

Requisitioned cargo ships lined up in the outer harbour.

HMS *Decoy* tied up against what is probably HMS *Tyne*.

Small craft tied up against *Decoy*. Viewing down the canal towards the dome of the Canal Company building.

Two of the cooks working below in the galley.

Stirring the Christmas pudding.

The padre transferring across to HMS *Diamond*.

David Packer, HMS *Striker*.

I was born in Richmond Road, Swindon, Wiltshire, in 1934 and went to primary school in the town before going on to Jenning Street Secondary Modern School in September 1945. When I was 14 in my last year at school I joined the local Sea Cadet Corps based at the training ship TS *Emerald* and went on to join the cadet band.

Leaving school in July 1949 just before my 15th birthday I got a job as an office boy with British Railways' Great Western works in Swindon. I had uncles and a grandfather who were skilled fitters and turners with the railway and it was decided that I would follow this family tradition.

Although the Labour Government nationalised all the regional railways on 1 January 1948 the old Great Western Railway Company managed to retain its identity for a further two years until being wound up at Christmas 1949. However, our rolling stock in the south-western region still continued to be painted with its familiar chocolate and cream livery for quite some time. On my 16th birthday I was accepted for a five-year indentured apprenticeship as a fitter-turner-erector.

Over the next few years I continued with the Sea Cadets and went on various training courses with them, one being on gunnery at the National Training Centre on Whale Island in Portsmouth harbour and another on seamanship aboard the battleship HMS *Vanguard*, also at Portsmouth. At *Emerald* I helped to run our drum and bugle band as the bandmaster teaching new recruits. By the time I was 21 after seven years with the cadets I had reached the rank of cadet petty officer.

I completed my apprenticeship on my 21st birthday and around this time was called to take my national service medical examination at Gloucester, following which, because of my cadet force service and being a mechanical engineer, I was assigned to the Royal Navy. Just before joining up I married my girlfriend Sally.

On 10 November 1955 I reported to HMS *Raleigh*, the large shore establishment at Torpoint in Cornwall near the mouth of the River Tamar opposite Plymouth where I underwent my first few weeks of basic naval training. On completion of the course I was transferred to the HMS *Victory* Barracks at Portsmouth to await a posting. Here we were asked, 'Which fleet would you prefer?' Being newly married I asked for the Home Fleet in preference to the Far East and Mediterranean stations. We noticed that no one got what he had asked for.

In about March 1956 I was assigned to HMS *Striker*, a tank landing ship (LST) of about 2,500 ton displacement which had been launched in 1945 as LST 3516 before being renamed HMS *Striker* in 1947. The following year she had taken on board the Royal Marines of 40 Commando at Haifa, the last British unit to leave Palestine after the Jews there had established the state of Israel. She was now part of the Mediterranean fleet.

I left Portsmouth by train and on my arrival at Liverpool Street Station in London reported to the Railway Transport Officer (RTO), a person found on all the main stations during the days of National Service, who drove me to Blackbushe Airport not far from Aldershot. Here I went aboard an Eagle Airlines flight to Luqa Airport in Malta. On arrival I reported to HMS *Ricasoli*, the naval shore base housed in an old fort on Gallows Point, a promontory jutting out into the eastern side of Valetta's Grand Harbour. Here I was to wait while *Striker* returned from its current exercise.

HMS *Ricasoli*, the shore base in Grand Harbour, Malta.

HMS *Striker* was part of the Amphibious Warfare Squadron with which we spent most of our time practising beach landings with NATO forces and ferrying troops from Gibraltar to our bases at Benghazi, Oran, and Tripoli. At the time I was the only national serviceman in the ship's company.

HMS *Striker* in Grand Harbour, Malta.

In late October 1956 after our usual practice exercises off the island of Sardinia we headed back to Malta, arriving there on about the 28th of the month. Immediately we began to load up tanks and take aboard Royal Marine commandos. From the radio we learned that the RAF was involved in bombing and rocketing various installations in Egypt so consequently, as we set sail, we had more than some idea of where we were heading.

We found ourselves to be part of quite a large convoy which included destroyers giving us protection as we headed eastwards. On the voyage we were instructed on how to administer morphine should we have to deal with any wounded during the action. Off Cyprus we met up with a fleet of French ships before sailing south towards the Egyptian coast off Port Said.

During the last couple of days of our journey we saw RAF bombers returning from their raids. Over the radio on 5 November we learned that paratroopers had landed on Egyptian soil – the English on the airfield near Port Said and the French on Port Fuad. At 5am the next morning, the sixth, we closed up for action and put our commandos ashore on the beach from landing craft. We then withdrew offshore until the quay area was cleared of the enemy before returning to the dock for tanks and other equipment to be off-loaded. While all this was going on I was in the engine room so failed to see any of the action although our skipper gave us a few commentaries over the Tannoy.

Over the next few days we saw more troops being brought in by various ships and ferried ashore on pontoons. However, it wasn't long before we heard that America was making waves and that the United Nations was getting involved. We soon had proof of this when we had to sail to Haifi in Israel which was where *Striker* had taken the Commandos aboard in 1948. Here we loaded up United Nations Land Rovers, trucks, and equipment and returned to Port Said with them. After unloading we pulled back out of the way to the Port Fuad side of the canal.

Sometime afterwards we were told that the last of the invasion fleet would be pulled out by the 22nd of December but that *Striker* would be staying behind as a UK salvage unit ship. Being under UN control we had to disarm our Bofor and Oerlikon anti-aircraft guns and all crew had to wear civilian clothing which, to the Navy, means number eights. We understood that the aircraft carrier HMS *Theseus* would be stationed out to sea for our protection should there be any attempt to board us by any Egyptian hotheads. Later some Swedish UN troops joined us to act as guards.

But for those on salvage duty the last ship finally pulled out of the canal in the early hours of 23 December. The next day we saw a large crowd of Egyptians milling around the De Lesseps statue. After a while there came a large explosion as they tried to dislodge the canal builder from his vantage point. When the smoke blew away he was still there looking down the canal. Of course we gave a big cheer which brought a few rifle shots our way. A little later they tried again and this time Ferdinand toppled off his plinth.

While we were here I learned that my daughter had been born on the 27th of December, an event which I toasted with sippers given to me by my shipmates.

This period became pretty boring so some of the chaps got together and gave a ship's concert which turned out to be excellent.

Members of the concert cast.

We also had events which included 'who can grow the best beard' and soon we were beginning to look like pirates. I sported one myself, keeping it until I returned home. We also received quite a number of films and other items to help with our leisure time.

Dave aboard HMS *Striker* in Port Said harbour

HMS *Striker* stayed on in Port Said until early in February 1957 when the first ship was able to make passage out of the canal. We had been aboard the ship since the middle of October four months earlier so we were glad to set sail and get back to Malta. On our return from Port Said the ship was first fumigated before we continued with our normal duties such as taking part in exercises with NATO forces.

Early in September 1957, with my National Service drawing to a close and having had considerable leave accumulate, I flew back to the UK and reported to the RTO at Liverpool Street Station again. Here I was supplied with travel warrants, money, and a leave pass for 62 days. When this came to an end I reported back to HMS *Victory* at Portsmouth from where, in early November after two days of paperwork and a medical had been completed, I was demobbed.

Back home I returned to my old job with British Rail as a die sinker toolmaker until 1959 when I left to join the Press Steel Company in Gypsy Lane, Swindon as a try-out fitter toolmaker. The firm later become British Leyland/Rover, and finally BMW. I stayed there until retirement reaching the grade of foreman/coordinator over the skilled and semi-skilled men. I retired when I was 65.

Soon after retiring I took up sequence dancing and have also continued with my lifetime love of coarse fishing. Our daughter Lynne, who was born while I was in Port Said, regularly visits Mum and Dad who have currently been married 55 years.

* * *

Victor Mallinson, HMS *Striker*.

I was born in 1937 in Nottingham but after a year we moved to Sleeford in Lincolnshire where Dad got a job.

After leaving school at Easter 1952 I started work nearby at Airworks Ltd, RAF Digby as an apprentice fitter. Airworks carried out flying training for the services. However, as we were flying about 100 Tiger Moths, most of our time was taken up with ground staff duties. Since these planes had no brakes we had to collect them from the field and guide them in by holding on to their wing tips. This kept us very fit but taught us nothing about maintenance. At the end of 1952 Airworks left Digby and went off to deal with more modern aircraft at Weston Super Mare so we were given our marching orders. I began work at Bass Malting but it was only seasonal so I left and went to work at Frank Kyme's Farm at Leasington Moor. It was while I was here, in May 1955 just before I was eighteen, that I received my call up papers for National Service.

I had every intention of signing on so that I could join the Navy but the shortest length of service at that time was nine years. My brothers Phil and Roy were both in the Army at that time and advised me just do the National Service. At the medical and interview in the Lincoln Drill Hall I was told that very few NS recruits were sent to the Navy so I expected to get my second choice. Therefore I was pleasantly surprised when on receiving my call up it was for the Royal Navy. I was to train as a mechanical engineer (stoker).

So, on 16 May 1955 I set out from Sleeford to report at HMS *Raleigh* at Torpoint near Plymouth. The national service divisions were segregated from the regulars on an island with a bridge joining us to the main part of the barracks. I joined my class in Granville Division and so began my three months training with the first two weeks mainly square bashing under the instructors who were mostly ex-wartime vets. Their main job was to hammer blind discipline into us. They weren't keen on national servicemen and I was called names I had never heard before. Part of the assault course was through a tidal river and at low tide we had to slog through two to three feet of mud and still parade for divisions next morning spick and span.

Our instructor was a P/O Matty who had had a bad time in the war, having been sunk three times, and this had left him with a very mean streak. Every morning the whole barracks had to parade in best uniform. On the first morning I was pulled up by the officer of the day for not wearing my best uniform but I managed to convince him that it was the one I had been issued with. So he gave me a pass to go to the civilian naval tailor in Plymouth and have a uniform made. Lucky me! I later found out that this was a fiddle as the tailor used to give the officers a back-hander for all the trade they sent him. The cooks, mostly ex-wartime, were also running a scam with the food and this meant that what we were given was atrocious.

After three months training we were passed out as mechanical engineers (stokers) and after leave I received a draft chit to join HMS *Striker* a landing ship tank (LST) of the Amphibious Warfare Squadron Mediterranean based in Malta. On the flight out I had a bit of a run-in with a commander who was taking his family out there. On my arrival I learned that *Striker* was at sea so I was billeted at a shore base, Fort Ricasoli, until her return.

A close-up view from aboard ship of Fort Ricasoli.

My first trip on HMS *Striker* was to Port Said to help withdraw some of our last Canal Zone troops to Cyprus following the 1954 agreement with Egypt to finally pull-out of our bases there once it had been decided to make Cyprus the base for MELF, our Middle East Land Forces. After that we spent most of our time on exercises doing landings in such places as Corsica, Sardinia, Sicily, Italy, Gibraltar and Cyprus.

HMS *Striker* (L3516) in Grand Harbour, Malta.

During the summer of 1956 after Nasser seized the Suez Canal we started to build up the squadron with more ships being taken out of reserve. A big build-up of all kinds of ships also took place both in Malta and Cyprus. Eventually, at the end of October, we headed out to sea to join a convoy and learned that we were heading for Port Said.

HMS *Rampart* (LCT L4037) in convoy to Port Said.

Early on the morning of 6 November the amphibious fleet protected by our destroyer escort proceeded toward the Egyptian coast. Eventually we lowered our LCAs (Landing Craft Assault) filled with marines and they made their way inshore to the long beach lying to the right of the canal entrance. We in the engine room were given a running commentary by one of the bridge party who would say something like, 'A gun has opened up on the beach.' There would be a bang as one of our destroyers fired a shell. The commentary would then continue. 'That gun is now out of action.' After the marines had secured the area lying along the western causeway we were able to enter the mouth of the canal and tie up at the fish dock to unload the rest of our troops with their tanks and support vehicles.

Unloading a Centurion tank from HMS *Striker*.

View from close to the De Lesseps statue towards the outer harbour and the cargo fleet.

Landing craft bow doors nosed in to the quay at the back of the Fish Dock. 40 Commando landing beach at left.

After we'd taken the town *Striker* was used as a ferry between Malta, Cyprus and Port Said. On one occasion we had to take a load of captured arms and ammunition out to sea and dump it overboard. Most of the troops had left Port Said by the middle of December but Striker was left behind to serve as one of the support vessels to the salvage fleet involved in clearing the sunken blockships. On 24 December we watched from the ship a large crowd of Egyptians on the quay taking part in an attempt to blow up the De Lesseps statue. After about two or three failed attempts they finally managed to topple it.

With the pull-out of the main British and French forces we had become attached to the United Nations peace-keeping force and not allowed to wear Royal Navy uniform or fly the white ensign.

The United Nations flag flying on HMS *Striker*.

Two boats used by the divers to traverse the 'wrecks'.

On 24 January the *Striker* departed for Malta, one of the last British ships to leave. I was at Malta only for a short time before returning to the UK where I had some leave owing to me. It wasn't long then to May 1957 and demob.

* * *

Patrick Edward Smeath, HMS *Ravager*.

Pat was born 28 January 1928 in Exmouth Devon but moved with his parents to Lympstone three miles away soon afterwards. He was educated at Lympstone Primary School then, from the age of 11, at Exmouth Senior School. He left at the age of 14, shortly before his father died at the age of only 42, and became apprenticed to a local builder as a carpenter-joiner.

Over the next few years he became quite an accomplished athlete and also a musician with the

Exmouth Town Band. In 1946 at the age of 18 he completed his apprenticeship.

The following year Pat joined the Royal Navy and signed on for 12 years. He carried out his training at HMS *Raleigh* the shore establishment at Torpoint, aboard the light fleet aircraft carrier HMS *Victorious*, and later at Plymouth barracks.

He then joined HMS *Vanguard* which was preparing for the royal tour to Australia but this was cancelled when the King fell ill. Instead the *Vanguard* went on a tour of the Mediterranean. After service on the *Vanguard* he went to HMS *Tyne* for a while until joining the Command Field Gun team for 1950. After this he joined HMS *Ocean* for a tour of the Far East where he visited Japan via Colombo and Hong Kong.

In September 1951, after being in the Field Gun Team again, Pat returned to the Far East on the troopship *Empire Pride* to join the Hong Kong Shore station HMS *Tamar*. After 15 months he was posted to the aircraft carrier HMS *Unicorn* operating between Hong Kong, Singapore, Japan and Korea. He returned to Plymouth after two years and two months away and in January 1954 married his fiancée Barbara before returning to Plymouth Barracks to join the Blue Jackets Band which played at many local and official events.

In 1955 Pat joined the minesweeper HMS *Pickle* on fishing protection duties in Arctic waters until early in 1956 when he was again required for the Field Gun Team which performed at Earls Court. In late July after leave he was sent up to Scotland to join the LST HMS *Ravager* at Gareloch on the Clyde which had just been taken out of 'mothballs'. She sailed for Devonport on about 2 August, obviously to prepare for 'Suez'.

Ravager (L3505), after being made ready and taking on stores and the Centurion tanks of A Squadron, the 6th Royal Tank Regiment, sailed for Malta to join the invasion fleet arriving there early in September. The convoy left for Port Said on 30 October sailing at about eight knots to accommodate the slow flat-bottomed amphibious craft.

HMS *Ravager* (L3505) in Grand harbour, Malta.

View of the LST *Puncher* (L3036) and, partly hidden, the RFA LST *Empire Gull* (3513).

Approaching Port Said on the morning of 6 November.

At about 0900 hours on the morning of 6 November *Ravager* lowered her ramp close to the beach near the smouldering remains of the Casino Jetty where the commandos had gone ashore earlier and began discharging her tanks into the shallow water. She then sailed round the western mole into the entrance of the canal.

The outer harbour served as the vessel's home whenever she was in Port Said. However, for most of her time spent in the eastern Mediterranean *Ravager* carried out a shuttle service of stores and personnel between Port Said and Cyprus.

View of the western mole from within the outer harbour.

View from *Ravager* in the outer harbour looking towards the western mole. *Portcullis* (L4044) on the right, the coastal minesweeper *Darlaston* (M1127) on the left.

View from the *Ravager* on the eastern side of the canal towards the lighthouse on the Port Said waterfront.

View from the *Ravager* looking directly across at the light-house situated just behind the waterfront.

The *Paul Solente* blockship. The Suez Canal Company domes partly hidden by its mast. The police station tower is on the corner of the Commerce Basin.

View across to the LCT HMS *Rampart* (L3037) nosed in to the quay by the Casino Palace Hotel

The LST eventually set off back to the UK on 9 December, having quite a good trip and being 'blown' through the Bay Of Biscay (Pat's tenth time) to arrive back at Plymouth on Monday 17 December. Early in 1957 Pat was due to join a survey ship going to Australia for two years but he decided to buy himself out of the Navy and left in the August after ten years service.

Back as a civilian Pat returned to work as a carpenter with the local council until he retired at the age of sixty-five. But he then continued to work at something he'd always enjoyed – restoration of antique furniture, until he retired again age seventy-five. He died on 16 February 2010, age eighty-two.

(Thanks to Barbara for this contribution.)

* * *

John Eastlake, HMS *Anzio*.

I joined up for my National Service on 10 October 1955 and after training as a signalman (ORD), known as a bunting tosser, I was drafted to the aircraft carrier *Theseus*. This was followed by a posting to the frigate HMS *Vigilant* which is where I was at the end of July 1956 when a signal came through asking for volunteers for an unknown draft. I thought, Why not, I'm only in the Navy for just over another year? I moved into Devonport Barracks on Monday the thirtieth.

On the following Friday, 3 August, I was told to pack my kit for a crash draft. On the Saturday, together with a number of other volunteers, I was given a series of jabs. Then there was a lull, while we just lounged around, until 2200 hours the following Thursday when we were assembled and taken to the station for a midnight train to London where we arrived at 0730 hours. We were then coached to Blackbushe Airport and a flight in a Dakota that afternoon, via a refuelling stop at Marseilles, to RAF Luqa in Malta where we arrived, very tired, in the early hours of Saturday morning.

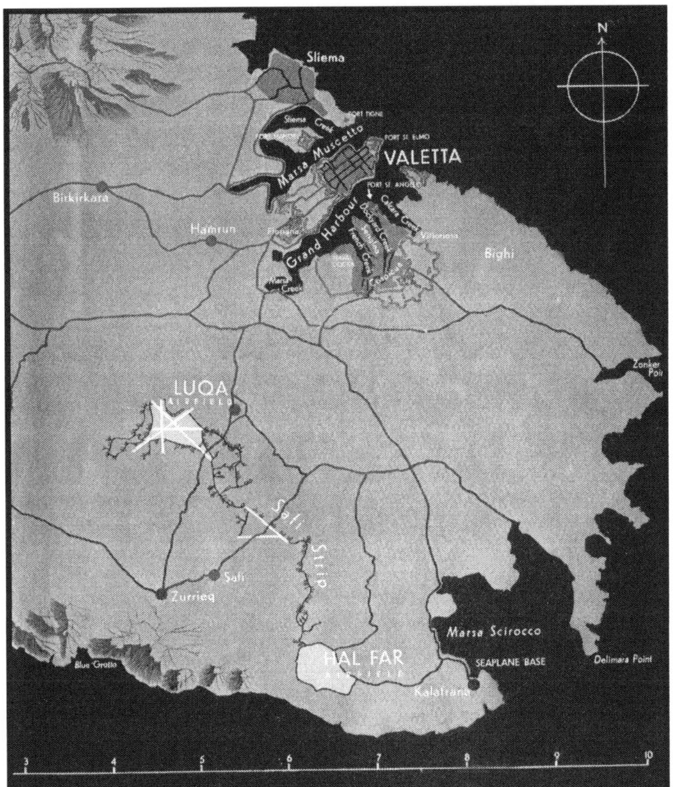

The location of Luqa Airfield in Malta.

At 0011 hours, after a short night billeted in the heavy repair ship HMS *Ranpura* in one of the Grand Harbour Creeks, we attended a draft routine and by 1130 I found myself aboard HMS *Anzio*, a tank landing ship (LST) and made duty signalman for the day although why, I don't know, as the ship was still in mothballs. We remained accommodated on the *Ranpura* while we worked on the *Anzio* each day along with some locals until she was ready to live in which was on the 23rd of the month. Starting on Monday the 27th we began sea trials, gun firing, and landing craft assault (LCA) exercises.

LST exercises off Malta. L3003 *Anzio* in the foreground with L3518 *Suvla* behind. Among the others would have been 3036 *Puncher*, 3505 *Ravager*, 3511 *Reggio, and 3156 Striker.*

The following day we carried out degaussing and compass setting. On the 29th we undertook more LCA exercises both during the day and the night. On the 30th we went on squadron exercises and on the last day of August we began six days of exercises of various types. This was followed by five 'nothing days' until Wednesday 12 September when we began three days of exercises, day and night, loading and unloading lorries.

Unloading and loading exercise with a three-tonner Bedford RL Navy truck.

Starting Monday 17 September we practised daily beaching to load and offload lorries. On an exercise taking place on Friday 21, while hitting the beach very hard while I was on duty on the flag deck I was sent flying and hit my face around my mouth on a solid piece of metal. I ended up in the Royal Naval Hospital at Bighi to have my teeth sorted out with one being removed. I had to wait until 10 May 1957 for a false tooth.

I was back for more exercises on 25/26 before we left for Syracuse in Sicily on Friday 28, arriving there at 0900 hours. I was not needed on watch for a couple of days so with several others went up into the hills where, with a great view of Mount Etna, we camped overnight. We arrived back aboard ship at 2100 hours the following night.

We left Sicily at 2000 hours on 1 October for more night exercises on our way back to Malta where we arrived at 0830 hours on Tuesday. Between then and 29 October we carried out a number of exercises but on Tuesday the 30th, at 2330 hours, after having earlier taken on board a contingent of 42 Commando and trucks, we set off eastwards in convoy. We were told the next day where we were bound.

Trucks waiting to be loaded aboard the *Anzio*.

The *Anzio* loaded 'to the gunnels'.

HMS *Meon*, the Headquarter ship for the landing craft on its way in the convoy to Egyptian waters.

HMS *Meon* coming close to the *Anzio*.

During our journey the convoy was apparently being shadowed by an American submarine. We arrived off the Egyptian coast on time to see the bombardment of the Port Said beach to loosen up the opposition for our Commandos early on the morning of the sixth of November

A Daring class destroyer being used to bombard the invasion beach before 40 and 42 Commandos went in.

We offloaded our commandos in their LCAs at 0245 hours then waited for instructions.

Members of 42 Marine Commando wading ashore.

The *Anzio* tied up at the quay by the Casino Palace Hotel.

View south down the canal from on board the *Anzio* near the De Lesseps Statue.

View from the *Anzio,* moored at the back of the Fish dock, towards the De Lesseps Statue and HMS *Forth* behind it..

Anzio at another of the harbour quays.

We went into Port Said harbour at 1100 hours to drop off supplies and retracted at 1400 hours to anchor off the harbour.

On the 8th we left for Cyprus where we spent some time refuelling and going ashore where we played in a hockey match against minesweepers and a football match against the LST HMS *Ravager*. On Monday the 12th while at Famagusta HMS *Theseus* arrived and anchored offshore nearby. This had been my first ship.

We set out on our return to Port Said on Sunday the 18th, arriving the following day. On Thursday 22nd some of us went on a bus tour of Port Said to view the damage. We then drove on south as far as we could to see something of the 'canal zone'.

The coast road on the way to El Cap.

On Sunday 25th we began four hectic days in which we loaded up vehicles and took them to Famagusta, returned and loaded up again then set out for Malta on the Thursday. On the Friday in strong winds one of the lorries caught fire and in the end we had to push it overboard. By Saturday the wind was gale force and our bow doors swung open. We hove to with our stern to the wind all day Sunday and most of Monday when we were joined by HMS *Wakeful* and HMS *Wizard.* We eventually arrived in the Grand Harbour at 1900 hours on Tuesday 4 December.

On Thursday 13 December, after having offloaded the trucks and having all the damage repaired, we returned to Port Said, where we moved berths a number of times and loaded more vehicles ready for the final pullout of our forces. We left Port Said for the last time at 2000 hours on Saturday 22 December, and spent Christmas Day at sea. We arrived in Malta on Boxing Day at 2300 hours. A better 'cruise' than the previous one! We left Malta for Plymouth on Friday 1 of February 1957.

After *Anzio* I somehow got myself into the Devonport 'sub smash' MTB unit for six weeks although I spent nearly four of these weeks on leave. Besides having to be ready for any submarine having trouble we would go to sea each day out of Plymouth Sound and, among other things, tow targets for gunners off the cliffs near Plymouth. Then I went to the frigate HMS *Undaunted* and during my time with this ship went on a course at the signal School HMS *Mercury* near Petersfield. I was demobbed on Friday the 13th of September 1957 and returned to Bristol.

* * *

Alexander (Alec) Watt, HMS *Parapet.*

I was born in 1938 in Karachi in what was then India where my father was the Chief Aerodrome Officer. I returned to the UK at the end of the war when I was seven and educated at a boarding school in Scotland. I elected for early call-up rather sit A-Level exams.

On 27 April 1955 I joined the London Division of the RNVR as a boy seaman and was rated Ordinary Seaman on 24 July. I completed part 1 training on the aircraft carrier HMS *Theseus* between the 8th and 22nd of August.

I was called up for National Service on 9 April 1956, attending the recruiting centre in Croydon, not far from Reigate where we lived. Here I was told that there were no vacancies in the Royal Navy but that I could settle for the Army. However, on explaining that I was already a member of the RNVR and had completed part-one training I was allowed to fast track through the recruitment process for the Royal Navy.

I was sent to Victoria Barracks Portsmouth and then, on 23 April, to HMS *Ocean* to complete my training. On 9 June I was drafted to HMS *Victory* at Portsmouth and on 19 June drafted to the coastal minesweeper HMS *Laleston* berthed at HMS *Vernon*, Portsmouth, where I stayed until 4 August.

My Suez experience began on 5 August when I was drafted to HMS *Parapet* (L4039). *Parapet*, along with her sister tank landing craft, was in mothballs up a muddy creek at Llanelli in South Wales. Our task was to make them seaworthy and then proceed to HMS *Drake* at Plymouth for refitting and taking aboard stores. This was the start of *Operation Musketeer* although none of us was aware of this at the time.

On 19 August this small fleet of five landing craft accompanied by a tug left Plymouth for the Mediterranean, destination Malta via Gibraltar. On the way we encountered a gale in the Bay of Biscay which made for the interesting experience of trying to keep an unladen landing craft on course even when the most experienced helmsman was unable to keep the bows heading within 10° either side of the agreed course. After a day at Gibraltar with shore leave we left for Malta but one day out we lost a rudder and had to complete the voyage under tow.

Following a spell in dry dock during which we took the opportunity to paint the sides of the *Parapet* we commenced training with the rest of the Amphibious Warfare Squadron for the task ahead. This included finding out how many vehicles of whatever size could fit on the loading deck of an LCT, taking on LVTs, (tracked amphibious armoured personnel carriers), and taking aboard various kinds of vehicles as well as tanks from the dockside.

The LCT HMS *Parapet* (L4039) and the requisitioned cargo ship *City of Brooklyn* in Grand Harbour, Malta.

In all the Amphibious Warfare Squadron totalled 17 craft, many of which, like *Parapet*, had been drawn from the reserve fleets in the UK and Malta. There were eight LSTs and nine LCTs in the squadron. A joint land and sea exercise had been planned for October but events overtook this.

With the landing craft being the slowest of the vessels the convoy we belonged to had to set out early enough to arrive at Port Said in time for the assault and we set sail on 30 October.

We arrived offshore from the canal entrance about nightfall on 5 November. In a letter to my father soon afterwards I described the Suez landing as follows:

Approaching Port Said. Action stations!

'We went in on Tuesday 6 November at sunrise, 3.30am GMT. The beach was a mass of fires where the Casino Pier and the beach huts were burning. The fires were caused by rockets which had been fired by planes and ship shellfire prior to us going in.

The small LCAs were the first to go in and they met with instant opposition as they started to approach the beach. However by the time we reached the beach the Egyptians were so busy with the commandos that they did not have much time to direct their fire in our direction although one or two stray bullets inevitably did come our way however, fortunately not causing casualties.

We, being the first LCT in, had the honour of discharging the first Centurion tanks ever to be beached from an LCT in action. After having ditched the 4 tanks we backed out and made our way round to the harbour where we put our nose to the De Lesseps jetty and got rid of 1 Land Rover, 1 Saracen Ambulance, 1 Scout Car and 3 three-ton trucks.

Immediately after this we started a non-stop ferry service of troops and vehicles from merchant ships to the jetty.

Unloading at the quay by the Casino Palace Hotel.

Meanwhile the tanks had met with immediate opposition on reaching the road at the other side of the beach. However a couple of 20lb shells soon cleared them. That night we got a good firework display with bonfires thrown in. (Pity it was the 6th and not 5th). There were three big fires including an oil fire. Also one or two ammunition dumps went up in flames adding to the display of fireworks.

A ceasefire took place at the end of the day although Egyptians sniping continued afterwards and persisted right through until the withdrawal just before Christmas.

Unloading the cargo ships.

Truck being lowered to the deck of *Parapet.*

Trucks coming ashore along the road at the side of the Casino Palace Hotel.

Troops and stores being gathered in the same place.

Landing craft nosed in to the quay at the back of the Fish Dock with the LST *Reggio* (3511) on the left. Tents have been erected on the quay at the back of which is the beach where 40 Commando came ashore.

We learned that some of the those fighting for the Egyptians were boys from as young as eight and women armed with Bren guns. They fought until they were either captured or killed.

Most of it is over but we are still ferrying troops and vehicles from ships to shore. For 3 nights so far we have been up all night and the others we have got up at 4 or 5 in the morning.

I don't think that I have any more news for now in any case I must turn in or we will get no sleep at all. We have already been worked to a standstill. I don't know how much more they can expect of us but we can't work much longer. The only rest we got today was 10 minutes for a short Remembrance Service.'

The French Hospital ship *La Marseillaise.*

Three LCTs with *Counterguard* (4043) the nearest. At the back is the troopship *Empire Parkeston*.

Viewing across the Port Said harbour from the back of the De Lesseps Statue where 45 Commando came ashore.

Just before Christmas the squadron left Port Said to return to Malta where it was disbanded. We celebrated Christmas at sea and the Commodore sent all ships the following message:

GOOD KING WHIRLWIND FIRST LOOKED OUT ON THAT SUNDAY EVENING, WHERE THE SEA LAY ROUND ABOUT DEEP AND WET BUT TRANQUIL

BRIGHTLY SHONE HIS LIGHTS THAT NIGHT, THO' THE BUNTS WERE TIRED WHEN A CONVOY HOVE IN SIGHT SLOW BUT AS DESIRED.

HITHER BARHILL STAND BY ME WHERE D'YOU THINK YOUR GOING, HITCH UP TO SAMSONIA'S STERN, SHE WILL DO THE TOWING

ANTIC LIES A GOOD LEAGUE AFT, UNDERNEATH THE SKYLINE, RIGHT AGAINST THE CHANNEL GATE, BY OLD NASSER'S HIGHLIGHT.

BASTION, BUTTRESS AND REDOUBT, COUNTERGUARD YOUR NEIGHBOUR, PORTCULLIS WATCHING THE OLD ONE OUT, SHE'S THE NAMELESS NUMBER.

PARAPET LAST ALONG THE LINE, KEEPS AN EYE ON SPABURN, THEN WE'LL MAKE VALETTA YET – PERHAPS BY FRIDAY MORNING.

(Bunts were signalmen responsible for flag, light, and radio communications, and referred to the days when all signals were by flags.)

Following two months of activity preparing the craft to be laid up in Malta I was then posted back to the UK, arriving at HMS *Victory* on 23 March 1957 via a troop ship to Liverpool and thence by train to Portsmouth. I was promoted to Able Seaman on 9 April and then posted on 22 October to HMS *Diligence*, a shore establishment on Southampton Water, where I became part of a trials crew testing fast patrol boats.

On 29 November I was drafted to HMS *Neptune* the Reserve Fleet HQ base at Chatham where I served out my remaining National Service until 8 April 1958 when I transferred to part-time service in the RNSR (Royal Naval Special Reserve which all naval National Service personnel were required to sign on to for a period of ten years.

Parapet crew photograph taken at Port Said against the side of probably HMS *Forth*. Note the Jack Russell ship's mascot.

Following National Service I did a three-year apprenticeship in the wine trade followed by four years as an insurance broker in Lloyds of London. I then joined Thompson Regional Newspapers as a Financial Advertising representative. Next I moved on to the Express Group as Financial Advertising Manager. After five years I joined Shandwick Public Relations working for one of their clients, Finance for Industry. I then went on to join another of Shandwick's clients, Dun & Bradstreet where I worked for 23 years eventually retiring as Director of Global Service Excellence. I now live in Reigate enjoying golf and mountain walking.

* * *

Keith Carne, HMS *Sallyport.*

In August 1956 whilst serving as a regular on HMS *Drake*, the Royal Naval Barracks at Devonport, I was a member of the team responsible for maintenance and general security of all the ships of the reserve fleet anchored in the River Tamar. This was at a time when we had a Navy.

One morning later in the month a party of about 30 of us was detailed to travel to Llanelli in South Wales. On arrival we were billeted in the drill hall of the local TA centre. During the next few weeks we attended the North Dock and set about bringing back to operational condition approximately six tank landing craft which had been moored there since the end of WWII.

Towards the end of July we sailed them back to Devonport where I was drafted to one of these vessels, HMS *Sallyport*, 4064. What a ship! It had a flat bottom and a maximum speed with a following wind and tide of nine knots. It rolled and tossed in dry dock. I was responsible for the maintenance of all the small arms and three Oerlikon guns which were the ships main armament

We sailed for Malta towards the end of August and then to Cyprus where we carried out practice beach landings with army personnel. By the end of September and the completion of the exercise our training was well advanced and we returned to Malta to find the Grand Harbour and all the other mooring areas full of Royal Navy ships which was when we realised that something was definitely going on, and soon.

We embarked several large wireless vehicles, trailers and army personnel and right at the end of October set sail as part of a massive convoy to

Egypt. Being the slowest ships the LCTs were right at the front and it took quite a while for us to converge on the mouth of the Suez Canal. (During the journey a man was lost overboard from *Portcullis* but fortunately he was found and fished out of the sea by *Counterguard.*)

The rest, as they say, is history. One of the photographs is of the LCT 4043 *Counterguard* taken from aboard *Sallyport* as we went in alongside to discharge the wireless vehicles and the army personnel. The other is taken from the *Sallyport* looking at the quay and the Casino Palace Hotel.

HMS *Sallyport* in Port Said harbour.

The Casino Palace Hotel.

* * *

Neville Brandish, RFA *Salvestor*.

I was born in Cowley in the city of Oxford in 1932, just down the road from the Morris motor car factory. From the age of five I attended the local primary school and then the Temple Cowley senior school which I left when I was 14 in 1946.

After school I worked as a college messenger at St Peters Hall, later a college of Oxford University, and worked there for three-and-a-half years before joining the Royal Navy as a stoker in July 1949. I did my initial training at HMS *Raleigh* at Torpoint in Cornwall.

On completion of my training I was drafted to my port depot at Portsmouth. My first ship was the cruiser HMS *Ceylon*. We sailed from Pompey on 11 April 1950 for a two-year commission as flag ship for the East Indies Admiral.

After a few months on station at Trincomalee, Ceylon, we were ordered to relieve HMS *Belfast* in Korean waters. On the way we had stopovers in Singapore and then Hong Kong before setting out for the port of Sasebo in Japan. However, after only a few hours at sea, we were recalled to Hong Kong where we tied up at the jetty in Kowloon harbour for four days.

On the morning of the fourth day we heard the sound of bagpipes getting closer and closer until the 1st Battalion of the Argyl and Sutherland Highlanders came in sight - 800 men and their kit. It took us a few hours but we embarked them all safely and took the first British Army troops to Pusan in Korea.

I left the *Ceylon* In April 1952 and flew home from Japan on compassionate leave after receiving news that my mother had been given only a few days to live. After leave I was drafted for twelve months to the old Royal Yacht *Victoria and Albert* in Scotland where I was based on HMS *Largo Bay*.

After this I spent some time in the reserve fleet until August 1954 when I was drafted to HMS *Bulwark* which at the time was at the Harland and Wolf shipyard in Belfast being prepared for its commission two months later.

I then spent another period in the reserve fleet until August 1956 when I was drafted to the salvage vessel RFA *Salvestor* anchored at Pembroke Dock in South Wales. *Salvestor*, which was a King Salvor class salvage vessel built by William Simons and Company Limited of Renfrew in Scotland, had been completed and commissioned in late 1942 during the Second World War. We sailed her to Devonport for a quick refit before making for Port Said via Malta and Tripoli in Libya.

We stayed at Port Said helping to clear the canal under the UN flag for some time after our troops left following the ceasefire. We finally left for home in February 1957 and I was demobbed in March.

Since I had been a stoker spending most of my time below deck I didn't have anything to do with the actual salvage operations we carried out but I obtained some photographs.

Sea Salvor on the left and LC11 on the right working on the blockship *Paul Solente*. At the upper centre is the blockship *Pollux* and at the top right the blockship *Peleuse*.

French hospital ship *La Marseillaise* and a number of requisitioned cargo ships anchored near the eastern breakwater.

Peleuse in the foreground with the *Paul Solente* flanked by the CL11 and *Sea Salvor* close to the Port Said waterfront.

HMS *Forth* in the foreground and two landing craft nosed in to the quay by the Casino palace Hotel.

* * *

David W (Tilly) Tyzack, Clearance diver.

I was born at the Royal Engineers barracks in Camberley Surrey where my father was based in the Army. Just before the war began the regiment was posted to India and married families went with them. We were there until 1947. I joined the Navy as a regular at the tender age of 15 years and six months in April 1951 and was sent to HMS *St Vincent*, the boys' shore training establishment at Gosport on the west side of the entrance to Portsmouth harbour.

I was a very good swimmer and played a lot of water polo for *St Vincent* so when the time came to choose a speciality I volunteered to become a clearance diver. The training for this took place at HMS *Vernon*, a barracks on the other side of the harbour near the Isle of Wight ferry terminal. In 1919 both the Royal Marines and the Naval Ordnance Department which were then based there had vacated the site and moved elsewhere allowing the shore establishment HMS *Vernon*, operating as the Naval Torpedo School, to take their place.

HMS *Vernon*.

During WWII, when some of Vernon's buildings were destroyed by German bombing and then rebuilt, the Navy's Deep-Diving Trials Unit and Clearance Diving training were also established at the barracks which is where the famous Buster Crabb was trained. My time at Vernon was 18 months of sheer hell but I made it, with just five of us out of the original 50-plus finishing the course and qualifying as clearance divers in 1955 with the rank of Able Seaman Clearance Diver 3rd class.

From here I was posted to the Assault Squadron Royal Marines (ASRM) which was the Royal Marine training base for swimmer-canoeists and light landing craft situated in Poole Harbour, Dorset. While there we worked hard and carried out a lot of exercises with canoes of the type depicted in the 1955 film Cockleshell Heroes, a true Second World War story in which a team of canoeists paddled ashore into German-occupied France to carry out a sabotage mission.

Our training involved the team being dropped off at intervals in the sea by a fast naval craft with a dinghy lashed to its side then collected again by means of a wire loop held over the side by a teammate. As the dinghy came speeding alongside we would thrust an arm through the loop (ouch!) and swing ourselves aboard and then up and out of the way onto the launch to make room for the next swimmer to be collected in this way. We all finished up with rainbow-coloured bruising to our upper arms.

In August 1956 I was on leave at Barnstaple in Devon and out for the day doing a bit of courting among the dunes at Saunton Sands when my name was called over a Tannoy System from a police car. Like a fool I popped my head up to see what was going on and was spotted. I was ordered to return to base forthwith, if not quicker.

Back at Portsmouth, the team, with all its dive equipment and explosives, etc., was quickly assembled and flown out in a bone-shaker of an aircraft from an RAF base to Malta where we underwent further training and work-ups with night beach attacks, recces, and more of the fast drop-offs and pick-ups. I think we were here about a month

Early in November, together with members of the Tank Corps, we went aboard a tank landing craft with all our diving gear plus heavy tanks and set sail eastwards for Port Said. Each night we kipped down with the Pongos under their tanks,

By the early morning on the sixth of November our LCT was lying off the Port Said beach which extends westwards from the entrance to the Suez Canal. Just a few hundred yards further to our right along the coast and behind the beach was El Gamel Airfield which the Paras had taken the day before. They were now waiting for the support of the Marines who were with the invasion fleet somewhere behind us. And in turn the Marines were waiting for us.

In the dark we assembled on the upper deck in our dive suits and breathing apparatus and said our last prayers with the army chaplain. Then, just as dawn was breaking, we boarded our small landing craft and made for the beach.

Ashore on the beach we checked for mines. Although we were wearing our dive suits and breathing apparatus we of course had no need for the latter at this time. Just over the top of the beach we came upon a long deep trench containing quite a lot of weaponry still in boxes with what appeared to be Russian writing on them; there were no Egyptians in sight. Cautiously we made our way over the bare terrain to the back of the Fish Dock adjacent to the De Lesseps Statue.

From here we dropped down into the harbour and began an underwater search for mines and booby traps but found it to be clear so that we were able to give the okay for the main landing craft to come in with their tanks and trucks.

On the beach I came across a marine and an Egyptian soldier who had been laid side by side after having been caught in the crossfire during the assault on the beach. I could only hold their hands and try to comfort them as they shared a cigarette together and then died together. About 30 years later at a Marines Association meeting ex Colour-Sergeant 'Tug' Wilson came over and introduced me to the son of that dead marine who asked me to tell him about his father's last moments.

As our own landing craft arrived to collect us we could see the first of the LCTs approaching from the canal entrance to unload at the Fish quay.

The only opposition we encountered was while going further into the canal to inspect the blockships and relaxing on the top deck of our landing craft. A sniper in a large building close to the waterfront began firing in our direction. A message was radioed to shore and in a short time a large tank came out of one of the streets nearby. We signalled a message to the tank commander who then ducked down inside his turret. Moments later the turret swivelled and a round was fired into what we believed to be the position of the sniper. It took out the whole front wall. No more problems.

On arrival at the blockships and after checking for explosives we made a start on positioning marker floats. We had made these ourselves back at Poole and they consisted of tennis ball-size spherical floats of orange plastic and had about sixty feet of line attached to them. They marked the places on the sunken ships that would have to be sealed up before the salvage vessel crews could make a start on lifting them. The depth of the water we found to be about 33 feet which is a safe depth for a frogman breathing pure oxygen. Below this depth though, it can become toxic.

Clearance divers passing dumped firearms to members of a Scottish regiment on the quay.

Bill Cornick, Reg Boyle, 'Andy' Andrews, 'Shorty' Ayres, Ted Butler, 'Baldy' Baldock, Lt 'Trunky' Parker, 'Dutchy' Dutchman, and 'Tilly' Tyzack.

'Tilly' Tyzack at Port Said after the search of the harbour.

From here we went on further down the canal to begin searching the backwater canals on the south and west of Port Said where we found army uniforms, ID cards, and weapons that had been thrown away by Egyptian soldiers. We also had the job, at regular intervals during the nights we were there, of checking the underwater hulls of the British and French warships to make sure that no Egyptian Navy swimmers had slipped in and attached limpet mines to these vessels. None was found.

I think it was on about the third day we went across to Port Fuad on the other side of the canal where we found a bonded warehouse with lots of booze in it. We decided that this would make a better base than sleeping on our LCT every night so we brought all our kit ashore and settled in here before continuing our duties. The following day a huge French battlewagon came into the canal and anchored close by. When we got back that evening we were greeted by a unit of heavily armed Foreign Legion troops off the cruiser and they made it clear that Port Fuad was theirs so sheepishly we departed, but with our tool boxes topped up with duty free booze.

After the ceasefire we headed up the canal towards Ismailia and the Bitter Lakes for the purpose of clearing any left-over Second World War and even more recent munitions until we were relieved by another clearance diving team that had been sent out from Britain.

During the rest of my Navy service I belonged to several dive teams in the UK, Hong Kong and Singapore where I was involved in bomb and mine disposal and training new divers. By the time I left the Navy in 1963 I had reached the dizzy height of Petty Officer Diver 2nd Class. In Civvy Street I became a policeman in Eastbourne.

HMS *Vernon* has now gone, its position having been taken by Gunwharfe, a posh shopping complex.

* * *

Ronnie H Hulton, Merchant Navy.

Ronnie, who was a merchant seaman for 39 years especially with the Atlantic Steam Navigation Company, was not actually involved in the Suez Crisis itself but came into contact with others who were and consequently acquired his own collection of photographs pertaining to *Operation Musketeer* which were circulating at that time.

The Atlantic Steam Navigation Company, which operated from 1946 until 1971, was founded by Lt Col Frank Bustard. It initially operated three ships for the Ministry of War Transport which were the LSTs *Empire Baltic* (3519), *Empire Cedric* (3534), and *Empire Celtic* (3512). These were used to transport armed forces vehicles between Tilbury and Antwerp for the British Army of the Rhine (BAOR).

(In August 2011, shortly after loaning me his photographs, Ronnie died of asbestosis. Many thanks to Ronnie's widow Norma for her assistance in helping me to complete this contribution.)

Light aircraft personnel shuttle used between Cyprus and Port Said landing on one of the aircraft carriers.

LCT *Redoubt* (L4001)

A line-up of 'Empire' vessels at the quay: *Empire Cedric*, *Empire Gaelic*, *Empire Petrel*, *Empire Cymric*, and the RFA LST 3037 *Evan Gibb*.

Children scavenging for food.

Malcolm F Green, No.3 Field Squadron, 22 Regiment, Royal Engineers.

Malcolm Frederick Green was born on the 9th of June 1935 at Great Yarmouth in Norfolk and went to primary school at nearby Gorleston-on-Sea except for during the war when he was evacuated for a while. At the age of eleven he passed the 11+ examination and went on to Great Yarmouth Technical High School for his secondary education and left in the summer of 1951 when he'd just turned 16 to become an apprentice bricklayer.

In about May 1954, three years into his apprenticeship, Malcolm was called for his National Service medical at Norwich. Shortly afterwards he learned that he was to join the Royal Engineers and reported to his training unit on his 19th birthday in June. Following training at Farnborough and some time spent in a holding unit his posting came through; it was to 22 Regiment in Libya.

At this stage Malcolm and his fiancée Jean decided to get married so that they could save the marriage allowance while she continued to live with her parents. They took out a special licence and made it just in time, tying the knot on 2 October during Malcolm's embarkation leave.

On the 27th of the month Malcolm went out to Libya where he joined his regiment at Gialo Barracks, Tripoli. Here he was assigned to No.3 Squadron. Malcolm also signed on for a third year's service to take advantage of the extra pay.

In January 1956, after 15 months of training and various desert exercises, 3 Squadron was detached from the regiment and posted to Cyprus to bolster the number of troops fighting EOKA. On its arrival in Nicosia the Squadron was installed at the CBS Barracks just outside the town.

For most of 1956 during that time of intense EOKA activity the squadron carried out the usual routines of patrols and searches together with some exercises including one in October when they went out to a coastal location to brush up on their Bailey bridge-building skills. By now they realised that something serious was imminent.

Bridge-building on pontoons at the beach.

Early in November the squadron was put on alert with the lads ordered to get all their kit together. The following day they were trucked to Limassol where they were ferried out on lighters to the *Empire Ken* for the journey to Port Said. A day later they were entering Port Said harbour.

The *Empire Ken* viewed from the *Empire Parkeston*.

Part of the convoy seen from the *Empire Ken*.

The French hospital ship *La Marseillaise* in the convoy.

Ashore Malcolm's troop was billeted for the first night in a cinema next to the waterfront park. They could look down from the balcony upon another troop below staying with their trucks.

Overlooking the south (left) side of the park is the three-storey cinema with semi-circular balconies. On the opposite (north side) of the park is the Casino Palace Hotel.

View from the third-floor cinema balcony of some of the No.3 Squadron lads bivouacking in the park below.

View to the left of the Casino Palace Hotel showing the flats behind the '40 Commando' assault beach.

Three sappers on the cinema balcony looking down and across the park and out towards the mouth of the Canal.

View from the cinema balcony of the Casino Palace Hotel and ships berthed in the outer harbour close to the mole.

The cinema on the south side of the park.

The view south down the Canal from the balcony. The nearby Lighthouse to the right. The oil tank is still burning.

The Lighthouse just to the south of the cinema..

Some of the sappers by the cinema building entrance.

Diagonal view to the right across the boulevard from the front of the Railway Station.

After that first night spent at the cinema Malcolm's troop moved its billet to the school immediately next to the Port Said Railway Station. From here they went out the following morning to begin building a pontoon Bailey bridge next to the Girder bridge at Raswa. This crossed the side canal that came off the Suez Canal and led to the Industrial Basin built to provide access to the town's inland wharves via the back of the prison as far as the Gas Works.

The Raswa Bridge passed over a narrowing of this canal which separated the Bassin De Raccordement, or Connection Basin coming off the Suez Canal just south of the Bassin Abbas Hilmi, from the main length of the Industrial Basin canal.

Although French Paratroopers had taken the Raswa Bridge undamaged early on day one of the invasion a smaller one crossing the short length of the Bassin De Raccodement had been blown up earlier. It was the job of the No.3 Squadron sappers to replace it, at least as a temporary measure.

The El Raswa Bridge.

Three sections of Bailey bridge built on pontoons.

A group of the lads taking a 'NAAFI' break. A Bedford RL three-tonner truck to the left and a low-loader behind.

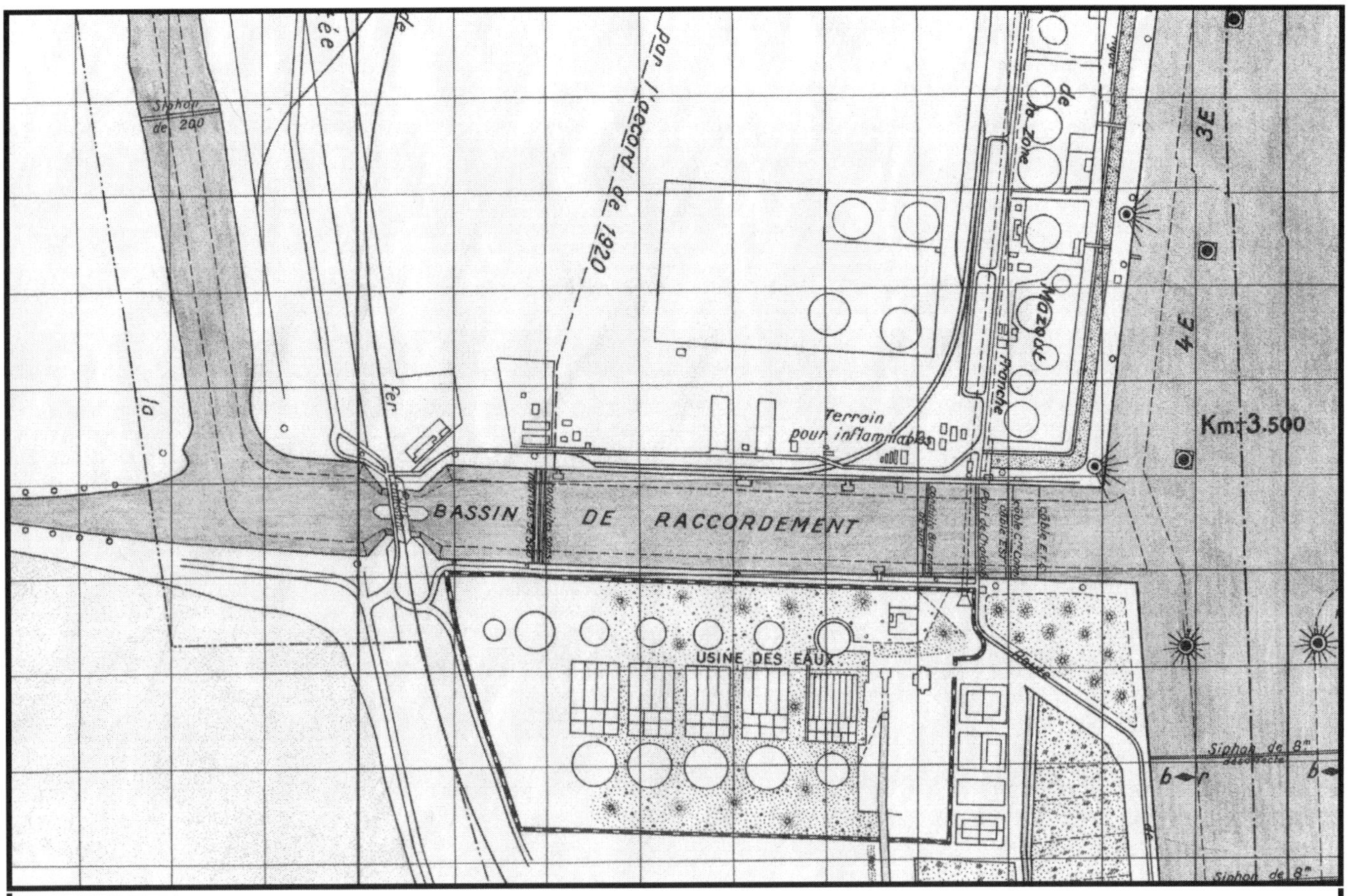

The Razwa road-rail bridge, captured by French paratroopers, can be seen resting on its elongated pier at the western (left) end of the Bassin De Raccordement. The bridge that was blown up is presumably the Pont de Chaland which carried the coast road over this side canal. It was close to this that 3 Squadron built their pontoon Bailey bridge. The Usine Des Eaux at the bottom of the map is the Water Works. The branch canal going north leads to the town wharves.

The Raswa bridge.

Looking north along the canal coast road towards Raswa.

At the end of the second day a ceasefire took place. After that it was mainly a matter of filling in time until the withdrawal which came about a month later when the squadron returned to Nicosia to continue in the struggle against EOKA.

Towards the end of his National Service Malcolm flew back to the UK on a chartered Britavia aircraft. This presumably was because there were insufficient national servicemen approaching their demob date at this time to warrant the use of a troopship. He was demobbed on the 8th of June 1957 after which he returned to the building trade to continue as a bricklayer in the Great Yarmouth area for the rest of his working life which he extended until he was about 68. Malcolm was released from the Reserve on 8 June 1969.

* * *

John Alan Page, No.3 Field Sqn Royal Engineers.

I was born in Islington, London on 9 August 1936 and lived there until 1939 when we moved to Highgate which is where I began school at Highgate Primary School in North Hill in 1941.

During the Blitz we were bombed out of our house in Archway Road but after a while it was repaired and we moved back in. In my last year at school I sat next to Rod Stewart's brother Bob with his sister Peggy in front of me. They all lived across the road from me.

When I left school I went to work at Industrial Electrical Ltd where my training included rewinding and repairing AC and DC motors and switch gear. I was here from 1950 until 1954.

In November 1954, three months after reaching my 18th birthday I was called up for my National Service. I don't know why but I signed on for three years, choosing to join the Royal Engineers. First I went to No.1 TRRE at Malvern Wells in Worcestershire for three months then to No.9 Training Regiment at Cove in Hampshire for my full training. After passing out I was sent to No.12 RSME (Royal School of Military Engineering) at Brompton Barracks, Chatham where I took the course to became a BII electrician.

I left Chatham on Thursday 2 February 1956 and spent the night at the transit unit attached to London's Goodge Street Underground Station. From here I was taken to Blackbushe Airport near Farnborough and flown out on an Eagle Aviation aircraft to join No.6 Field Park Squadron at Tripoli in Libya with a stop at Malta on the way. I stayed with the unit for about three months before sailing to Cyprus on the troopship *Charles McLeod* with a stop along the way at Benghazi. On arrival I was trucked to Nicosia where I became part of No.3 Field Squadron based at the CBS (Cyprus Broadcasting Station) camp. Also there was a unit of the REME and one of the KOYLI.

The 3 Field Squadron tent lines at the CBS Camp.

I worked as an electrician at Nicosia Prison and on detachment at a new outdoor prison at Pyla, Larnaka where we erected poles and overhead lines to supply power. I also wired up the lights of Government House in Nicosia for the Queen's birthday party held there.

Accommodation built for the prison at Pyla.

John setting up security lights at Pyla prison.

I think it must have been perhaps in early to mid -October that most of the squadron went out to a tented camp somewhere on the south coast of the island where we were to carry out a period of training in watermanship and Bailey bridge assembly. We didn't know at the time that we were in fact getting in some practice for the Suez crisis. While there I was in charge of the diesel generator which was handy because I could put my washing to dry on the radiator.

View to the mountains from the camp on the beach.

As well as being an electrician I was also the troop storeman so shortly afterwards when the order came to prepare for the invasion of Egypt it was my responsibility to supervise the loading of the troop stores onto a Bedford RL lorry. I accompanied the driver to Famagusta where we drove onto the troop carrier *Charles McLeod.*

The ex-LST, now troop carrier, *Charles McCloud* at Famagusta. Operated by the Atlantic Steam Navigation Co.

The *Charles McLeod* loaded to capacity with trucks.

On 4 November we sailed first to Limassol and then to Port Said the following day. The rest of the squadron went on the *Empire Ken* troopship.

View from the *Charles McCloud* as it arrives in the outer harbour of the Suez Canal on the 6th of November.

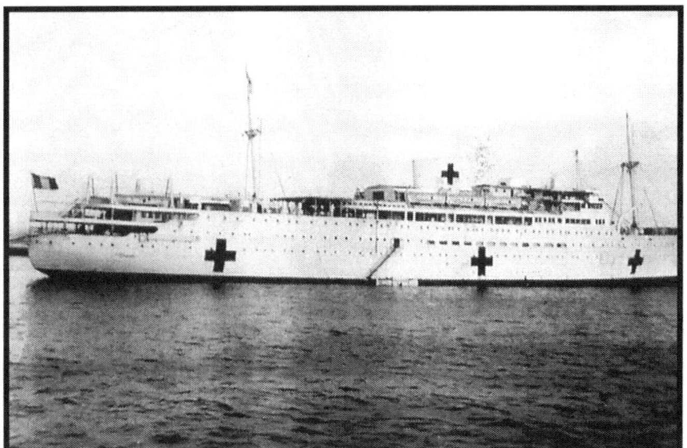

View from the *Charles McLeod* of the French hospital ship *La Marseillaise* anchored in the outer harbour.

After waiting some time in the harbour we landed on the quay at Port Said during the afternoon of the 6th with the sound of some small arms fire still echoing around the town. I was quite lucky really since we just drove the Bedford RL 3-tonner off the landing craft near the Casino Palace Hotel while the rest of the lads had to clamber down nets hanging off the side of their ship into smaller craft before they could go ashore.

My troop made camp for the night in a small park on the waterfront next to the Casino Palace Hotel which was very close to where we went ashore. Some of the other lads in the squadron commandeered a cinema in the street at the side of the park. There was still some sniper fire taking place which led to our captain calling on the Marines, or it may have been ten or so of our lads, to sort it out. After a while the firing stopped. None of our unit had been hurt.

While we were there in the park some civilian lorries arrived with the bodies of Egyptians who had been killed in the fighting. We soon got fed up with the flies they were attracting until they got buried.

The following day we left the cinema and the park and moved to a school building alongside Port Said railway station. I still slept in the back of the truck to look after the troop's gear. Late that night the ceasefire took place.

Photograph taken from a balcony at the secondary school next to the railway station.

John on one of the platforms at the railway station.

Some of our lads were called on to clear up the lines in the station sidings while others had to remove stuff that had found its way into the Sweet Water Canal. Luckily I didn't get that job because I had to stay with the truck.

On the 8th we heard that one of our squadron officers, 26-year-old, Sandhurst-trained, Lt Arthur Hercy Pipe-Wolferson, had just been killed clearing a mine or some explosives.

On 24 November a train arrived at the station carrying wounded Egyptian soldiers from their lines south of El Cap. They were presumably coming for treatment. Their Para escorts who took them through the station to the road outside came under siege from a mob of locals. The situation started to look nasty and our sergeant called us out of the school in support. A ceasefire had come into effect on the 7th and consequently we were not allowed to fire so we were ordered to fix bayonets instead. Things soon quietened down.

The crowd of locals outside the railway station. Photograph taken from the balcony of the adjacent school.

On the 10th of December I flew back to Nicosia as part of the advance party and remained there with 3 Squadron for the second year of my National Service during the continuing EOKA terrorist campaign. In summer we used to go on swimming trips to Kyrenia. As they needed a lifesaver on these occasions they sent me on a course which was held at Golden Sands Camp in Famagusta. At the end of the course I got a medal. On these outings to Kyrenia I patrolled the bathing area with a collapsible boat powered by a Petter's engine. Just by the castle there was an area of the sea that was just a fraction shallow for satisfactory games of water polo so we attached some explosives to the sea bed and made it a little deeper.

When my three years service was drawing to a close I joined some other Cyprus servicemen coming up for demob and flew out from Nicosia to Southend Airport on a government charter flight. From there I went to Barton Stacey transit camp in Hampshire and left the Army a few days later. Sometimes afterward I was sent the General Service Medal with a bar for taking part in the Suez crisis.

Back home I got a job at the Pye Radio factory in Islington N7 where I started as a coil winder. Later I was made up to foreman in charge of the radio and television assembly shop. When the factory closed down I moved from Highgate, where I lived, to Dagenham and went to work at the Thorn Consumer Factory at Chigwell, Essex. I worked on Ferguson radios as superintendent of the coil assembly cabinet. After a while I was made redundant because of the factory closing down.

Then I got a job as a foreman at Gould's in charge of assembling marine oscilloscopes. I was made redundant again when this factory closed down. This time I found myself a job at Labcraft as foreman in charge of making low voltage lights. I was made redundant yet again when the factory closed down.

From here I went to Rose Green Hospital as the maintenance electrician until the hospital closed down. At this stage I retired but then began working two days a week at Harold Wood Hospital at Havering, until that closed down too.

* * *

Harold Bentham, 3 Field Sqn, Royal Engineers.

The sunk Canal Company tug *Hercule* was finally raised by the converted French LCT 525 and the RFA vessel *Kingarth* on 29 December. The Canal Company building behind.

A blockship opposite the Port Said Engineering Works.

View from the *Empire Ken* of the Casino Palace Hotel.

Sailing ships in the yacht Basin.

Three Field Squadron's pontoon Bailey bridge built across the Bassin de Raccordement at Raswa.

Just good friends! Note the factory again.

Harold Bentham and Frank Shepherd in Port Said.

Local 'bobby' getting involved. A squaddy's rifle appearing in the photograph to the lower right.

Disturbance outside the Railway Station. The Paras and the sappers of 3 Squadron help the crown to disperse. Note the factory on the right and in the next photographs.

The platforms of the station seen from the side of the adjacent school. A United Nations train has just arrived.

UN peacekeeping troops waiting to detrain at Port Said.

* * *

Frank Church, 3 Field Sqn, Royal Engineers.

I was born on 25 September 1935 in a small terraced house in Alexander Road, Denton, a district of Gravesend in Kent on the side of the River Thames.

I can recall from when I was only five, which was the time I began attending Whitehill County Primary Mixed School, a battery of ack-ack guns being set up at the bottom of our road. They were placed there to intercept the aircraft of the Luftwaffe whose crews used the Thames estuary as a guide into the heart of London at the time of the Blitz. The Germans soon knew the guns were there and replied by trying to knock them out. As a result we were constantly bombed.

In one raid a time bomb landed in the road outside our house and we were evacuated to a nearby school. When the bomb exploded it blew out the front of the house leaving us homeless. Eventually we were taken in by family friends at Kings Farm in Poplar Avenue until the authorities were able to find accommodation for us. Soon after this I started to witness the dog fights that use to take place above our heads and since Gravesend had its own fighter aerodrome I spent the rest of the war watching the comings and goings of the aircraft based there.

In 1946, a year after the end of the war, I went to Whitehill County Modern School for a couple of years until, in 1948, I passed the second-chance 13+ examination and was given a place at Gravesend Technical College where I joined the boxing club and particularly enjoyed it. On leaving I obtained an apprenticeship as a carpenter and joiner with Edward Brothers, a Gravesend joinery firm. Over the next five years I attended night school and ended my time in May 1956 after taking the exams and obtaining an Ordinary National Certificate in building construction.

With the completion of my apprenticeship I married my girlfriend Joyce. We needed to get permission to marry because we were under 21, the age of consent at that time. Our honeymoon period didn't last long. That brown envelope containing the words 'You will report to Military Road, Chatham for a medical,' dropped through the letterbox and onto the mat. This was the beginning of an eventful two years.

My National Service started on Empire Day 24 May 1956. I joined the Royal Engineers at Merebrook Camp at Malvern in Worcestershire and spent the next 12 days undergoing a further medical check, haircut, kitting out, drill, getting fit, and getting used to a routine to prepare us for what was still to come.

On 6 June we were transferred by train to Cove in Farnborough, where we joined No.9 Training Regiment RE as group 910 (No.9 TRRE's 10th fortnightly intake of the year) where the real sapper training began. This included bridge-building, explosives, ropes and knots, barbed wire entanglements, watermanship, weaponry and the like, together with much bull and sweat expended in square bashing. After tests most of us passed as BIII Engineers.

Following the pass-out parade sometime in August we were moved to a transit area locally to await a posting. This was a very boring time doing just menial tasks around the camp although we were able to get 48-hour passes every fortnight which allowed me time with my wife who was worried about where I would be sent.

Eventually, after about two months, our postings came through; mine and some of the others were to Cyprus. On 22 October we sailed from Southampton aboard HMS *Theseus*. It was a great voyage. We called at Gibraltar then Malta where we left the carrier and transferred to the troopship *Empire Ken* for the final part of our journey to Cyprus.

We disembarked offshore at Famagusta and went by smaller boats into the harbour where a number of lorries were waiting to take us to our new unit, No.3 Field Squadron RE, based just outside Nicosia, the capital of the island. This was to be my unit for the rest of my National Service.

Apart from the office block, the dining room and the NAAFI, we were all housed under canvas, about 300 of us I think. Our OC was Major Kenneth McTaggart.

Our stay in Nicosia was short-lived, *Operation Musketeer* was about to start. In early November, after just two days, the whole squadron was transported to Limassol where we met up with the *Empire Ken* again and sailed for Port Said at the entrance to the Suez Canal where we arrived on the sixth.

Eventually we were able to anchor in the harbour and when they were ready for us ashore we disembarked onto what seemed to be a chaotic quayside. After quite a wait our troop and one of the others were marched just a short distance along the quay, accompanied by the smell of smoke in the air and the sporadic sound of small arms fire, to a building which we found was a cinema where we were to spend the night. We spread our single blankets on the concrete floor, ate our emergency rations, and then tried to sleep.

The following morning we went on parade and learned that it was going to be our job to build a Bailey bridge over the Interior Basin Canal which led off the Suez Canal to the south of Port Said at Raswa. It was at this time that we saw two or three trucks arrive on the wide long road near our cinema and some squaddies beginning to unload a great many dead bodies and stacking them on the grass verge. The dead from the fighting over the past couple of days had to be buried somewhere, and soon.

Some chaps from the RAMC had been given the job of searching the bodies for dog-tags or identification of some kind, presumably so that the Egyptian authorities could notify the next of kin; what a job it must have been for them. A digger also arrived at this time and began excavating a trench in the central grassy area of the road nearby and this is where the squad that came with the lorries put the bodies to rest, if only temporarily.

When we got to Raswa we found that the Bailey bridge was to be erected on pontoons to replace the one that had been destroyed the previous day by the Egyptians on their retreat south. The French paratroopers had managed to capture intact the permanent road/rail bridge crossing this canal a short distance away.

Construction of the bridge was really heavy going and took us three days. However our tanks and heavy armour never needed to use the bridge because a ceasefire came into affect soon after we got it started.

By this time we were billeted not in the cinema but in a school adjacent to the Port Said Railway Station. The classrooms made ideal billets although we still had to sleep on the floor. The flat roof of the building with a parapet made a good place for guarding the building and watching the surrounding area. I had my share of guard duties on this roof, some of them at night when it got quite cold. After a few days we had set up a cookhouse for ourselves in the teachers' staff room using portable ovens fired by oil. For the first few days we lived mainly on corned beef and porridge.

View from the school of one of the platforms and the rear of the main concourse building of the railway station.

Although the conflict was quickly over we found that we were not going to be withdrawn for some time. Those of us who were carpenters were taken each day to a deserted builder's yard some distance away which was stacked with 4 x 2 lengths of timber. We were given the job of making up double bunk beds whose supports for the mattress were made of pieces of one-inch wide metal strapping normally used to hold packing cases together. These were for the use of the squadron personnel and the job kept us busy for quite some time.

After a while we were allowed to take a walk in the town as long as we were in pairs or more. One day while some of us were out and about a voice called from across the road, 'Churchy, what are you doing here?' It was my brother-in-law Jack, a sapper reservist who had been called back and was billeted in the German Consulate.

After about four weeks at Port Said we sailed back to Cyprus and arrived at our camp in Nicosia on 2 December. We remained on the island for a further year during which, among our several duties, was the construction of a number of small Nissen type huts used for various purposes including office storage and accommodation for EOKA prisoners. We also participated in two exercises in the Troodos Mountains. Also during my time in Cyprus a new officer, 2nd Lt Roger Kirk, joined the squadron. I discovered he was the brother of Peter Kirk, our Gravesend MP.

We left Cyprus on 2 December 1957 aboard the troopship *Dunera* and sailed to Tripoli in Libya where the other 22 Field Engineer Regiment squadrons came aboard to join us before we continued on to Malta and the UK. The voyage was great with plenty of sunshine and good food until, that is, we sailed into the Bay of Biscay and met waves that must have been 20 to 30 feet high. The storm added a couple of days on the journey to Southampton.

After Christmas leave I reported back to Chiseldon on the south-east of Swindon where the regiment was based and that is where I served out the rest of my National Service until discharged on 24 May 1958. In the time I was here Lt Kirk got permission through his brother to take a number of us up to London for the day where we were able to visit the House of Commons.

For a while I went back to my old firm but soon realised, perhaps after my time in the Army, that being inside all day was not for me so I left and teamed up with a bricklayer I knew and started a small building company. This brought in a modest income for six years until we parted, each going our own way.

In 1995 my brother, also a carpenter, found himself over-extended with work and asked me to finish off some jobs at Gillingham Football Club ground for him. After a while the club chairman Paul Scally invited me to work for the club permanently. This was the time when Tony Pulis was the manager. I accepted and remained with the club until the year 2,000 when I retired.

* * *

John Challis, 8 Squadron, Movement Control, Royal Engineers.

I was born at Wembley in January 1935 and educated through primary level at St Mary's School, Twickenham before attending The Quintin Grammar School in Regent Street, London W1.

As far as I was concerned, the main advantage enjoyed by all those who attended Quintin was the superlative sports facilities available. I spent more time at the sports ground at Chiswick than at the school buildings in Regent Street, especially when I was the school cricket captain. I have to admit that all the prizes and trophies I won were sports connected. Despite this, however, I went on to take 'O' and 'A' Levels, finishing at Quintin's in the summer of 1953.

My medical examination for National Service was taken at Bromyard Avenue, Acton, where I was persuaded by a recruiting sergeant to sign on for 22 years with a three-year option: well, what else did I have to do? This decision had several awkward consequences.

Firstly my father, who had been a Lt Colonel in the Royal Engineers during the Second World War, having served in Jaffa, Alexandria, Port Said, and in Cairo as AQMG by the war's end, went apoplectic. 'How can you get a short-service commission if you have signed on as a regular?' he wanted to know.

Secondly, after being kitted out at Norton Camp near Worcester I was sent for three weeks basic training to No.1 TRRE at Merebrook Camp, Malvern. and it was here that I had my most embarrassing moment in the army. When I was asked, after two weeks of my initial training, what trade I would like I replied that I wanted a commission and to serve in Movement Control. When the sergeant asked me why I wanted a commission I replied, 'My father said that I should ask for one.' The sergeant turned to the sergeant major and said, 'Oh, Daddy says he should have one!' I still blush when I think of it. How naïve I was then!

John during his three week's basic training.

Eventually I went to one of the RE training camps at Cove near Farnborough for what seemed an eternity. I don't think I realised at first that this was also serving as pre-WOSB training, not that it made any difference in the end because when I eventually went to face the War Office Selection Board at Barton Stacey I failed. That was when they stopped calling you sir.

From here I went on a cadre course back at Cove after which I gained a stripe and was posted to Longmoor in Hampshire, the military railway headquarters run by the Royal Engineers. Here I started a 12 month trade course as a traffic operator with the training squadron.

The first part of the course involved learning to be a shunter. When I was given a shunting pole and enquired if this had anything to do with Movement Control, which is what I was interested in, I was told with a smirk that if I didn't move my arms quicker I would lose one of them. However, despite moments like this, I enjoyed my time at Longmoor. Little did I realise then that a few months later I would operate a signal box, what we referred to as block posts, with more than 50 levers and emerge as a traffic operator with promotion to full corporal controlling a line at the Longmoor Military Railway.

Looking back I remember learning a very valuable lesson when I first took over the Longmoor Downs Box. When a civilian platelayer named Jock saw my initial concern at the responsibility I'd been given he said, 'Look Sapper, if you don't know what to do, put all the pegs (signals) at danger, then if there is a crash it's not your f…ing fault.' Good lesson that!

John in the signal box at Longmoor, Hampshire.

Well, just as my three-year option to leave the army fell due in the summer of 1956, and which I was going to take, Colonel Nasser in Egypt decided to nationalise the Suez Canal. Being a traffic operator I was one of those 'selected' for service in Egypt. Before long the reservists started arriving at Longmoor and I was put in charge of them, including a couple of lads who had been corporals at Guillemont Barracks when I'd been undergoing training there and who had given me a hard time. Now I was the corporal and they were back as sappers. The palliasses they got weren't the best.

There were about 32 of us from 8 Squadron chosen for the Egypt draft. They included Captain Richardson, S/Sgt Harrison and S/Sgt 'Bull' Stevenson. Towards the end of October we were transported to Southampton where we went aboard the troopship *Empire Orwell* and set sail for the

The *Empire Orwell*.

John on the *Empire Orwell*.

John again, on the left.

The room in the dome of the Port Authority building.

Two of the salvage vessels attending to a blockship.

Mediterranean, stopping briefly at Malta before continuing on to Cyprus.

We arrived offshore at the port of Limassol where we disembarked down the side of the ship via scrambling nets into lighters that appeared to rise and then fall about 20 feet as we were about to let go.

Once ashore we were taken by trucks to the nearby Akrotiri RAF base where we boarded a flight bound for the El Gamil airfield at Port Said. By this time *Operation Musketeer* had already begun and the airfield was secure. As we went aboard the Valetta aircraft, which was one of those that had recently taken 3 Para and 16 Independent Parachute Brigade there before us, I asked the pilot for a parachute. 'You won't need one,' he replied, 'We never get that high.'

On arrival at the airfield we were driven into Port Said and billeted in the Suez Canal Port Authority building on the canal side. I decided to make my living quarters in the dome at the top of the building. This led to an altercation with a staff sergeant in the RASC who felt that since he was on General Stockwell's staff I should have sought his permission first. However, to cut a long story short, we eventually discovered that he was engaged to the girl who had introduced me to my future wife. Small world! Alan Williamson would become best man at my wedding. Unfortunately Alan died earlier this year (2011) to bring an end to the regular lunches we had enjoyed together since the time we were demobbed.

Eventually we got down to the business of operating the railway line between Port Said railway station and El Cap on the cease-fire line. The track was just a single line and I was told to keep a record of the number of axles moved (the army term used for the number of journeys made by a train) because we were going to get reparation from Nasser, presumably for the diesel used. Some hope! I was involved in the running of a train from

View to the rear of the Port Said railway station building.

Viewing along the frontage of the railway station. Protruding beyond are the three adjacent secondary schools.

The El Raswa road-rail bridge on the line to El Cap.

View from the eastern side of Port Said railway station overlooking the covered platforms.

Four of the squadron lads on a locomotive somewhere between Port Said and El Cap.

the station in Port Said to El Cap about once a day. Apart from that I wasn't over busy.

The most notable event for 8 Squadron, apart from when one of our drivers, Geordie Foster, was shot in the knee by a careless French legionnaire, was bringing the first UN troops, who we called Bluebells, into Port Said on the train from the cease fire line at El Cap.

A Sikh (UN?) soldier and the Deputy Stationmaster of El Cap station enjoying a conversation on the platform.

A group of UN peacekeeping troops recently arrived at El Cap before continuing their train journey to Port Said.

However, where they were concerned I didn't cover myself in glory on that occasion after sending them to one canal-side basin when the reception party waiting for them was at one of the others. No wonder I didn't get an MBE like S/Sgts Stevenson and Harrison.

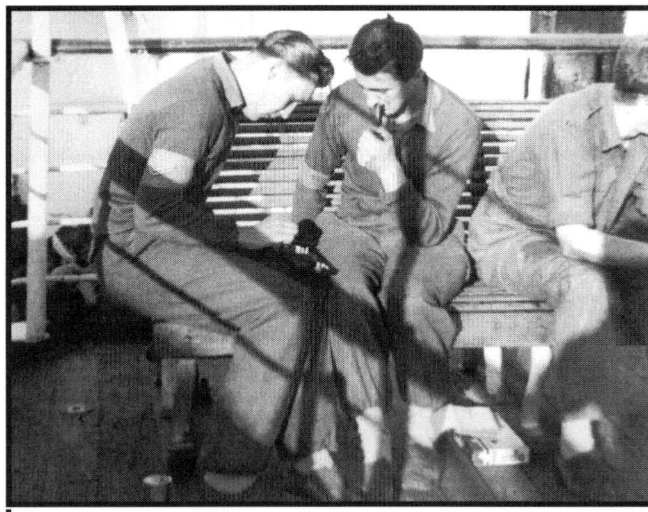

John playing chess on the *New Australia.*

We left Port Said towards the end of December on the *New Australia.* As we were preparing to depart I remember seeing a Cadillac being lifted aboard one of the ships. On our arrival at Southampton we were made to stand for hours and hours while customs made sure that we weren't smuggling valuables. I wonder if they caught the 2nd Lieutenant who nicked the Cadillac. Of course, belonging to No. 8 Squadron, we had a train laid on that took us directly to Longmoor from where I was demobbed the following day.

Before I arrived home from Egypt I had already obtained a position in a department of the Foreign Office in Whitehall where I spent an enjoyable three years until I decided to go into commerce to try and earn some real money as a salesman. At least the firm gave me a car and I became the national sales manager of a multi-national food company for a while until I decided to try running my own business – without a great deal of success I have to say. Eventually I found myself in financial services, becoming a branch manager until I retired at the age of 60.

During this period I played cricket at Teddington and Chertsey until I was 50 at which time I took up golf. Now I'm retired I do that all the time, except when my marvellous wife and daughters tell me what I should be doing with my time. What I really like is playing granddad to my two granddaughters. Little did I think that an argument with a staff sergeant in the dome of the Suez Canal Company building in Port Said would have such a beneficial effect on my future life.

* * *

Dave J Brewer, Royal Engineers, Movement Control HQ South West, Camp 10, Southampton.

David John Brewer was born on 3 July 1936 in Margate, Kent but six months later the family went to live in Exeter. When he came up to the age of eleven he passed the Scholarship Examination and entered Exeter Hele Grammar School. After taking 'School Certificate' when nearly 16 Dave left school in the summer of 1952 and was engaged by the Western Region of British Railways at Cullompton.

Dave was called up at the age of eighteen-and-a-half and reported to No.1 TRRE at Malvern Wells in February 1955 for basic training. He found the anticipated two years separation from Mary, his girlfriend of two years, unthinkable and he vividly remembers writing '730 days to do' on his enlistment day and religiously going on to mark off the remaining days for the whole two years. It was a bitterly cold February in Worcestershire and the whole area was blanketed in snow for most of the six weeks Dave spent at Malvern.

Among conscripts it was generally thought that whatever one's civilian occupation happened to be the services did their utmost to put you into something completely different. So, having worked as a junior clerk with British Rail, Dave was somewhat surprised when he was allocated to a branch of the Royal Engineers called Movement Control and sent for trade training at Longmoor in Hampshire, the home of the Military Railway. It was a 'sod of a place' to get back to whenever Dave had been home on leave in Exeter – all the way to Waterloo Station in London, then to Liss where he caught the Royal Engineers' own train, the Bullet, to Longmoor Camp.

Dave spent several months at Longmoor and one of many memories he has of his time there is helping to stand night guard over the set of the train crash scene in the making of the film Bhowani Junction starring Stewart Granger and Ava Gardner. Dave didn't even see Ava during her time at Longmoor and much of the crash scene was made of timber and cardboard anyway.

Eventually Dave was given his official posting which was to Movement Control, HQ South West, at Gate 10 Southampton. The camp consisted of rows of very basic Nissen huts situated on a strip of wasteland between the railways station and the civilian docks. The job entailed providing the clerical back-up to all the movements of military personnel and freight to and from the ports between Portsmouth to Plymouth which incorporated all the troopships, naval vessels, and civilian liners involving a military connection. The work hours were unsociable to say the least. Ships arrived and departed according to the tides and it was not unusual to be on duty for two or three days and nights continuously. Occasionally it was possible to just snatch a 'kip' in the back of one of the thousands of cars lined up on the wharves for shipment abroad.

Dave (front), and his mate Dave Burton, at Gate 10.

Surprisingly quickly, Dave feels, he rose to the 'dizzy heights' of lance corporal and his most outstanding memory of this period is of the degree of responsibility and decision-making that was thrust upon him. Through the summer and autumn of 1956, because of the Suez Canal crisis, a huge number of military personnel and amounts of equipment had to be transported from England to the Middle East in the shortest possible time.

A normal Movements Control embarkation detail consisted of a major, captain, staff sergeant, corporal, lance corporal and three or four sappers. However, the demands on the Southampton-based unit far outweighed the staff available. Consequently, on the second of August, Dave, now Corporal Brewer, was transferred to H M Dockyard at Plymouth with two sappers to 'kick-start' the loading of personnel, tanks and arms onto ships for transportation to what would become a war zone.

He had left Southampton with the promise that within forty-eight hours a full complement of officers, etc., would follow to take charge. However, the scale of the operation never allowed the higher military echelons to appear with any consistency. Consequently this nineteen-year-old corporal, assisted occasionally by two sappers, was basically left by himself to mastermind the complete embarkation of men and loading of materials at Plymouth docks.

Dave returned to Southampton on 4 of September. Events then returned to relative normality for a while until early November when the invasion of Port Said took place and Dave began travelling to and fro between Southampton and Plymouth again. It was at about this time that Gate 10 Camp was transferred to an ultra-modern camp at Botley just outside the town.

Just prior to his demobilization in February 1957 Dave was called before the colonel and offered a third stripe to sign on as a regular. By now, however, he had got the 730 days down to single figures and his mind was made up to return to Civvy Street. In the Queen's birthday Honours List a few months later Dave was awarded the British Empire Medal for outstanding unsupervised work with considerable executive responsibility during the Suez Emergency.

BUCKINGHAM PALACE

I greatly regret that I am unable to give you personally the award which you have so well earned.

I now send you my congratulations and my best wishes for your future happiness.

Elizabeth R

Corporal David J. Brewer, B.E.M.

Corps of Royal Engineers.

Letter sent to David Brewer from Buckingham Palace following his award of the British Empire Medal

The medal was presented by Major General H A Borradaile, GOC South-Western District at Topsham Barracks, Exeter.

From Major General R.A. Bramwell-Davis,CB,DSO.

Telephone: Aldershot 380

HEADQUARTERS
ALDERSHOT DISTRICT
ALDERSHOT

1st June,1957.

Cpl. D.J. Brewer,BEM,
i/c Freight Section
(Stores Ships),
HQ (MC) Port of Southampton,
Southampton, Hants.

I am very pleased to hear that you have been awarded the British Empire Medal in The Queen's Birthday Honours. I offer you my congratulations on the award and am very glad to know that your services to the Army have been recognised by Her Majesty.

R.A. Bramwell Davis
Major General,
General Officer Commanding,
Aldershot District.

Letter to Dave from Major General R A Bramwell-Davis.

* * *

Major Angus I M Gregor MacGregor, FACI, MInst RE, 16 Field Squadron, Royal Engineers.

At the time of the Suez crisis I was commanding 16 Field Squadron Royal Engineers which was part of 35 Corps Engineer Regiment based at Ripon in Yorkshire. The regiment was moved down to Marchwood, the base of 17 Port Training Regiment RE, for stevedore training. Here we 'absorbed' 653 Port Operations Squadron into our No.16 Field Squadron.

The troopship S S *Asturias*.

Early in November we embarked on the troopship *Asturias* in Southampton which stopped at Malta for a few hours to take aboard extra supplies. While we were there I ordered 500 pars of socks, a number of battle batteries, and complete kits for two reserve officers who had been allocated to the squadron at the last moment and who had turned up at Southampton at the last minute with only what they stood up in. Their luggage had been sent in accordance with instructions as 'passenger luggage in advance' but they arrived first and we sailed without said luggage in advance. The other squadron commanders laughed at my order for 500 pairs of socks and asked me what I was going to do with them all.

The troopship came into Port Said past the long breakwater at the entrance to the Suez Canal and we disembarked at the quayside close to the Casino Palace Hotel. All the squadron's transport came

The lads of No.16 Squadron assembling some hundred yards along from the quay and the Casino Palace Hotel 'conservatory' after coming ashore.

to Port Said in an LST and had to be landed on the beach that extends behind the western breakwater. This included our 10-ton workshop lorry and the generator trailer behind it. This had been loaded last and was directly behind the bow doors. Trapped behind it were the tanks and armoured vehicles of the Royal Tank Regiment. The 10-tonner driver drove down the ramp and out of the way while the RTR vehicles came ashore to go where they had been instructed. Eventually our driver, a staff sergeant, got bored with the waiting and jumped down from his quite high cab, breaking his leg in the process. He was our only casualty

Initially we spent some time near the Governate building, some three-quarters of a mile west of the Casino Palace Hotel, until I decided to move the squadron back closer to the harbour area. We set up our marquees on the grass of the central reservation of the dual carriageway of Sea Road, a couple of hundred yards or so from the hotel.

Not long after our arrival in Port Said the CO of the regiment made contact with me pleading for some of my supply of socks. He also ordered me to hand over some of the battle batteries too.

Many days before the end of the final withdrawal Regimental HQ and the other squadrons of the regiment left Port Said and gradually the perimeter closed in towards us. My squadron was nearly the last to leave but I left part of one troop behind to escort General Stockwell to his ship the following day.

I managed to get the whole of 16 Squadron loaded into an LST at the quay and we sailed to Cyprus. On our arrival we couldn't enter Famagusta harbour as it was full and we waited at anchor in the bay for some hours until a storm warning was given when we upped anchor and went out to sea where we weathered the force 12 gale for over five days. Eventually, as the storm subsided we managed to enter the harbour where we went ashore and were transported to the NAAFI's Golden Sands holiday camp where we found the rest of 35 Regiment.

My squadron we given the task of clearing a large warehouse, known as Jack's House, of all the equipment the Reservists had left behind. We lived on the flat roof of the building. After some weeks we moved back to Britain and returned to Ripon.

* * *

John Burn, 16 Sqn, 35 Engineer Regiment, REs.

I was born on 12 October 1936 in Croydon, Surrey which is now the London Borough of Croydon. Because I lived in South London all through the Second World War while attending primary school I saw a lot of the bombing that took place there. One night while we were in our Anderson shelter in the back garden a bomb destroyed three houses only three doors away from us.

In July 1952 at the age of 15 I finished my education at the local secondary modern school and soon afterwards joined Samuel Stephens Ltd, a printing firm in Upper Norwood, South London, for a five-year apprenticeship in photogravure retouching, for which I signed the papers on 12 October, my 16th birthday.

As my 18th birthday approached, the time for National Service call-up, I had the opportunity to transfer to another department to train as a planner which was what I wanted to do. The management asked me to apply for a deferment from National Service for one year which I did. This was granted and I finally entered the services twelve months later at the age of 19 when I was called up to the Royal Engineers.

I reported to the RE training camp at Malvern in

Worcestershire on the 5 January 1956 as part of the 5601 intake. Here we were kitted out and given two weeks of basic training before being transferred by train to No.3 Training Regiment RE at Guillemont Barracks, Cove near Farnborough in Hampshire. This was where we began our real training to become field engineers and to carry out mine laying, mine detecting, bridge building, bridge destruction with explosives, and boat handling on Hawley Lake. We finished off this three months of training with a passing-put parade which my parents attended, receiving our postings, and being taken on a trip up to London for a show before going on leave.

John Burn.

The passing out parade at Guillemont Barracks, Cove.

John Burn on the extreme right of the photograph.

My posting was to 35 Engineer Regiment based at Ripon in Yorkshire where I joined No.16 Squadron at Deverell Barracks. The regiment had just returned from a tour of duty at Limassol in Cyprus and was being built back up to full strength with newly-trained sappers. After a while some of the sappers went off somewhere to help repair what I think was some flood damage to a river bank which left us a bit short-handed on camp. One day after parade some of us were ordered to report to the Sergeants' Mess to help at one of their evening functions. I ended up serving behind the bar, something which I found quite enjoyable. This led to my being offered a permanent job there which I accepted. From then on my only parade was the pay parade once a week.

By the end of July everyone realised that things were soon going to be happening following Nasser's nationalisation of the Suez Canal Company. It seemed obvious that the British and French Governments were intent on doing something about it because soon afterwards our squadron was sent off to the Royal Engineers Port Operations base at Marchwood near Southampton to train as stevedores which indicated that should we invade Egypt to take back the canal this was what we would be involved in.

At Marchwood, which lies on the bank of the River Test opposite Southampton, we joined up with 653 Port Operating Squadron, part of 276 Port Regiment (AER) whose personnel included reservists who mostly worked at the London docks. We trained at the water's edge on Cracknore Hard using winches and jibs to load and unload cargo and vehicles from a small 750-ton previously Africa Corps' stores ship, the KT3. This had been 'liberated' by the Royal Engineers in Hamburg harbour at the end of 1949 and brought across to Marchwood where it was renamed the *Empire Stevedore* and used as a training ship.

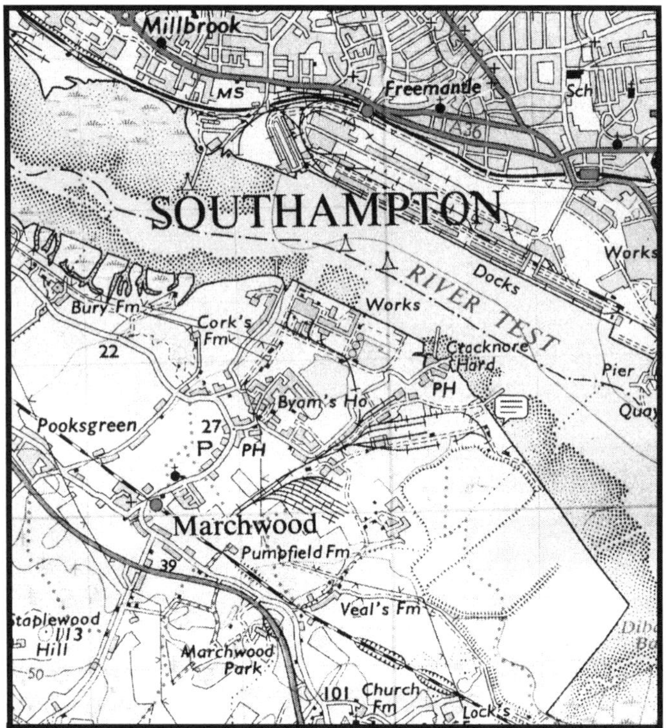

Extract from the 1960 one-inch to one-mile Ordnance Survey map of the Southampton-Marchwood area. With thanks to the Ordnance Survey.

The *Empire Stevedore*.

It rained fairly continuously throughout August and September and our training eventually came to an end when we were washed out of the tented accommodation and taken to Aldershot where we moved into permanent barracks. This had recently been vacated I believe by the Parachute Regiment which was now on its way to either Malta or Cyprus to be ready for the invasion, should this ever take place.

During October we did some weapons training with Sten guns which it was thought would be the best weapon for stevedores to use. Then, towards the end of the month, we were told that if we could get home and back in one day we could have a day's leave as we would be leaving for Southampton by train the following day. Since South London was not far away I managed to get home and back on time. I understand that some of the lads went AWOL. Just before departing we were each issued with a bandolier of 50 rounds of ammunition and a .303 Lee Enfield rifle, none of which, obviously, had been zeroed in to our personal requirements.

We sailed from Southampton aboard the troopship *Asturias* and called at Malta on the way to restock with supplies before continuing on to Port Said at the mouth of the Suez Canal.

Picture postcard sent by John to his parents just before sailing from Southampton for Egyptian waters,

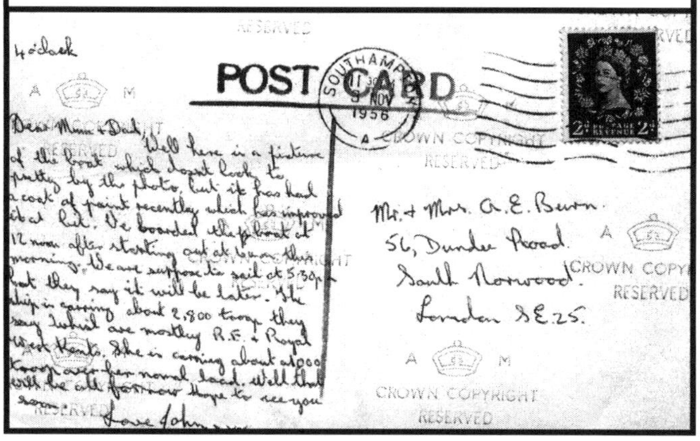
POST CARD

SOUTHAMPTON 1956

4 o'clock

Dear Mum & Dad, Well here is a picture of the boat which doesn't look so pretty by the photo, but it has had a coat of paint recently which has improved it a lot. We boarded the boat at 12 noon after starting out at 6 this morning. We are supposed to sail at 5.30pm but they say it will be later. The ship is carrying about 2,800 troops they say which are mostly R.E. & Royal West Kents. She is carrying about 1000 troops over her normal load. Well that's all for now. Hope to see you soon. Love John xxx

Mr + Mrs A.E. Burn.
56, Dundee Road.
South Norwood.
London SE.25.

CROWN COPYRIGHT RESERVED

We arrived at Port Said on the 9th of November shortly after the ceasefire had taken place. The area around the mouth of the canal and inside its entrance were full of Allied ships.

La Marseillaise anchored in the outer harbour.

Upon coming ashore we assembled on the road running up the side of the Casino Palace Hotel until we were taken to our billet in a school building situated along a road leading west a short distance across town that had been commandeered by the Army at some time before our arrival. I don't know

A photo that John came across on his arrival at the school.

why the earlier occupants of the school shown in the photograph should have taken furniture into the school yard and be stoking a fire.

Once settled into our billet we were taken to the quay where we made a start on the job of unloading supplies from the various ships anchored in the harbour.

Much of our work involved unloading jerrycans of petrol from the holds of ships into barges drawn up alongside just as we had done at Marchwood using each ship's own jibs and winches. On one occasion I was working on a barge taking jerrycans off the pallets while, unbeknown to me, the barge had drifted out of position. As the now empty pallet was lifted for its return it immediately swung to the vertical and hit me in the rib cage. I was knocked down and became unconscious for a while. After reporting to the MO I was strapped up in sticking plaster and put on light duties. To this

View eastwards along the Rue du Vingt Trois towards the area of the quay by the Casino Palace Hotel. In the middle distance on the right is the Cathedral tower and on the left the minaret of a mosque.

day I still think I cracked a rib..

The accident led to my starting a cooking career in the Army because my light duties involved working in the ship's galley helping to prepare meals for the rest of the sappers working the ships.

A Port Said street scene.

When it was known that we would not be remaining long in Port Said we were moved out of the school and into a tented area set up on a dual carriageway near to the Casino Palace Hotel and the waterfront where it would be easier to control the shrinking area of occupation when we started reloading the ships again ready for our departure.

The lads at the quay waiting to embark.

When this finally took place we sailed from Port Said, Cyprus-bound, on the *Empire Grebe*. This was a ship originally launched in 1945 as the LST 3038, renamed *Fighter* in 1947, then renamed again as the *Empire Grebe* when brought back into service for the Suez crisis after being mothballed in the River Clyde. The vessel was crewed and managed by the Atlantic Steam and Navigation Company on behalf of the Ministry of Transport.

Sailing aboard this ship was quite an experience since it normally carried just tanks and their crews which meant that the accommodation was quite limited. Most of us had to sleep on the steel deck in the hold where the tanks would normally be. Flat-bottomed boats like LSTs were not designed for long voyages and what made it worse was the weather. A trip that should have taken about 26 hours took five days. Every time we tried to enter Famagusta harbour it was too rough and dangerous so each night we had to anchor in the lee of the land. Eventually we made it.

The *Empire Grebe*.

Ashore we were billeted at Golden Sands Holiday Camp which I believe used to serve as a leave camp for members of the forces in the Canal Zone in the early fifties and was still employed for the same purpose by those serving in Cyprus. I was soon allocated to the cookhouse while the rest of the squadron went out each day to a large warehouse to sort out equipment that had been loaded rather badly in the rush to leave Port Said. The sooner we got this job done they told us the quicker we would return home.

On our return to the UK we went back to Ripon where we arrived about 25 January 1957. I was assigned to the cookhouse until I was offered a six-week regimental cooks' training course at the Army Catering Corp training camp at Catterick which I accepted and really enjoyed.

Soon after my return to Ripon some other cooks and myself were posted to Ollerton in Nottinghamshire to become the permanent staff at a TA camp where each fortnight we would have a different unit arrive from anywhere in the country. With another regimental cook I became responsible for the Sergeants Mess meals.

One of the things I enjoyed there was the trips out that were laid on for us. I found the excursion to the Ollerton Coal Mine interesting and we also visited the John Player cigarette factory in Nottingham although, being a non-smoker, that didn't interest me a great deal.

One of our jobs was to carry out town patrols with a truck to pick up the late night drunk servicemen and get them back to camp. I remember a unit of Geordie WRACs from Newcastle seeming to enjoy themselves a great deal during their time with us. When the TA season finished we returned to Ripon where we learned that in October the Regiment would be posted to Osnabruck in Germany.

Meanwhile I went back into the main cookhouse and soon afterwards we were told that those national servicemen with no more than three months still to serve would not be going to Germany. Since I was due out in January I would be one of them and as a result I was posted to the permanent staff of the Royal School of Military Engineering at Chatham in Kent where I ended my army service back in the cookhouse and carrying out fire pickets. I was demobbed on 2 January 1958.

Returning to the print trade I finished my interrupted apprenticeship and continued in the trade for 49 years although switching between firms and areas. I retired at the age of nearly 64 in August 2000.

* * *

John (Ginger) Bowden, 16 Field Squadron, Royal Engineers.

I was born on the 1st of December 1935 in Bexley Heath, Kent. This was the year my father, who was in the Coldstream Guards, transferred to the Reserve. On the 1st of September 1939, the day the Germans attacked Poland, Dad was recalled to the Colours and served for much of his time at Regimental Headquarters, Birdcage Walk in Central London. Soon after Dad's recall we went to stay with friends of my mum at Bletchley. This was not with the intention of getting away from any bombing but because my younger brother had developed a severe whooping cough from the dampness of the air raid shelter we spent time in. It was while at Bletchley that I started school.

After a while we moved to Horsforth near Leeds, again to friends of the family. Move number three was to Five Lane Ends at Bradford where my maternal grandfather was now the County Court Usher. This was followed by some time spent at Weston-Super-Mare where we lived with Dad's mum. Our final move was to Kingswood at Bristol where we lived with my dad's eldest sister. Towards the end of the war we finally moved back home to Bexley Heath. Dad, meanwhile, remained with the Guards until 1960.

When I was eleven in 1946 I went to Graham Road Secondary Modern School, leaving at Christmas 1950 after I'd turned fifteen. I started work in London in the Publicity Printing Office at Macmillan, the book publishers. After a while I left and went to work for Associated British Pathe, first in the news department, then in the documentary section, and finally in distribution.

As I was getting towards my 18th birthday and knowing that I would have to do National Service I decided to enlist for the three years and get my choice of service which was the Royal Engineers. However, there was a problem. Being the son of sergeant in the Coldstream Guards and the grandson of a retired drum major in the Grenadier Guards I had a lot of pressure put on me to go for one of the Guards regiments. But I stuck to my guns and enrolled in the Royal Engineers for three years on 12 September 1953.

On the 24th of the month I reported to No.1 Training Regiment RE at Malvern where, with the others of the intake, I collected my uniform, etc., and learned the very basics of drill. I remember we seemed to do a lot of potato picking locally during the short time we were there. We were then transferred to No.6 TRRE at Norton Camp near Worcester for more basic training, square bashing, and use of the rifle.

My final spell of training took place at No.8 TRRE, Pinefield Camp, Elgin which is north of the Cairngorm Highlands in Scotland. Here, in the middle of winter, we learnt all the things that make you a Royal Engineer: Bailey bridging, digging trenches, demolitions, and so on. Some of this training took place at Findhorn Bay on the Moray Firth coast and after each time there we were made to march back to Elgin, which was quite a considerable distance.

Our passing-out parade took place in March 1954 and with great anticipation we waited for our postings. I found the idea that I might go abroad very exciting and when my posting was listed I discovered it was to 16 Field Squadron, Minden Camp, Fayid, in the Canal Zone of Egypt.

In April, after a short stay at the Barton Stacey transit camp in Hampshire, I sailed from Southampton on the troopship *Empire Ken* bound for Port Said. I remember we stopped briefly at Algiers where I went ashore and visited the Casbah. In Port Said, before we even got on the train to go south, one of the chaps had his watch stolen. Welcome to the Canal Zone! At Fayid I joined my squadron whose parent regiment was 35 Corp Engineer Regiment currently based in Cyprus. So for the time being we were attached to 22 Field Engineer Regiment.

Life now started to get a little easier than during training with trips into the desert to blow things up, plenty of swimming in the Great Bitter Lake, and, the highlight of my time there, a trip to Mt Sinai for an exercise. We also had guard duties of course as well as escort work up and down the famous Canal Road which included escorting prisoners to MCE Moascar, the Military Corrective Establishment.

Eventually the squadron joined its parent 35 Regiment in Cyprus which was based at Polemidhia Camp near Limassol. This posting had to be the icing on the cake – possibly the best posting in the forces at that time. We had the freedom of the whole of the island, swimming every day in the summer, 48-hour leave passes, coach trips, football matches, and work detachments to Akrotiri, Episcopi and Famagusta.

On 22 November 1954 I returned to Egypt to attend a clerks' course at Moascar, flying from Nicosia to Fayid. I completed the course on 18 December and flew back to Nicosia.

Some time later I went on a cadre course following which I was promoted to lance corporal. On my return to Cyprus I became the orderly corporal to Squadron Sergeant Major Wildgoose and also had a spell as the squadron MT corporal.

Suddenly the peaceful atmosphere in Cyprus changed overnight. EOKA, a terrorist organisation wanting union with Greece had set itself up and was responsible for a co-ordinated series of explosions that took place all over the island on the 1st of April 1955. The rest of the year saw us doing patrols in the streets of Limassol and carrying out very early morning raids in the Troodos Mountains. By now the fun of being in Cyprus had passed.

In December 1955 the regiment's tour overseas ended and we set sail for England, again in the *Empire Ken*, and from Southampton travelled up to Deverall Barracks at Ripon. Still the orderly corporal I settled down to soldiering in England. I passed my army driving test, went on the ranges at York, did church parades, and started to look forward to demob. Then, late in July, the Suez crisis began. Towards the end of August, with just 18 days of service to do I was told that I would not be demobbed for the time being. The regiment was to train as dockers and stevedores. Reading between the lines we could guess why.

The regiment left in convoy for Marchwood near Southampton and a life under canvas while we trained. We were joined by other sappers posted to us as well as reservists, many of them London dockers who were not a happy lot. They had mostly been out of the Army for some time and were earning good money. Now they were back on army pay. There was considerable unrest and I believe it made the national papers. But I found them a great bunch to work with and I made a lot of friends among them. The weather was quite wet at this time and conditions underfoot at Marchwood were particularly bad. After a while we were transferred to permanent barracks at Aldershot.

On 1 November we set sail on the troopship *Asturias* from Southampton and, via a short stop in Malta, made our way to Port Said where we disembarked on 10 November. Despite the ceasefire there was still a bit of shooting taking place here and there as we took up residence in a school which, having had my memory recently jogged by seeing a 1956 street plan of Port Said, I think was situated near the western end of a boulevard called Rue du Vingt Trois Julliet which is fairly close to, and parallel with, the beach that had been stormed by the Marine Commandos that morning.

We were soon put to work on 12-hour shifts unloading the supply ships that came into the harbour. We moved backwards and forwards along the quay to wherever we were needed on a ship. After a while, for reasons unknown to us, we were withdrawn from our billet in the school and housed instead in tents erected on the grassed area in the middle of our dual carriageway boulevard.

It wasn't long before we began loading the ships back up again. We were very grateful for the help of the Navy during our time working at the quayside. They made us welcome on board HMS *Forth* for the use of their laundry and shower facilities.

Some time in December when our work was done and it was time to leave Port Said we departed on three fully-loaded flat-bottomed tank landing craft making for Famagusta in Cyprus, a journey of about 300 miles which took us four days. We were billeted in the old Golden Sands holiday camp and I stayed there until the arrival offshore, yet once again, of the *Empire Ken* on which I sailed back with the Reservists to the UK and demob from Barton Stacey. By this time I had served three years and 128 days, enjoying every minute of it.

After leaving the Army I worked as a fitter's mate on various building sites around the London area installing heating systems. During this time I earned very good money and during October 1959 got married to Joy. A year or so later I gave way under pressure from my father and grandfather to get a job with a pension and enrolled in the Fire Service in December 1960. I retired in 1991.

My wife Joy and I have two daughters and two granddaughters and have just celebrated 52 years together.

* * *

John, third from the right, and some of his mates in Port Said.

Albert Hallett, 42 Field Squadron, REs.

I was born 2 March 1934 in the small village of Kilham six miles north-eastwards out of Driffield in East Yorkshire. I went to the village school from the age of five through until I was fifteen when I went to work in nearby Driffield as an apprentice electrician. Being an apprentice allowed me to obtain deferment from the services until the end of my apprenticeship. On 15 February 1955, just before my 21st birthday, I attended my force's medical at Jameson Street, Hull. About a month later I received a travel warrant to report to No.6 Training Regiment, Royal Engineers, at Norton Camp, near Worcester to begin my two years of National Service.

After being fitted out with the uniform and other gear and receiving a briefing on the Royal Engineers we were sent to No.3 TRRE at Morval Barracks, Cove in Hampshire. Here we were taught how to march, handle explosives, make knots and lashings, practise boat handling and Bailey bridging, etc. We also spent time close by at Guillemont Barracks which was also a 3 TRRE base where we did more drill, mine laying and detecting. When all this was over and we were classed as trained Royal Engineers we had the passing out parade which was followed by our postings. I was one of those posted to 42 Squadron, 35 Field Regiment based at Limassol, Cyprus, BFPO 53.

We were first taken to Goodge Street underground station in London, part of which had been an air raid shelter during the recent Second World War and was now used as a London transit unit. It consisted of tunnels with rooms off to each side, each sleeping eight to ten men, and the unit was fully equipped with a kitchen and other basics.

The underground trains were continually rumbling through above our heads. Our first duty was to carry iron bed frames down the spiral staircase, not in the lift. When this was done we learned that the beds had only just been taken upstairs by the departing previous intake. A week later we were taken to Blackbushe airfield in Hampshire from where we flew to Nicosia. Shortly afterwards we were trucked to our regiment at Polemidhia Camp just outside Limassol.

Among our first duties, with EOKA terrorists recently having become active, were town patrols, as well as guard duties both at the camp and at the officers' retreat in the Troodos Mountains. After a while ten of us were selected for detachment to various localities around the Cyprus coast building radar sites for the Royal Signals.

Explosives had to be used on the solid rock when digging the deep trench latrines. Gravel for the concrete was brought from the beach on three-ton lorries. On one occasion while passing through a village near Cape Plakoti in the Kyrenia area we had a missile thrown at the truck. Fortunately it missed otherwise, with plastic explosives on board at the time, the four of us sat on the load of gravel in the back could have been in serious trouble.

We had some good times though and since in the heat of the summer we began early and finished early we were able to go swimming and fishing in the afternoons. After about six months the regiment's tour was over and we returned to the UK and took up residence at Deverall Barracks, Ripon.

Here we found ourselves on evening town patrols again but this time it was because of trouble between our lads and the Royal Signals who were based just across the road. The days were taken up with drill, demolition training, visiting the rifle range at Strensall near York, map reading, and Bailey bridging, etc.

In August 1956, following the recent takeover of the Suez Canal by the Egyptians, the regiment moved in a convoy of lorries to Marchwood, across the river from Southampton, stopping on the way at various army camps to refuel. We were under canvas as we trained to become stevedores and crane operators at Cracknore Hard.

Fortunately, by the time the weather deteriorated and conditions among the tents became really bad, we had more or less completed our training, and were moved to permanent accommodation at Aldershot which had recently been vacated by a unit of the Paratroop Regiment that had flown out to Cyprus.

While here we carried out various jobs, one of them being at Sandhurst, the officers' training college, where we levelled the playing fields. On another occasion we were involved in picking up soldiers and reservists from the Red Cap depot at Pirbrite who had been brought back there after going AWOL.

Sometime in October we moved to Netley Hospital near Southampton, then being used as a transit centre for those awaiting their turn to board a ship bound for Egypt. We filled in some of our time with map-reading exercises around the area.

Sometime over mid-October we drove our vehicles to the docks where they were loaded onto various commandeered boat. The one we went aboard was the MV *Huntsland* on which extra accommodation had been fitted in the form of hammocks and a galley.

Trucks being parked at Netley Military Hospital.

Trucks parked in the grounds of the hospital.

Albert with one of the Land Rovers in the Netley grounds.

While at sea we passed some of the time with target practice over the stern of the boat using balloons. We had quite a quantity of surplus ammunition owing to the armourer having given us 2,500 rounds instead of 250. I often wonder even now if he managed to cover up the mistake.

Scammell tractor unit being loaded aboard the MV *Huntsland* at Southampton.

The requisitioned SS *Sunkirk* being loaded at Southampton preparing to sail with the *Huntsland* for Egypt.

After a short stop at Malta we arrived at Port Said on about the 5th of November during the night and in thick fog. By daylight the fog had cleared and on deck we found that we were surrounded by what appeared to be hundreds of ships most of them waiting to enter the canal to unload their urgently required cargos and troops. Ashore there were flames, smoke and lots of noise from the shelling and shooting. When our turn came to move into the canal and along the mole we were able to see many of the sunken vessels that had been used to block the canal. However we were able to get close enough to unload the ship.

A part-view of the harbour from a Port Said quay.

Ashore we were first taken to our base, a commandeered school close to other buildings that had been taken over by our forces.

View from the roof of the School billet of other buildings commandeered by the various invasion units.

Each day we were taken to the canal at Bassin Abbas Hilmi, where some masted Egyptian vessels were moored. This was situated a few hundred yards further down the western side of the canal from the Canal Company building. Here we unloaded the boats that could manage to get down this far which were the smaller kind of boats such as landing craft, lighters and barges, and brought ashore their cargoes of tinned food and jerrycans of petrol.

Because of the invasion food was in very short supply for the locals. When we were at the school for a meal young children used to appear at the

The Egyptian ships at one of the basins.

wire fence begging for food. Bacon butties were sometimes passed to them but their religion didn't permit them to eat bacon so they fed it to the dog and ate just the bread. On one occasion a can of beans was thrown off a balcony to the children below. It burst open on impact and they just scooped up the mess since they were so hungry. Water was scarce too since the town supply had been cut during the invasion. For washing we were issued sea soap and went to the beach.

The children at meal times outside the school.

View from the back of the school billet of shell damage to nearby buildings.

View from the school roof in another direction.

After the United Nations peace-keeping force arrived we started to prepare for the withdrawal which in our case would initially be to Cyprus

Some of the United Nations peacekeeping force on a Port Said street.

On a designated day sometime after mid-December we moved down to the quay and embarked on a ship for the return to Famagusta.

Troops sleeping on deck in transit to Cyprus.

In Cyprus we were housed under canvas with not much to do except guard duty and occasional tasks that had to be carried out. One of these was serving as an escort to a load of explosives for use in the copper mines. We would actually be sitting on the explosives in their narrow gauge railway wagons that went underground. At least we were able to use the miners' shower block.

On another occasion I had to drive ten reservists to Nicosia for their flight home. Unfortunately the petrol in the vehicle was from a jerrycan that had been at Suez and stored for quite some time. This meant that the inside of the can had started to rust and the bits were being drawn through the carburettor so that every ten miles or so the engine would stop. We had to clean the carburettor quite a number of times, and on the return journey too.

In January 1957 it was our turn to be released and we returned to the UK and Ripon. Owing to the amount of leave accumulated by many of the men it was quite some time before the regiment was back to full strength.

I then learned that in April I was to be posted to Christmas Island. This didn't please me at all since I was due for demob in March. A visit to the squadron office was arranged where I learned that I was to go as an electrician. However, I had never taken the army trade test, because whenever one had been arranged I had been on the move. Consequently I wasn't officially qualified and my name was taken off the posting. This was quite a relief and more so later when I learned that during May and June 1957 they had tested hydrogen bombs close to the island. So I was demobbed in March after what was really a great experience.

Back home I returned to my old job and stayed there for a further 14 years before moving to another firm where I spent 25 years and became chief electrician. I retired in 1999 although I still do a couple of hours per day as a handyman at the local surgery.

* * *

Jim Gow Clark, 24 Field Squadron, Royal Engineers.

I was born in Johnstone, Renfrewshire, Scotland on 15 September 1935. I finished high school in the summer of 1950 when I was coming up to 15 and began work more or less right away as an apprentice joiner. Towards the end of the year, after a three-month trial period during which I was cheap labour at 28 shillings a week, I started a five-year apprenticeship and took night classes leading to the City and Guilds of London Institute examinations. In May 1955 I took the Final Examination in Carpentry and Joinery and passed with flying colours which was more than useful since eventually it was to give me an extra two shillings and sixpence a week as a soldier. I completed my apprenticeship at the end of 1955.

On 4 March 1956, I reported to No.6 Training Regiment of the Royal Engineers at Norton Camp near Worcester for kitting out and basic training, not forgetting all the injections in both arms. Because I was a joiner they kept me back for a further fortnight to carry out maintenance work on the camp while the rest of the intake went off to their various destinations for further training.

Early in April I was posted to No.3 Training Regiment at Morval Barracks, Farnborough in Hampshire for the field engineering, weaponry, drill, explosives, and all the other skills that make a recruit into a sapper. This was completed in July and after some leave I was posted to 3 Troop, 24 Field Squadron, part of 36 Core Regiment based at Roberts Barracks, Osnabruck in Germany. Our troop officer was 2/Lt. Watson supported by Sgt. Eames.

I felt this was the best posting any squaddy could wish for. It was a huge military complex built during the First World War for the German Army and was far superior to any barracks I had ever been in or even seen in Britain. We lived in luxury.

During September 1956 while out on manoeuvres 24 Field Squadron was ordered back to barracks and warned to be ready to move out at a moment's notice. This came in October and, leaving the rest of the regiment behind, well someone had to guard the West against the Russians, we returned to the UK via the Hook of Holland and Harwich, then boarded a train to Southampton where, together with the Highland Light Infantry and the Pioneer Corps, we boarded the troopship *Dilwara* and set sail down the channel. Our destination was supposed to be a secret but we all knew where we were going of course. The Suez crisis was on.

On the *Dilwara* making for Egypt.

We landed at Port Said just after the ceasefire had taken place and marched from the quayside to the pipes and drums of the Highland Light Infantry before taking up residence in the Port Said railway station.

The Port Said station concourse.

Out in the sidings we found a hand car, a manually operated rail cart used by the railway workers which some of the lads converted to operate off a motor cycle. They named it the Rockin' Roll Express. This was the time when Bill Haley and the Comets had recently come into prominence. I don't think anyone took the cart too far with Egyptian snipers still active in the area.

Some of the lads on the Rockin' Roll Express on the lines in front of a locomotive.

After spending the first night sleeping on the floor of the main hall the squadron was allocated quarters in one of the three school buildings situated at the side of the station. We were even provided with beds, and mosquito nets.

On the roof of the school. Back: Alan Smith, Pete Croft,?, Mike Barry, Jim Clark, ?. Front row: Jeff Parker, Taffy Norris, ?, Brian Pollard.

One of the first jobs I was involved in was as an escort on the train carrying supplies down the line to our troops in the El Cap area. Each of us was given just two clips of five rounds for this task. I don't think we would have been able to defend the train for very long with just ten bullets each.

The lads of 24 Squadron serving as the escort on one of the trains operating between Port Said station, shown here, and El Cap.

The next project which some of us took part in was to give a helping hand to another unit of sappers (16 Field Squadron) in the building of a pontoon Bailey bridge across the Bassin De Raccodment. The reason for this, so we were told, was to serve as a backup in case the existing Raswa swing bridge was ever sabotaged.

Lifting the heavy Bailey panels into position.

A section of the bridge now aboard the pontoons. Water tower at the Port Said Water Works in the background.

Egyptian fishermen near the new Bailey bridge in the Bassin De Raccordement with two 16 Sqn sappers looking on.

Photograph of the Port Said waterworks taken from the top of the water tower shown in the map below. Beyond the far end of the waterworks is the start of the Sweetwater Canal which is fed with water following its treatment at the works. On the far side of the Sweetwater Canal is the coastal road south which lies on the western bank of the Suez Canal. Beyond are the southern outskirts of Port Fuad.

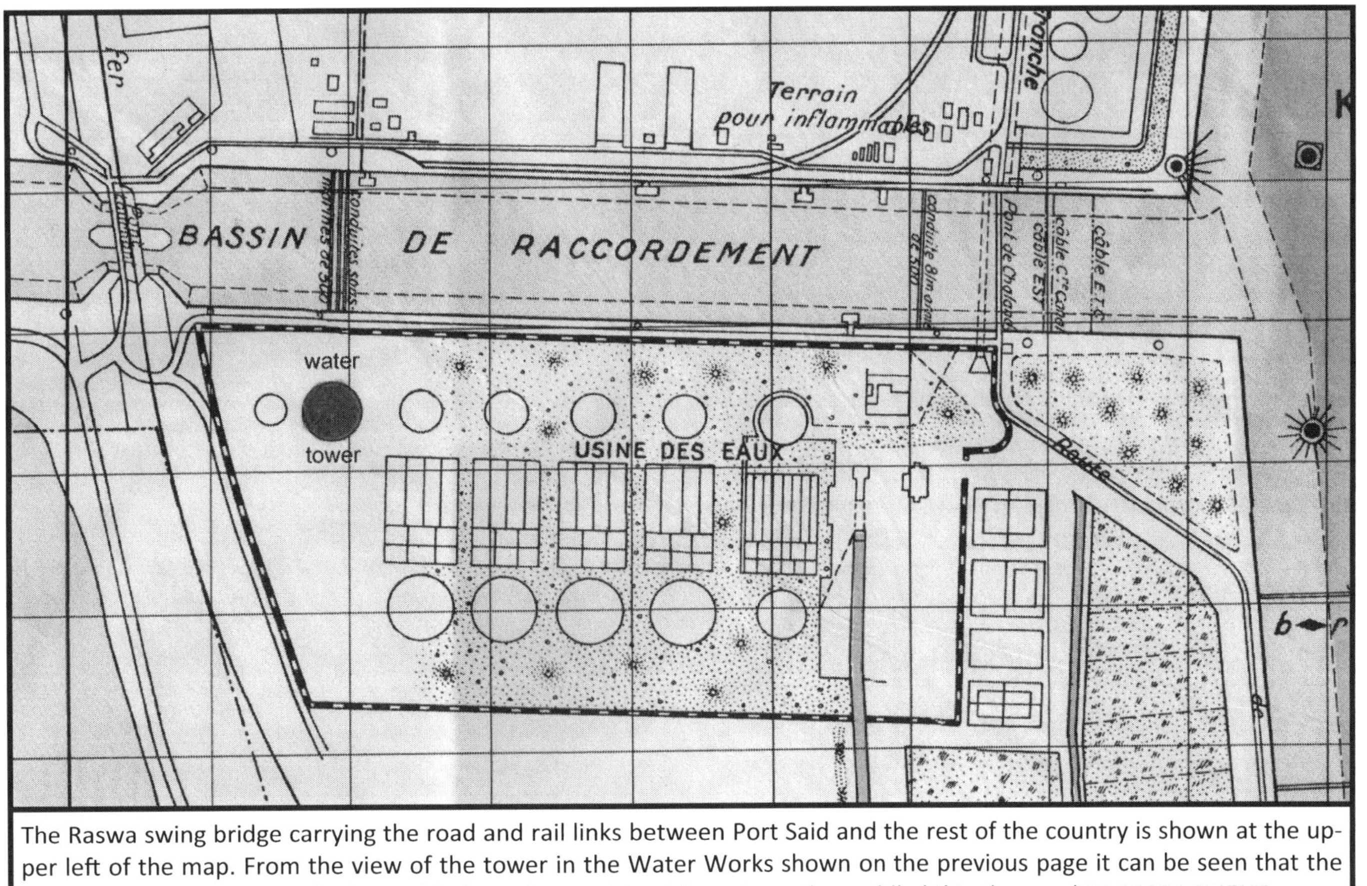

The Raswa swing bridge carrying the road and rail links between Port Said and the rest of the country is shown at the upper left of the map. From the view of the tower in the Water Works shown on the previous page it can be seen that the pontoon Bailey bridge was built roughly from the canal bank just above the middle 'R' in the word RACCORDEMENT.

Being one of the smaller ones in the squad my job was to hammer in the steel pins that connected the Bailey panels. This suited me fine because even some of the big lads found it hard lifting these great heavy frames and manoeuvring them into position. In the end I don't think the bridge was ever used. In fact, as far as I know, when we withdrew from Port Said I think the bridge, as well as our trucks and the despatch rider's motor cycle, may have been left behind.

Close to where we were working on the bridge we came across what appeared to be a grave. We were never sure if it really was a grave or a hoax but it was close to where the French paratroopers had landed although the helmet looked British. However, we always treated it with respect and it was left undisturbed.

The grave at Raswa.

Further jobs carried out by other troops in the squadron included guarding the new waterworks which was quite close to the swing bridge, and searching for landmines at the beach. It seems that another unit had checked the beach before us so there wasn't really anything to find. I guess the officers used the search as a useful training exercise to keep the lads on their toes.

On one occasion, while I was on guard duty at the main entrance to the station, I was approached by an Egyptian chap who had with him a woman dressed from head to toe in black. The man told me that I could have Johnny Johnny for 200 cigarettes. I knew what he meant. I tried to wave them on but to no avail. It was only when I pointed my rifle at them that they got the message. The possibility that this was some sort of diversionary tactic quickly passed through my mind. For all I knew it could have been a bloke under all that black carrying explosives or a gun.

About half way though our time in Port Said Norman Fletcher and myself, because we were joiners, were picked up one morning and taken to a joiner's shop owned by two brothers and given the job of making sections of latrines and small cookhouses for easy transportation and then erection on site. We found that there were men there from just about all the units in town doing the same job. An officer kept a record of every stick of lumber and all the nails, etc., that we used so that the brothers could be suitably compensated afterwards. Between us we used up their entire inventory very quickly and left them with nothing but sawdust and a pile of firewood off-cuts.

During our last week in Port Said as the occupation was coming to an end we began to enjoy a lot more free time although while billeted at the school we got caught for plenty of guard duties.

On one occasion 2/Lt Watson managed to acquire a jerry can of petrol and took five of us down to the canal side where he commandeered a small motor boat for a tour of the various sunken ships littering the entrance to the canal. We were also allowed to see a bit of the town on our own as long as we were armed and in groups. This was when we had a photo taken by an Egyptian street photographer with an old-fashioned wooden camera. We had to stand frozen for about 15 seconds while he removed the lens cap to expose the film.

The photograph taken by the street photographer. Jim Clark (Johnstone), Ted Balmer (South Shields), Len Brown (Rochester), and a mate whose name Jim couldn't recall..

Port Said street vendor.

Transporting trucks home as well.

Large mural of the action drawn by one of the sappers.

Homeward bound on the aircraft carrier *Theseus.*

When the time came to leave we went aboard the aircraft carrier HMS *Theseus* where, because of a lack of space for all the troops crammed into the ship, I found myself accommodated with the crew. I dined with them, slept in a hammock, and even got a tot of rum which was still the tradition in the Royal Navy at that time.

Troops being accommodated in the aircraft hangar.

The ship docked at Portsmouth just in time for Christmas. After leave we returned to Osnabruck in Germany from where I was discharged on 3 March 1958.

Back in Civvy Street I returned to the building trade until 1963 when I immigrated to Ontario in Canada. I continued as a joiner over there, eventually becoming a construction superintendent on schools and hospitals all over the province. In 1974, tiring of this and only getting home at weekends, I started my own business specialising in home renovations and additions. My son now runs things with my daughter's son as his apprentice.

(Jim died in December 2011.)

* * *

Norman Rose, 33 Squadron, Royal Engineers.

I was born on 6 March 1938 in Cleve House near Exwick, which is about two-and-a-half miles from Exeter, and attended the small local school there until I was twelve when I went to a secondary school in Exeter. I left School in December 1952 and became an agricultural student on a farm 35 miles away on the edge of Dartmoor.

I got my call up papers in December 1955. I could have got deferred but with my military family background – my father was an RSM in the Royal Engineers – I decided to join up straight away. I had to register at the nearest Labour Exchange, as it was called in those days, which was back in Exeter. After the interview I was told that I would be called for a medical in the New Year.

This said medical eventually took place in February, again in Exeter, where I had to cough and all that. I signed on for 22 years with a three-year option. Shortly afterwards I was sent a rail warrant with instructions to report to No.6 Training Regiment of the Royal Engineers at Norton Camp near Worcester.

For someone who had hardly been out of the county of Devon this all became quite an adventure. On the train I met a few other lads going to the same place where we were put in wooden huts. The following morning after breakfast we were issued with our kit and over the next three weeks while waiting for the intake numbers to build up we were taught how to 'bull'.

With this intake of regulars complete we were transferred to No.1 TRRE close to Hanley Swan near Malvern where training began in earnest. Although it was tough it was also a lot of fun and the comradeship that we built up in the party was great. The parade ground at the camp was very open and gave spectacular views of the nearby Malvern Hills. With the training over we had a pass out parade and I felt quite proud on the square as Mother and my father, the RSM, were both there. We rounded all this off with a trip to London to see a show.

After leave at home I reported to the Barton Stacey transit camp near Andover where our group was issued with KD kit while we waited for our posting, which was to No.33 Squadron, 37 Field Engineer Regiment at Limassol in Cyprus. After a few days we were taken to Stansted Airport in Essex for the flight which entailed a brief stop in the South of France and then Malta before our arrival at Nicosia Airport. From here we were trucked to the nearby Wayne's Keep Camp which was lit up red from the early morning sun.

Shortly afterwards we loaded all our gear onto a truck and set off on the long dusty journey to Limassol with a guard riding 'shotgun'. What the hell have I let myself in for! On arrival at Polemidia Camp we were issued with bedding to take to the tent lines but no mattress and had to sleep on the bed springs. Apparently we were moving out the next day. Although it was dark by 8 pm it was still very hot. The loos were a route march away and in the dark not easy to find.

The regiment was involved in several projects at this time. At Happy Valley close to Episcopi a tunnel had been driven through the headland to what had been a land-locked beach and was well on its way to being finished. However, out at the beach close to the Akrotiri RAF base, jet fuel tanks were being erected, each by one a different squadron of the regiment and this is where we newcomers were sent. It was blazing hot at this time of the year and at the end of each day it was a great relief to have a nice swim at the adjacent Ladies Mile beach where we were billeted in tents.

While I was there one of the lads was emptying his rifle in the tent and, not realising that there was still a bullet up the spout, pulled the trigger and shot one of the lads through what I think was the thigh. There was quite a stink about that. One guy in either 1 or 2 Troop was Lofty Squires who was six feet eight inches tall and always served as right marker at parades. He had to have two beds welded together.

About the beginning of October, with the oil storage tanks and the pipeline leading out to a tanker terminal point offshore well on towards completion, the recent arrivals returned to Polemidia where we were offered various courses, presumably to keep all these extra bodies occupied. I joined a plant course that was to be run by 18 Field Park Squadron and on the following Monday morning began learning how to operate and service a small Caterpillar D4 bulldozer.

Suddenly, towards the end of the month, with the Suez crisis in the news, rumours began flying about and then 33 Squadron was put on standby and the course put on hold. Then the standby became the real thing and on what I think was 4 November we were taken down to the jetty at the Limassol waterfront and ferried out to the Troopship *Empire Ken* for the journey to Port Said. Not all the squadron went. Those in sick bay were left behind of course and apparently not all the troops made it to the ship on time before it had to sail.

We arrived offshore from the entrance to the Suez Canal at Port Said just at dusk on the fifth to the sound of gunfire and jets screaming overhead. Several plumes of smoke blown on a westerly wind were rising from a number of places in the town with a particularly large one coming from an oil storage tank to the south.

View down the canal from the troopship *Empire Ken*.

We remained on the ship for a second night and through to the afternoon of the following day when the *Empire Ken* was given permission to move and slowly edged into the canal entrance while we waited to be ferried ashore. We could hear bullets from small arms fire hitting the ship while those who had cameras took shots of the action taking place around them.

Smoke rising from Shanty Town.

View down the canal of two blockships and the fire from an oil storage tank hit by a stray rocket from a French jet early in the assault on the town.

The Port Fuad side of the canal.

The canal waterfront where the 42 Commando were ferried ashore by helicopters from the aircraft carriers.

Ships of the size of the *Empire Ken* were far too big to berth at the quay and to disembark we had to wait while barges came to collect us and ferry us ashore to the quay on the western side of the canal which was the continuation of the canal mouth breakwater, with its Fish Docks and the De Lesseps statue promenade which ended at the Casino Palace Hotel.

The De Lesseps statue and the currently empty Fish Dock.

Casino Palace Hotel on left. The top right-hand flat in the six-storey apartment block was taken over by senior staff.

After disembarking our troop marched to an abandoned consulate where we spent the night, Despite our being the invaders of their town it didn't stop some of the locals joining us in a game of football during the short time we were there.

Egyptian lads joining the squaddies in a game of impromptu soccer near the billet.

The next day we were taken to a school next to the railway station and this became our billet for the rest of our time in Port Said while our troop carried out the tasks allotted to it.

The opposite side of the wide boulevard outside the schools and the adjacent Port Said Railway Station.

One of the 33 Squadron billets in the school. The beds were the concrete floor and a poncho/groundsheet.

One of the first jobs given to some of the 33 Squadron lads was to occupy the waterworks further down the canal on the far bank of the side canal crossed by the Raswa road/rail bridge. This had been captured by French paratroopers on the first day of the attack on Port Said.

I was among those who helped to run a train from the station as far as El Cap to repatriate the wounded Egyptian prisoners who had been released. Firstly though we had to make sure that the carriages were cleared of all the rifles and other arms found on board.

Train ready with the repatriated Egyptian wounded.

The Red Cross train between Port Said and El Cap.

Our No.3 Troop's Sgt Blake was sat on the roof of the train with a Bren gun on one of these journeys when he was swept to the ground by a wire crossing the line. He was returned to Cyprus to have his injuries treated, We never saw him again and when we got back to Cyprus he had been replaced by a Sgt McGibbon.

Another of the many photographs taken of the diesel locomotive and the carriage used to repatriate the wounded Egyptian prisoners.

Coupled locomotives on the Port Said to El Cap line.

View of the Canal road looking north. The Suez Canal on the right and the Sweetwater Canal on the left.

Following the spell on the railway I was one of those who then went to the docks to unload stores and rations for 33 Squadron. It was while I was here that I passed out with a bug of some kind and woke up in the Casino Palace Hotel which early on was serving as the allied front line hospital.

A local disturbance somewhere in Port Said.

I wasn't well enough to return to Cyprus with the rest of the squadron and followed some time later aboard the French hospital ship the

Marsellaise. From Limassol I rejoined my unit at Polemidia Camp where in the New Year through January and February of 1957 I completed the plant course I had started in October.

From then on it was routine duties for a while until I went on a blacksmithing course which proved very useful indeed since on my return to civilian life it became my vocation.

At one stage 3 Troop spent three days at Wayne's Keep in Nicosia waiting to be flown to Jordan in support of King Hussein against some faction or other but nothing came of the emergency and we were stood down. Our troop frequently acted independently and later, when 37 Field Engineer regiment was disbanded, 33 Squadron would be retained to become an independent unit.

Some months later we embarked on a tank landing craft and sailed to Tripoli for desert warfare training and bridge building. We were stationed just outside Tripoli in the old wartime Italian Ghurgi Barracks. During our stay we also enjoyed a trip to Wheeler Field, the nearby American air base as well as a visit to the old Roman ruins of Leptis Magna 80 miles east along the coast from the capital.

Back in Limassol I spent some time with the Regimental Police and also took an eight weeks NCO's cadre course at Polemidia under the RSM and a sergeant and afterwards was made up to full corporal.

In May 1958 I was put in charge of the G10 stores. On the 15th of the month the Squadron went out on the seven-weeks-long *Operation Kingfisher* which was intended to surround the whole of the Troodos area and flush out the EOKA terrorists believed to be hiding there.

After having served almost three years of the 22 I decided to take the option to leave since my father was not well and I felt I should be at home. In February 1959, on the day six of us left Limassol for Nicosia Airport on our return to the UK it snowed there for the first time in twenty years.

We landed in Germany and spent six days, on what must have been a junket for someone, at Sennelager to view changes that were currently taking place in heavy bridging practices before returning to Chatham from where I should have been demobbed. But my papers had been sent down to No.10 Railway Squadron at Longmoor which was to be my AER unit. I made my way there and was demobbed from the Army two days later. Since I was a regular I was paid a small amount per week for being in the Army Emergency Reserve until I was released from it.

After demob I became a blacksmith for the next 45 years thanks to my army training, first with the Ministry of Public Building and Works and then privately. I represent the Worshipful Company of Blacksmiths as an accredited judge.

*   *   *

Eric A Pegg, 33 Squadron, Royal Engineers.

I was born 27 November 1934 very close to the centre of Manchester at 23 Upper Jackson Street, Hulme, a street now obliterated by the Mancunian Way. Dad was a greengrocer, fruiterer and fishmonger, while Mum had been trained as a milliner.

In 1937 we moved over the invisible city boundary into Salford and the district of Pendleton known as Hanky Park from Hankinson Street, the main thoroughfare of the slum, close to where Dad now had a lock-up shop. In 1939, just before WWII began we moved again, this time to Lower Broughton Road in Salford where we had live-in premises. Mum ran the shop here while Dad kept his lock-up in Boundary Street going.

I began school in September 1940 at North Grecian Street Infants just as the war began. The first thing we learned was how to operate a stirrup pump – at five. Not long afterwards I arrived home one day to find I great pile of bricks stacked on the pavement outside the shop. We soon had a bricklayer working in the cellar creating a very sturdy alcove with heavy baulks of timber laid across the top of the new supporting walls and this was where Mum and I were to sleep for the next few months until we thought our Blitz had finished.

After breakfast on 23 December Dad went off on

the tram to the lock-up at Pendleton to prepare the Christmas poultry orders for his customers. A couple of hours later he arrived back. During the night a bomb had fallen on Boundary Street and demolished the shop and some of the surrounding property as well as killing a number of people. Dad had survived those horrendous four years in the trenches against the Germans during WWI and had now been lucky again.

With the end of the war in Europe in May 1945, and the war against Japan in August, I went along to the local street parties laid on to celebrate these VE and VJ days. At sometime in the next school year I sat the 11-plus Examination and failed as did all the others in class 4B. The 'streaming' had been very accurate.

In September 1946 I began my secondary education at Broughton Modern Secondary School but spent only about two months there. Mam and Dad had decided that they wanted something better for me than a Salford slum and just before Christmas we moved to Blackpool where they had spent holidays during the 1920s and 1930s. I transferred to Tyldesley Secondary Modern School where a length of covered bicycle stand across the middle of the playground separated the boys school from the girls school, and never the twain were supposed to meet … but did.

At Tyldesley I enjoyed most of the subjects, especially woodwork, metalwork and English in which the teachers were disciplinarians. I also developed my soccer skills and became a member of the junior and then senior school teams. When I was 13 I suddenly discovered an interest in the girls at the other side of the bike shed. I started to get to know a number of them and one year later, by which time I was a prefect and deputy head boy, I was going out with Theresa Nuttall who eventually became my wife. During that last year at school I joined the school youth club housed in the school premises and remained a member until I was twenty-one.

I left school at Christmas 1949 and early in January began an apprenticeship as a carpenter and joiner on the princely sum of £1 8s per week. Since we had a cabinet-maker, Jack Kershaw from Todmorden, on the staff I began learning his skills too.

With the beginning of the new academic year in September 1950 I was allowed one-day release at Blackpool Technical College for instruction which would eventually lead to the City and Guilds of London Institute examinations although I had to attend two evenings as well.

After a good season of soccer in which I led the junior youth club soccer team to victory in the Hogan Cup I was invited to play for the Blackpool Colts. However I needed to attend night school three nights a week which was at a time when a consistent attendance was required in order to be allowed deferment from National Service until the end of one's apprenticeship at the age of twenty-one. Consequently with this, study, and time to see Theresa, I couldn't manage the training sessions so reverted to youth club soccer which I could manage without training.

Towards the end of 1953 I was transferred to Fieldings, a house-building company, to widen my experience. I obtained the final City and Guild's certificate in the summer of 1955 and in October, just before my 21st birthday, was called for my national service interview and medical at Fulwood Barracks, Preston, where I asked for the RAF. On my 21st birthday in November I at last started to receive the tradesman's £12 a week. In December I received my calling up papers and learned that I was to join the Royal Engineers.

On 5 January 1956, as part of the 5601 intake, the first of the year, I reported to No.6 TRRE at Norton Camp just outside Worcester for two weeks of kitting out and initial training. Norton camp was made up of timber buildings situated as an annex at the side of the brick-built Worcester Regiment Norton Barracks. At pay parade I discovered that I was now back on £1 8s a week, what I'd started work with six years earlier. I know I was getting bed and board but I thought with such a pittance the government was taking a real liberty as well as putting my marriage on hold for two years.

At the end of two weeks we were trucked to Worcester Station to join a train that had just arrived from Malvern with the 5601 intake of sappers from Merebrook Camp there. Together, about 150 of us, we were taken to Farnborough in Hampshire and then to No.3 TRRE at Guillemont Barracks, Cove, where we underwent fourteen more weeks of training and field engineering. Along the way I obtained the LMG patch and one for being a 'B' tradesman because of my City and Guilds certificate. Apparently both gave a small pay increment. After the passing out ceremony we were taken to London with the choice of a number of different West End shows. I saw Kismet.

Since I had come reasonably near the top of the course I was invited to take a training NCO's cadre just down the road at No.9 TRRE and this is where I returned after a week's leave for course No.118, Southwood Camp. After ten weeks of intense bull, further field engineering, learning to give a ten-minute lecture in the classroom, taking drill sessions on the parade ground, all to the snarling of the RSM and the junior NCO's, those of us who passed were supposed to be ready to replace the NCOs going on demob at the training camps.

Although I came 13th out of the 49 on the course I wasn't given a training camp to return to after the week's leave that was now coming up. I was to return to Cove. Just before going home I saw a notice on the board inviting candidates for a Royal Engineers No. 9 Parachute Squadron course. I put my name down since I saw it as a means of ensuring that I remained in the UK for a further two or three months by which time, I hoped, it wouldn't be worthwhile sending me abroad. However, when I went on leave and told my father-in-law-to-be what I'd done he pointed out that if there was an emergency of any kind, and this was the period of the cold war, then the Paras and the Marines would be the first to be called back. On my return to Cove I saw one of the clerks and told him that if anything came through I'd changed my mind.

By now it was the end of July and Nasser had just nationalised the Suez Canal. Instead of becoming a training NCO I was sent off with a number of others to Barton Stacey holding/transit camp in Hampshire.

I remained at Barton Stacey for weeks on end , shovelling coke, on cookhouse duties, and carrying out many other being-kept-busy tasks. Each weekend unless on guard duty I would hitchhike home to Blackpool and then on Sunday evening tell Theresa, 'I'll see you next Saturday.' But after the last weekend in August there wasn't a next Saturday.

One miserable cold and misty morning early in September about 35 of us were transported to a very primitive wooden-hutted Heathrow Airport and put on a Bristol Britannia 'whisper' jet and flown on a non-stop six-hour flight to Nicosia in Cyprus. After about a night in a transit camp just near the airport we were collected by a couple of 3-ton Commer trucks and armed escorts to take us across country to the south coast and Polemidia Camp, the home of 37 Field Engineer Regiment just outside Limassol. Our accommodation was arranged in parallel lines of square tents. I was allocated to 33 Squadron. The OC of the Squadron was Major McKay.

I think we'd been at the camp only about two days when we were listed for an anti-EOKA patrol in Limassol. After the evening meal we were escorted by a full corporal to the armoury where we each drew a rifle and five rounds of ammunition which were carefully counted out and signed for. A covered three-ton Bedford RL truck then took us down into the town by which time it was dark. The only person breaking what I assume was a curfew was a prostitute of rather doubtful vintage. One of the lads who had been at Farnborough with us was so desperate however that he had her in the back of the truck and out again before the corporal and the driver at the front of the truck had decided where to go next.

Over the next few days we did a couple more of these patrols before being told to gather our gear together and be ready to move out on detachment. We were going to join up with the rest of the squadrons which were working on an oil-storage project on the shore of the Akrotiri Peninsula adjacent to the air base.

We drove down the hill to the edge of Limassol then swung right along the metalled road until it petered out into a sandy track running along the back of the beach. Within half an hour we arrived at Ladies Mile Camp at the water's edge. As soon as we had been allocated to tents so that we could stow our gear we were rushed back onto the trucks and taken on a little further round the shoreline to where the fuel storage farm was being built. I was told that each of the squadrons, 33, 34 and 40, had its own tank to build. I assumed, like everyone else not privy to what was going on behind the scenes in Whitehall, that the work was just a normal part of modernising the facilities at the air base. It was of course in preparation for the invasion of Egypt.

Eighteen Field Park Squadron had begun excavating the foundations for the first of the five tanks on 28 August. This involved digging out a level-based pit to take a thick bed of sand on which the tank would rest. Number 33 Squadron, which during the summer had been working on a tunnel driven through the coastal cliffs near Episkopi, was transferred to Ladies Mile towards the end of August and given the job of erecting the British-made kit-set tanks. Another squadron was allocated the job of building the ship-to-shore pipeline. The pipeline was needed because Limassol is a shallow -water port where vessels have to offload their cargo onto a lighter offshore.

The first two tanks, each of them storing 350 tons or 3000 barrels of aviation spirit, were required urgently because of the imminent invasion. This amount of fuel was needed as an initial reserve and since the pipeline was unlikely to be finished by then it was planned that the fuel stored in the tanks would be brought in, and then collected as required, by bowser.

The stores and materials for the construction of the first two tanks arrived on the third and fourth of September and work began right away. The tanks were assembled under the supervision of a Major E W Kenworthy, RE, who had been flown out from the UK with the kit-sets especially for the job. They were made of Meccano-like curved panels which were joined at their overlapping edges, with sealing strips between them, by means of nuts and bolts – 12,000 to a tank. The nuts had to be tightened to a uniform degree with ratchet torque wrenches. Floodlights had been set up so that work could continue at night. (Source: History of the Royal Engineers, 1948-1960).

According to Geoffrey J Wilcock, ex-Royal Engineer who was there at the time, quite a number of sappers were hospitalised during the erection of the tanks.

When we arrived on the site in mid-September the first two tanks were almost complete. We were to be part of the day shift and immediately put to work in the searing heat. It was hottest summer Cyprus had had in eight years. Those of us fresh out from the UK were thirsty all the time. We were forever sloping off to get a drink at one of the large earthenware jars of water set up on the site but if we broke off too often the 2nd Lieutenant would shout, 'Get back to work.' The first two tanks were completed on 18 September. Although work then continued on the other three tanks our small intake was sent back to Polemidia. I wasn't sorry..

Soon after our return we were all interviewed in alphabetical order by Major McKay, the OC of 33 Squadron who had decided to lay on a number of courses to keep his new arrivals busy. Apparently we were all excess to the regiment's requirements at this time but of course the numbers were being built up for the attack on Egypt.

The oil storage tank farm under construction at Akrotiri.

When it was my turn the Major wanted me to go straight to the workshop but I managed to persuade him that I'd been there, done that, and could I go on one of his courses. With the truck-driving course already full he mentioned a plant course and I snapped it up. I discovered that in fact there were two courses, both about ten weeks long. One dealt with the more mobile vehicles such as bulldozers, scrapers, graders, road-rollers, and dumper trucks. The other involved cranes and their conversions into face-shovels, back-actors, and draglines. I opted for the bulldozers. The courses, with about twelve of us on each, were run by 18 Field Park Squadron Plant Troop..

Eric, on the right, awaiting his turn to operate a Caterpillar D4, after a week in the classroom. (Photo N Rose).

Eric 'cabbying' one of the D4 bulldozers.

With the arrival of October we were seeing cloud for about the first time since landing in Cyprus. The sweltering heat had now dissipated and the nights had started to become quite cool. At the end of the month, only about four weeks into the course, 33 Squadron was suddenly put on 24-hours notice for *Operation Musketeer*, the invasion of Egypt. Now we realised the real reason for building the fuel-storage tanks in such a hurry and our spending so long at Barton Stacey wasting taxpayers' money. All demobilisation was cancelled until further notice.

I think it was on 4 November that those of us chosen to take part in the attack on Port Said were trucked down the hill to the docks and ferried out to the troopship *Empire Ken* from the jetty.

The Limassol jetty.

The troopship *Empire Ken*.

We set sail in the afternoon. When we were shown our quarters down below we found that the ship was packed. Later, after we'd settled down for the night some of us were unable to sleep because of the heat and took our groundsheet and blanket up on deck where we tried to make ourselves comfortable on any spare bit of deck we could find in the damp salty air. No one challenged us and that's where we stayed for the rest of the night. Soon after dawn, with hair and blanket somewhat damp, we were woken up by the crew beginning to move about. It was then we noticed that during the night we had been joined by another troopship – *the Empire Parkeston*. That morning, the fifth of November, British Paratroops attacked el Gamil airfield, some three miles to the west of Port Said.

During the day we had become part of a large convoy of ships and as we came in sight of the Egyptian coastline towards nightfall we could see smoke rising on the horizon. Despite being so close to Port Said we spent another night aboard ship with the same group of us sleeping on deck again. Soon after this second dawn the Commandos went in by which time we were close enough to the coast to see the crenulated profile of Port Fuad and Port Said.

Later, as the time drew closer for our unit to land, we were assembled in what was possibly the ship's dining room where the CO of the regiment gave us a pep talk. I have forgotten all but one thing that he said and this I remember well. Since hardly any of us had been in action before, he said, fear could sometimes cause us to have an accident in our pants, or words to that effect. To avoid this, he continued, 'Have a bloody good rear before you go ashore.' I'd not heard it called that before but then lieutenant colonels probably have a different vocabulary than joiners.

During the afternoon we assembled on deck in full kit and took in the scene of smoke and scuttled ships as the *Empire Ken* crept between the breakwaters and anchored inside the entrance to the Suez Canal.

The *Empire Ken* entering the Suez Canal.

The people of Port Said had been warned apparently that troops would soon be landing and that it would be dangerous to be in the port area. It became dangerous for us too. Suddenly there was a metallic-sounding clang just above our heads and then another. We had all heard enough ricochets in cowboy films not that much earlier in our lives to know that someone was shooting at us and there was a rapid move by many to find something to stand behind even if it was only one of the other squaddies. The town had still not been cleared of snipers even though making the waterfront safe enough for the ships to enter had been one of the objectives of the Commandos.

The few quays where all but small ships could berth were now denied us since they lay at the far side of the blockships and we had to use lighters and other small vessels to make the transition from ship to shore. After a while someone got organised and we started to disembark and line up on the quayside on the flat area behind the De Lesseps statue and just north of the Casino Palace Hotel where we were allowed to stand easy while it was decided what to do with us.

As we stood chatting and trying to take in all that was happening around us a very smart unit marched past us and came to a halt close by. They were so obviously a French outfit and we thought they were the Foreign Legion. Then someone said, 'Bloody Hell, take a look of that!' I'd already seen what he was referring to.

Interspersed at regular intervals among the ranks of men, and dressed exactly the same, were a number of young women, I wondered what their job description was. The kindest answer I heard was that they were probably nurses.

After a while our troop was marched though part of the town into a wide boulevard with central reservation, past the modern railway station on our left, and through a gateway of the grounds of one of three requisitioned three-storey secondary schools situated side by side..

Two of the schools, a low-loader, and two three-tonner Bedford RLs.

We took our gear inside and were left for a while to choose groundsheet space on the concrete floor of the upstairs classrooms which were quite devoid of furniture. I found a spot that for most of our time in Port Said I was glad to call my own at the end of each day. Before we settled down someone arranged a meal. When we awoke the following morning, the seventh, I can't recall being told that a ceasefire had come into effect the previous evening. I thought we were still at war.

View from the school balcony of the road and the station.

View to the front of the school.

No school today, and enjoying the break from routine. Still in their pyjamas or is this the way they always dress?

One of the first jobs my particular group of sappers was involved in was to assist a few lads from the Field Park Squadron in pulling down an unsafe building that had been damaged during the air attack on the town. We passed a steel cable through one of the shattered ground floor window openings and back out of the adjacent one. The two ends were then attached to a bulldozer. After we'd all moved well back the operator drove his D8 away from the building and proceeded to make the two openings into one. There was dust flying everywhere. In no time at all what had once been a rather fine building was just a large heap of rubble with a gradually-settling thick white cloud hovering above it. It was all very spectacular. Even the locals thought so, we had quite an audience.

With this job done we were allowed to make our own way back to the school. On the way we were waylaid by a street photographer who was obviously treating the invasion as just another business opportunity. We formed a group and let him take our picture.

Eric standing second from the right. Alan Lloyd from Gateshead standing second left.

I personally saw no sign of resentment at our presence in the town despite the killing that had taken place and the damage we had caused. In fact, some of the locals were, or feigned to be, positively friendly and were treating the arrival of large numbers of fresh faces as an Allah-sent opportunity to market their selection of trinkets and postcards, dirty or otherwise. The events of the last few days seemed to have just washed over them. Some of the population strolled about as though it was the usual Sunday afternoon promenade and we the entertainment. Others were so relaxed about the whole business that they hadn't bothered to get dressed that morning – they were still in their 'nightshirts' and lounging about in the sidewalk cafes smoking their communal pipes through flexible hoses and drinking coffee thick enough to hold the spoon like Araldite. They'd seen it all before.

A pavement-side café and its local clientele.

For the very poor people of the town things were not so good. Port Said, being a trading port, has always been a multicultural town with many of the Arab population able to speak English. Consequently we were able to chat to a group of the locals who explained that the shortage of food had nothing to do with the invasion; it had always been like this, especially under Nasser. Cairo wasn't interested in them. Of course this could have been just ingratiating talk but we saw signs of poverty everywhere.

A part of Port Said's Shanty Town that managed to survive the shelling from one of the ships.

One morning, the adjutant, a captain whose name I am unable to recall now, came into the school and told three of us to bring our rifles and follow him. He led us out of the boulevard and in among the streets until he came to a stop at a large and flash left-hand drive American car parked against the pavement. It was unlocked and he told us to get in. He seemed oblivious to any thought of a booby trap although he may well have checked the vehicle previously. After some initial trouble finding the position of the gears on the steering column shift he drove us off somewhere. I can't remember where we went or what we were supposed to be doing other than acting as his bodyguard but it was certainly more interesting than replacing the sash cords in a Blackpool boarding house.

The Royal Engineers contingent at Port Said seemed to be mainly employed in helping to get the public utilities infrastructure of the town – water, electricity, sewage, telephones, etc., back into working order or guarding them against any further damage by saboteurs or looters.

One morning four or five of us from Three Troop of 33 Squadron were picked out and taken to Marconi House telegraph office overlooking the canal. Because of its association with the British establishment there had been attempts to break into the building, presumably to sabotage the radios, teleprinters, telegraphic and communications equipment, or just generally loot the place. We were armed and were to live on the premises until further notice for the purpose of discouraging any more mischief. Our food would be brought to us each day.

After organising the guard-duty roster for the night we started to explore, inspecting the electrical equipment and rummaging through the cupboards and drawers. After we'd done this a couple of times, then again, looked out of the windows, had a read, a brew up, tried out the typewriters and written letters home, it all became a bit tedious.

I have to admit I removed from a drawer an envelope containing a small collection of used foreign stamps torn from letters received by the company; a little something for Theresa's album. I think we had about five days of this before being relieved and taken back to our little areas of concrete floor space in the school.

As well as serving as stevedores to load and then eventually reload the ships, the sappers were also responsible for running the trains backwards and forwards between Port Said Station and El Cap Station some thirty miles to the south on the bank of the Suez Canal.

This was the point the Army had reached by the time the ceasefire came into effect at midnight on the sixth of November. From then on El Cap served more or less as the demarcation point between the two sides until the United Nations peacekeeping force took over. It was by this route that the lads guarding the village were supplied with food and other necessities, and the Egyptian wounded and prisoners, repatriated.

According to an entry on the Internet site *britains-smallwars, units at Suez*, by Vincent Cassin, when a subaltern of No.2 Troop insisted on taking over the driving of a diesel locomotive against the driver's advice on a stretch of suspect line near El Cap he managed to derail it by driving too fast. The attempt to lever the 80-ton giant back on the track was unsuccessful and it was left to another sapper unit with a crane to deal with later.

Sappers attempting to lever the locomotive back on track.

As the time came close for the United Nations to take over and the Allies to depart, our troop found itself with less to do than of late except for the odd patrol such as on the one shown below.

Some of the lads keeping an eye on a scramble for food.

On close to the last day we were driven out to the water works at the south side of the town. We were given a time to report back at the truck and then left to our own devices for a few hours. I don't know whether this was just a convenient way of keeping us occupied or a genuine desire by the OC or the troop subaltern to let us do some sightseeing while we had the opportunity. Whichever, it was an interesting experience and provided us with some extra memories of Port Said. The waterworks is the source of the Sweetwater Canal which was originally built during the construction of the Suez

The water works layout and filter beds as seen from the top of the water tower. The Sweet Water Canal supplying drinking water to the villages and towns to the south exits the site to the right (south) just beyond the raised black tank.

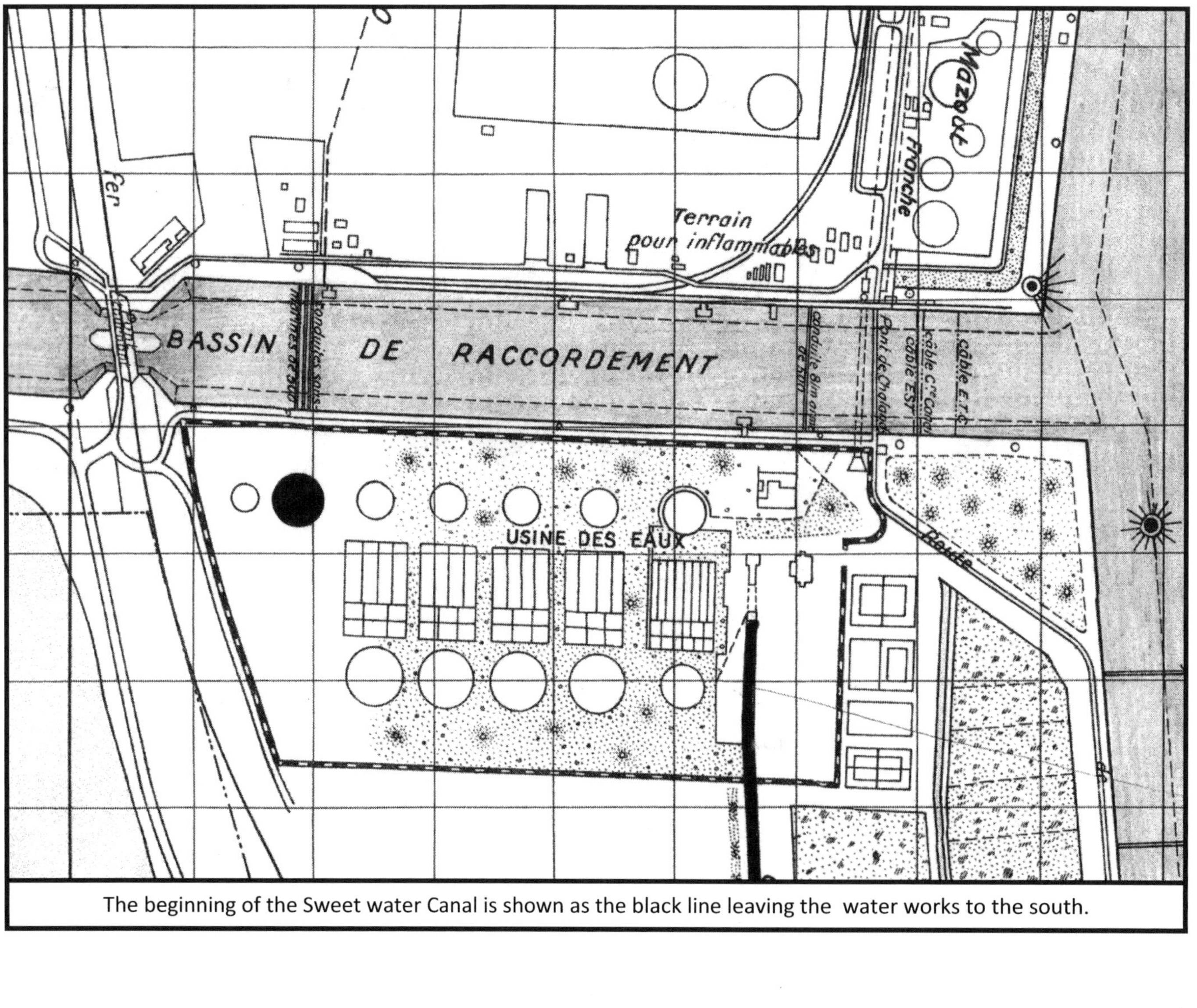

The beginning of the Sweet water Canal is shown as the black line leaving the water works to the south.

Canal and parallel to it just a few yards away to provide drinking water for the vast labour force and then afterwards for the inhabitants of the various villages and towns situated along its length. We managed to get out and about again in Port Said before we finally joined the withdrawal.

An undamaged part of town with Woolworths on the left.

On the 16th of December we learnt that the sappers from Polemidia Camp were to leave Port Said the next day for their return to Cyprus. We spent our last night on our concrete beds and soon after breakfast made our way to the quayside to be ferried aboard what I think may have been the *Empire Ken* again. Units were not necessarily kept together for their return to Cyprus or Malta.

We stowed our kitbags and weapons in the sleeping area, and went back up on deck to watch the ship's departure. As we slowly eased our way out of the canal we had an excellent view to starboard of the French hospital ship and an aircraft carrier that had accompanied us at the landing. We passed the De Lesseps statue on our left.

While we'd been away in Egypt the lads back in Cyprus had experienced the blackest period of the emergency. In just over a fortnight EOKA terrorists had killed thirty-eight people – twenty-one Britons and seventeen of their fellow Cypriots.

On Saturday, 24 November, a week or so after our arrival back in Cyprus, those of us who'd been away were treated to a day out. Coaches were laid on and we were taken, well armed with rifles, Sten guns, cartons of cigarettes and crates of booze, to Kyrenia on the north coast of the island. The cigarettes from the NAAFI were so cheap that it tended to encourage those squaddies who didn't already smoke to start. On the coach someone threw me a cigarette so I lit it up and had a puff. It did nothing for me apart from make me cough so I saw no point in acquiring the habit and it costing me money for the rest of my life.

Near the summit of the Kyrenia range, which has a high point of some 3,340 feet, we stopped and had a look round what was left of St Hilarion Castle. It had been built on what must have been an already fairly impregnable site to start with. From here we were able to look down on the port of Kyrenia below us and out to a smudge of Turkish coastline fifty-odd miles away on the horizon.

The Department of Antiquities keeper who showed us around said that Walt Disney had once shot some of the outdoor scenes here for one of his movies. After a while we piled back into the coaches and continued on, descending the winding road down into Kyrenia. This northern part of Cyprus tended to be a mostly Turkish area so when we were given a few hours to explore the town we felt reasonably comfortable. At one stage we found ourselves outside the police station so made it the backdrop for a photo-taking session.

One of the 3-Troop sappers with a Sten gun, name forgotten, and Eric, outside Kyrenia Police Station.

Back at Polemidia I completed the remaining few weeks of the plant course which ended with examinations sometime in January 1957. When the results were posted I found that I had come second. For a while those of us who had been on the various courses and waiting permanent assignments found ourselves in limbo and became fair game for anyone needing spare bods to do jobs around the camp. We got lumbered for night guard duty on what seemed to be an inordinate number of times. I hated the tedium of those two 2-hour spells patrolling a pathetic excuse of a boundary fence. The boredom though was tinged with an element of apprehension and a feeling of vulnerability in which, from the blackness of the hillside, we must have been silhouetted against the lights of the camp. We also carried out more after-dark patrols and the odd exercise.

At last, with the approach of spring and drier weather, it was decided to start up the Episkopi tunnel project again and this time, hopefully, get it completed. No.33 Squadron was transferred to the Episkopi cantonment for the duration of this work. Soon after our arrival there I was posted to the Plant Troop of 18 Field Park Squadron so that I could take charge of one of the D4s needed on the project. A vacancy for a dozer operator had arisen when one of them went back to Blighty on demob or reposting. He was an older full corporal regular called Beecroft who'd done some instructing on the course.

The large Episkopi cantonment was gradually being developed as Britain's new military headquarters in the Middle East. Although we were accommodated in tents the main buildings on the site were two- and three-storey-high blocks constructed of permanent materials and with more to be built. It certainly appeared that the British were planning to be here for a considerable time to come despite the hopes of the Greek Cypriots.

In April, Archbishop Makarios was released from exile in the Seychelles and flown to Greece. This was on the understanding that he didn't try to return to Cyprus. Also in April EOKA declared an unofficial truce against the British which lasted until September. A response to the release of Makarios possibly.

It wasn't long now before all the junior NCOs in the Plant Troop had been released on demob and I was made a lance corporal. A relatively elderly Sgt Herbert was the only other troop member with stripes and our only officer was Captain Orange-Bromhead who, I learned many years later, eventually became a lieutenant colonel.

I took over one of the D8 caterpillar bulldozers and with an attached scraper widened the road from the Akrotiri RAF base down to the fuel tank farm on the beach. At intervals along the fence there were signs stating that photography was forbidden. I took three photographs: one of two Vampire fighters, another of a Canberra fighter-bomber, and the third of a Valiant bomber. They didn't show enough detail to make it worth my while approaching the Russians with them.

An RAF Valiant bomber at Akrotiri.

I also did some levelling work around the rather grand house which had just been built, I believe, for the C-in-C of MELF. This was situated on the Episkopi limestone plateau behind Beach Five. The house had been provided with its own private track leading down to the beach. However, there was still some further work to be done on improving the turning circles on the hairpin bends.

Sgt Herbert took me to the site in his Austin Champ and explained that he wanted me to try out a new bulldozer that had just been received from the UK. When it arrived on site it turned out to be a Mark 3 Challenger made by Fowlers of Leeds – the firm that also made tanks for the Army. In terms of power the Challenger, with a Meadows engine, was an English equivalent to the D8 and the Sergeant wanted to know how it reacted to a prolonged hard workout in the hot weather. (Fowler's was actually now owned by Thomas Ward of Sheffield who had integrated the company with Marshall tractors of Gainsborough ten years earlier.)

During the Suez' crisis six months before, the government had been most disappointed, to say the least, in America's hostility to the venture rather than supportive. Whether the purchase of a British machine was a reaction to the government's perception of how we'd been treated by the Americans, or simply part of a policy to buy British if the quality and price was right, I don't know. I liked the machine and it handled well. its main difference to the D8 was that it had a higher revving engine. Whether it would have the longevity of the rugged D8 remained to be seen.

The Fowler Challenger Mark 3.

Over the next few months we carried out a number of other jobs on detachment around the southern area of Cyprus, some of them on behalf of local communities.

Frequently the crane drivers and the operators of the more mobile machines would find themselves on a project together and would invariably treat these occasions as an opportunity to learn each other's jobs. At lunchtime, as soon as we had finished our sandwiches, someone would say, 'Let's have a cabby on your machine.' And after a bit of tuition the dragline or Coles crane operators had learned the basics of how to control a bulldozer, grader, road roller or dump truck while in turn we were soon getting the hang of manipulating their machines. This eventuality was something perhaps not foreseen by the plant course organisers but would be of great benefit to the Army in an emergency.

One or two of these young National Service operators at little more than eighteen took to their machines as to the manner born. Lifting and swinging the dragline bucket, for instance, became one smooth flowing motion and a joy to watch. Our late teens and early twenties were a wonderful time for learning as testified by the young age of heavy bomber pilots during World War Two.

With the arrival of the hot weather it was the practice to start work early and then finish early in the afternoon. With our being next to the sea. Ladies Mile Beach became very busy at this time of the year. The transport section back at Polemidia would lay on a truck each afternoon for those lads and members of married families who wanted to go down to the beach.

As a consequence of all this and other traffic between Limassol and Ladies Mile the track had deteriorated badly and sergeant Herbert decided that upgrading this would be my next job, which, appropriately, would be with a grader.

Eric on the beach road to Ladies Mile and Akrotiri.

National Servicemen were allowed two weeks' leave while in Cyprus, that's all I got anyway. Some of the lads went home to Blighty for this fortnight. Others decided that with a relatively short time of their service left they would be better off seeing something of the Middle East while they had the opportunity and went to Israel. A few may have gone to Turkey while others just lounged around the camp for the fortnight.

I discussed the subject with a few of the lads and four of us thought we'd like to see something of the island while we were here. We checked with the squadron office and since EOKA seemed to be still honouring its truce with the security forces we were allowed to plan something as long as we went out in pairs or more and the situation didn't alter in the meantime. This resulted in four of us, Charlie, Denis, Mike and myself hiring a car and doing a circuit of the island. We set off on the last Saturday in August in a hired Morris Minor and encountered no problems.

Despite operating heavy earthmoving equipment I didn't hold an ordinary driving license. I had a word with the RTO, a captain, about the possibility of giving up my second week's leave to go out with the lads of the transport troop to get some experience. He readily agreed and offered to put me through the test afterwards.

On the Monday morning of my leave I went down to the MT pool and introduced myself to the sergeant. He put me with the driver of a three-ton Bedford QL for the day. This had a 'crash' gearbox that made the most awful sounds if you didn't get things right. I think I'd been put on the QL on purpose. No doubt the idea was that if I learned how to change gear on this I'd have no problems with the other vehicles, all of which had synchromesh gearboxes. I watched and listened for a while before being given a go myself on the open road. After creating the odd screech or two, and with a 'Oops, sorry!' I managed to sort it out.

A Bedford QL three-tonner truck at Polemidia Camp.

On another day I went out in Bedford's modern and smarter-looking version of the three-tonner, the RL. This had an air-compressor under the side of the vehicle which was connected to the engine so that you didn't need a foot pump to put air in the tyres. It was a nice truck to drive.

Bedford RL with the 35 Regiment number still showing. 37 Regiment had replaced 35 Regiment two years earlier.

For great gearboxes you couldn't beat the one on the Austin Champ. It had the smoothest action I've ever encountered since. The vehicle I suppose was the British equivalent of the American Army Jeep and was powered by a sealed Rolls Royce engine. It was a most enjoyable drive.

An Austin Champ at Polemidia Camp, near Limassol.

Towards the end of the week I got my hands on the big stuff. One of the lads had to take a Scammell tractor and low loader to Famagusta to return a D8 from our plant yard and the sergeant sent me with him. The Scammell, with its big multi-geared Gardner engine made at Patricroft, Salford, was no longer a novelty for the driver near demob so he let me drive nearly all the way there and back. At one place the road ran parallel to a river then curved to the right to cross the one-lane bridge and then to the left at the other side. Cyprus bridges weren't built for this kind of truck and I couldn't quite get the back end of the trailer round the end of the parapet. The driver sorted it out for me and I managed it on the way back.

Scammell tractor, low-loader and D8.

One day the following week the captain took me out on a test. He passed me on the practical then started asking me road code questions. I was taken somewhat unawares. No one had mentioned the road code, either the British or the Cypriot one, if there was such a thing. 'Get the book from my clerk,' he said, 'and come and see me in a week's time.' After the oral test I was given a license and a letter for the authorities in Britain.

One day near the end of my service, Captain Orange-Bromhead caught up with me in the plant yard and invited me to sign on for the extra year. If I did he would make me up to full corporal right away. I felt flattered but had to say no thanks. Theresa already had the wedding organised with the vicar at St John's Church, Blackpool.

My demob group went down to Limassol docks sometime early in December and was taken out to the lighter drawn up against the foot of a rickety stairway leading up onto the deck of the troopship *Dilwara*. After stowing our gear aboard we returned to the lighter and spent the rest of the afternoon assisting the married families to clamber up the swaying stairs with their kids and luggage. We sailed in the evening by which time I had been appointed the NCO in charge of washing up. We stopped briefly at Tobruk to take aboard more mar-

Returning to the *Dilwara* after the afternoon in Tripoli.

ried families, then Tripoli for more of the same but getting shore leave for a few hours.

Two weeks after our departure from Limassol we tied up at the quayside in Southampton just behind the liner *Queen Elizabeth*. We transferred to a train and set off for Andover Junction, and then by truck to Barton Stacey. After a few days, during which our time was filled with a number of pointless 'keep them occupied' chores we went on Christmas leave.

Back in Blackpool, with the remnants of my Cyprus tan, bleached blond hair, and corporal's stripe I became the centre of attention – for about three minutes. I returned to Barton Stacey early in the New Year just to be demobbed. I was now deemed to have been enlisted for Part-Time National Service into the Royal Engineers and posted to 111 Plant Regiment, 227 Squadron, Ripon, on 27 January 1958. I was later transferred to the Army General Reserve on 4 July 1961 and discharged from Reserve Liability on 28 February 1964. However this was all on paper. When I was demobbed the annual camps had been discontinued and I never had anything to do with the Army again.

Theresa and I were married early in February, two days after the Manchester United air crash at Munich, and honeymooned in London. Initially I'd thought about taking an earth-moving job at Preston on the by-pass, Britain's first length of motorway. But it was February, very cold, and I didn't fancy getting up at about 5.30 a.m. to travel there in time for work by eight. So I drifted back into the building trade with my old firm. I discovered that my army driving license converted into heavy goods, PSV, and virtually every other category except for tramcars and motorbikes.

In the summer of 1960, two-and-a-half restless years later, I was doing some bricklaying at the front of the house when George Braithwaite, one of my old tutors from the technical college, happened to be passing and stopped to talk. He asked me why I didn't get out of the overalls and go teaching. Apparently with my Final, and now my Full Tech City and Guilds Certificate, I could go into technical college or secondary teaching as a technical subjects teacher without any further ado. After twelve months' probation I would become permanent if satisfactory. By September I was a secondary school woodwork teacher in Whitefield near Manchester and a night school tutor at Blackpool Technical College. After two years of travelling daily from Blackpool to Whitefield I was 'head-hunted' by the Blackpool authority which wished to expand the amount of technical education taught in the borough.

In the staff room I was soon advised that promotion in teaching would come only with a degree so from 1962 onwards, in order to gain university entrance, I began to collect O- and A-Levels at evening classes at Blackpool Technical College and and Wigan Mining College for geology. Three years later I registered with London University for one of their external degrees. In the early 1970s I acquired a B.Sc honours degree in Geology and Geography.

Meanwhile, in 1968, now with Stewart and Letitia and widowed mother-in-law Thyra, we moved for promotion, first to Maidstone and then to Telford. In 1974 we went to live in New Zealand and that was where I retired. I lost Theresa in 2003 and two years later I returned to the UK where I eventually married Margery who I had known, together with her late husband, at school and youth club.

*   *   *

Alan Phelan, 33 Squadron, Royal Engineers.

View from the *Empire Ken* troopship on entering the canal. Fire from Shanty Town hit by a destroyer shell.

View from the *Empire Ken* just before it dropped anchor in the outer harbour. Smoke from a ruptured oil tank at the Standard Oil Company site about three miles away.

View of the dredger *Paul Solente* sunk as a blockship close the Port Said waterfront about opposite the lighthouse.

* * *

Ray Alan Rudkin, 57 Squadron, Royal Engineers.

I was born on 14 February 1935 in Leicester and have lived there ever since. I took to cricket at a very early age and have a photo of me at about the age of eight or nine in cricket whites when I played for my primary school. At the age of eleven I went to a secondary modern school and soon got into the school cricket team. On leaving school at 15 Dad put me as an apprentice bricklayer starting at £1 a week. I found that I liked the job so went to night school for the City and Guilds course. I finished my apprenticeship at the age of 21 early in 1956 by which time I had acquired the Final Certificate in Bricklaying and was married with a young son.

I now had to do my National Service and was put into the Royal Engineers. With initial training over I went on to do more training as a field engineer which I found fairly easy since much of it was just like being in the building trade. My posting was to 36 Engineer Regiment in Germany, part of a large garrison of sappers housed at Roberts Barracks, Osnabruck, an ex-SS camp during World War Two, which we shared with 38 Regiment. There were North and South Camps and we were the engineers for No.1 Division and the other regiment for No.2 Division. As can be imagined there was fierce competition between the two colonels in all that we did such as schemes and exercises and consequently we probably had more square-bashing, parades and kit inspections than the Guards at this time.

Lots of the guys hated the disruption of going out on exercises, especially during the harsh German winters, but I quite liked them. There was an agreement between the NATO Allies and the Russians that allowed observation teams in each other's territories to monitor any possible build up of forces that might herald an attack by the other side. The Americans had a mobile atomic cannon which had a steering cab at both back and front to help it get round tight corners. I went on only one scheme where this 80-foot giant was present and it had to try to keep moving at all times so that it became difficult for the Soviet observers in what I think were called their 'Sox Mex' cars to radio accurate co-ordinates back to base. Sometimes it could move only a very little distance because accompanying teams had to take down telegraph poles and other obstruction on roads. There was always one of these Soviet cars following the canon.

I wasn't long in Germany before the Suez flap got serious. No leave had been allowed for quite some time because of the uncertainty surrounding the situation. However, being a married man, I eventually got some leave back in the UK but had been home only two days when a telegram arrived instructing me to report to Southampton Docks to go aboard the *Dilwara*.

The American 'Nuclear Canon' in Germany.

The troopship *Dilwara*.

During our transfer aboard ship not long before sailing I discovered that my kit had gone missing. I was the fifth person allocated to a four-berth cabin. Fortunately we took turns at sleeping on the floor. We called in at Gibraltar and Malta on the way to Egypt. I found the trip quite exciting since I loved boats and had asked for the Navy when interviewed for National Service.

Lazing on the deck on the way to Port Said.

When we got to within two or three miles out from Port Said we waited. We were mustered on deck in the early morning, about 5.30 I think. then, together with another lad, I was ordered to scramble down the nets hung over the side of the ship to a naval craft to stack the kitbags thrown down to us. We then sat about for what seemed hours waiting for further orders until the sergeant major told us we were not going ashore this early after all so for some reason we were made to get all the kitbags, and then ourselves, back up on deck again where we continued to wait at muster.

In the early afternoon the sergeant major returned and told us it was our turn to land so down the nets the two of us went again and started stacking the kitbags a second time in the landing craft. We hadn't had anything to eat or drink since early morning and by now we were hungry, very tired and hot. A sailor took pity on the two of us and mashed us a cup of tea.

Finally we were joined down the nets by the rest of the squadron and were taken ashore where we landed at the quay on the canal waterfront at about 6 o'clock in the evening having passed the blockship *Pollux* and other ships on the way in.

The scuttled salvage vessel *Pollux.*

Everyone seemed to land close to the Casino Palace Hotel where there was plenty of space to assemble on the wide side street and on the area at the back of the De Lesseps Statue. From here we were marched to the railway station where we were each given a field pack on which we heated

The mural at the western side of the station concourse.

The mural at the eastern side of the station concourse.

View of the station entrance and the first two of the three school on its far or western side.

The plaza fronting the station and the three adjacent schools. The mosque with its minaret is directly opposite the school adjacent to the station.

our food. After this supper and mounting a guard the rest of us were all too ready to get our heads down after having been got up quite needlessly early as it turned out.

The following day, except for HQ Troop which stayed in the station, we moved to a building down the railway yard behind and slightly to one side of the station. We stayed here, 12 of us to a room and just one blanket to a soldier, for almost the rest of our time in Port Said.

This view, two photographs joined together, is from the roof of the building to the rear and western side of the station which was allocated to Ray's troop and in which they were billeted for most of their time in Port Said.

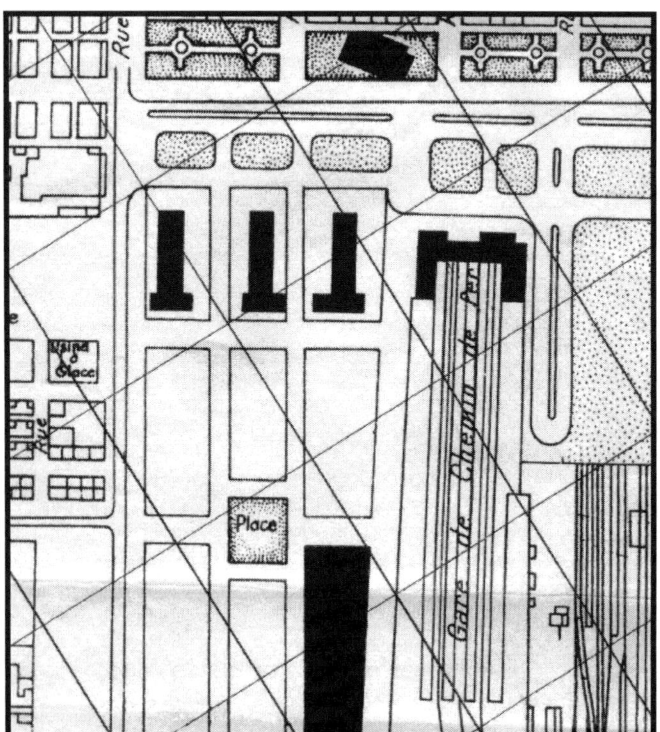

Various buildings highlighted.

The building down the station yard used as a billet. The photograph of the station was taken from this roof.

We were allocated duties each day including guards of course. The area between the back of this block and the building shown behind it on the right is shown in the following photograph.

One of the lads on guard.

Combining guard duty with sunbathing on the roof?

Being 21 rather than 18 like most of the lads, and a fully-qualified tradesman, I tended to be given jobs where I could be left alone to get on with them. Consequently I missed out on many of the things the troop did together.

The lads detailed for work on the quays and basins on the canal side would turn right along the plaza on leaving the station and pass along the street known an Rue Mustapha Kamel.

Viewing left across the plaza from the right-hand side of the station front. Mosque and minaret across the road.

French soldiers on the Rue Mustapha Kamel.

Army truck on the Rue Mustapha Kamel.

This was the street where Egyptian traders would hawk their wares. The MPs used to cordon off the street most nights at about just before the six o'clock prayer call, and confiscate any goods that the soldiers had traded in – boots, berets, fags, etc. However, the traders would come again the next day.

One day when most of the squadron was out on a job another sapper and myself were working in the station when the HQ Troop billeted in the station shouted to us to come and bring our rifles to the front entrance of the station. We grabbed them and ran out to the pavement to join our mates where we found what looked to be hundreds of Egyptians shouting and coming towards us.

An officer suddenly appeared from somewhere and told us to fix bayonets. He grabbed a rifle off one of the squaddies, advanced to what looked like the ringleader of the mob, and jabbed the bayonet in his arm. This calmed them down and believe it or not the crowd slowly started to disperse. I went back to change my underwear and returned to what I'd been doing.

One of the troops of the squadron went down the line to the furthest point of the army's advance, El Cap, and built a small bridge over the Sweetwater Canal there.

Small bridge built by the sappers at El Cap.

Towards the end of our stay in Port Said while we were just waiting for the withdrawal and no longer had much to do except for basic duties we began to get more free time and as long as we were armed and there were at least two of us, we were given permission to go out into town.

On one occasion while I was out with another sapper I'd met up when with we were approached by an Egyptian chap with a camera who began pestering to take our picture. In the end we said okay and he took a couple of snaps. He then rushed off to develop his film but was soon back.

Alan and his mate posing for street photographer.

Ray with a bit of free time.

When the withdrawal drew close we began reducing the perimeter of the occupied area of port Said and moved from the station area to a block of flats close to the quay by the Casino Palace Hotel.

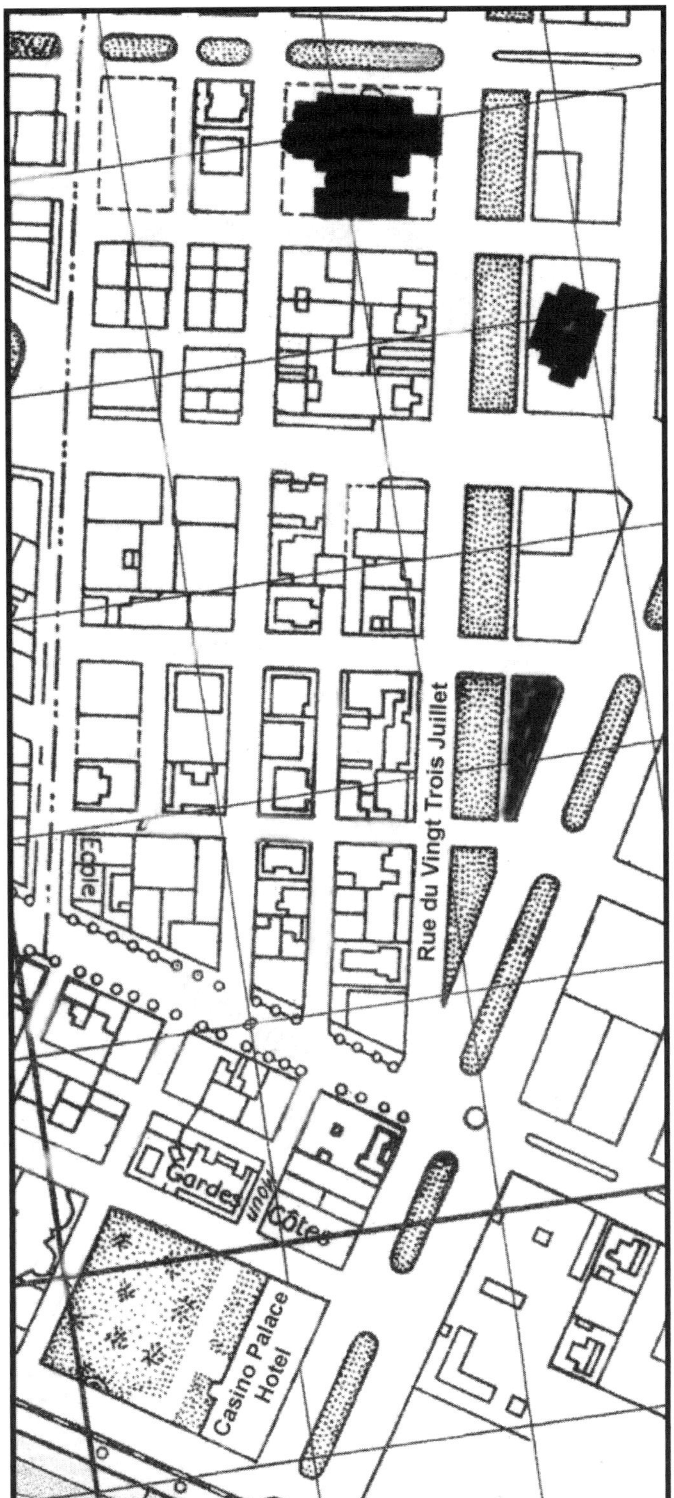

The new billet was the triangular building at the beginning of the Rue du Vingt Trois Juillet. The features with a dotted shading are grassed areas of parks and central reservations of the wide street. Vingt Trois Juillet translates to the 23 of July, the date of the military coup in

In the map the triangular block of flats, a mosque, and the Catholic Cathedral have been highlighted to locate the following photographs.

View west along the Rue du Vingt Juillet from an upper end flat in the apartment block billet. A mosque straight ahead and the Catholic Cathedral on the left of the street.

View west from a front balcony on the first floor.

View from an upper rear flat looking out over the ground where No.45 Commandos landed by helicopters, the De Lesseps Statue, and the Fish Docks.

While we were here many went down with gippy tummy but me especially. I was rushed into hospital with this extreme gastroenteritis, according to my medical records. Then the RAF flew me to Cyprus, just me, a nurse, and the pilot in a rather small aircraft. The RAF managed to lose my kit again, this time including my rifle and 55 rounds of ammunition. I remained in hospital there for three to four weeks where I was pampered by the ladies of the QARANCs, bless 'em.

I came back from Cyprus after Suez on the *Dilwara* again. It took us three days to get aboard the ship. Day one was rough and when a flat-bottomed naval craft ferried us to the ship which was about a mile out to sea it managed to get under the stairs in the swell and rip them off. The next day we had to sit out the weather ashore while the sea calmed down. A Cypriot guy saw what was happening and brought a camel to the beach and sold rides. The third day we managed to start getting aboard the ship.

We arrived at Southampton quite early in the morning and I was about the first off the ship and into the customs hall. Having lost all my kit I only had a small knapsack, razor, knife and fork so was through right away. I was waiting for the other six sappers who'd come on the boat with me when all hell broke loose. RPs and officers were running all over the place. The reason was that a Pioneer Corps soldier had been found to have a pistol and rounds in his kitbag. From then on everyone had to empty his kitbag out onto the table. Some Pioneer lads were found to have no kit in their kitbags, just cartons of cigarettes. It was evening before we finally got away on the train to Chiseldon Camp near Ogbourne St George in Wiltshire where we were given a meal, three weeks' pay and leave, and told to kip down for the rest of the night. We just went AWOL and made our way to the station and slept on the benches until the first train for London arrived.

* * *

Andrew B Ramsay, 57 Sqn, Royal Engineers.

During my National Service I was stationed at Roberts Barracks, Osnabruck in Germany with 57 Squadron, 36 Engineer Regiment, Royal Engineers. When the balloon went up for Suez we had already been on standby for a while. We were soon on a train to the Hook of Holland and then on a ferry to Harwich. On the ferry I met one of my apprentice friends. We had both been deferred from National Service until we'd completed our training. He was in the Argyll and Sutherland Highlanders.

At Harwich there was a special train waiting to take us directly to Southampton docks where we had to parcel up our civvy clothes to be sent home. We sailed for Egypt on the troopship *Dilwara* and on reaching Malta learned that a ceasefire had taken place. Nevertheless we continued on to Port Said where, on our arrival, it was like being in a film. We had to disembark over the side down rope ladders and into a smaller boat and with not enough rifles between us. I had been issued with a bazooka with bits missing; it was little more than an empty tube.

View of the blockship Pollux on the way to the quay.

From the quay we marched to the railway station which was to be our squadron barracks. This was next to a row of three schools where other units of the Royal Engineers were billeted. To start with we slept on the roof of the office block of the station down the yard but later went inside but on beds with no mattress.

View on the roof looking west away from the sidings. The three sappers are George Summer, Preston; Andrew; and Bobby MacGregor, Glasgow.

View of the station taken from the central reservation opposite the first of the three adjacent schools

Someone broke into the ticket office of the station and we were able to purloin tickets to various destinations as souvenirs.

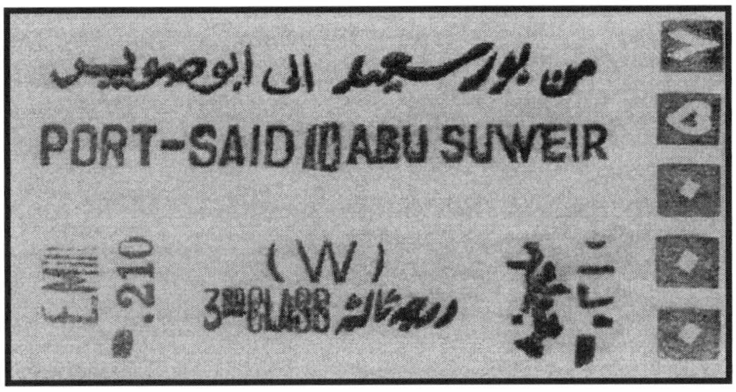

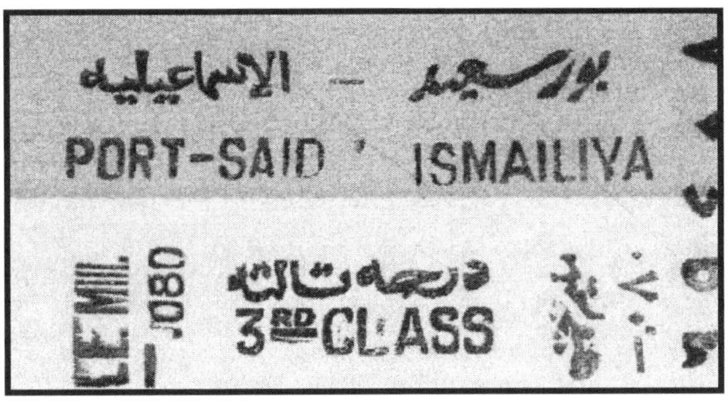

During one of the night shifts at the quay we were unloading equipment, including batteries, from a cargo vessel to a smaller boat. This smaller boat was quite a way below us and some of the batteries missed and went into the water.

After while we had to start loading everything back on the ships again in preparation for leaving the United Nations to get on with things. As things wound down towards mid-December we managed to get out and about on our own a bit.

These two photographs are of the same corner,

Another street in Port Said.

In December the UN troops arrived at the station and we started to hand over responsibility for the town to them.

A United Nations officer entering the station.

As the evacuation of Allied troops began to take place we moved closer in to the quay and slept in a block of flats that had been abandoned for the time being by the occupants. All their possessions were still there. We slept on top of the beds and left things as they were.

After my two years National Service I was for 30 years senior technician at Glasgow University Engineering Department working on the corrosion of various metals and building rigs for students. I was offered early retirement at 60 which I gratefully accepted.

* * *

Maurice C Lockyer, 323 Electrical and Mechanical Squadron, Royal Engineers.

I was born 19 December 1931 in my parents' flat at Oxford Gardens, Chiswick in London although we actually resided in another property in Ealing.

I started at Little Ealing School when I was five and continued there until 1940 when I was evacuated to Weston-Super-Mare because of London being a war zone. Since my father was a master butcher and couldn't take time off from the shop we had never been able to take holidays away. Now, however, I was living in a holiday resort.

I remained in Weston until April 1942 when bombing raids on London had tailed off somewhat. However, on my return I managed to see the occasional aerial dogfight. Soon afterwards I sat and failed the examination for grammar school but at thirteen I passed the entrance examination for Acton Technical College.

I left college in the summer of 1946 and joined the Lightfoot Refrigeration Company at Wembley as an apprentice. The start pay was 27 shillings for a 48-hour week. It was during this period that I joined the Air Training Corps. Being an apprentice I was deferred from National Service until I was 21 in December 1952 when I took my medical at Acton. I had heard that having sugar in the urine made one medically unfit for service so when it came time to provide a sample I added a few grains of sugar to the specimen glass. These didn't seem to be dissolving so I flushed this attempt away. I had to drink another glass of water and hang about for a while until I was able to produce a further specimen.

I then tried 'plan B' and when my name was next called I continued chatting to the chap sitting next to me and waited until the third and much louder request for my presence before I responded. In the hearing-test room it was only after the specialist's first three whispers that I answered. This led to my being given a grade-two rating on my hearing but despite this my services were still required.

On Thursday 15 January 1953 I reported to No.6 Training Regiment of the Royal Engineers at Norton Camp near Worcester for kitting out and initial training at this wooden-hutted cold and damp unit. At the end of a fortnight we were taken to Worcester Station and put on a train to take us to Farnborough in Hampshire where we were trucked to No.9 TRRE at Southwood Camp, Cove.

The Bailey bridging took place fairly early in the four-month course so we spent a lot of time in the freezing cold and ankle-deep in mud. The course ended in May when we went on a week's leave. I returned to Cove briefly before being posted to Brompton Barracks, Gillingham, for No. 209 refrigeration mechanics course with B Squadron. The course final examination took place on 18 February 1954 after which I was given a posting to Egypt. Following a week's embarkation leave I returned to Gillingham where I prepared for my eventual departure overseas

On 4 April, after a night at the Goodge Street Deep shelter Transit Centre with the others on the posting to Egypt, I flew out to Egypt from Lydd Airport in Kent. We had a two-hour stop in Malta at about 2am for both the aircraft and us to be refuelled. Then we continued on to a transit camp at Fayid in the Canal Zone where I was given a lift by the night-mail collection driver to my posting at the Engineer Base Group at Fanara.

By the end of the year when my demob was approaching the whole British Army was preparing to leave Egypt with the transfer of HQ MELF to Cyprus. We were told to smash all the spare parts we had accumulated through the cannibalisation of written-off machines and which were not covered by paperwork. We scrapped thousands of pounds worth of parts this way. What a waste! We were also instructed to put sand into the refrigeration systems of all equipment selected to go to auction in Cairo. I often wondered afterwards how the locals in the Canal Zone survived after 90,000 troops pulled out. Apart from the money we spent locally hundreds were employed in the various garrisons. Whole villages probably died from lack of income.

I flew back to the UK from Fayid RAF base. After a refuelling stop at Luqa in Malta we landed at Lydd in Kent. From here we were sent to Barton Stacey from where, in January 1955, after two weeks' leave, I was demobbed.

To start with I couldn't find a job I fancied so I went back to my old firm. I passed my driving test in April, got married in May after a six-year courtship, and in the summer was called on to do my first and what proved to be my only two weeks of annual reserve service at Ripon.

In the spring of 1956 the firm transferred me to the service staff. At the time I was living with my wife as a happy civilian with my wife in a caravan about three miles from Staines. On the morning of 9 August while I was starting up the van ready to drop my wife at the station on my way to work she returned from the site's communal letterbox with a letter marked OHMS. I had been recalled to the Colours and was supposed to report immediately to No.9 TRRE at Cove.

Although the letter didn't say so this mobilisation of reserves was obviously a consequence of Egypt's recent seizure of the Suez Canal Company. I came as a bit of a surprise though because I'd formed the impression from the papers that only ex -regular reservists were to be called up. I reported for duty two days later and found myself a member of No.2 Troop, 323 Electrical and Mechanical Squadron which had just be mobilised as a reserve unit. This was an independent outfit capable of doing almost anything and comprised a few tradesmen of many kinds and the rest supplying the labour.

One of our first duties was to drive to Bicester in Oxfordshire to collect our new transport. This comprised ten-ton workshop wagons down to Land Rovers with five-cwt water tank trailers. On our return we painted the vehicles with sand-coloured paint and a large letter H on roof and sides. I hadn't been comfortable driving this kind of three-ton truck, the Bedford QL, which needed double declutching at every gear change and instead was given a Land Rover. Soon afterwards I was made the CO's driver.

One day in September the drivers left Cove in convoy at about midnight and drove to Barry in South Wales. The following morning as we approached the docks through the streets of a rundown area dozens of scruffy urchins bombarded the convoy with stones and half bricks. Great fun, for them!

After the vehicles were loaded aboard the ship we were taken to Maindy Barracks in Cardiff and installed in a large gym lined with bunk beds spaced about two feet apart. As well as the sappers there were thirty military policemen, all reserve RAC and AA patrolmen, recalled for traffic control duties.

After a night out at a fairground I returned to Maindy to find a message from my wife telling me that the local council was trying to evict her from the caravan site because it wasn't licensed. There was also a problem with the finance company over the repayments on the caravan. I was given four days' leave to sort things out before rejoining my squadron which by then had moved to Tilshead on Salisbury Plain. The squadron then moved again, this time to Bovington in Dorset where we spent several days replacing a number of telegraph poles, the originals having been erected about 1910, so we were told.

One early afternoon at the end of October we were told to return all equipment to stores and to pack our kit. We then boarded a convoy of trucks and set off following the leading vehicle. After dark we reached our destination which we discovered was Lydd Airport on Kent. We were told that we would be flying out in about two hours' time but not to where. We had a fair idea though and this was confirmed when one of the Shackleton's aircrew mentioned Malta.

We landed at Luqa Airport after about five hours and were trucked the four of five miles to the docks at Valetta Harbour to board the aircraft carrier *Theseus*. Once settled in we were allowed back ashore and enjoyed an evening in Valetta. The following day we had a pleasant sightseeing tour round the city and then, a day or two after that, the third of November, we sailed.

We slept in hammocks, or tried to. There wasn't much to do aboard except to wait for the next meal. On one occasion someone tried to keep us occupied by having us line up on deck to watch the gun crews practise with their pom-pom ack-ack guns firing at Verey flares. Then I was given a stint up a tower about sixty feet above the deck on anti-submarine watch with the largest pair of binoculars I have ever seen. It was very windy up there and I lost my beret overboard. When I came down a naval officer saw me with the binoculars and asked where I'd been. He was not impressed when I told him 'Upstairs looking for submarines.'

Early on the 6th the *Theseus* dropped anchor some way out from the mouth of the Suez Canal and our contingent of commandos began to be ferried ashore by helicopters. Apparently this was the first helicopter-only operation carried out by an aircraft carrier.

I was one of seven sappers sent deep below deck via a vertical iron ladder to send ammunition up from the ship's magazine. It was a very primitive operation and carried out with just rope and pulley in a temperature of about 100° F. While the other lads worked in pairs I was the odd one out and had to work on my own so had a job keeping up with them which led to a bit of good-natured banter from the lads up on deck who said I must have been idling. Unfortunately our officer, Captain Oatley, overheard this and took it seriously and from then on he became very much anti-Sapper Lockyer.

In the afternoon we were ordered to come up on deck to watch the battle ashore. It was a remarkable experience watching a war in Cinerama and Technicolor. Close at hand we were deafened by the clatter of engines and rotor blades as helicopters took off to take the marines ashore then return with the wounded.

During the evening we were each issued with seventy-five rounds of .303 bullets in clips of five carried in light brown bandoliers. I wore mine across the chest feeling like a Mexican bandit. We were told that if any of us got shot the man next to him was to use the wounded man's field dressing to bind the wound and then leave him for the medics to deal with. None of us had had even the most basic of first aid training, not by the Army anyway.

At about 11pm we were ferried ashore in a landing craft and spent a cold and uncomfortable night trying to sleep on the pavement by the edge of the canal and were happy to rise with the sun. Our kitbags and blankets were in transit on another ship and we were to be cold at nights for another ten days.

A short walk away on the central reservation of the Place de la Gare, a very wide and open boulevard, we each cooked breakfast in our mess tins using mini stoves and combustible blocks. While we were eating an Egyptian passed us pushing a handcart carrying a body wrapped in a sheet.

'Is he dead mate?' one of the lads shouted rather unfeelingly. Shortly afterwards an English expatriot type walked by taking his Jack Russell dog for a walk. Smartly dressed in blazer, flannels, brown brogues and trilby, he raised his hat and said, 'Good morning Gentlemen. I'm glad to see that the sappers have arrived.' He didn't seem to be bothered by the sounds of nearby small arms fire or the whine of the occasional bullet overhead. Mad Englishman!

One of our sergeants and a few of the men found a showroom with new vehicles on display. They broke in and drove a three-ton Bedford cattle truck straight out through the plate glass window and a Morris Minor too for the CO to use. We clambered aboard the truck and a Marine captain arrived as our guide.

We drove into the central area of town and round a corner where we almost ran into the back of a tank which had just done an emergency stop. At that moment a young Egyptian civilian came crashing down onto the rear nearside of the tank then rolled off onto the road where he lay spread-eagled on his back with a horrible red gunge oozing from his stomach and through his shirt.

'Get that f------ wog off the road,' shouted a commando sergeant. Two of his lads heaved the body into the doorway of the Woolworth's store with a little more strength than was necessary and its head and shoulders crashed through the glass leaving the neck impaled on the jagged remnants of glass protruding from the bottom rail.

One of the balconies above was packed with cheering commandos, some wearing a fez. They were clearly the ones responsible for throwing the man, possibly a sniper, off the balcony. Having done some work at a mortuary I had at least seen a dead body before but some of our lads were looking distinctly white. Further along there were more bodies lying in the road although, surprisingly, the most upsetting sight for me was coming across a number of dead horses and donkeys with their stomachs spilled out. These animals have a lot of intestines.

At our destination just out of town to the south we found we were at the water works. This was a very smart looking facility with pumping station and a number of raised storage ponds set in several acres of 'woodland' and grass. We weren't sure that the facility had been secured and when we came to some open ground the corporal had us spread out in line abreast instead of making for the more protected area of the trees. A Bren-gunner could have wiped out all ten of us with one burst.

We made it to a tarmacadam road bordered on the far side by a tall hedge. There could have been Egyptians on the far side so far as we knew. We lay down and took cover among some trees and faced the hedge. Robin, the chap next to me at the end of the line, found himself close to a pile of dead Egyptian Special Policemen who had been thrown up on top of each other. He didn't like this one little bit and asked me to change places with him. We learned later that the policemen had fired shotguns at the descending French paratroops. Even though they eventually surrendered they paid for this indiscretion with their lives.

After lying in this defensive position for about half an hour we saw a legionnaire ride past on a bicycle. He was whistling to himself and completely ignored us. It was then we realised that the waterworks had already been brought under Allied control.

One of our lads, a dour Scot who rarely spoke, even to us, climbed up on the bodies to empty pockets and take off wristwatches. We found a way round to the other side of the hedge where we saw that it was just open sandy waste.

Our task at the works was to ensure that Port Said's water supply was maintained, both for us and the local population. On a patrol around the plant I came across a legionnaire washing his clothes in one of the ponds. I tried to explain that he wasn't to do this but he couldn't understand me and became somewhat aggressive. I called the corporal who, in his schoolboy French wrote a note to carry with me explaining that the water in the ponds was strictly eau potable. As I went round I showed this to every Frenchman I met. I also went into the main pump house which, with its windows right up to the ceiling, could have belonged to any waterworks in Britain. Here I found a shortish man in a French officer's uniform and wearing an eye patch. He was looking at a large map on a table in front of him. I saluted and he spoke to me in French. I assumed he wanted to know what I wanted so I showed him my bit of paper. He read it, smiled, and nodded okay. Later I discovered I had been speaking to General Gilles, one of the French parachute commanders.

That night my friend Robin and I found ourselves on anti-saboteur stag patrol around the ponds. As we walked I thought I saw some movement in the shadows ahead of us so I arranged to go around the back of the building while Robin came in from the front. As I circled the building I saw Robin talking to another person and thought I'd done well until I received a blow in the kidneys from someone behind me. It was a legionnaire. The French were also doing stag duty in the same area without anyone informing us. It could have been fatal. The Frenchie was a far more experienced soldier than I was.

While at the waterworks we discovered that there were several Englishmen among the legionnaires. They told us that now the fighting was over all they wanted was to get back to Algeria and kill more wogs. By this time Britain and France had been forced to call a halt to the invasion following pressure from home and the Americans. All we were doing now was keeping the infrastructure of the town operating and preventing sabotage and looting until the UN peacekeepers arrived.

Although I had acquired a discarded parachute on my first day in Port Said and wrapped myself in it at night I was still cold without a blanket especially since we had to sleep on a concrete floor in an outbuilding. After a few days we moved into quite a modern looking school back in the Place de Gare. The upper balconies overlooked the central grassy area of the road which was covered with the small brown bivouac tents of the legionnaires. It was quite strange to see them on parade; an officer would slap a sergeant who in turn would strike a man in the ranks.

One of the first things we did at the school was to remove all the desks and books from the classrooms and take them out to the playground. We were instructed to smash the desks and burn the books. I don't know what the idea of this was or who gave the order. What brave soldiers we were!

In a nearby council yard we found trucks, tools, and timber and we quickly set to making ourselves some makeshift beds. We used the canvas covers from the trucks to stretch between the bed sides. From then on we slept better.

While working in the council yard which was overlooked by tenement blocks, a veteran infantryman of Korea I was chatting to kept edging away from me. I asked him if I'd got BO or something. 'Don't come near me,' he said. 'You're an obvious target for a sniper from the apartments with that white scarf you're wearing.' I thought I looked quite flash with the piece of parachute material round my neck but should have realised the danger. In fact just before leaving the UK we had been instructed to blacken all our webbing and brasses. I thanked the bloke kindly for not having warned me earlier but it demonstrated the difference between an engineer and a trained infantryman.

Most days we went out on working parties although our anti-Lockyer captain tended to send me out on my own. One job I had, on 16 November, was to erect a five-foot diameter canvas water tank on the rook of a multi-storey building being used as 40 Division HQ. This was to give the water pressure plenty of 'head'. The supply pipe was connected to a Petters petrol engine pump down at the bottom of the central well of the building. I had to sit with the engine all day to see that it kept running and to top it up with fuel when necessary. I was sitting on a doorstep writing a letter when an officer about four floors up emptied the dregs of a cold cup of tea out of his window right onto my letter. 'Thank you very much sir.' I shouted up the well – or words to that effect.

A day or two after this the ship finally arrived with our transport and kitbags. We went to the docks in a commandeered refrigeration truck. The cook was with us and while aboard the ship helping with the unloading managed to steal about a dozen of so compo ration boxes hiding them among the kitbags. Back at the school he gave the other helpers a box each so that from now on with lived well, swapping say a tin of mutton, scotch style, for perhaps a tin of peaches. One day some time later what was left of our cache of food disappeared while we were out. We heard that the MPs had been around and confiscated the remnants of our booty.

Another day, again on my own, my task was to check right through an abandoned tower block of flats leading to the airport. The whole place had been vandalised. I had to go right through the building to make sure all the taps had been turned off. Water was apparently seeping through walls and ceilings down to lower levels. When I was dropped off looters were using ropes to lower furniture from windows down to carts and trucks. Not my concern!

The building was opposite a military barracks that had been blasted by the RAF the day before the Paras dropped. Inside I found that there was considerable water damage. Every flat door was open and all remaining furniture overturned and smashed. I started at the top and worked my way down, turning off taps as I went. There was little of value left worth taking or small enough to fit the pocket. However, I did make a collection of coins from under drawer and shelf liners remembering that this where Mum used to hide odd bits of change.

Although the captain was sending me out on what were only one-man jobs I felt very exposed and vulnerable on my own among Egyptian civilians. However, I was still only a young lad and tended not to question an officer's orders. In the afternoon I explored what was left of the barracks. This overlooked the sea on the way out to the airport. I found odd mounds of .303 bullets with their lead tips cut off with pincers to make them into dumdums, ammunition banned by the Geneva Convention. I found a few letters in kit boxes and removed the stamps for my own collection. All in all it was a pleasant day out. (Overlooking the sea on the way to the airport suggests it was the Coastguard Barracks.)

On another occasion I was given the job, again on my own, of guarding a large isolated locked-up detached house set in about half an acre of ground and surrounded by a high wall with double wrought-iron gates. I found an old chair and settled down outside against the gates. After a while several friendly Egyptians came along in ones and twos and began to chat. But as the group began to grow so did their confidence and one grasped hold of my rifle and asked me how much I wanted for it. I told him to sod off in a friendly way and moved inside the gates with a bullet up the spout just in case.

When I was picked up to return for lunch I was surprised to find that no one took over from me. It was then that the thought crossed my mind that the captain was sending me out on so many time-wasting and potentially dangerous jobs on my own that he must have wanted me out of the way for some reason. This was confirmed a morning or two later on works parade when he allocated everyone jobs for the day except me then walked away so I took the day off sitting in the sun reading a book. Some years later, back at my job in Civvy Street, I did a day's work at an Esso oil refinery and discovered that my old adversary was now working there in personnel. I learned that he had acquired a reputation as a mean-spirited and arrogant man who was disliked by most of those who had to deal with him

One day, at last, I was given a job where I wouldn't be on my own. Four of us were sent to the El Gamil airfield to build a number of wooden crates, each to carry a zinc coffin.

Our dead from the action had been wrapped in blankets and buried locally. Now they were being exhumed for transportation to the UK. Six of them were to be flown home that day accompanied by a REME lad who would carry out any re-soldering if any variations in air pressure should cause a split seam in the zinc. If this were to happen the smell would have been awful since by this time the bodies had been buried in the ground since the fifth and sixth of November. Nevertheless I am sure the REME lad would have soldered on. However, when we arrived at the airfield we found that the crates had already been made so we spent the rest of the day there just watching the comings and goings.

Our unit's only casualty was Jock who had taken my job as the CO's driver back in the UK at the time when I had had to go home to see about the eviction business. In Port Said he had been driving the CO in their new Morris Minor when the car had come under attack from snipers. The CO decided that they'd better stop and take cover in a doorway. As they ran at a crouch Jock had taken a bullet which had just missed his spine at waist level. It passed right through his stomach and came out low down without hitting bone. It could easily have been me

One afternoon the captain informed me that I was to report to the Chief Royal Engineer's office as I had been 'volunteered' to become his driver. The following morning, all spick and span, I duly reported for duty not particularly looking forward to driving his Fiat limousine. However, he had been called out early and had needed to find another driver at short notice. It was just as well really since a few days later he returned to his HQ in Tripoli and took his driver with him. I didn't want to leave our outfit and in any case I may have had my demob delayed.

On one occasion when I was left guarding the camp, alone, a food riot took place nearby when a shop was being looted. The Arabs were fighting each other for tins of food and other goodies with men knocking down children to relieve them of their loot. The shopkeeper, his nose split open from top to bottom, asked me for help but there was nothing one man could have done to restore order without shooting at the mob.

We had been given no guidance whatever on dealing with this or any other type of disturbance and anyway, I couldn't have left the premises unguarded. Shortly afterwards about twenty lads from a Scottish regiment arrived in a large armoured personnel carrier to confront the crowd of about sixty. A corporal walked into the mob and smashed his rifle butt into the face of the largest Arab. The crowd just melted away and within a minute the street was deserted.

Another time about ten of us had the task of clearing the Place de la Gare of possibly 500 to 600 people which, much to our surprise, we managed to do without any unpleasantness. With some good-humoured pushing in a not too forceful way while the sergeant major told them to 'Go home gentlemen, your wives are waiting for you and your teas are ready,' we cleared the whole area in thirty minutes. Amazing!

Half pay was issued once a fortnight in army paper money BAFVs (British Armed Forces Vouchers) and there must have been many pounds worth of it circulating in the town. An invasion does not stop an Arab trading and all he sees are those thousands of extra customers who arrived with money to spend. The Army informed us that it was illegal to carry sterling so the Arabs had to accept army money since it was the only means by which he could do business with us.

For the Arabs BAFVs became a second currency since so far as they knew, at least initially, we could be around for quite some time to come. As soon as it was known that we were leaving panic set in and they were offering us £5 army money for £1 sterling. Unfortunately we had no sterling, having changed it all into BAFVs before we landed. The British Government, apparently, had no obligation to redeem the BAFVs circulating among the civilian population. One Arab I came across showed me some Monopoly money that he had taken in payment for goods. Now why hadn't I thought of that?

One evening we were able to enjoy some entertainment when a large screen open-air cinema was set up in the railway goods yard. I sat with some others on the roof of a railway goods truck to watch it. I can't remember the name of the film now but I know the sound as distorted and that it was a bitterly cold night. We also managed to get to a cinema on another occasion.

When it was learned that the first UN contingent of troops was expected to arrive at Ismailia by air on 15 November we had the task of preparing a camp for them, erecting tents and digging trenches to run in a water supply to standpipes and washing troughs, etc. I didn't witness the incident myself but I was told later that the dour Scot previously mentioned for relieving the corpses of their valuables at the water works had been one of a party digging trenches for running the pipes when he had come across a shallow-buried body. Rather than reroute the trench or remove the body he had simply chopped through it where it interfered with his navvying.

When the nearly 100 Danish UN soldiers arrived in Port Said they seemed to be a happy group of men in well-tailored smart American style uniforms. They contrasted sharply with the Yugoslavs who followed. They appeared to be sixteen-year-old boys, miserable, bewildered and, through the wire of their compound, looking like prisoners not knowing what it was all about. They were dressed in uniforms that looked as though they had been made out of grey army blankets. Apparently we were to guard the UN camps and also to supply their ammunition. We discovered that they had no equipment or transport of any kind and in effect the British and French remained in charge.

By 16 December all British and French troops had withdrawn from their billets to the waterfront area in preparation for embarkation. From then on we never saw any of our officers again and were left in charge of the SSM.

We moved into a hotel located on the sea front and when it went dark my spell on guard duty took place on the white-painted flat roof with a three-foot high parapet. By now the sniping had resumed again and every so often there were bursts of automatic fire coming in our general direction. The moonlight was almost bright enough to read by so I thought it prudent to sit with my back against the parapet wall and to have a quiet smoke. I took just an occasional look over the wall; no sense in being a silhouette target.

On the night of the 16/17th a patrol of the Royal Scots was fired on from a building. In the firefight that followed their major, (Major David Pinkerton) and twenty-seven Egyptians in the building, were killed.

The next day I had a raging toothache. I had to find four armed volunteers to go with me to a dentist located in a building about 100 yards from where we were billeted. The tooth was extracted. No problem!

One morning shortly afterwards a group of us went out along the breakwater jetty where the statue of Ferdinand De Lesseps stood covered in Verdigris. In a brick building nearby we found a large generator in beautiful condition, all polished and painted. The date on the casting I believe was 1922 although I can't now remember the name of the British manufacturer. It must have weighed a ton but we managed to manoeuvre it outside onto the jetty to await the Royal Navy to lift it into one of their ships with a crane.

On my twenty-fifth birthday, 19 December, my unit went aboard the *New Australia*, an immigrant ship commandeered as a troopship. Just before they embarked two young officers had nailed the Union jack to the mast on the jetty and then greased to pole. We heard after we'd all left that the Egyptians had been unable to climb the pole to remove the flag and had been forced into sawing it down. Later three squaddies were brought aboard on stretchers. It was rumoured that they'd been shot in the legs by French soldiers for attempting to loot the Johnny Walker warehouse. Soon afterwards we sailed.

Our first stop was Oran in Algeria to refuel. We watched the French offloading their tanks and equipment as well as some large American cars which they had taken as being 'the property of French citizens.' By the same token we had crated up some very large carpets from a hotel and these were being shipped back for the Sergeants' Mess as squadron stores. There would be no custom's check on these. One man had in his kitbag compressed motorcycle telescopic front forks, another a lathe chuck, and several had liberated Czech-made rifles.

We passed Gibraltar on Christmas Day and when we entered the Bay of Biscay the sea began to develop a considerable swell. Walking up the stairs became quite difficult. One moment you felt as though you weighed a ton and the next almost as though you were floating on air. One day we were told to throw all our personal ammunition overboard. I'd started with 75 rounds but had lost one so 74 went over the side. I felt relieved that I had not been put in the position of having to kill a fellow man.

At Southampton we disembarked and entered the customs sheds where we started to have our kitbags emptied and our belongings inspected. Then someone shouted that the train had arrived and an instant mass exodus took place leaving the customs officials bewildered. Unfortunately by this time I had already paid £5 duty on free issue cigarettes. On the train men were taking watches and jewellery out of their rifle magazines and replacing the springs.

On the way to Barton Stacey by double-decker bus from Andover station I sat at the front upstairs and was amazed to see in the bus headlights what seemed to be hundreds of both dead and dying rabbits strewn across the road . I had not heard of myxomatosis before. At Barton Stacey transit camp most of the staff were away on Christmas leave and there were only six of them there. The following morning the sergeant major found a local elderly doctor and brought him to the camp. The SM assembled us together and shouted, 'Is everyone fit?' We all chorused, 'Yes sir,' upon which the doctor set about signing all the forms which said that he had examined each man and

turned to Valetta. At one stage the garrison was put on standby and we had a visit from the General Officer MELF, Lt Col Ledger based in Cyprus. He also visited our Army Post Office HQ in Valetta.

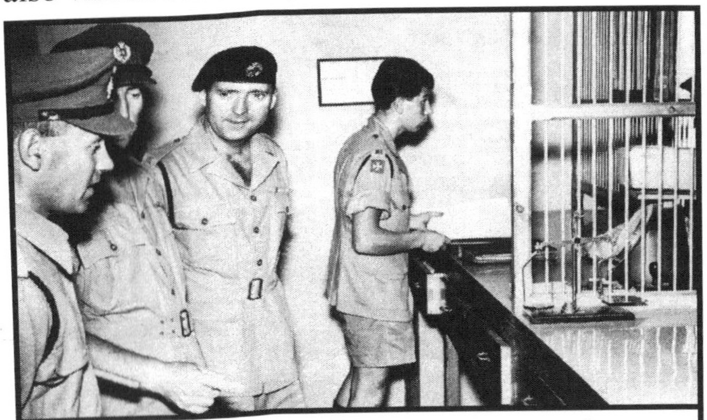

Visit of Lt Col Ledger to the postal unit at Valleta.

On my demob in 1958 I returned to my old Post Office in Spalding as a postman and soon met Gillian. We were married just before Christmas and went on to have a daughter, Denise, and two granddaughters, Amy and Chloe.

Later I took postman high grade and did work as an inspector and at one period chief inspector during a flu epidemic. In May 1994 I took retirement at the age of 56 after 43 years of service.

* * *

Charles Eric Farrar, No.8 Railway Squadron, REs.

I carried out my National Service in the Royal Engineers from 1955 until 1957. After training I was posted to No.8 Railway Squadron, a self-contained Railway Operating Unit based at the Longmoor Military Railway Depot in Hampshire.

We served as a standby unit and were expected to be able to go anywhere required at short notice so when the Suez business blew up we were confined to camp and put on 24-hours readiness. Although we weren't told as much over the next few weeks, if at all, I suppose the intention in high places was that we would operate the branch of the Egyptian railway system that ran from Port Said down the length of the canal if and when we invaded Egypt to take back the Suez Canal Company into its rightful ownership.

At Longmoor we painted our vehicles sand brown and added a large Letter 'H' on both the sides and the tops so that this agreed code letter could be recognised by the Allied aircraft.

After a while an advanced detachment was sent out to the Mediterranean, I don't know whether it was to Malta of Cyprus, to prepare the way for the rest of the squadron when it followed.

The No.8 Railway Squadron detachment sent ahead. Back row: Blaxill, Edwards, Taff Simcock, Foster, Tony Dewey, Haynes. Front row: Tucker, Abbott, Stiff, Gibson. Some of the lads are showing off their newly-issued bush hats just before flying out.

After several false alarms when it got into October those of us left behind at Longmoor were stood down. The MOD had mobilised Reservists and the AER to make up the numbers for Egypt so it became our job to arrange traffic control and serve as storemen in kitting out the reservists and then reversing the process on their eventual return.

* * *

Sam Ainsworth, Port Operations unit, REs.

I was born on 24th November 1934 in Liverpool where my father was a charge-hand working at the New Dock. Two sisters came along later.

I left school in the summer of 1949 while I was still only 14 and started working at a bike shop, followed by a spell on a building site and then a couple of other jobs, the last one being with Dunlop's at Speke before being called up for National Service in the Royal Engineers when I was eighteen-and-a-half. I'd had my 18th birthday the previous November so why it was the 5th May 1953 before I had to report to Norton Camp near Worcester for initial training I have no idea.

After passing out from there I was sent to No.4 Training Regiment RE at Gibraltar Barracks, Aldershot, for driver instruction. Following this I was posted to another training regiment at nearby Farnborough to learn about mines, demolition, Bailey bridges, watermanship at Hawley Lake, and acquire the various other skills required by a sapper. On passing out from here as a B3 field engineer I was sent back to Gibraltar Barracks.

I spent the next five months as a medical orderly

found him fit for discharge. We were given the choice of waiting for the camp staff to return from leave after the New Year or filling in all the appropriate forms ourselves. We opted for the latter of course, marking most entries n/a (not available). Then, with our travel warrants signed, we were trucked to the nearest railway station for our trains home, waving goodbye to a great sergeant major as we left. He remained behind eventually having to explain his action of demobilizing us without higher authority.

This little war took 155 days of my life out of my control and left me unemployed for two months afterwards. I felt at the time that part of my life had been wasted since I contributed little to the 'Suez' operation other than making up the numbers. The jobs of reservists were supposed to be protected but in my case this would have meant sacking my stand-in, a married man with four children. Eventually though I found a job.

On 19 November 1959 I received a general service medal with the Near East clasp and a letter to say that I had been transferred to class N Reserve until November 1960 or age 45 years whichever was the sooner.

Generally most of my work since demob has been in refrigeration service installation in supermarkets, cold rooms, mortuaries, on air-conditioning of operating theatres, computer rooms, and nuclear shelters.

Meanwhile my wife and I went on to have two sons and one daughter as well as four granddaughters now all grown up. These days I'm involved in genealogy, browsing around car boot fairs, and collecting model vans and buses.

* * *

John Mepham, Postal unit, Royal Engineers.

I was born 8 September 1937 in a small cottage which backed on to our main river, the Welland, in Spalding, Lincolnshire, which runs out into the Wash. In September 1942 I started at St John's Infants School which was during the middle of the war in which Lincolnshire, lots of which is flat, was covered with numerous bomber bases so there was always plenty of action taking place.

In Spalding the town's largest fashion store was hit by a bomb and totally destroyed. We also had a Spitfire crash land nearby after it was damaged in a dog fight as well as the crash of a Lancaster bomber with the loss of all on board. Twice during the war we were flooded out and each time temporarily moved to a council house.

I remember standing with my mum in the garden on 6 June 1944 and watching hundreds planes pulling gliders heading for the D-Day in sion. Our cottage has since long gone. In the S tember I moved on to the juniors at Willes School for Boys.

In 1948 I went to the Sir John Gleed seconda school. I left school in the summer of 1952 wh coming up to the age of fifteen and joined the Po Office as a telegram boy with two other lads until was called up for National Service early in 195 when I was eighteen.

I reported to No.6 Training Regiment RE at Norton Camp near Worcester for basic training before being moved on to Mill Hill in London for postal training after which I was sent to Gunsite Camp in Ducane Road next to the Wormwood Scrubs Prison with the other 23 in the group. It was in perhaps in the May that I was posted to Malta while the other 23 in the group went to BAOR Germany. I was a replacement for a chap on demob and was billeted in Valetta with the Royal Malta Regiment.

On the morning of the departure of the invasion fleet for Egypt Grand Harbour was full of every type of ship in the Royal Navy. It was a wonderful sight!

View taken from the Barrakka Gardens in Valetta of part of the Grand harbour as it began to fill up with ships .

During the conflict I was sent to RAF Luqa to set up a post office for the transfer of mail coming in and out of the island by air which I collected or delivered to the ships in the harbour.

On 10 November the aircraft carrier HMS *Theseus* arrived back in the Grand harbour with the dead and the wounded from the fighting at Port Said who I saw when I went aboard the ship to collect and deliver mail. Following the conflict I re-

before being transferred for the rest of my National Service to the stables where I was put in charge with promotion to acting-lance corporal. The stables belonged to the Saddle Club used by the officers and their wives.

Sam on the right with some of his mates at the stables on his return from riding out with the officers.

On leaving the Army I returned to my job at Dunlop's and also joined the TA which held its camps at the Royal Engineers military railway base at Longmoor. However, my time back at work didn't last long because after about 15 months the Suez crisis came up in July 1956 and soon afterwards I got a letter calling me back to the Royal Engineers and to report for duty the following month. My father, a sapper sergeant who was also in the TA, said he wished it was him going instead of me. Three days later he got his call up too. I found myself in the same outfit as Dad and lots of other reservists in a Port Operations unit at Marchwood across the water from Southampton where we prepared for the call to Egypt.

On the first parade in which it was my Dad who took the roll call prior to giving out the day's jobs, he went along the ranks asking for names until he reached me. When he asked for my name I told him to sod off and that he should know it by now since he gave it to me. This raised a lot of laughter from the lads. He asked me again and I told him to get lost. At this point there was a tap on my shoulder from behind. It was the officer of the day with his silver-handled cane. 'This is my parade,' he said, not Sergeant Ainsworth's, tell him your name.' 'You must be joking sir,' I replied. 'I'll deal with you later,' he said, but I heard nothing more about it.

Father went out to Malta before me, by air. I followed him on the troopship *Asturias* from Southampton, arriving eight days later. In the Grand Harbour at Valetta we blacked out the ship before continuing our journey to Port Said.

The troopship *Asturias*.

In the entrance to the canal, we went over the side and down nets into landing craft to be taken ashore on the quayside close to the famous Casino Palace Hotel and to join up with the Port Operating units that had come over from Cyprus.

I met up with my father a day later. Soon afterwards a newspaper reporter and his photographer came to see us with the news that we were the only father and son to be serving together in the 'Suez' campaign. A photo they took was shown in the Sunday Pictorial on 25 November.

PORT SAID THANKS DAD . . . I MEAN SARGE. Sergeant Sam Ainsworth and his son, also Sam, are in the same Royal Engineers unit. They're billeted in a millionaire's mansion at Port Said—but Sam and Son would rather be home in Liverpool!

While in Port Said I was mostly involved in administration duties around our billet which was in one of the requisitioned buildings. It was a large mansion set behind a wall and gates and belonged to a shipping magnate I believe. It was situated on the opposite side of the road to the Casino Palace

Hotel but a bit further along from the quay. It had been cleared of everything valuable.

Sam on guard duty outside the 'mansion' billet.

On the only occasion we got a bit of free time we went to the cinema aboard HMS *Forth*, the fleet depot ship which was anchored just off the esplanade between the de Lesseps statue and the Casino Palace Hotel.

I think it was well into December after the United Nations took over from us that we went aboard the aircraft carrier *Theseus* and sailed back to the UK where we arrived at Southampton just before Christmas. I was demobbed and returned to my job at Dunlop.

I got married on 2 April 1960 and we went on to have firstly a daughter who in turn had two children, and then a son who is disabled. Meanwhile I continued with Dunlop for 25 years until its works at Speke closed down. We then bought a small shop in St Helens selling fruit and veg. Eighteen months later we bought a second and bigger shop and developed a very good business until retiring when we were sixty-one. We still keep busy, dancing three nights a week as well as playing crown green bowls.

*   *   *

Geoffrey Ponsonby, 51 Port Operations Squadron, 176 Inland Waterways Transport (IWT) REs.

Geoffrey was born in Buxton, Derbyshire on 16 July 1932 and was eventually followed by a brother Stuart. From the age of five he attended Hardwick Square Infants School before going on to Kents Bank Secondary School for Boys until he was 15 in July 1947.

Even while still at school Geoff's ambition was to work in a circus and to be a trapeze artist. He always opened any of the school's concerts or shows by 'flying' across the stage.

He would practise his act in the wood near his home swinging from the trees. A viaduct spans over the main street where Goeffrey lived and he prided himself that he was the only one in his gang daring to walk along the parapet hoping someone would have the nerve to follow him.

On leaving school in 1947 Geoff was taken on as a plumber's apprentice at Heathcote's, a family firm of builders in the town. After a while he became indentured and two or three times a week had to travel something like 20 miles to Stockport Technical College for day-release classes and night school. He was deferred from National Service for the length of his apprenticeship.

During this time Geoff was involved with the local congregational church where he would appear in the concerts and pantomimes they laid on from time to time. He was also a member of the YMCA which is where, when he was about 18, he met his future wife Eileen, the niece of one of the helpers at the club.

Geoffrey was called up for National Service in July 1953 and assigned to the Royal Engineers. He reported to Norton Camp near Worcester for his training after which he was posted to Germany for the remainder of his two years until his demob in July 1955 when he was put on the Reserve.

Geoffrey at Norton Camp near Worcester in July 1953.

On his return to Buxton Geoffrey went back to his trade as a plumber and in March the following year he and Eileen were married. In May he went off to the required two weeks annual camp.

Two months later, when Egypt's Colonel Nasser took over the Suez Canal Company, the government began calling up thousands of those belonging to the Army Emergency Reserve (AER), including Geoffrey and he returned to the Army in the middle of August. After just two weeks back in the Army he was given 48-hour leave before being sent out to Cyprus to join 176 Inland Waterways Transport (IWT) Workshop Squadron attached to 51 Port Squadron at Limassol as part of the big build up of the armed forces there.

In the last letter Eileen received from her husband he said how beautiful Cyprus was and that they would go there for a holiday one day.

On Tuesday 16th of October she received a telegram telling her that earlier in the day, at the village of Akhna, her husband had been killed in a traffic accident and that the funeral would be held the following day, 10am, Wednesday, 17th of October, at Wayne's Keep Military Cemetary in Nicosia. Akhna is situated just north of Dhekelia which lies between Limassol and Famagusta in the southern part of Cyprus.

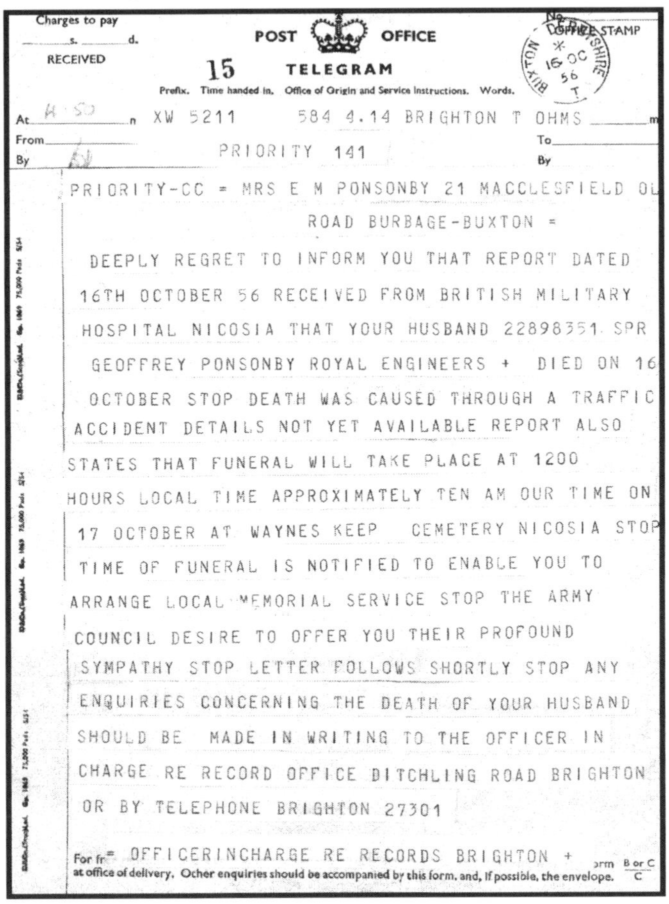

Charges to pay ____s. ____d.
RECEIVED

POST OFFICE
15 TELEGRAM

Prefix. Time handed in. Office of Origin and Service Instructions. Words.

OFFICE STAMP — BUXTON DERBYSHIRE 16 OC 56

At H 50 m XW 5211 584 4.14 BRIGHTON T OHMS
From
By
PRIORITY 141
To
By

PRIORITY-CC = MRS E M PONSONBY 21 MACCLESFIELD OL
ROAD BURBAGE-BUXTON =

DEEPLY REGRET TO INFORM YOU THAT REPORT DATED 16TH OCTOBER 56 RECEIVED FROM BRITISH MILITARY HOSPITAL NICOSIA THAT YOUR HUSBAND 22898351 SPR GEOFFREY PONSONBY ROYAL ENGINEERS + DIED ON 16 OCTOBER STOP DEATH WAS CAUSED THROUGH A TRAFFIC ACCIDENT DETAILS NOT YET AVAILABLE REPORT ALSO STATES THAT FUNERAL WILL TAKE PLACE AT 1200 HOURS LOCAL TIME APPROXIMATELY TEN AM OUR TIME ON 17 OCTOBER AT WAYNES KEEP CEMETERY NICOSIA STOP TIME OF FUNERAL IS NOTIFIED TO ENABLE YOU TO ARRANGE LOCAL MEMORIAL SERVICE STOP THE ARMY COUNCIL DESIRE TO OFFER YOU THEIR PROFOUND SYMPATHY STOP LETTER FOLLOWS SHORTLY STOP ANY ENQUIRIES CONCERNING THE DEATH OF YOUR HUSBAND SHOULD BE MADE IN WRITING TO THE OFFICER IN CHARGE RE RECORD OFFICE DITCHLING ROAD BRIGHTON OR BY TELEPHONE BRIGHTON 27301

For fr= OFFICERINCHARGE RE RECORDS BRIGHTON + orm B or C
at office of delivery. Other enquiries should be accompanied by this form, and, if possible, the envelope. C

Eileen expected that more detail about the accident would follow but it never did, other than that Geoffrey had been travelling in a truck which had overturned at a road block and that he had been buried in Wayne's Keep Military Cemetery, Nicosia. Plot 23, Row B, Grave 17.

Geoffrey's coffin being brought into Wayne's Keep Cemetery on the back of a Land Rover.

The coffin being carried to the graveside.

Six of the lads, the Padre, and Geoffrey's coffin.

More of Geoffrey's burial ceremony at Waynes Keep.

The headstone on Geoffrey's grave in Nicosia.

Eileen had known Geoffrey about six years in all although since she lived six miles out in the country from Buxton where Geoffrey lived, and during his apprenticeship he had attended night school three nights a week, she didn't see all that much of him. For nearly all the time Geoffrey was doing his National Service Eileen's only contact with him was by post.

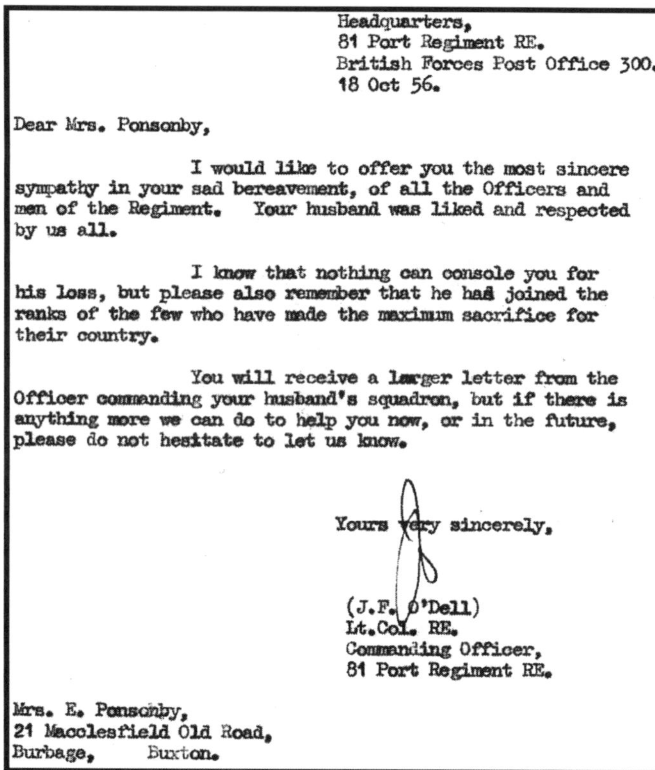

Headquarters,
81 Port Regiment RE.
British Forces Post Office 300.
18 Oct 56.

Dear Mrs. Ponsonby,

I would like to offer you the most sincere sympathy in your sad bereavement, of all the Officers and men of the Regiment. Your husband was liked and respected by us all.

I know that nothing can console you for his loss, but please also remember that he had joined the ranks of the few who have made the maximum sacrifice for their country.

You will receive a larger letter from the Officer commanding your husband's squadron, but if there is anything more we can do to help you now, or in the future, please do not hesitate to let us know.

Yours very sincerely,

(J.F. O'Dell)
Lt.Col. RE.
Commanding Officer,
81 Port Regiment RE.

Mrs. E. Ponsonby,
21 Macclesfield Old Road,
Burbage, Buxton.

Letter written to Mrs Eileen Ponsonby on 18 October from the CO of 81 Port Squadron based in Cyprus.

Eileen received three more letters of condolence in a similar vein. One was from Captain H F R Mason, RE, of 2 Troop, 51 Port Squadron RE, BFPO 53, in a letter written on 17 October.

Major H A T Rosser ERD RE, OC of IWT Troop, 81 Port Regiment RE at BFPO 300 wrote a letter to Eileen on 26 October.

Major F J C Linnell of Headquarter, 176 IWT Workshop Squadron RE, Marchwood near Southampton also sent a letter to Eileen which was undated.

There was no official recognition of Geoffrey's death until the time of the Afghanistan war when the parents of a young marine killed while serving there applied to have their son's name added to the Buxton War Memorial. This request was successful. Through the efforts of the British Legion Eileen managed to have Geoffrey's name added too. It was placed under the heading of the Cyprus Emergency. Appropriately, this ceremony took place just in time for Remembrance Sunday in November 2010. It had taken 54 years for Geoffrey to be remembered.

Eileen eventually remarried and became Eileen Thompson after which she moved away from Buxton. Later she was widowed again.

(Many thanks to Eileen for this contribution.)

* * *

William (Bill) Avis, 165 Port Squadron, REs.

I was born on 2nd August 1935 in Greenwich, London, SE10, where my home was 4 Idenden Cottages in Tunnel Avenue. I began school in September 1940, attending Dreadnought Infants until it was damaged during the Blitz. While repairs were being made to the building we went temporarily to the Glenister School. On one occasion my friends and I had to take rapid shelter when a German aircraft came down to strafe the street. Fortunately none of us was hurt. During the six years of the war our house was also damaged. In September 1946 I went to the Glenister Secondary School and finished there in the summer of 1950.

In the September I started my first job which was as a storeman with a firm that made cables for undersea communications. I remained there until I was eighteen and called up for my two years National Service on 15 October 1953 when I reported for training with the Royal Engineers. After the usual square bashing etc., I did trade training in port operations and was then posted abroad where I served in Tripoli, Port Said, Adabiya, and Aqaba in Jordan. I was demobbed in October 1955 and shortly afterwards returned to my previous employer.

On 19 June 1956 I reported to Marchwood near Southampton for my annual AER fortnight's training on Port Operations with 165 Port Squadron, 81 Port Regiment. A month later, on 26 July, the Egyptian leader President Nasser nationalised the Suez Canal and I was recalled to the Colours, reporting on 13 August to the Royal Engineers at Longmoor Camp in Hampshire where I joined up with 165 Port Squadron, 81 Port Regiment again. Here we were fitted up with uniforms and equipment and started to carry out port duty training again. On the 20th I was promoted to lance corporal.

After about a month we were transported to RAF Lyneham in Wiltshire for a flight to Cyprus. We flew in a York aircraft via Nice and arrived at Nicosia Airport at 4 am on 26 September and were taken to a nearby camp.

Later that day we left for Golden Bay at Famagusta in the south-east of the island where we got settled in under canvas. Later that evening, after being fed, we were taken down to the docks to begin a ten-hour night shift unloading ships. This went on until the end of October. We had to leave the camp every night at great speed because we were frequently sniped at by EOKA.

On 3 November we left Famagusta on the troopship *Empire Ken* bound for Egypt, arriving at the entrance to the Suez Canal on the firth. We were told to go to the starboard side of the ship to be ready to board the landing craft even though this was the side under sniper fire from the Port Said buildings. When the landing craft arrived we went aboard down rope ladders. As soon as we reached the quay and the gate was lowered we came under sniper fire again.

Corporal John Fisher and I were ordered to fire at the buildings from where it was thought the Egyptians were firing at us. This went on for quite a long time until the firing suddenly stopped. I don't know if we hit anyone or they were sorted out by another unit. When some French paratroopers arrived by sea we noticed that they had a number of females among them. I asked one of the paratroopers what the girls were doing with them and learned that they were there to provide 'comfort' when the men came back from the front line.

With the sniper silenced for the moment we were now able to move on and find accommodation for the unit. We found a place but blood was everywhere and we had quite a lot of cleaning up to do to get rid of the mess. We could still hear the sound of firing. At about 10pm, once we were installed and had had something to eat we went back to the waterside and began to unload essential supplies such as jerrycans of water, petrol, diesel and the like from the ships.

Over the next few weeks when not required for unloading and then loading the ships we were sent out on patrols around the streets of Port Said. We saw some awful sights and by the time the United Nations troops arrived to take over patrols I for one was looking forward to coming home.

On 16 of December all 81 Port Regiment left Port Said on the aircraft carrier *Theseus*. My sleeping area was in a hammock in hangar three. We arrived at Portsmouth on 22 December but were unable to land right away because of fog. When we did eventually go ashore there was no media about. From here we entrained for Longmoor. The camp was actually closed for the Christmas period and nobody seemed to know we were coming. Our CO telephoned whoever was supposed to be in charge of the camp and told him to get it opened up. At last we were able to hand in our kit and equipment and receive our travel warrants.

I arrived home early on the morning of 23 December. The family were all asleep and had no idea when I was coming home and certainly didn't expect me for Christmas. In January I went back to work again and on the 10th I transferred back to the

Army Emergency Reserve.

I got married in September 1959 and we went on to have a boy and a girl. Later we moved to Wandsworth in London where I joined Civil Defence Communications for weekend and evening duties.

In November 1965 we moved to Eastbourne where I again joined the Civil Defence, this time as a Scientific Intelligence Assistant. During this period I went to many locations, sometimes overnight and sometimes for the weekend.

I didn't have a camera at port Said but before returning home I was given just a single photo as a souvenir. It shows the Royal Engineers erecting the Bailey bridge at El Raswa of which I had no involvement.

The El Raswa Bailey bridge.

* * *

Vic Wernham, 167 Port Operating Squadron, REs.

Vic carried out his two years National Service in the Canal Zone of Egypt from 1954 until 1956. In August 1956, not long after his demob and shortly after the nationalisation of the Suez crisis, Vic was recalled to the Colours with a number of others who had been with him in Egypt. After kitting out they were flown to Nicosia in Cyprus and then by road to Famagusta to join 167 Port Operations Squadron which was billeted at Golden Sands holiday camp.

Each day from quite early in the morning until well past 1800 hours for the next couple of months or so the lads were transported out to ships moored in the bay to unload cargo in preparation for the invasion.

They seemed to operate almost totally on gallons of tea and bully beef sandwiches which eventually led to some protests, an event in itself..

Vic operating the winch during the unloading of supplies.

Vic bringing a truck out of the hold of a ship.

Bringing up another vehicle from the hold.

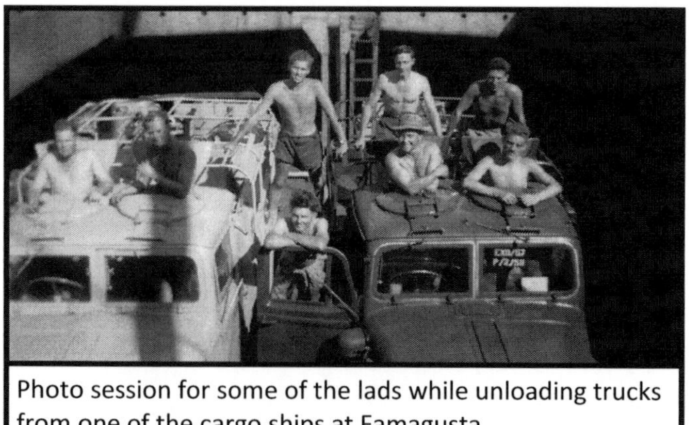

Photo session for some of the lads while unloading trucks from one of the cargo ships at Famagusta.

An Austin Champ being raised from the hold.

Four of the sappers working in the hold of a ship.

Mostly Land Rovers ready for being taken ashore.

Three of the lads working as deck hands.

Some of the squadron lads finding time to relax in the sea at Golden Sands beach, Famagusta.

The Squadron assembling for the journey to Port Said.

All kitted out and ready to go.

The squadron on the landing craft.

The LCT *Counterguard* (4043) by the De Lesseps statue promenade. In the outer harbour in the mist are La *Marseillaise*, the *Ocean*, and the *Theseus*.

The squadron went in with the invasion and did its bit to help for the length of time it was in Port Said.

Back at Famagusta it wasn't long before the Reserves were found flights back to the UK.

* * *

Anthony Gathercole, 1207 Port Operations Squadron, Royal Engineers.

I was born at Crayford, Kent on 15 October 1932 and left school in December 1946 soon after my 14th birthday when I took a seven-year apprenticeship as a waterman and lighterman on the River Thames.

I was called up to begin my National Service two months before my twentieth birthday and reported to Guillemont Barracks, Cove in Hampshire, on 20 August 1952 where I underwent six weeks of basic training with the Royal Engineers.

My posting was to Egypt and after spending a night at the Goodge Street underground transit station in London I flew from Blackbushe Airfield in Hampshire to Fayid in the Canal Zone via Marseilles and Malta.

Before take off we were given a talk by one of the aircrew about the Hermes aircraft we were to fly in. It had been taken apart, rebuilt and checked out so there was nothing to worry about, he told us. There was no explanation as to why we needed to know about the Hermes; we were going on it anyway. Apparently, however, about three months previously a Hermes had crashed in the Sahara Desert after flying off course for hours and running out of fuel.

Following my arrival at Fayid I was trucked to No.1207 Port Operations Squadron, Inland Waterways Transport, at Ismailia and allocated a tent with three MT drivers. As soon as they found out that I had a Civvy Street driving license the office soon had me driving in the MT Section. They were good lads! I soon got the hang of driving the 15 cwt and three-tonner trucks. There was no Treaty Road for us, it was the Canal Road only, except for a few occasions. The Treaty Road was poorly maintained as many will remember. My time with the MT lasted about two months.

In January 1953 I was made up to lance corporal and went aboard the tug *Helen K Henges* as the skipper in charge of a crew of about six or seven. I had been a tug mate and relief captain on the Thames for two years. The work was mostly towing various craft from A to B along the Suez Canal which was between Adabiya in Suez Bay in the south to Port Said in the north. We also acted as convoy escort to civilian-manned craft.

During 1954, by which time I had become a full corporal, we were working in Lake Timsah when the tug's propeller came off. I had to take a Z craft with a diving team to the spot to try to find it but had no luck with that.

Unsuccessful search for the propeller.

I finished the remaining eight months of my National Service as the skipper of the Z72.

At last the day I had been waiting for finally arrived and I was going home after a very long 22 months. I flew home on an AVRO York and that was me finished with the Army – or so I thought. Back home in Civvy Street I completed my apprenticeship and became a Freeman of the Company of Watermen and Lightermen of the River Thames.

In July 1956 the Egyptian leader Nasser nationalised the Suez Canal. A month later while I was on holiday touring the west country a telegram arrived back home recalling me to the Colours with instructions to report to the RE Port Operating base at Marchwood just across the water from Southampton. Here we were kitted out for duty in the Middle East then taken the short distance to Southampton to board the troopship *Empire Parkeston*. There were about 100 of us sappers together with perhaps 100 lads of the Tank Corps.

The troopship *Empire Parkeston*.

We sailed through the Bay of Biscay in a force nine gale during which the ship's ventilation system broke down and the state of the troop decks was terrible. We stopped at Gibraltar for about a week while it was all sorted then continued on to Malta where we transferred to the troopship *Empire Ken* to continue our journey to Cyprus via Tripoli in Libya. We arrived in Cyprus at the port of Famagusta and went ashore to be billeted in the Golden Sands R and R Camp. Our job for the next few weeks was to operate Z craft between the waterfront and the ships lying offshore to unload various cargos.

On about the 1st or 2nd of November our crew was ordered to Limassol to man a Z craft that was not quite ready for immediate service after having had a refit. She was a twin-screw vessel and both had been playing up. Everything was being done in a rush. HMS *Warden*, an Admiralty Bustler Class rescue tug newly arrived from England, eventually took us in tow, firstly to collect another Z craft at Famagusta which we in turn would tow, for the journey across to Port Said for *Operation Musketeer*.

The Royal Fleet Auxiliary (RFA) tug HMRT *Warden*.

With foul weather and being towed in a flat-bottomed boat at a fair speed by a tug with a 3,000 HP engine, the journey was not the best and sleep was just about impossible. By the time we were close to Port Said we had both our engines working properly and were able to operate fully under our own power. HMS *Warden* then returned to Cyprus to tow a heavy lift barge back to Port Said to help with the removal of blockships.

On arrival in the canal we went alongside the carrier HMS *Ocean* and loaded Centurion tank ammunition which we were able to take to Abbas Quay for unloading after navigating between the blockships at night. After this we were kept busy ferrying men and vehicles from ship to shore.

On about the second or third day at Port Said we picked up some 50 or 60 of our paratroopers, including their walking wounded, who had dropped on the El Gamil Airfield on the first day of the invasion, also some French paratroopers. The French we took over to Port Fuad then our lads to one of our ships which I think was HMS *Theseus*.

After the ceasefire took place it all seemed a bit confusing. We continued carrying out various tasks with our LCT for a couple more weeks getting about here and there.

El Cap Railway Station some 20 miles or so south of Port Said as seen from the canal.

When we returned to Cyprus we were put in a tented transit camp up in the mountains. It was December with snow on the ground so we were very cold. From the camp we were able to see aircraft landing at Nicosia Airfield way below us. We weren't here for long though and soon on our way home on a good flight in a turbo-prop Bristol Britannia aircraft which landed at Heathrow just in time for Christmas.

Once more back in Civvy Street I continued my work as a waterman and lighterman for several different companies. From the 1970s the dock industry went into decline. Finally I became skipper of high speed passenger craft on the Thames before retiring in 1995. We have three children, seven grandchildren and three great grandchildren. My interests are Art, Golf, and Gardening.

* * *

P R (Bob) Jordan, Port Operation Squadron, Royal Engineers.

I was born on 16 July 1934 at Chalfont St Giles in Buckinghamshire where, at five, I went to the local council school in the village and then on to the comprehensive school at nearby Chalfont St Peter.

I left school in 1950 and managed to get a job in the goods office at Gerrards Cross station on the line into Paddington. After a while I was promoted to the ticket office where I met several famous people passing through such as the England cricketer Dennis Compton and the actress Flora Robson.

When I came due for call up my father, who was ex-military, said I should volunteer otherwise, with my height, they would put me in one of the guards' regiments. He called them glasshouse soldiers. So in July 1952 I went to reading and signed on for three years with the Royal Engineers.

For my basic training which began shortly afterwards I was sent to Aldershot Barracks on Queens Road, Aldershot which, it was claimed, had the largest square in the country. Once training was over I was sent to the Longmoor Military Railway training camp in Hampshire where I was put on and passed a checkers course. A posting to Singapore followed and I left the UK from Southampton at 8.30 am on 31 December 1952 aboard the *Empire Trooper*, the one-time German ship *Cap Norte*.

While aboard the ship I made friends with a lad from the Wiltshire Regiment who was on his way to Korea. He showed me a photograph of two sisters who lived in Exeter, one of whom he was going out with. He suggested I write to Georgina, the other one which I did, not thinking that anything would come of it. However I got a reply while in Singapore and we continued to write to each other for the next two-and-a-half years.

Due to a hold-up in the Pool of Suez we took 30 days to reach Singapore. On our eventual arrival I joined the Port Operating Squadron which, I discovered, also employed local labour. I found it all very interesting and managed to earn a stripe while I was there.

After about three months I was posted to Kuala Lumpur in Malaya where I was billeted in a transit camp for a while during which I was made up to a full corporal then sent on detachment to Port Swettenham, some 24 miles southwest of Kuala Lumpur where I lived in the Seaview Hotel. My job was to check military stores arriving in the country. For a while just before my demob I served as the RTO (Rail Traffic Officer) on Kuala Lumpur Station.

After serving two and a half years in Singapore and Malaya I returned to the UK by air on 14 July 1955 and was demobbed on the 18 August 1955 from Goodge Street Station in London. Two days later, after having scanned the London papers, I had found myself a job at a sports shop in the City of London just by the Stock Exchange. I soon found that it was quite a journey from Chalfont into London six days a week. Meanwhile I made contact with Georgina and started courting her properly, if you can call it that from the best part of 150 miles away.

A year later, after Colonel Nasser of Egypt seized control of the Suez Canal, it soon became apparent that many of those on Reserve were going to be called up. Sometime in August, a Friday I think it was, I heard on the radio an announcement that all the reservists required for the emergency had already been sent for. I'm home and dry I thought, until a brown envelope marked OHMS dropped through the letterbox. I was to report to Barton Stacey, the sapper transit camp in Hampshire to be fully kitted out.

After two weeks a number of us were taken to Blackbushe Airport and flown to Valetta in Malta where we stayed for a short while before continuing on to Nicosia in Cyprus. This was at a time when the EOKA terrorists were highly active. The night we arrived they blew up a six-ton ammunition truck.

Shortly I was assigned to the Port Operating Squadron at Famagusta which was camped by the beach under canvas on a hard standing. We were reasonably comfortable though and the food was quite good too. Our job was to travel from Famagusta to Limassol each day where we loaded coastal vessels with diesel, petrol and ammunition before travelling back to camp in Famagusta. We carried out these duties for about a month, being escorted along the roads, many of them little more than dirt tracks, by Land Rovers and armoured Scout Cars.

One of the ships we loaded was a coastal supply ship, the RASCV *Malplaquet* and another, the *Mull*. Both of these ships would be loaded, set off somewhere, and then return two days later. I don't think any of us had any idea where they had been to unload their cargo because the invasion of Port Said hadn't yet begun. It remains quite a mystery to this day, certainly to me.

The *Malplaquet* .

Finally, on 3 November, we found ourselves gathered on the jetty at the Limassol waterfront waiting to be taken out to the *Empire Ken*. Someone had placed a little transistor radio on top of one of the bollards and while we were waiting we heard the broadcast of Prime Minister Eden's speech in which he explained why we were invading Egypt.

The jetty at Limassol.

Aboard ship and on our way we were given deck watch duty. We didn't know what we could expect on our arrival at Port Said and shortly before the ship made its way inside the entrance to the Suez Canal on the 6th the sappers were gathered together for instruction on the rules for using our rifles and given pre-battle pep talk in which we were told to mind our backs.

Entering the Suez Canal. Fish Dock on the right.

The blockships *Pollux* and *Peleuse*.

Cargo vessel and *La Marseillaise* in the outer harbour.

Two aircraft carriers in the outer harbour at Port Said.

Bob on the *Empire Ken* with a carrier in the background.

When we finally got ferried ashore and were on the quayside we came under fire from a sniper in a domed building nearby. Our Bren gunner fired back using a whole magazine. The officer was not best pleased.

Our unit was billeted in a block of flats situated not far from the quayside and normally occupied by some White Russians until we turned up, so one of the officers told us. We were able to spread ourselves about the building and the top floor windows gave us a good view over much of Port Said.

From the rooms at the back we were able to look out to the Fish Dock, the De Lesseps Statue and the entrance to the canal. From the front balconies of the end building we were in on the Rue du Vingt Trois Juillet we had a good view down the length of the street.

The Rue du Vingt Trois Juillet.

The first building in the Rue du Vingt Trois Juillet.

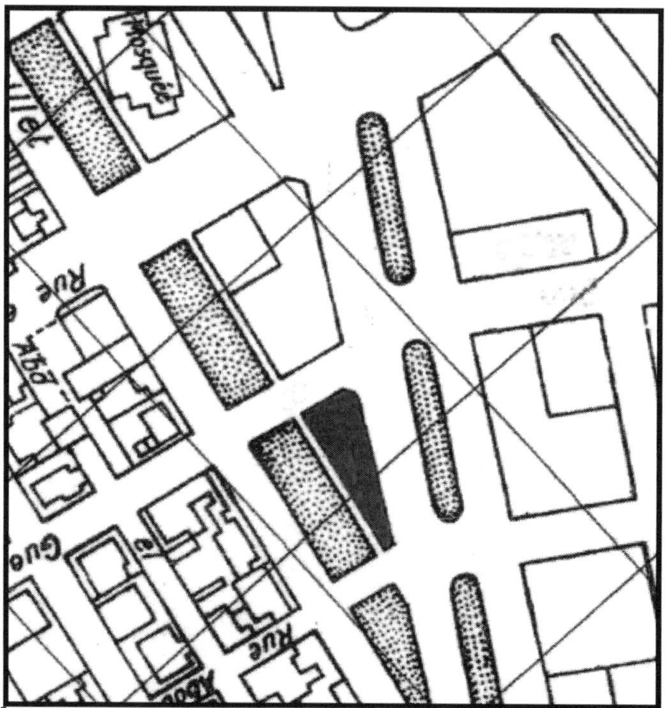

Apartment block billet marked in black.

Later in the day we began unloading the cargo from some of the ships we had previously loaded only a short time before while in Cyprus. There were about 20 of us in our troop and we were split up into shifts working around the clock. No cookhouse had been set up for us so we were issued with enough 24 hour ration packs to keep us going. I think we were luckier than most though because while we were on the ships we frequently got offered meals by the crew.

At the flats I came in contact with a washing machine for the first time. Once we learned how it worked it was a real luxury. I had a watch that Georgina had given me and happened to have it in the top pocket of my shirt. I put the shirt in the wash, forgetting about the watch which wasn't as waterproof as they are now. It never worked again.

When things quietened down a bit, and we were able to get some time off to look at the town, we were told to have a bullet 'up the spout' and not to go out alone. I had the feeling that there was quite a bit of tension in the air and this may have been caused by the French paratroopers who had previously been in Indo-China. We were told that they had shot some Egyptians over an argument. I also heard that our paratroopers had raided a warehouse on the waterfront and taken quite a lot of whiskey and beer.

Horse and carriage taxi service on a Port Said street.

More trouble arose when later we were ordered to begin reloading all the stores back on the ships. This didn't go down well with the reservist London Docks stevedores who just wanted to get back home for Christmas. They were demanding answers from the officers which at this stage they didn't have. It got as near to a mutiny as you can get and for a while some of the officers were looking quite frightened.

We eventually left Port Said on the 12 December aboard the aircraft carrier HMS *Theseus* where we found places to sleep on the flight deck between the aircraft and the vehicles.

Bob aboard HMS *Theseus* on the journey back to the UK.

After an uneventful journey we arrived back at Southampton at about 8am on 18 December so were home for Christmas.

Welcome home.

After I'd had a break I returned to my job at the sports shop but eventually found the travelling each day too much and got myself a job as a despatch clerk at the Watford branch of Pickford's, the well-known removal firm. A couple of years later I got a job in the tyre business

Georgina and I got married in September 1959; she forgave me about the watch and we went on to have three wonderful children. Due to Georgina being ill I retired in February 1999 after 38 years in the tyre trade, the last 15 as manager of our Exeter depot. Georgina passed away in 2000.

* * *

John B Talbot, IWT 172 Port Maintenance Squadron Royal Engineers.

In 1953, after not having received my National Service call up papers for several months following the completion of my engineering apprenticeship in the Black Country I decided to volunteer and signed on for three years with the Royal Engineers at Wolverhampton with very specific requests about what I had in mind regarding courses, all of which were honoured.

I reported to No.3 TRRE at Cove, Farnborough for my basic training then commenced an engine-fitting course at No.12 SME, Chatham very soon afterwards.

I came top in that and was posted then as an NCO instructor for the rest of my time until my demob in the spring of 1956. By this time my family had moved to Bristol which is where I was living a few weeks later when the Suez crisis blew up. I was called back into the Army in August.

When we mustered on 13 August 1956 at the Royal Engineer's railway depot at Longmoor in Hampshire, I knew only two sappers in 172 IWT Port Maintenance, both from my 12 SME days. (See same date for Bill Avis.)

After having prepared and despatched a veritable fleet of Jones KL 66 mobile cranes to Cyprus we flew out to Nicosia, then went by road to our unit headquarters at Famagusta.

About two weeks after our arrival, and duty in the gear store and on the docks there, a small group of 16 of us was sent on detachment to Limassol to reinforce 51 Port Operations Squadron who came in daily from Polemedia Camp just outside the town where they were based with 37 Field Engineer Regiment. Their OC was Major Young from the Port of London Authority.

We were initially billeted there too and travelled to the docks for our work each day for about two weeks until, with the help of the RAMC lads, we 'renovated' the old abandoned Custom House down at the port waterfront where our Z craft had already arrived, so that we could become more independent and, without the travel twice a day, be less at risk to ambush by EOKA. We also enjoyed the protection of an infantry detail assigned to us. After some time spent billeted in the Custom House we moved into tented accommodation.

In our new IWT base sapper Davies built us a bar out of dunnage timber. I sketched a mural for its wall which was painted by one of the clerks, and we stocked up on Tennents lager, Keo beer and other beverages. The bar became a focal point for visitors of all the services and was tended each evening. Card schools took place nightly and by mutual agreement there was no differentiation of rank. It was all very agreeable.

IWT 172 and 51 Port Squadron headquarters at the port with three KL66 Perkins P6 diesel cranes and a Neals 10 ton hammerhead Meadows diesel crane.

A slightly different view of the yard.

I remember that at one stage there were some serious discipline problems occurring with an operating squadron manned by sappers mainly from Liverpool and they were 'disgraced' by being 'corralled' at a site outside Limassol, presumably because Q Movements couldn't rely on them. So far as I can recall they were subsequently shipped back to Famagusta.

Because of the EOKA threat we were unable to explore the town when not on duty since it was out of bounds. However, not far around the coast close to the Akrotiri Peninsula was a secure beach known as Ladies Mile and I went there several times on army transport and in fact learned to swim there.

Since the waters of the Limassol waterfront were quite shallow ships had to anchor out in the bay. Their cargos had to be loaded and unloaded onto lighters towed by tugs and Z-craft.

A Ford ambulance coming overside from a cargo ship to Z craft-14. The SS *Salinas* is in the background.

The Cargo ship SS *Senator,* of Liverpool, with Z-craft, Z-3, Z -8, and Z-14 alongside.

The troopship *Empire Ken* at anchor in Limassol Bay. This ship took large numbers of sappers to Port Said.

View from a cargo ship in Limassol Bay of Lighters full of equipment ready to be taken aboard.

Z craft-8 out in Limassol Bay.

Lt D Jeffries of 172 Port Maintenance Squadron boards the *Empire Parkeston* for detachment to Port Said

Royal Fleet Auxiliary (RFA) vessel *Surf Pioneer* in the bay.

The RFA *Surf Pioneer* was a 12,000-ton tanker whose normal cargo was aviation fuel. Following the Nasser's nationalization of the Suez Canal the ship was diverted from its normal service to the Mediterranean to support the Suez campaign by supplying water to to British naval units.

The *Surf Pioneer* visited us twice and each time it arrived in Limassol Bay it took us four-and-a-half days to fill her tanks since she had only a 4-inch diameter pipe.

The ship's Captain Hult would generously entertain our RE teams by putting on films and supplying refreshments. Sapper Pond and myself were permitted to use the Captain's dark room and he also supplied all our chemicals and papers. I have fond memories of the captain and his ship.

Ten-ton Neals crane discharging a Ford ambulance from the Z-14 at Limassol quay.

The *New Australia* emigrant ship, chartered as a troopship, arriving back at Limassol from Port Said with the Paratroop Brigade, including the 9th Independent Parachute Squadron, Royal Engineers.

When the Paratroopers were brought to shore on 51 Squadron vessels all their prize AK47s were seized by the Royal Military Police before they were allowed to board their transport for the journey to camp at Nicosia..

Following the end of hostilities in Port Said it was the reserves that were among the first to be demobbed and we flew back to the UK in a DC4 Air charter plane. I was demobbed from Longmoor on 22 December.

* * *

Thomas George Gilkes, Sixth Royal Tank Regt.

I was born in the Liverpool Royal Infirmary in November 1936 and all my early life was spent at nearby Huyton. Amongst my earliest memories are those of the war years and the bombing of Liverpool which we could see ablaze with the sky lit up. Very few bombs dropped locally near our home yet we had to spend many nights in the Anderson shelters. We young lads however managed to get out and about to find bits of shrapnel where there had been bombs.

During the war we had an internment camp in the town for a while. German and Italian POWs were also held at Huyton and when American troops began arriving at Liverpool they too were housed at Huyton till they moved on.

At the age of ten I won a scholarship to Prescot Grammar School and spent the next six years preparing for O-levels of which I achieved eight. I left school in 1953 and started work with Martins Bank. The bank's practice was to place new entrants at a branch for two years until they were called up for National Service. My salary was £175 per annum.

In 1955, following my medical I was summoned to report to the 5th Inniskilling Dragoon Guards at Waitwith Lines, Catterick on 2 June. I had specifically asked for a tank regiment to avoid being drafted into the Pay Corps and so that I could have a dramatically different experience for two years. At the end of May a mail strike was called and on 2 June, just as I was leaving the house, a telegram boy arrived with an instruction not to report until the ninth. The strike was still in force on the 9th and no further reprieve was received. The journey to Catterick took 12 hours via Manchester, Huddersfield, Leeds and Darlington where we were collected by three-tonners and taken to our various regiments.

Basic training during a hot dry summer was

tough and tiring but a tremendously maturing experience. Two of the lads eventually realised that they had earlier met each other in Wormwood Scrubs. While at Catterick I played cricket for the regiment.

After passing out six weeks later we all had a 48 -hour pass then returned for trade training. In tanks it is imperative to have two trades and I chose to be a gunner/signaller. In fact I had higher marks for signalling but preferred gunnery as my first choice since the signaller had to load the 20 lb shells into the breach of the gun and dispose of the red hot shell cases, as well as carry out his signalling duties.

At the end of October I was posted to the 6th Royal Tank Regiment based in Munster in Germany. The Ex-German officer barracks were excellent and the medieval town had been left virtually untouched by the war. I was detailed early on to take over the accounts of the officers mess which I did until the whole regiment moved back to the UK in April 1956 to prepare for service in the Middle East where we were to take over from the Queens Bays at Aqaba in Jordan. We were based at Tidworth on Salisbury Plain where, soon after our arrival, I was promoted to lance corporal and, as well as my officers mess job where I was given a room of my own, I was also given responsibility for all the batmen. The summer was spent painting our tanks yellow and being kitted out for a hotter climate. By August I had become a full corporal.

Late that month we were called back from leave to prepare urgently to move out which we did over the course of a week. The tanks and all the B vehicles journeyed by convoy down the A303 to Seaton Barracks in Plymouth where we were based for a week or so while we waited for the LSTs to come down from Gairloch where they had been mothballed since the end of WWII. After cleaning, victualling and swinging the compass we embarked the whole regiment on four LSTs - three fighting squadrons and HQ Squadron. By that time we had been joined by many reservists and I had been assigned as wireless operator on the regimental wireless control vehicle in HQ Squadron, an Alvis Saracen.

HQ Squadron were allocated to the LST L3036, *Puncher*. The journey through the Bay of Biscay was pretty testing for landlubbers in flat bottomed ships with a maximum speed of four knots. It took a week to reach Gibraltar and a further six days to Malta where we arrived in the Grand Harbour on 12 September.

The LST *Puncher* entering the Grand Harbour, Malta on 12 September 1956 with HQ Squadron of the 6th Royal Tank Regiment

Our camp was under canvas on Marsa racecourse at the head of the Grand Harbour and we remained there for nearly two months. There was no running water but we had compulsory swimming each day. We also had weekly loading/ unloading practice with the LSTs and short voyages around the island to enable the Royal Marines we had aboard to take to the small landing craft and attack the beaches. By the following morning we would be back in Valetta to unload and return to routine.

Early in November we awoke one morning after yet another of our loading exercises to find that we were not arriving back in Valetta but travelling eastwards with no land in sight. We had not been kept abreast of developments regarding the Suez business but gradually we found that a large fleet of British and French ships was sailing with us and a day or two later we were joined by a large contingent of ships from Cyprus.

View from *Puncher*, in convoy, of one of the escorts, HMS *Alamein* of the 4th Destroyer Squadron

We were briefed on 5 November that we were to be landed in Port Said the following morning. We were woken at 3 am on the 6th to unshackle all vehicles as we slowly moved towards Port Said.

View from *Puncher* of another LST and the smoke rising from the fires in Port Said as they gradually approach the entrance to the Suez Canal on the morning of the sixth.

With mounting excitement we watched fighter planes from the aircraft carriers launch rockets on strategic targets ashore followed by broadsides from the destroyers and cruisers which had been escorting the fleet. Smoke and flames were much in evidence as we approached the coast and then we saw flights of helicopters taking the Marine Commandos ashore.

Helicopters from one of the aircraft carriers taking teams of 45 Marine Commando ashore

One of our squadrons was equipped with specially waterproofed tanks capable of being launched in shallow water and these went ashore from their LST at the beach just behind the Fish Dock where 40 Commando had landed earlier.

Our HQ Squadron made its landing within the canal on the Port Said waterfront with *Puncher* nosing into the quay by the famous Casino Palace Hotel. Once ashore our tanks made their way through the city streets while the occasional Molotov cocktail was dropped on us from the balconies of tenement buildings. Progress was slow in reaching the Canal Company building. Afterwards we moved back to the beach area to dig trenches and establish headquarters.

Dingo Scout Car in the foreground with Billy Steele, looking at the camera, sitting on his Centurion tank. Damaged and wrecked buildings on the far side of the road.

Tanks of B Squadron on the cleared ground between the De Lesseps Statue and the Casino Palace Hotel.

Meanwhile one of our squadrons had travelled 21 miles down the canal road to El Cap unaccompanied by infantry which had missed the rendezvous. My job was to ensure that all vehicles in the regiment were in contact at all times, to give out fresh tuning and netting calls at midnight each day, to change frequencies, and to make sure no vehicle was missing.

On the 8th, following the ceasefire, we requisitioned a school in Port Said where we remained until about mid-December. During this 'waiting' time, despite the ceasefire, we had to take care following the Moorhouse business. Occasionally, armed and at least in twos or more, we were allowed into town where we searched for trinkets and other souvenirs being offered by the local street vendors who were quickly in evidence. Having no cash and only BAFS vouchers which we found difficult to unload on the locals we were forced into trading with the only thing of value we had, our cigarette ration.

Groups of squaddies taking the opportunity to explore Port Said. Tom with Sten gun and his mate with camera.

British troops bartering with Egyptian street vendors.

One of the regiment's tanks awaiting its turn to be loaded aboard the *Empire Cedric*, one of a number of chartered ex-LST Bustard boats.

A sergeant with Sten gun looks on as two tanks wait to back onto the *Empire Cedric*.

The BAFS vouchers tended to become the currency of the card schools that naturally enough sprung up all over among those with time on their hands. I was fortunate enough to do quite well with the cards and won enough to buy a camera in Malta on our way home after cashing in the vouchers.

As the UN troops gradually took over in Port Said and the perimeter of the area occupied by the Allies shortened around the canal waterfront we reloaded our tanks aboard various LSTs.

Not long before Christmas we embarked on the *Empire Baltic* for the voyage home. Christmas was spent at sea, Boxing Day at Malta, New Years Day passing Gibraltar, and we arrived at Tilbury a week later. In convoy we travelled to Bulford in Wiltshire with the London lads in Land Rovers occasionally breaking off to deliver jerricans of petrol to relatives who were on rationing because of the closure of the canal.

In April the regiment was posted to Benghazi in Libya but regrettably I didn't have enough time left to serve to go with them. I was demobbed in June 1957 from Bovington. On the following day back home I had to report to the local TA Centre but that was my only contact with the Territorials as by then the requirement to attend TA parades had been phased out. I returned to my employment at Martins Bank.

In June 1961, three month before my scheduled marriage, I received a rail pass, a postal order, and a letter telling me that I was to be recalled to the Army. This was a precaution taken at the time the

Russians began building the Berlin Wall. In the event an emergency call did not come and I was even able to use the postal order.

In September Eve and I were married and later went to live in Surrey whilst I was working for an international bank in the City of London. This job involved extensive travel around the world to over 50 countries including, in 1978, Egypt which didn't look much different than in November 1956. The flies were just as bad.

We have recently (2011) celebrated our 50th wedding anniversary with our three children, grandchildren and other family members in South Devon where we retired to 16 years ago.

* * *

Maurice G Arden, 24 Port Workshops, REME.

I was born in the Lincolnshire Fens in December 1934 and attended school there until I left in 1949. In 1951 I ran away from home due to family problems and got a job on a farm where the foreman made life very difficult for me at every opportunity. By the following year I'd had enough of this and went into town and joined up, volunteering as a three-year regular.

I desperately wanted to be a vehicle mechanic so chose the REME. When I got home to my relatives where I had taken refuge my Aunt Liz announced to the others with much alarm that I had joined up for nine years. I had to explain that it was for three years, and the nine years was with the reserve. It never occurred to me that one day I would actually get called back while on the reserve.

I suppose I didn't have a clue as to what to expect when I arrived at Warminster on that September day in 1952, but at that age one is a bit naive to say the least. Between then and final demob quite a bit of growing up took place which wasn't a bad thing.

After all my training and becoming a driver and motor cyclist I was posted to No.6 Battalion REME at Bordon. At the end of my three years I returned to Civvy Street where I worked as a welder.

In August 1956, during my two weeks annual holiday from Aveling-Barford, the manufacturer of earth-moving equipment at Grantham in Lincolnshire where I was living at the time, I went on a pleasant motor cycling tour of Wales with my good friend Dave Gowler. We made many B and B stops along the way and danced the evenings away.

On my arrival home on the Friday evening Dad told me the police had been round looking for me, 'You've got to go back in the Army as soon as you get home,' he said. I mentioned to Dad that I was riding in a scramble on Sunday at Cambridge.

'What if you come off and break a leg?' he said.

'I won't be able to go back in the Army.' I replied.

In actual fact, Dave and I had been haring up and down the Pendine Sands near Tenby on our bikes when we heard the news that all reservists were to report in but we didn't see any point in breaking our necks to get back.

However, all went well at the Cambridge Scramble and when I got back home I washed the bike and with the help of my brother and Dad manhandled it upstairs into my bedroom and covered it up for the duration. It was a brand new 197cc Francis Barnet.

On Monday morning I took the train from Grantham station for my trip to the REME depot at Arborfield near Reading. On arrival I was immediately set upon by the duty guard for being late reporting for duty. I was made to parade in front of three or four officers sitting behind a table on the edge of the parade ground and told to explain my reasons for being late reporting.. I told them that I had been in darkest Wales on a motor cycling trip and for the most part away from any form of communication.

They were about ready to throw the book at me until the old gentleman of a colonel piped up, 'He's here now; there's no point in having him back if we're going to clap him in irons. Case dismissed.' I gave them my smartest salute.

I collected my kit and caught a train to Warminster then took local transport to 24 Port Workshops REME at Sutton Veny on the edge of Salisbury Plain. Arriving late in the evening, I grabbed a bed and got my head down and awoke the next morning to find Jim Youngson from Newcastle sitting on my bed with a big smile on his face. We had been mates in the army previously at 6 Training Battalion, Bordon, in Hampshire, so that was a surprise.

Then I met the rest of the reservists who had been called up. Names I remember are Senior, Hayward, Sergeant Nobby Noble (Peterborough), James, O'Keefe, Barlow (Birmingham), Lofty Carr (Preston), Darby, Clarke, Haslam (Manchester), Tom Batey (South Shields), Ron Lumbard (Grimsby), and Smith. There were twenty four of us in total. The OC was Captain Fleming from Edinburgh. I was known to my army mates as Geoff.

There had been two of us on the intake at Warminster with the name Maurice and the corporal asked if either of us had a second name. I volunteered mine and it stuck throughout.

There wasn't a great deal to do in the early days of the Crisis. We dashed around the countryside in one of our recovery vehicles which was a 6x6 Scammell, or spent time at the workshops in Warminster on one course or another. I found myself an evening job with a small garage in Warminster doing panel beating. It paid a few bob. We also made the odd foray into Midsomer Norton 20 miles away for the local dance.

Sometime in October we all went home on a weekend 48 with a reminder from Captain Fleming that if the balloon went up we had to return. And to get back pronto without fail. Sure enough it happened and every man played fair and arrived back on Monday morning.

Later on, following a great deal of activity, about six or eight of us were put on a truck and taken to Southampton docks where, in the dark, we offloaded our kit onto a small launch then went out into the Solent until a large black shape loomed up in front of us. It was the MV *Huntsland*, an 11,000 ton cargo ship requisitioned during August for the Suez crisis. It became our home for the next ten days.

The MV *Huntsland*.

I remember from schooldays that the Bay of Biscay could be a pretty rough place but it turned out to be just the opposite with a placid sea and blue skies. We saw the lights of Lisbon and, as we passed through the Straits of Gibraltar, the lights of car on the roads near the Rock. In the Mediterranean half a dozen porpoise joined us by the bows of the ship and seemed to stay with us for a couple of days or so.

We had our turn at spud peeling and also took part in target practice with our .303s. I got invited below by one of the ship's engineers and marvelled at the size of the engines. All this was very exciting and new to me. Since we had lorries on the deck we could recline on their canvas covers and take in the sun.

On reaching Malta we sailed into Valetta Harbour and witnessed the bumboats that came out to try and sell us stuff when we had anchored up, Sadly we were not allowed ashore and soon were on our way again with seamen suddenly appearing, paint brush in hand, to black out every port hole in the vessel. I remembered the blackout from the Blitz. Blimey! I thought. This is war!

We arrived early at Port Said and had to stand off whilst the Commandos and infantry dealt with the opposition. We could see all this going on and the firing taking place. We were to see the aftermath of these actions later when we finally got ashore. It was not a pretty sight. Later we passed some properties with large gardens and saw bodies stacked like sacks of potatoes. It was quite a shocking sight for us who'd never witnessed anything like this before.

Our job at 24 Port Workshops REME was to unload the vehicles from the tank landing craft and ensure as quickly as possible that their engines were ready to start. Some of them had been aboard ship for many weeks. However we never had any trouble and four of us could unload one of these vessels in twenty minutes.

We were split up into three working groups with the one I was in being situated in a very nice garage which we had commandeered in one of the main streets and was large enough to take a Jeep

A group photo of the lads taken outside the garage.

and our three-ton workshop vehicle with tools and supplies on board. There was just enough room left at the side to take an army style camp bed on which I could sleep at night.

The lads in one of the other groups were at Sherif Quay where they had made some sort of a billet in a wooden shack where they seemed to be constantly fly-bitten. Not very nice! The third group had had to dig a hole at the side of the canal on Abbas Quay which was the next basin down the canal from Sherif Quay. This hole was covered by whatever sheeting the lads could find and that was it; also not very nice at all. Compared to them our garage was heaven. However we were all able to go onto one of the supply ships anchored in the canal where they had showers and put on the odd film show for the lads.

While at the garage Sgt Nobby Noble and I found that we could access a cellar in the property next door where there was a spare bath which we hauled out into the street and round into the garage where we set it up. Then from somewhere we acquired a water tank and a field burner like a massive blow lamp and hey presto we could have a shower. There were very nice toilets at the rear of the garage too so we were well set up and the envy of our mates who used to pop in to use the 'facilities'.

One Saturday afternoon about four of the lads were taking apart and cleaning the Bren gun at the front of the garage with the doors open. We all remembered that having re-assembled said item and before putting the magazine back on one should cock it and pull the trigger to make sure there is nothing up the spout. Well, the lads didn't do that. They put the magazine on and pulled the trigger. BANG.

Now, imagine, Saturday afternoon, about 2 to 3pm, and the street full of passers by. Right opposite the garage was a property with a large open window on the first floor with three ladies side by side, arms folded, leaning on the sill, taking in the scene of everyone going about their business. That .303 bullet went right across the road and embedded itself in the wall about four inches below the sill. It was quite noisy in the street and not one of the ladies realised there was anything amiss.

I was at the rear of the garage when I heard the shot and came rushing forward to see what had happened. There was lots of confusion, surprise, and words like 'Oh shit. What have we done?' Captain Fleming happened to be with us at the time and came rushing in from somewhere to see what all the commotion was about. Everything was very quickly put away and after some very sharp words from the captain the matter was forgotten. But the incident could have proved very nasty indeed. 'Phew!'

One night about midnight, Captain Fleming requested me to get off down to Sherif Quay which was about two-thirds of a mile away from our garage on an errand of some kind. After all these years I can't remember what it was for but the Captain said better take someone with you so young Noble came with me in the Jeep and, carrying the same Bren gun mentioned earlier, sat in the opposite rear corner of the vehicle while off we went down to the quay.

We did what we had to do then set off back. The main street was dead straight and must have been a mile in length. About half way along it someone let fly from a rooftop to our left with an automatic weapon. The bullets hit the road in front of us and up the walls to our right. I put my foot down and drove as fast as the Jeep would go to our garage. We shouted to the chap on guard outside to 'Kindly open the jolly door if you wouldn't mind old chap' or words to that effect. We shot into that place of refuge like there was no tomorrow. I can tell you, I was 'frit' to death. Nowt had ever happened to me like that before.'

Towards the end of our time in the town I was sent to an open area south of the beach in order to set to and spray some 30 cwt vehicles. These were destined for the UN peacekeeping force which had now arrived and my job was to spray them white with help from a young lad in the Swedish Army. He didn't speak English and I certainly didn't speak Swedish. However, we seemed to manage all right. Funny that two such people should be put together by the powers that be. I guess the final job on the vehicles was okay as I later saw some of them trundling around the town but now with UN stencilled on their sides.

Despite the ceasefire and our imminent departure there was still a lot of anger among some of the Port Said population. We used to get harassed by young fourteen-year-old kids as we marched in fours down the street to the cookhouse on the beach close to the scene of the 'spray shop' area. We just had to keep our cool and not be drawn by them.

One day there appeared to be a lot of activity in the street outside the garage and we as bystanders watched as a few platoons of our infantry chaps marched by accompanied by English civilian types some of whom were journalists. I heard one of them shout towards us, 'If we don't sort this lot out now, there will be trouble in the Middle East forever.' What made him say that I don't know but it has stuck in my mind ever since.

Another of my errands was to collect a young serviceman who had just arrived from Abbas Quay on a ship from Cyprus and take him to El Gamil airfield to the west of Port Said along the coast road. He told me his task was to line the coffins of about 12 British servicemen from the early assault on Port Said with lead prior to their return to the UK by air. I left him at the airfield to get on with his job.

On another of the days when I had to go down to Sherif Basin I could see there was something going on with the French Foreign Legion lads who were quite a bit active. Apparently an Egyptian had shot one of their chaps and had been caught. He was tied up to one of the cast iron vertical supports of the open warehouse on the wharf. He was still there two hours later as I was returning to the garage. From what I found out later his future was not to be envied.

As operations were coming to an end it once again fell to us to reload all the equipment back onto the LCTs and it all went ahead at full speed and without any mishaps. We then went back to the garage for the last time. We set to and swept the place clean and left it in fine condition although we did leave the home-built shower setup in place for whoever to enjoy before we motored off down to the Sherif Basin for the last time to join our transport, a TLC which was to carry us and our vehicles to Cyprus. So far as I was concerned it had all been quite a learning curve.

We docked at Famagusta after a very pleasant crossing through water so clear one could see the hull of the ship well below the water line. We offloaded the vehicles and drove them to Dhekelia which appeared to be a large ordnance depot. We left them there and were then transported to a tented transit camp next to Nicosia airfield. We were there for quite some days including Christmas when we had a very nice festive dinner laid on for us.

When it was time to go we embarked on a Bristol Britannia for the flight home to Lyneham I think it was, got rid of our gear at Arborfield, then I took a train home to Grantham. Soon afterwards I went to see my boss at Aveling and Barford and re-started work in the welding shop. I quickly got back into motor cycling. I married in September 1960.

* * *

Brian Spearen, Royal Army Ordnance Corps.

In April 1954 (5407 intake) I reported to Blackdown Dettingen Barracks, No.2 Training Battalion, RAOC, at Deepcut near Camberley in Surrey and became Private Brian Spearen, 23018383, for two years National Service. After six weeks of basic training and trade training with No.4 Battalion, I was posted to Bicester near Oxford to 16 Battalion. This is where I spent the rest of my National Service, getting thoroughly bored with the duties and the bull for most of the time. At one stage I volunteered for an overseas posting but nothing came of it. Then I got talked into taking a pre-parachute training course at Aldershot where the bull was even worse. But while I was there I took a nasty fall and had to be returned to unit at Bicester in April 1956 just in time for demob. On release I found that I had been allocated to the AER (Army Emergence Reserve), which is what I had wanted rather than the TA.

Back in Civvy Street I returned to my job as a cabinet maker and also met the girl who was to become my future wife. In late July the Suez crisis began and in August I had to report to Chillwell in Nottinghamshire for my two weeks of AER training. In the first week we fired five rounds each on the 30 yards range, had a day out in Skegness, and spent the evenings in the local pubs. It seemed like an extra holiday. In the second week we were sent back home where, we were told, there would be a postcard waiting for us telling us we were to be called up again. Sure enough, there was. So, with my discharge book, voucher with my first day's pay, and a railway warrant, I duly reported back to 16 Battalion RAOC Bicester where we were greeted with cheers and laughter by other national servicemen who had been called back and had arrived there before us. After a refresher course and firing on the ranges etc., we expected the crisis to fade out.

However, it didn't, and in October we were granted seven days' leave and then put in an advance party. After a few days we caught the 4am train to Southampton where we embarked on the *Empire Fowey* and on 31 October sailed for a destination unknown. I think we had over 3,000 soldiers on board, mostly infantry, with some of them having to sleep in gangways and the water being rationed. After about seven days we arrived in Malta where more supplies came on board. We left Valetta harbour the same night and were told that we were sailing for Port Said. This journey took three days and we arrived on 11 November surrounded by other ships although, because of a shortage of space in the harbour and quays, we weren't able to find a berth until the fourteenth. During our time on the ship we were kept busy with fatigues. Letters we wrote home were censored.

It was at this time that we learned that a ceasefire had been signed back on the sixth so we didn't think we would be needed and expected to be sent home. Eventually though a message came over the speakers telling us to prepare to disembark. We were each issued with 50 rounds of .303 ammunition, compo rations, and a bag of cheese sandwiches. We were transferred from the ship by landing craft and, passing the De Lesseps statue on the way, came ashore on the quay to gather together by the front of the Casino Palace Hotel.

After a while we were marched to the walled market place of shops where we slept, and washed in a cattle trough. This was a holding area of captured Egyptian ordnance. I think there was a prison opposite.

This photograph shows troops that have just come ashore from the troopship *Empire Fowey* climbing aboard their transport on the street leading off the quay at the side of the Casino Palace Hotel

On my 21st birthday I found myself on guard duty and realised that I knew the orderly officer from basic training when he was just a private. He was now a 2nd Lieutenant. One of the jobs we were involved in was clearing out a bonded warehouse in the dock area. Cigars and cigarettes were in plentiful supply.

As Port Said was gradually taken over by United Nations troops we were allowed more free time and during an excursion into the town, armed and with mates, we were approached by an Egyptian street photographer who asked to take our photo. We agreed and when he'd finished he developed the film there and then in the street under a black cloth.

Brian, in the middle, and two mates.

After about a month we learned that we would soon be going home in an aircraft carrier and on 15 December went aboard HMS *Theseus* where we were accommodated in hammocks in what was normally the ship's cinema. We sailed for Malta where we were transferred across the harbour and onto the troopship *Empire Ken*. We slept on the floor of the second-class lounge and arrived back at Southampton just before Christmas. A train took us to Bicester from where I was demobbed. On my arrival home my mum said to me, 'Get in the bath. You're filthy!'

* * *

Ken Jones, Royal Signals.

After leaving school I served my time as a cabinetmaker. In March 1953, after the completion of my apprenticeship, I was called for National Service and served in the Royal Signals where I was trained as a keyboard operator until March 1955.

As a reservist I was recalled for the Suez Crisis in August the following year and reported to Catterick for kitting out before being sent down to Ogbourne St George just south of Swindon in Wiltshire. It was from there at the end of October that a small party of us was trucked to Lyneham a few miles to the west for a flight to Cyprus via Malta.

After about four days in Cyprus we went aboard the troopship *Empire Ken* at Limassol, on the third of November I think it was, and sailed for Port Said where we arrived offshore on about the fifth.

The following day, after things had quietened down a bit the *Empire Ken* was allowed to enter the canal and anchor temporarily in the harbour by the De Lesseps promenade to discharge its contingents of troops.

Our signals group was directed to a block of flats at the back of the piece of spare ground in front of us where 45 Commando had landed that morning. All we had to do was walk along from the ship with our kit, turn in along the street at the side of the Casino Palace Hotel, then right again to where the apartment blocks lay on our left.

The photograph below, taken later, shows an unEgyptian-looking child wearing war paint and what appears to be a feathered head-dress like a Red Indian chief. He/she had no braves or cowboys to play with so soldiers were probably the next best thing. The innocence of children!

The apartment block where Ken was billeted. His flat was the one with the washing hung up to dry.

When it was time to go on duty six of us from the Royal Signals were sent to HMS *Tyne* which had been fitted out as the headquarters ship for the task force communications and was berthed close to the northern end of the Fish Dock.

Antenna mast on HMS *Tyne*.

View through more of the Tyne's communications antennas at ships anchored across the harbour.

Another view on HMS *Tyne*.

View from HMS *Tyne* across to ships in the outer harbour.

View from HMS *Tyne* of passing traffic in the mouth of the Suez Canal.

The Depot ship HMS *Forth* and its entourage.

While we were billeted in these flats I acquired one or two spoils of war in the form of old photos I admired. One was a postcard of the Suez Canal Company building, current I would guess. in the early 1930s. The other was a more personal one of three smart gentlemen posing in front of the Suez Canal Company building. A caption in French had been written on the back together with the date of 27 October 1932. The original photo was in sepia.

Gents' fashion of 1932.

In the early days of the soccupation the French ship *La Marseillaise* anchored out of the way by the eastern breakwater. Towards the time to leave she had moved across to the western breakwater facing the open sea.

Closer view of *La Marseillaise*.

The troopship *Asturias* preparing to depart the canal.

With their job complete the Paras departed Port Said for Cyprus on about 12 November aboard the *New Australia*. The main evacuation of the port began on 7 December and over the following week something like a half of the 22,000 allied troops occupying Port Said had departed for Cyprus, Malta or the UK aboard the ships *New Australia*, *Asturias*, *Dilwara*, *Ascania*, *Theseus*, and the *Dunera*. The *Tyne* remained almost to the end when the Destroyer HMS *Duchess* ushered the last remnants of the task force out of the canal mouth on 22 December.

The good thing about serving on HMS *Tyne* was that if we were aboard when the rum ration was given out we got it too. It was a pity that we didn't remain on the *Tyne* to come home instead of on the troopship *Dunera*. Christmas was spent still at sea.

* * *

Norman M Gant, Royal Signals.

I was born in November 1936 at Norwich and went to school there until I was fifteen when I started work in a small engineering workshop with the hope of an apprenticeship. However I didn't get much encouragement and also realised that I didn't particularly enjoy working indoors so I left when I was 17 and went to work for a haulage firm doing all sorts of jobs as well as learning to drive.

As I was approaching my 18th birthday in November 1954 I got the call to attend the medical and interview for National Service at our local recruitment centre in Colgate Street. I was given the normal tests, ie., reflexes, checked for height and weight, etc., and a questionnaire on engineering to fill in which was not very technical stuff. I wanted to join the RAF to train as a motor engineer but found that to be certain of getting this I would have to sign on for three years, which I did.

In November, when the big day arrived, I travelled by train to RAF Cardington in Bedfordshire where I was required to take some sort of oath of allegiance. The next day in an interview I was told that I could not train as an engineer but could go into the RAF Regiment or train as a cook. I said that I wouldn't do that since I'd joined up to train as an engineer. But they insisted and said that I'd signed the oath. This was happening to another chap as well. So I then told the officer that if they didn't release me I'd go to the papers and tell them that the RAF was recruiting people under false pretences. We were both released the next day with travel warrants to return home. Mother was most surprised.

I still had my National Service to do of course but it was a further seven months before I was sent for by the Army and I finally joined up in June 1955. At this particular time there were both rail and postal strikes taking place. It took me seven hours to get to Catterick Camp in North Yorkshire. While I was there a lot of the lads got involved in helping out the postal service.

Towards the end of my military training I was asked to choose the branch of the Army I'd like to serve with. I chose the REME with the Royal Signals my second choice. I got the latter and remained at Catterick for the signals course after which I was posted to the MT section of the Royal Signals at No.5 Training Regiment, Harper Barracks, Ripon for driver training. We were taught by local authority driving instructors and did our training on the roads around Harrogate and on Ilkley Moor as well as learning about repairs and servicing from our own instructors. I passed the test and was issued with my heavy goods license on the 1st of September 1955. After 14 days leave I was posted to No.1 Corps Royal Signals at Herford, BOAR 15, in Germany.

My driving was mostly on left-hand drive Jeeps, and Champs which had just come into service and could be used to go through water up to four or five feet deep when the extended exhaust pipe and air vents were put in place.

Throughout my time in Germany I was involved in a lot of driving while on manoeuvres and training exercises during which we slept in bivvies which were small tents. After a while I became the CO's driver and sometimes drove the adjutant, Captain Bonnard, which got me all over the place.

Sometime in August 1956 we received orders to spray all the vehicles yellow ready for going abroad, not that we were told where. When this was completed some of the drivers took their trucks to Antwerp ready to be loaded onto ships. The rest of us returned to Aldershot for intensive training which included lots of route marches around the district. Then, in September, by which time our outfit had its name changed to 23 Corps, we were taken to Lyneham in Wiltshire and flown to Cyprus.

We hadn't been in air long and flying over Brighton when the captain sent a message back to us saying that we would be returning to Lyneham because an engine had failed and that we were not to be alarmed if we saw fuel being ejected. We landed safely with just a bit of a wiggle as we hit the runway. Fire engines were parked close by just in case. We were taken straight to a Nissen hut and not allowed out until much later when the aircraft had been repaired and they were ready for us to get back aboard.

We landed at Luqa Airport in Malta for refuelling and then flew on the rest of the way to Cyprus, coming down at RAF Akrotiri just west of Limassol. From here we were trucked a short distance further west to the Episkopi Garrison where we were quartered in bell tents. It was cold at night and the toilets were not the best, just deep pits dug out of the limestone with wooden seats arranged across them. These were enclosed within a primitive shed and gave off quite a pong. However, there was quite a large NAAFI where we could buy the strong Keo beer.

While we were here we carried out a normal routine of parades and went on marches. I was also involved in a truck dispatch service that went to various places in Cyprus. Because of EOKA we had to have an armed guard standing on the passenger seat with his head protruding out of the circular hole in the cab roof.

Sometime near the beginning of November I was chosen to be part of a Royal Signals advanced party on active service going to Port Said to set up communications for *Operation Musketeer*. Early on the 5th we were taken to Limassol where we went aboard the minelayer *Manxman* for the journey to Port Said. I noticed that some of the buildings on the Limassol waterfront were boarded up because of trouble with the EOKA terrorists.

We had to walk to the end of the timber jetty to where the ship was moored and this wasn't easy with all the kit we had to carry. Lighters were normally needed to reach the anchored ships lying off this shallow water port. Manxman however, being a minesweeper, had a fairly shallow draft and was able to get closer in.

Once we were on our way we couldn't go on deck because of the spray. The Manxman, arguably the fastest ship in the Royal Navy at that time, was speeding along at 39 knots and giving us quite a rough ride. I was lucky in meeting some members of the crew who were from Ipswich which is not far from my home town. They took me aft to show me how they laid mines. It was quite stable in that part of the ship and gave us a much smoother ride. This, and a tot of neat rum which went down like a red hot poker, helped me avoid being seasick.

We arrived off Port Said in the afternoon in time

to see a second wave of 3 Para dropping into El Gamil airfield. It looked to me as though one of the chutes didn't open properly since it seemed to go down at quite a speed. Before going ashore a meal was laid on but most of the boys were too ill to eat. I was able to tuck in though.

After dark we nosed into the mouth of the Suez Canal and moored against another ship lying alongside the quayside and which we had to clamber over to go ashore. After being issued with Sten guns and ammunition we made our way along the waterfront as far as the Suez Canal Company building which had become the Forces HQ. In front of the building stood the remains of an anti-aircraft gun wrecked by an RAF rocket earlier. Some of the signallers remained here but about eight or nine of us left the area of the canal building along a nearby street to a large house which we were told was normally used by the Canal Company managers. We searched the building and, finding it empty, moved in. The officers slept on the ground floor and the other ranks upstairs. Some of the cooks stayed there and so did I since I was the Adjutant's driver as well as his batman. When I was not needed I helped the cooks, not that this involved much since we were eating from 24-hour compo ration packs issued daily. I remained here for the rest of my stay in Port Said.

During this first day tanks were still rolling along the streets and advancing. After they'd passed through the snipers began operating again. I still have the bullet that I dug out of the wooden door jamb where it had ricocheted off the wall just above the floor where I slept that first night. If we were required to go out after dark to the Canal Company building we had to go out at the back and climb a ladder to go over a wall into another street where it was safer in case there were snipers still about.

The next day we went out looking to secure a billet for the rest of 23 Corps. Captain Bonnard was leading the armed group and took us into a hotel that seemed to be deserted until we got to the top floor where the owner and his family or friends were drinking and smoking just as though it was a public house and everything was quite normal. The Captain went and had a word with the owner and asked him to remove everyone from the building. The following day our unit took over the hotel. Even for us this was intended to be only temporary accommodation since we were supposed to be moving on to follow the moving front line. However we then heard that our government had called a ceasefire and that El Cap a few miles down the canal was as far as our troops would be going.

During the days things now became quite peaceful but at night, even though there was a curfew for both the citizens of Port Said and the troops, snipers were operating. One evening, as a break from the daily routine, we were taken out to the waterfront where we went aboard HMS *Dalrymple* for a film show on deck. It was while I was there that one of the sailors gave me a photo of one of the blockships in the canal.

The scuttled bucket dredger *Paul Solente.*

What little spare time I had after this I spent watching naval divers sinking large metal tanks on either side of the scuttled ships, fix wire hawsers to them, then pump the water out of the tanks so that the ship would rise until it floated again after which the divers would close the sea cock valves. There were quite a lot of French soldiers around the port at this time and they were willing to swap 50 of their cigarettes for 20 of ours. I tried some of theirs; they were horrible!

We left Port Said on the SS *New Australia* on the 22nd of December and dropped anchor outside the port of Oran in Algeria on New Year's Eve. We were hoping that we would be able to go ashore to do a bit of drinking but no luck, we had to stay aboard. The ship was so overloaded, I was told, that some of the men had to sleep in the swimming pool area. I think that this was because we were among the last people to leave Port Said and everyone had to be aboard. One thing I remember about the voyage was enjoying the sight of the porpoises following the ship to feed on the waste jettisoned from the galley.

We docked at Southampton on New Year's Day, were transported to Aldershot, and then had two weeks leave before returning to Herford in Germany which, for me, was for my final few months of service. I was demobbed from Chester in June 1957.

On my return to Civvy Street I went to work for a builder as a buyer and got married in 1960. Later I was promoted to services manager and worked for the company for 43 years until I was 65 when I reduced my hours to two days a week for a further five years until I finally retired.

* * *

Derek Tuckey, 106 Company, RASC.

After leaving school at 15 I started work as an apprentice at a branch of International Stores. This was a two-year apprenticeship and as soon as it was over, with National service not far away I applied for early call up to get it over with. I enrolled in Her Majesty's forces at RASC Blenheim Barracks, Aldershot, which was not far from my home in Basingstoke. I suppose I was placed in the RASC because my job in civilian life was in the retail trade.

After training I was posted to Dusseldorf in Germany and then, later, to 106 RASC Company at Bielfeld where, after some induction training, I was put to work in the stores. Eventually I was made a full corporal and put in charge of a platoon.

Later I was sent on an air dispatchers' course which I did not enjoy. The thought of dispatching consignments from an aircraft did not appeal to me one little bit, so in the autumn, by which time I was corporal in charge of Composite Platoon, it was with some relief when we were told, with no prior notice, to pack our bags and get ready to depart for the Middle East.

We took a train and ferry across the North Sea to Harwich where we joined a troop train to Southampton via a very circuitous route that took for ever to get round London into the southern rail region. En route we passed along the line near Basingstoke that was adjacent to the bungalow where I lived with my parents and was amazed to see my mother in the garden.

At Southampton we embarked on the troopship *Dilwara* and left port early the next morning, the 1st of November. We stopped at Gibraltar for a day, then a day at Malta and on to Cyprus before arriving off Port Said late in the day on 14 November. We had to disembark via scrambling nets into small landing craft which were bobbing up and down considerably on the swell. With my fear of heights I don't know how I did it; I just remember landing in a heap in the bottom of the boat.

By now it was getting dark and as we approached the beach we could see tracer bullets flashing across the sky. After the front of the landing craft ground onto the beach we ran for the Bedford trucks which took us to El Gamil Airfield where we spent the night in tents behind a low wall. We got very little sleep as aircraft seemed to flying over the top of us for most of the night.

The next morning our unit made a trip to the quayside to get some breakfast from the Navy and then began the task of making up food supplies for distributing to the units. Other than having to go on some patrols in the town from time to time this was pretty much our routine until we were informed that we would soon be homeward bound. We were taken out to the *Asturias* on about 14 December and arrived back off the Isle of Wight early on 30 December amid very rough seas. We had the Argyle and Sutherland Highlanders on board and there was some concern that if they were not on their way home for the evening of the 31st things could get a bit lively.

The problem was that it had not been possible to get the pilot aboard in the rough sea. Fortunately, however, the weather eased a little and early on the 31st we berthed at the dockside where the Jocks were the first off and away. I remember looking over the side of the ship whilst waiting to disembark and being amazed to see numerous packs of 200 cigarettes and an assortment of other bits and pieces floating in the water. The word had got around that kitbags were being checked.

Our 106 Company was sent to Greys in Essex and from there we were sent on two weeks leave, having to take rifles and kitbags with us, before returning to Germany. Back at Bielfeld I seemed almost surplus to requirements so was sent on a drill instructors course. Consequently I ended my army days drilling fresh arrivals and others at the barracks. I was offered a third stripe to stay on but enough was enough. I had enjoyed my service and felt that it had made a man of me but could not see myself being a soldier in the long term.

I returned to my life in the retail trade and became a branch manager with International Stores for two years until I could see that I would be making better progress with a company operating the modern supermarket set up and joined Budgens where I enjoyed a few years managing stores for them. However I had a hankering to be in business by myself and took on a Spar franchise. Although this was much smaller than the stores I was use to I enjoyed the challenge. I remained a store owner in various stores for the rest of my working life.

* * *

Dave Green, 106 Company, RASC.

I was born in Suffolk at the Beccles Hospital on 26th August 1937. Just two or three weeks later we moved from my parents' terraced house in Beccles to Gillingham, a lovely little village of about 300 people about two miles away across the border in Norfolk.

I hadn't turned much more than four when my parents found me climbing the trees near our local primary school so that I could wave to the children there. Since I was showing an interest they managed to get me in there by the time I was just four-and-a-half.

When eleven I left primary school in the summer of 1948 and in September began attending the Beccles County Secondary Modern School. While I was there I joined the school boxing team and went on to win the Suffolk Schools Boxing Championship in the 6 stone 11 pounds category. I also represented the school at football and cricket until I was 14 when I broke my left leg playing football. I didn't play again until I was 17 when I began playing for Beccles Town.

In July 1952, after leaving school at 15, I went to work at Church Farm, Alderby which was a couple of miles away from where I lived learning to do just about everything. After a while I moved on to Hill farm close to home in Gillingham where the tractor was a Field Marshall model made by Marshall's of Gainsborough.

Towards the end of 1955, after working on the land for nearly three-and-a-half years, I received notice to report to Colgate Street Norwich for my medical and interview for National Service. By the time I went I had decided to sign on for the extra year so that I could join the RASC, the same corps that my dad had belonged to during the war.

They allowed me to have Christmas at home and I joined the Corps on 9 January 1956 at Aldershot for my initial training. I then went to Houndstone Camp at Yeovil in Somerset for some more training and learning to drive vehicles other than tractors. After eight hours tuition, two hours a day on the old crash gearbox Bedford QL, I was the fourth to pass and was offered a staff car driver's post in Australia but turned it down. What a fool!

I returned from Yeovil to a camp at Borden just outside Aldershot where I remained for a while not doing much prior to eventually receiving a posting to Germany. My elder brother Noel who had been called up in 1954 was stationed nearby in Aldershot with his parachute regiment so while I was waiting for my transportation date I spent a week with him at his barracks. What a crazy lot they were!

On 2 May I set off for Germany with a number of others who'd also been posted there, first by train to the port of Harwich in Essex then by boat to the Hook of Holland before going on by train again to Beilfeld where I joined 106 Company RASC, BFPO 39. I'd been there about two months when I was offered a job in the gym as a PTI. I took it; it was just up my street. I was sent on a two-week PTI course at Sennelager near Paderborn and passed it so that I was eligible for my first stripe.

Dave in Germany.

In August, I think it was, following the trouble the government was having with the Egyptian leader Nasser, we had a succession of reluctant reservists come to join us. For some reason it didn't strike me then that I would get involved in all that business.

During the latter part of October I went home on leave to see my parents but part way though my stay I received a telegram telling me to report to Southampton. By the time I arrived some of the company had already left on the *Empire Parkeston*. The rest of us boarded the troopship *Dilwara* and followed soon afterwards. I remember the Argyll and Sutherland Highlanders were on board the ship too.

I think we sailed on 1 November. During the voyage I discovered that about a third of the troops were reservists with some of them being real old soldiers who had seen service in Korea. I led a number of PE sessions while we were at sea and some of us passed the time playing open pontoon. We called in at Gibraltar on the way before continuing on to Limassol in Cyprus where we stopped briefly to drop off one of my company who had fallen ill on the journey. This was so that he could be taken to BMH at Nicosia for treatment. We then set off south for Port Said. The whole journey was really slow and by the time we began disembarking at the waterfront on the 14th a ceasefire had already been in place for a week. Ashore we were taken south out of the town to a tented camp that had been set up just beyond the water works between the road and the Sweet Water Canal. On the way we saw a building with a sign for Brooke Bond Tea.

The big thing for me though was meeting up with my brother with the 33 Parachute Field Regiment of the Royal Artillery. While in Port Said I served as the Mail NCO, collecting the mail for the lads and posting their letters home. On one of these trips I saw Noel coming into town driving his CO, Lt Colonel 'Guy' Fawkes. I pulled over and after giving the colonel a salute told my brother to stand to attention when talking to an NCO.

'I'm glad you can control him,' said the colonel, 'we cannot.'

I won't mention Noel's reply.

(Brigadier 'Guy' Lindsay Valentine Francis Fawkes died in 2003 aged 90).

What a surprise it was! Brothers in different units but from the same little village meeting up like that in a place overseas. Noel's unit had come over from Famagusta on the *Empire Gull* and was in position down south at El Cap.

The waterfront at Famagusta. (Photo Roy Hulmes.)

Dave's brother Noel and unit boarding the *Empire Gull.*

The L3513 *Empire Gull.*

As well as my brother I also met another chap from a unit of the Paras while I was going for the mail. Together with a mate he began to collect me in his Champ for the journey back into Port Said when mail was in. He was an Irishman and what a mad sod he was although he had a heart of gold. We took some chances by taking a tour round the Port Said streets with Paddy just managing to keep a street ahead of our military patrol. We even got chased by about 50 Arabs who had gathered to make a protest of some kind but got away, thank goodness.

Among our duties was keeping guard at the docks as well as at several warehouses to prevent looting. After things got a bit quieter we were able to relax a bit and the company played football against the Navy. We got beaten 6-3 although I had the satisfaction of scoring all three of our goals. While at Port Said I bought a Swiss Helvetia watch off an Arab for a few hundred cigarettes.

One of our RASC units in Port Said was the 65 Field Bakery which set up its oven trucks in an old warehouse and its yard not far from the canal side although I don't know where exactly. This outfit, together with a bakery on one of the ships was responsible for supplying fresh bread to the troops.

65 Field Bakery of the RASC in Port Said. Photo supplied by Mick Loder of 57 Field Squadron Royal Engineers.

We got withdrawn from Port Said just before Christmas and sailed for Famagusta in Cyprus, again on the *Dilwara*, and were put ashore on smaller boats.

From here were taken in trucks to Akrotiri RAF base near Limassol via Nicosia. Until we were passing along Nicosia's Ledra Street, the infamous Murder Mile, I hadn't realised that the old Bedford QLs could go so fast. On arrival at the RAF base we were put up in tented lines.

We spent the festive season at Akrotiri and my favourite meal while we were there was chip butties eaten with a bottle of Keo beer. We were kept busy for a while ferrying trucks around the island until early in the New year when we returned on the *Dilwara* to Southampton and dear old Blighty for some well-earned leave. We then went back to Germany where 106 was disbanded and we were incorporated into 107 Company housed at the same barracks.

Since I was listed in the records as a driver my PE career was now over. However I was soon made up to full corporal and given a platoon of my own and also became the captain of the company football team which went on to win the Minor Units Knock-Out Cup.

In the middle of 1958 the squadron moved from Bielfeld to a place called Hilden to become the transport unit to the KOYLIs. With seven lorries we were given the job of transporting all their supplies and equipment from their camp to ours at Hilden.

During the journey we were close enough to call in at the site of the Belson extermination camp. I have never been to such a quiet place in my whole life. We didn't see a sign of an animal or a bird anywhere in the vicinity.

On our return to Hilden Captain Pledge congratulated us on having done a great job. He then told me that if I would sign on for three more years he would give me my third stripe immediately since he was about to become a major in charge of his own company. I thanked him but explained that my mother and father meant too much to me for me to stay on longer.

At the end of 1958 I had my last Christmas with the lads and returned to the UK in early January 1959 via the Hook of Holland to Harwich and then to Borden. At Borden I spent my last few days with the RASC and to finish off my service they put me on guard for the last night. The following morning, for the last time, I climbed aboard the Borden 'Bullet' which is what we called the train to Aldershot, then to Waterloo, underground to Liverpool Street, and home to Gillingham. The end of three wonderful years! God Save the Queen, hello Civvy Street. I then spent the next eight years as a reservist.

When I started work again it was as a lorry driver for Vitovis Ltd who provided provender food for farmers. I also began playing football for Bungay Town and in the 1960/61 season we won the Senior Cup at Portman Road, Ipswich I also played for Suffolk County against Cambridge at the same venue.

In 1963 I got married and then two years later changed jobs, going to work for Richard Clay (printers) at Bungay until I took early retirement 30 years later in 1995. But I then went on to work for a while driving a recovery vehicle for A W D Hammond the Ford agency at Halesworth until 2002. Joan and I have now been married for 48 wonderful years.

* * *

Gordon Harry Ball, Army Catering Corps

I was born on September 6, 1935 at Royston near Barnsley in Yorkshire where I lived with my mum and dad on a railway workers estate. My dad was an engine driver.

When war was declared in September 1939 I had just started school at Royston C of E. Whenever the air raid siren sounded we were all taken to the shelter that had been built on the school playing field where we would sit on long forms while we sang songs such as Old Macdonald and Ten Green Bottles, etc., until the all-clear sounded. Sometimes we hadn't been back in the classroom for very long when the siren would sound again and off we would go back to the shelter.

Every house on our estate was issued with an Anderson shelter which had to be dug partly into the ground. Dad did this with ours. There was no door, just a bit of old carpet hung down. When there was a raid we took our gas masks with us to the shelter, and a blanket because we didn't know how long we would be in there as we tried to keep our feet out of the water that seeped up though the earth floor.

I can still remember that sometimes during a wartime evening while we were listening to the BBC radio the broadcast would get interrupted when a propagandist in Germany nicknamed Lord Haw Haw would break into the programme to tell us how badly the war was going for the British. Sometimes he would even announce the Luftwaffe's target for that night.

About a mile away from where we lived was Monkton Colliery which had had pit head baths recently installed. Soon afterwards Lord Haw Haw announced that the target for tonight would be the new pit head baths at Royston in Yorkshire. Sure enough we got the raid and could hear the explosions from home. Fortunately they missed the baths by about 50 yards and no one was injured. The next day everyone went to see the craters left behind.

In 1946 my dad was transferred to the Normanton loco sheds about seven miles away near Wakefield so we went to live there where I attended Queens Street School for a short while until I left in the summer of 1946. Having failed the 11-plus examination for grammar school I went to Normanton Secondary Modern which I never really liked although I enjoyed a few of the subjects.

With my 15th birthday being on September 6 1950 I missed leaving school in the summer by three days. However, I was told that if I got a job I could leave at Christmas. In Normanton at that time there wasn't a lot of choice of jobs except for the colliery. Coming from a railway family I wanted to become a fireman so my dad made some enquiries and discovered that I couldn't work at the loco depot until I was 16 but could get a job meantime as a junior porter or train recorder if I passed the medical. I passed this in November at Manchester, left school at Christmas, and began work on New Year's Day 1951 at Goosehill Signal Box as a train recorder.

A year later on nearing my 16th birthday I transferred to the engine shed as an engine cleaner. After three months I passed a test which made me available for firing trips on the footplate. There wasn't much opportunity at that time for becoming a permanent fireman but I stayed on until I was 18 when I was called up for National Service.

I went to Leeds on about September 4 1953 to register and take the medical. I was told to cough a couple of times, had my ears syringed, and passed A1. When I was asked which regiment I preferred I said the Royal Engineers since I knew they ran the military railways. I was then informed that to make sure of this choice I would have to sign on for the extra year. I refused their offer and when I received my papers the following month the travel warrant was made out to Aldershot where I was to join the Army Catering Corps at Ramillies Barracks on 5th November.

Since I hadn't ever been away from home on my own before I wasn't looking forward to the next two years. My apprehension was justified. After taking the 10.00 am London express to St Pancras, crossing London to Waterloo Station, taking the Southern Railways train to Aldershot, and exiting the station, I was immediately pounced on. 'Are you for the ACC? Right then, get on the lorry.'

After arriving at the barracks I was fed and shown a bed while for the rest of the day more recruits arrived. The next day began at about 6am when a corporal roared into the billet and woke us up by banging on a steel locker and shouting, 'Out of bed you lazy lot, you're in the Army now. Get dressed; last one cleans the latrines.'

In no time at all we were outside, at the cookhouse, fed, given a haircut, and kitted out. Then we met the drill sergeant who explained that we were now a number, that he knew all the tricks had all the answers, hard men would be tamed, and that before the end of the next two weeks we would all hate him.

The next two weeks passed quickly and we were all posted to various ACC training camps across the country.

The first week in training. Gordon back row second right.

Gordon in the middle.

I was fortunate enough to get Catterick in North Yorkshire. On the first morning we were woken in the usual way – with a big stick rattling the locker. The sergeant was Sgt Thompson and his sidekick Cpl Lester. We began life here with six weeks of square-bashing during which all of us resolved to accept the next two years come what may, all of us except one lad. He told us that on his Christmas leave he intended going AWAL which he did, sending the billet a Christmas card from Southern Ireland.

With this out of the way we began 12 weeks training to be cooks throughout the first three months of 1954. We were issued our cooks' whites and introduced to our civilian chef, a Mr Dobson I think it was, who was going to train us. I passed the course and became a B3 Army cook.

Gordon, Kneeling on the left, and some of his mates on the B3 cooks' course at Catterick

In April our postings came through and I found that I'd been allocated to the regimental depot of the Durham Light infantry at Brancepeth Camp just outside Durham City. I was there for about six months before being sent to 58 Medium Regiment of the Royal Artillery for a four month spell at Otterburn in Northumberland after which I received an order to report back to the DLI at Durham from where I was to go on three weeks leave before being posted to Korea.

Whilst at Otterburn I had sent in a pair of boots for repair and when I reported to Aldershot to prepare for embarkation after my leave they did a kit check and discovered I was deficient one pair of boots. As a consequence they took me off the draft. It is one of the regrets of my life. I'd have bought a replacement pair of boots myself if I'd known that was going to happen.

After eight weeks of odd-jobbing in Aldershot I was sent back to Brancepeth and then put on a B2 cook's course at Catterick which I passed. I returned to Brancepeth and spent the rest of my National Service there before being demobbed on November 5 1955.

I returned to my old job on British Railways with its anti-social shifts which made it almost impossible to arrange or keep dates with girls. It was quite a regular thing to be at work 12 or 14 hours, especially working a slow coal train into Lancashire on a foggy winter's night. Relationships with railwaymen tended to be something of a no-no with local girls.

However, in July 1956, soon after carrying out my two weeks AER training at Marchwood near Southampton with 169 Port Operating Squadron which had a lot of Reservist dockers and stevedores from the Liverpool area, I eventually got married to a railwayman's daughter. Afterwards we went to Scarborough where we spent our two weeks honeymoon in her parents' caravan. When we got back I read about the Suez trouble in the paper. Some of my mates at work were in the Territorials and I told them to be getting their kit ready.

On the Saturday lunchtime as I was getting ready for a local 2 pm to 10 pm shift there was a knock at the door. I answered it and found a GPO lad there with his pushbike. 'Telegram for G H Ball,' he said. I was to report immediately to 169 Port Operations Squadron RE at Longmoor in Hampshire. I couldn't believe it. I'd only been married a fortnight and here I was, back to the Army again. I decided I was going to have the weekend at home.

I set off to Longmoor on the Monday morning and met up with lots of my old mates. I was assigned to the officers' mess with another cook and for a few weeks the time passed with nothing happening and all the lads wanting to get back home. Then, suddenly, we were given orders. We were to move to a camp nearer Southampton. Before we left we were marched off for injections, two in each arm. 'We haven't got time to mess about,' we were told. Lads were keeling over everywhere, myself included, and we were laid out in rows till we came round.

I can't remember exactly where our temporary camp was but once there we were told to parcel up our civilian clothes for despatching home. Shortly afterwards we were put on a train which took us directly onto the Southampton dockside where we joined thousands of other troops and boarded the troopship *Asturias*. Since we boarded just about last we were berthed on one of the top decks. Conditions on the lower decks were bad with squaddies having to sleep on the floor in what during the day were walking spaces. Even the cinema was turned into a sleeping area. After dark the ship quietly slipped away from the Southampton quayside with nobody to see us off to war; no waving, no flags, no band.

Out at sea the ship began rolling and in the Bay of Biscay it got even rougher. One of the crew tried to cheer us up by telling us that it would get better as soon as we entered the Med. We went through the Straits with Gibraltar on the port and Africa to starboard and called at Malta where we posted our letters home. These were censored to make sure no one gave the game away. But of course, ever since the end of July when Nasser nationalised the Suez Canal, everyone in Britain knew where we would be going.

When we went up on deck on the morning of 6 November we could see smoke rising on the horizon from the fires in Port Said. We were nearing our journey's end. Our OC, Major Allan, informed us that we would be going ashore in the next few hours and tried to prepare us for what lay ahead by explaining that we would probably see dead bodies littering the streets and there would be sniping from the buildings. It didn't help when we then had to make out our wills before being issued with a .303 Lee Enfield rifle each and a bandolier of 50 rounds of ammunition.

We were the first to go down the gangway and into large landing craft. As I stood in the bow waiting for the vessel to fill up behind me I thought to myself, here I am, just 21-years-old, armed, invading a country which we have bombed and no doubt killed people. I don't think we will be welcomed. When that bow door lowers for us to go ashore, owt can happen. I was actually more concerned about what the effect on my family would be if anything happened to me than I was for my own safety.

When we landed on the quayside near the de Lessep statue it was fairly quiet We lined up and marched along a road parallel to the beach nearby on the right. We saw a few burned out and damaged building and Arabs standing about who didn't seem too concerned that they were in the middle of a war zone. After some distance we came to a large flat-roofed building on the left in its own grounds with iron gates at the entrance. This, we were told, had once been King Farouk's seaside palace and for the moment was to be our headquarters.

Before we took it over we were told not to drink the water – it could be poisoned, not to touch anything – it could be booby-trapped, and sleep where you can. Sentries were posted and we made a meal of our personal dried emergency rations unless we'd already eaten them on the ship which is what some of the lads did. Our group then settled down on a stone landing where we spent the night each with his single blanket. There was just one WC nearby which didn't work properly.

The following day one of the first priorities was to dig latrines in the garden while we, the ACC lads, prepared a meal using petrol burners blowing into steel sheet tunnels which was a very effective means of heating the food which came in tins of all sizes. As can be imagined, the great heap of these empty tins which were eventually piled up outside the gates became an immediate attraction to all the children in the area who swarmed over them searching for every last morsel of food.

After a while I was transferred to an old police station on the waterfront just a little way down from the famous lighthouse as cook for some of the sappers billeted there. One morning I was collected early while it was still dark to be cook for a squad of sappers from the 'palace' where I'd recently been and who were now working at the waterfront each day unloading the ships bringing in supplies.

At the quayside I were ferried out to a large merchant ship anchored in the middle of the canal. The only access to the ship towering above me was via a massive net hanging down its side. With all my cooking gear of knives, ladles, spoons, etc., a bandolier of 50 rounds, as well as a .303 Le Enfield rifle slung across my back, I started to climb.

Because of the curve of the ship I found myself dangling in mid-air and by the time I got to the top and scrambled over the rail onto the deck I was exhausted.

One night we worked very late aboard the ship and by the time we got back to shore it was after curfew. The lads were all returning to the 'palace' in a truck but as I was duty cook the following morning at the police station I had to get back there but the driver wouldn't go out of his way to take me. So I had the choice of either going to the palace with the lads or to the police station on my own. I decided I would have to walk the six or seven hundreds yards along the side of the Suez Canal back to the police station on my own. I set off in the dark, rifle across my front, a bullet up the spout, safety catch on, past dark alleys, and made it to the police station.

I banged on the door and got no answer. I banged again. A voice asked, 'Who is it?' I gave him my name, rank and number. 'Password,' he said. I'd left before they gave out the password for the day so they wouldn't let me in. I even told them the OC's name, Major Allan, but they still didn't want to know. Eventually, after a lot more dialogue, they opened the door to take a look at me then let me in. They'd somehow got the idea into their heads that all this was leading up to an Arab attack. Stuck out there for ages on the street on my own in the dark in a foreign city and feeling abandoned by my mates was the worst experience of my life.

By this time however the United Nations had got themselves involved and the sappers were now busy loading up the ships again that they'd only just unloaded.

Eventually we went aboard the troopship *New Australia* and set out for the UK. On the way we called in at the port of Oran in Algeria where we picked up a number of French families. By now the Arabs were seeking their independence from France and things were getting quite dangerous there.

We spent Christmas at sea and eventually landed at Southampton one morning just before the end of the year. There were no bands and streamers to meet us, just the customs men. Some of the lads who had gone ashore earlier had been found with Russian Kalashnikov rifles stuffed down their kitbags. I didn't smoke but I had saved up my entitlement of pipe tobacco for Dad. They took it off me. When customs had finished with us we boarded a special train and were taken off for the night to the camp we'd embarked from just a few weeks earlier.

The following morning we were told to get breakfast and then we would be going home. Those of who were cooks intended to go straight into the cookhouse instead of queuing with the Royal Engineers. When we got inside we found the place full of sappers banging their tin mugs and eating irons and shouting for their breakfast, and just one very terrified-looking ACC lad on duty. 'What's for breakfast?' we asked. 'Eggs, bacon and beans.' We told the lads to give us ten minutes and they'd have their breakfast. A big cheer went up and we got stuck in. Later a captain came and spoke to us and thanked us for helping out. I was demobbed shortly afterwards and arrived home at about 8pm that night. It was New Year's Eve 1956.

I went back to the railway as a fireman until Dr Beeching made a lot of us redundant in the sixties; moved to Bridlington; worked at a piggery; at a fruit and veg wholesale firm; with a village joiner/undertaker as a labourer, gravedigger, and coffin bearer; and at a builder's merchant driving and glass cutting until I retired in 1988 when I had my right hip replaced. In 2007 I had my left hip replaced and in 2011 had the right hip replaced again.

I am at present writing a diary of my life for the family – a son, a 30-year-old grandson, a 25-year-old granddaughter, and two great-grandchildren aged ten and five.

* * *

Derek Thomson, Army Catering Corps.

I was born at 43 Orchard Street, Norwich on 21 September 1934, one of eleven children, nine boys and two girls. Dad came originally from Aberdeen while Mum was from Winchester in Hampshire.

At the time of the Norwich Blitz in April 1942, the Baedeker reprisal raids, we were living at 96 Magdalen Road. Despite the corrugated-iron Anderson shelter we had in the garden I immediately got evacuated to Aunt Lily in Winchester for a while but when she wanted to keep me Mum brought me back home. Not long after that Dad fell ill with bronchitis and died. During the war each of my five elder brothers gradually became old enough to join the forces, four in the Army and one in the Navy. All five of them survived to return home afterwards.

While I was at secondary school I got a part-time job as a butcher's boy making deliveries to customers on the trade bike. I left school in 1948 to begin working for the butcher full time but since I was only fourteen it was very unofficial. Since my 15th birthday wasn't until September I should have continued at school until Christmas but they let me leave in the summer.

As I was coming up to my 18th birthday in September 1952 I received instructions to report for the National Service medical at Norwich and shortly afterwards was called up to join the Army Catering Corps at Aldershot with the number 22739037.

After an initial six months training with the Corps I was detached to the King's Shropshire Light Infantry at Gottingen, Germany, until my demob in 1954 when I returned to my trade as a butcher.

In the summer of 1956 I was called back to the Army with a letter telling me to report to an ACC unit in Hampshire where I got kitted out and was held for a while. Eventually, with other reservists I was transported to Southampton where I went aboard a ship and sailed for the Mediterranean. We stopped at Malta for a short while without being allowed to go ashore. We then continued on and when we went up on deck the morning after leaving Malta we discovered that there were ships all around us and realised we were part of a large convoy; we thought we had been on our own.

We were on deck playing cards when the Egyptian coast came in sight and a voice on the speaker system told us that we would soon be going in and to collect the ammunition for our .303s. Soon we saw smoke rising from the fires in Port Said. The smell in the air reminded me of the Blitz back in Norwich all those years ago. As we sailed into the Suez Canal entrance we could see the ships that had been sunk by the Egyptians.

Ashore I was billeted in a secondary school next to the Railway Station and attached to the Royal Engineers. Instead of being stacked out of the way to make room for us to sleep on the floors nearly every bit of classroom furniture had been taken outside to make a bonfire. I don't know why that was necessary.

There were two of us from the ACC and we did our actual cooking for the sappers in the open air at the back of the school on diesel burners. As well as cooking we had to dig pits for toilets with poles across for sitting on. We built timber walls around the pit and fastened canvas to the sides for a bit of privacy but the top was open to the elements and we were also overlooked by one or two tall buildings. I remember too that we were instructed to swallow a big salt pill every day.

Cooking out of doors at the back of one of the schools. Derek on the right by the tea urn and the Jerrycans.

When we discovered that the locals were trying to break into our store of food, which was kept in an old building in the school grounds, we had to line up with our loaded rifles to make them go away. Eventually, when things quietened down and we were not on duty, we were allowed out as long as we were in groups of at least two.

While we were out and about I saw some sights that have never left my memory. It was upsetting to see how we had treated the people in Port Said, particularly the women and children who had got caught up in the Canal business. It was their land and their town.

Just before Christmas our unit was withdrawn and we went aboard a ship and sailed for Famagusta in Cyprus and spent Christmas there. We returned to the UK in January and landed in Liverpool. I went straight from the ship and right through customs to the railway station and a train home to Norwich. I heard later that the boys on one ship had been given a real going over by customs.

I returned to my job, married Valerie in 1958 and we had two sons. We were divorced in 1980. I married again in 1984, to Pat who had three children of her own. Between us we have ten grandchildren.

*   *   *

Les Frampton, The Queen's Own West Kents.

My life began in the East Sussex village of Isfield near Uckfield on 11 August 1929, the youngest of four brothers and a sister. Father was foreman at the local flour and general cattle feed mill.

When I was four-and-a-half we moved to Uckfield where Dad had taken a new job and a few months later I began attending the Parochial School in Belmont Lane.

In 1938 Father went into the Army, joining the King Edward VIII Defence Corps which later became part of the Royal Sussex Regiment. On September 3 the following year, just after I was ten, Britain declared war against Germany and my brothers George and Frank joined up.

George was called up as a reservist having recently spent three years in the Army as a regular. He'd only been out since July. He went to France as part of the Expeditionary Forces and came out via Dunkirk. Frank also went to France and came out via Calais.

During the Battle of Britain we used to watch the dogfights taking place in the sky above us. On one occasion John was in the allotments at the back of our house watching the spectacle overhead when he saw a line of machine gun bullets making its way along the ground towards him and he turned and ran towards us as fast as he could. Another time an enemy plane dropped what was called an oil bomb and it killed a donkey in what is now Olives Meadow. Brother Peter, who had joined the ARP when he was old enough, later came home with the head of the bomb which we began using as a doorstop. Eventually Peter was called up too and he went into the Signal Corps.

When the raids on London started, 35 miles away, we spent nights outside at the back of the house looking north to the glow in the sky from the fires and the ack-ack guns firing at the enemy aircraft. We spent a lot of time watching the spectacle. School continued of course and if I had been up all night I would frequently fall asleep the following day at my desk. One day during the war while I was going to school a German plane flew close overhead and I saw it drop bombs on the army camp at Maresfield about three miles away.

On another occasion Uckfield itself was raided with incendiary bombs. Mother, my brother John and I heard the noise and Mother opened the front door to see what it was. She called out for us to run across the road to the air raid shelter by the laundry which we did with bombs falling all around us. One of them fell underneath John's trade bike which was propped up outside and it was blown right across the road. However, despite the large number of bombs dropped on the town the only damage, apart from my brother's bike, was to a house at the top of the town where a bomb went right through the roof. It was soon after this raid that a number of stirrup pumps were issued to the village.

Sometimes a gang of us boys went to the pictures during the evening and if a raid took place while we were in there a message was flashed on the screen and everyone had to leave the building and make for home in the blackout to the sound of ack-ack guns firing.

On 3 January 1941 Father died of natural causes while serving at Newhaven Fort. I remember him once telling me the story of how a local friend of his who had joined up with him at the same time, when arriving home on leave used to put his rifle and bandolier of ammunition into the coal cellar for safety. After he'd returned to camp his wife was making up the fire one day and didn't notice that a clip of .303 ammunition had fallen in among the coal. Soon after she lit the fire this exploded and blew out the front of the fireplace.

I left school in the summer of 1943 at the age of 14 and went to work at Blundell's Farm. One of the proudest moments of my life occurred when I was walking home for lunch one day when I saw my brothers George and Peter coning down the High Street wearing the red berets of the Airborne Forces. George, after his return from Dunkirk, had eventually joined the 1st Airborne Division which was formed in 1941, and when the 6th Airborne Division was established in April 1943 Peter had transferred to it from the Signals. It was about this time that John was called up leaving just Mother, my sister Helen, and me at home.

One day while I was hoeing in a field next to the cemetery in Snatts Road an anti-aircraft shell landed just behind me. It had come from a single anti-aircraft gun positioned in the nearby village of Buxted which was firing at enemy planes passing over East Sussex on a raid.

I stayed at Blundell's for 12 months before going to work at Hammonds Green Farm as under cowman. We used to start milking at 6 o'clock in the morning which meant I had to leave home by 5 o'clock. When the milking was done I went on to hedge-cutting or other jobs that needed doing around the place. I also learned to drive a tractor. It was while I was working here that I saw my first Doodlebug as we used to call them. I didn't know what it was at the time but thought it might have been one of our planes in trouble.

In April 1954 I was called up for National Service and reported to Brighton from where I was posted to the Queen's Own Royal West Kent Regiment at Maidstone in Kent for training. When this was over I was given my choice of posting which led to me joining the 1st Battalion of the regiment which was then serving at Luneburg in Germany. It wasn't too long before I was playing rugby for the battalion.

About a year after my arrival in Germany I received a letter from my sister asking if I could come home because our mother was seriously ill with cancer and was dying. She died three days after my arrival home and I was able to stay to attend the funeral and her burial at Uckfield.

I continued to serve in Germany where we went on manoeuvres on Luneberg Heath and also patrolled the bank of the River Elbe across which was the Russian zone. Eventually, possibly sometime in the spring of 1956, the Battalion returned to the UK and I was in the advance party that left Germany and sailed from the Hook of Holland for Harwich and then went by train to Old Park Barracks, Dover, where we were soon practising for a big parade that had been arranged for us in the county town Maidstone in front of the local bigwigs in which we would be dressed in our 'blues'. This was to mark the centenary of the regiment. As soon as the parade was over we were to go on leave.

However, this did not happen because in Maidstone, the evening before the parade was to be held, we learned that we would be returning to Dover instead to prepare for a move to Salisbury Plain to undertake training ready to go abroad. When the day came we left Dover by train and finished up at Bulford Camp. It was while we were here, on 13 August 1956, that I got leave to marry a girl I had known since 1948 when we both belonged to the Uckfield Bonfire Society, an organisation which had its beginnings in 1827.

Sometime in October 1956 we returned to Dover quite early in the day and learned that if we could get back by midnight we could go home. I got a lift with another chap who was going to Tonbridge. His father dropped me off at home and then picked me up again in the evening when returning his own son to Dover.

On arrival back at Dover we were told to pack everything we didn't need for storage and at about 4 o'clock in the morning left on a train for Southampton where we boarded a troopship and sailed for the Middle East. We learned that we were making for Egypt. We called at Malta on the way for fresh water and other provisions before continuing our journey east.

I shall never forget the sight of the ships that had been sunk in the entrance to the Suez Canal and the shell holes in the buildings when we arrived at Port Said and went ashore on 10 November. There wasn't a lot of time to look around before we were boarding trucks and making our way south to the front line at El Cap.

On our arrival there we were directed to the forward position at El Cap some miles down the canal where we spent two days in slit trenches. The digging was quite hard work with the temperature being about 70 degrees. However we were able to cool down in the canal which was quite pleasant. The only support we had was a small naval vessel close by which had managed to weave its way through the sunken blockships and was moored behind us. Occasionally groups of us were allowed to go back to the school on the local village which was the only concrete building. Here we were able to have a good wash and enjoy a laze around in the sunshine.

View north from the station of part of El Cap village.

One day I was sent to intercept a couple of men who we saw walking past us down the Treaty Road. I went across and asked them who they were and where they thought they were going. One of them showed me a letter which stated that he was a major general from the United States Army and he had been sent there as a representative of the UN. I warned them not to go too far to the Egyptian front line. Soon after this we heard on the grapevine that the UN would soon be arriving at El Cap and on 20 November we were replaced by the Royal Fusiliers and returned to Port Said where we were billeted in a school close to the sea front.

While there we were called out one day to a riot that had broken out by the local police station where a large crowd had gathered in protest at the destruction of their homes in which acres of Shanty Town had been burned to the ground. The story was that 45 Marine had got rather fed up of being shot at from the houses still remaining there after the main destruction and ceasefire had taken place and had retaliated by using petrol to get rid of them. We hadn't been given any training in riot control but luckily some reservists from the Hampshire Regiment who came to our aid, had. In all we spent about two weeks in Egypt.

According to the Queen's Own Gazette, Jan 1957, page 12, 'At 0400 hours on Sat. Nov. 24th 9 Platoon took out the last patrol of the Arab town; we sailed in the *Dilwara* the next day. All ranks enjoyed the two day rest on board and we disembarked at Limassol, then on to our camp at Dhekelia. Ten days later we learnt that the Battalion was to remain in Cyprus for a tour of 3 years. The company then moved to Famagusta on detachment. On Dec. 22nd our reservists left and at the time of going to press the platoon totalled twenty-two, all ranks included.'

I was demobbed in April 1957 at Maidstone and went on to join the East Sussex Fire Brigade and served for a total of twenty-seven years.

* * *

Stephen Hartley, 1 Battalion, West Yorkshire Regiment.

Stephen was a first lieutenant carrying out his National Service with the Ist Battalion of the West Yorkshire Regiment. He has supplied a number of photographs from the time he spent in Port Said during the Suez Crisis and one of immediately afterwards.

The troopship *Empire Fowey* which took the First Battalion of the West Yorkshire Regiment to Port Said.

View from the *Empire Fowey* of the De Lesseps Statue and the Fish Dock housing the fleet of French coastal minesweepers on loan from the USA under the Military Defence Assistance Pact. From the right are M683 Liseron, M687 Mimosa, ?, and M638 Acacia.

The Police Headquarters on the corner of the canal and the Bassin du Commerce commandeered by the 1st Battalion of the West Yorkshire Regiment.

First Battalion's commandeered harbour runabout *Tewfik* at the head of the Basin Du Commerce.

Contingent of UN Scandinavian troops just arrived from El Cap at Port Said railway station.

Stephen explains that while he was taking this photograph of these smart and well-organised and lined up troops a Columbian contingent was still on the train in a complete shambles trying to get themselves sorted out.

Lt Hartley and his platoon waiting to escort the first UN troops from the station to their designated areas.

Stephen came across a pamphlet that had been put out in Port Said as a warning to the Allies.

A Warning To
English & Frenchmen

DEATH TO YOU IF YOU DO NOT GO OUT OF OUR COUNTRY OR WE WILL THROW YETT ONT INTO THE SEA.
BE QUICK AND SAVE YOUR LIVES.
LONG LIVE EGYPT.

Another pamphlet was put out by the 'Egyptian underground'.

COMPLETE FIASCO

SOLDIERS OF FRANCE AND BRITAIN

Do you wander why Mr. Eden sent you to Egypt?
Do you realise now you are fighting for a lost cause?
If you entered our country toput an end to the Communist influence in this part of the world, as Eden pretends, you are wrong.

If you invaded Egypt because of NASSERS's Seizure of the Suez Canal you are still wrong for the Canal will always remain Egyptian,... or it will never be "SUEZ CANAL" after all.

If you came to destroy NASSER's Regime, you will fail because we believe that te is strong and God always protect. Besides, our revolution is based on prinsples and faith,.. not individuals, things which are not existing any more in your country.

Taking off PORT SAID, is not a Brilliant victory for you... as we had not chosen this town for the final and deceisive battle... NASSER's Army has not yet moved.

Britain & France ignore our plants... wait for the next step. We, are Taking our land itwill too late.

Now shall escape with draw our your forces after the arrival of the Uniterd nations Police or else.

The Canal is blocked... no more Arab oil for you and you lost the world respect.

Now you gave us reasons to wind up our British Empire. You are weak in Europe, in Asia & and in the MIDDLE EAST.

The spellings and grammar are all the original.

Also in the First Battalion of the Yorkshire Regiment carrying out his National Service at this time, was a friend of Stephen, 2nd Lt Anthony Gerard Moorhouse of Leeds, the son of Francis Gerard Moorhouse who was currently running the family business, Moorhouse Jams based at Beeston, Leeds.

Lt Moorhouse lost his life in Port Said and Stephen later attended his funeral in Leeds.

Lt Moorhouse's funeral held at Lawnswood Cemetery, Leeds on 10 January 1957. Following the gun carriage is Anthony's father and, on his left, Anthony's brother Peter. Lt Stephen Hartley is partially obscuring Mr Moorhouse's figure.

* * *

Anthony Gerard Moorhouse, 1 Battalion, West Yorkshire Regiment.

Anthony Gerard Moorhouse was born in 1935, the son of Francis Gerard Moorhouse, the proprietor of the jam-making company William Moorhouse and sons, and his wife Dorothy, of Beeston, Leeds..

Anthony was educated at Stonyhurst College to the west of Clitheroe in Lancashire after which he took a two-year food technology course. This brought him up to the time for his National Service when he was conscripted to the West Yorkshire Regiment. After training he was allocated to the First Battalion which, late in October, as part of the Suez Crisis invasion force, sailed in the troopship *Empire Fowey* for Port Said. When they arrived, by which time the ceasefire was already in place, they were allocated a billet in the police building on the canal side, with the officers setting themselves up in a luxury flat close to the Simon Arzt department store jus a few yards away. (See the Internet site 'Britain's Small Wars, Last Man Standing, by Peter Hinchcliffe.)

A month later, on 10 December, with preparations for the withdrawal already under way, Anthony was instructed to lead a raid that evening on the premises of an Egyptian dentist, Dr Gheude, presumably on the basis of intelligence received, where seven, (this is the usual number quoted), Egyptian Commandos were found to be hiding out during the ceasefire. These were taken into custody.

The following morning, on the 11th, Anthony departed alone, against orders, from the police station, so far as can be guessed, to check again on the dentist's safe house. It was the last time he was seen alive by anyone on the British side.

On 22nd January 1957 in Parliament, Mr Biggs-Davison, MP for Chigwell in Essex, '… asked the Secretary of State for War (John Hare) whether he will make a statement on the circumstances of the death of Second Lieutenant Anthony Moorhouse of the West Yorkshire Regiment in Port Said.'

John Hare replied,

'On the morning of 11th December Second Lieutenant A. G. Moorhouse of 1st Battalion The West Yorkshire Regiment, visited the area in which a patrol had been carried out in Port Said on the previous evening. According to an Egyptian witness, he was alone in a vehicle and stopped to speak to an Egyptian; a crowd assembled and one

man seized the officer's pistol. Moorhouse was then abducted in a civilian car. He was not again seen alive by any member of the British forces, but there was a report on 22nd December that Major Wiks, a Norwegian officer of the United Nations Force, had been taken blindfolded to a house and had seen him alive and well.

On receipt of the contradictory information that Second Lieutenant Moorhouse was dead, urgent representations were made to the United Nations to obtain the true facts, and on 31st December, the Secretary-General of the United Nations received a report, originating from the Egyptian Army Authorities, that Moorhouse after capture by Egyptians was kept with the intention of exchanging him for some Egyptian "resistance" prisoners. The report continued that when British troops began combing the area he was locked in a small metal cupboard; his captors returned once to feed him but, as the search intensified, they felt it unsafe to return and he was left for two days; on return they found him dead, apparently from suffocation, and buried him in the house where he had been kept prisoner.

On 4th January, a representative of the United Nations organization handed over at Naples a body which was said to be that of the officer. *An examination of teeth, scars, measurements, etc., established beyond doubt that the body was that of Second Lieutenant Moorhouse.*

I know I speak for the whole house in expressing sincere sympathy for the family of this young officer in their loss. In particular, I regret the uncertainty about his fate which continued for so long in spite of all our efforts to obtain the true facts from the Egyptian authorities.'

(With thanks to Hansard for permission to reproduce this 22 January 1957 extract.)

A United Press News Agency report carried by the Sunday Herald of Bridgeport, Connecticut, in the United States on 23 December 1956 had this to say about the end of the Allied occupation of Port Said.

'The Anglo-French troops evacuated Egypt yesterday in a blaze of gunfire ... under cover of low-flying planes and left the city in control of UN emergency forces. UN troops were forced to fire repeatedly to prevent infiltrators from getting into the tiny evacuation perimeter enclosed in barbed wire.

The Egyptian Nationalists ignored orders from Cairo to hand over Lt Anthony Moorhouse but sent word to the British via the UN Command that he was alive and well.

... The British who had threatened to hold 200 Egyptian prisoners hostage for his safe return said that when Moorhouse is released he will face court martial on charges of being AWOL, driving a Jeep without escort and allowing himself to be kidnapped by Egyptians who seized his weapon..

Heavy fire was heard inside the debark perimeter as the last man clambered aboard ship.'

On 7 January 1957 TIME MAGAZINE included an article on the Moorhouse affair with the title 'The Kidnapped Lieutenant.'

"I wish something exciting would happen," Lieut. Anthony Moorhouse, 20, wrote his family from Suez. Life after the ceasefire was getting monotonous for a young officer doing his national service with the British forces in Egypt. His father, a prosperous jam and preserve manufacturer from Leeds, read the letter in a taxi en route to a business engagement in London and smiled at his eldest son's restiveness. For the moment the headlines on the news vendor's sign just across the street seemed remote and unimportant. BRITISH OFFICER KIDNAPED IN PORT SAID, they read. It wasn't until he reached his hotel and got an emergency call from Leeds that Francis Moorhouse learned that his son had found the moment of excitement he sought.

Tea & Sympathy. The anguished father went to call on the M.P. for Leeds, who happens to be the Opposition Leader Hugh Gaitskell. Gaitskell poured him tea and got busy at the War Office. Lieut. Moorhouse, Gaitskell learned, had led his platoon through the back streets of Port Said on a night raid in which nine Egyptian terrorists were rounded up. He had gone back alone to the scene of the arrest next morning in an open Land Rover. The car had been found deserted on a side street. Lieut. Moorhouse was not seen again. That night Commanding General Sir Hugh Stockwell sent out search parties to comb every house in the district, but they found no sign of the young lieutenant. Francis Moorhouse's first instinct was to seize a telephone and put a direct call through to Egypt's strongman Gamal Abdel Nasser. It failed to get through.

But there were other ways of reaching the Egyptian dictator. Cyril Banks, a Tory M.P. who had quit his party in protest over the Suez occupation, was a close friend of the Moorhouse family and also knew Nasser from his days as a Middle East hand. "What would you really like me to do?" he asked Moorhouse. "Get over to Cairo," was the answer. " I believe that you could bring my son back if he is still alive." Banks promised to do what he could. By now the War Office, the Foreign Office, U.N. Headquarters and 10 Downing Street were all at work.

Preparing for the Worst. Bit by bit the story of the kidnaping was fleshed out. An Arab boy admitted having seen a crowd of Egyptians surround the British officer when he left his car. One of them had seized his pistol from its holster and held it to his ribs. Others had hustled him into a big car. The car was found later, abandoned, with a length of rope, a gag, a cloth bag and some bloodstains on the back seat. Some days later a U.N. intelligence officer had gone into the Arab section in an attempt to negotiate Moorhouse's release and had seen a man in British Uniform. The U.N. officer reported that Anthony Moorhouse was "alive and well." General Stockwell confidently ordered a destroyer to stand by at the Port Said quayside to pick him up. As the last British troops evacuated Port Said, the young lieutenant failed to materialise. But that night, Francis Moorhouse got a telegram from the War office telling him that his son was "safe and well," along with a personal note from Sir Anthony Eden. "This," said the lieutenant's mother, "is the most marvelous Christmas present." Then a cable arrived from the old family friend, Cyril Banks, who was in Beirut. RETURNING HOME," it said, "PREPARE FOR THE WORST." On Christmas Eve, Cyril had at last got to see Colonel Nasser for three hours. Nasser told him that young Moorhouse was dead.

According to Nasser, during General Stockwell's house-to-house search of Port Said, Egyptian guerillas had hidden Moorhouse in a steel clothes locker with a gag in his mouth, and when they returned he was already dead of suffocation. "Thus," said Cairo's government newspaper, Al Gumhuria, "did General Stockwell, with his foolishness and recklessness, cause Moorhouse's death." All of Britain's pent-up frustration over its troubles in Egypt focused last week on the story of Lieut. Moorhouse. Papers that had supported the invasion of Egypt and those that had condemned it, alike joined in angry outcry. Nasser's explanation that he had no responsibility, said the Manchester Guardian, opens up equally grim prospects for the future, when, as Colonel Nasser hopes, these marauders can once again operate from the Sinai and the Gaza Strip—and when their actions can be subsequently be disowned."

On 11 December 1959, the third anniversary of the Moorhouse abduction, Australia's Melbourne's Age newspaper carried an article taken from Cairo's official newspaper Al Gomhouria of the day before.

''CAIRO, December 10.—The head of the Government newspaper, "Al Gomhouria," Major Salah Salem, today published an open letter in the newspaper blaming General Sir Hugh Stockwell for the death of Second Lieutenant Anthony Moorhouse in Port Said during the Suez crisis.

The former National Guidance Minister said in the letter to Moorhouse's parent's that the British forces had blockaded the area where Lieutenant Moorhouse was imprisoned and General Stockwell had refused to let an Egyptian officer contact the resistance forces, insisting on conducting a search instead.

The letter said: "We do not harbor an atom of malice or hatred towards Lieutenant Moorhouse, nor do we intend at all to gloat over his death. The person responsible for your son's death was General Stockwell, the British commander at Port Said during the aggression.

"After Moorhouse's abduction, British forces blockaded the area where he was imprisoned and the popular resistance – which had taken him in retaliation for British kidnappings – could not reach the house so that he died three days later."

Major Salem said General Command, Armed Forces in Cairo, attempted to send one of its officers to contact the resistance forces in Port Said in order to help save the life of Lieutenant Moorhouse.

"But the British occupation forces there refused to allow a representative of the Egyptian command to enter Port Said. General Stockwell insisted on conducting a large-scale search and this prevented the resistance forces saving your son's life.'

On Saturday 8 July 2006, the 50th anniversary year of *Operation Musketeer*, the Guardian newspaper published an article by Jonathan Steele and Ian Black in which they re-examined Egypt's invasion by Britain, France and Israel, by interviewing survivors from both sides. One of these was Ali Zangeer who was one of the abductors of Lt Moorhouse.

'Ali Zangeer remembers every detail of his role in kidnapping a young British officer in Egypt half a century ago. He drove the getaway car that took the captured lieutenant to a safe house where he was trussed, gagged and hidden under the floor.

"The British had taken a lot of prisoners," Zanyeer says. "We wanted to capture one of them to do an exchange. We were driving round and found this officer on his own outside the police station. He had a pistol, but we had no weapons in case we were searched at roadblocks. I waited, then drove up, gave a small beep, and they seized his gun and bundled him into the back. There was a scuffle. He tried to grab my arm, but I punched him in the face."

The police station on the Suez Canal waterfront is certainly where the West Yorkshire 1st Battalion was based but it takes some believing that security on these streets on and around the waterfront by the police station was so lax as to make an abduction possible.

The punch in the face would account for the blood found on the rear seat of the abandoned getaway car. If Moorhouse's nose had been made to bleed from the punch, and the blood had later congealed, breathing by the nose may have been limited or impossible. With a gag in the mouth perhaps suffocation was inevitable. The report of the autopsy eventually carried out on the body may well have shed some light on this possibility.

According to the Internet web site Wikipedia, Moorhouse's body, after being disinterred from his temporary resting place in Port Said was handed over to United Nations representatives and on 4 January 1957 flown to Naples, Italy, for formal identification. The following day British pathologists from Scotland Yard formally identified the body as that of Moorhouse and it was flown back to the UK on 6 January.

Back in December 1956 the last of the Allied ships had left Port Said on the 22nd except for HMS *Duchess* which remained at the quay until the early hours of the 23rd in case the abducted Lt Moorhouse was released in time for the final departure of the British.

When it was at last accepted that this was not going to happen the *Duchess* raised anchor and slowly eased its way along the western mole and out into the open sea to join the departing fleet.

In 2006, the fiftieth anniversary year of the Port Said invasion, Saga Magazine put out an appeal to its readers to write in with stories of their memories of the occasion. Mrs Pat Tarrant, the sister of Lt Moorhouse, was one of those who replied and she has given her kind permission for her response to be reproduced here.

Loss of a brother

How a young National Serviceman's life ended in tragedy in Port Said

Lt Anthony Moorhouse, left, and his close friend Lt David Dodd. The picture was taken in Suez and was in Anthony's camera when his possessions were returned to his family

IN THE HUGE RESPONSE TO SAGA'S appeal for accounts of National Service experiences at Suez, one of the most poignant e-mails was from Mrs Pat Tarran (née Moorhouse), of Wetherby, Yorkshire, who wrote: "I am the sister of one of those young National Servicemen sent to Suez in 1956. While he was there he was kidnapped and lost his life. He was Lieutenant Anthony Moorhouse and he is buried in Leeds in the family grave. My younger brother, Peter, and I miss him to this day and visit the grave frequently."

Lt Moorhouse, 21, of the West Yorkshire Regiment, had raided a flat in Arab Town, Port Said, to arrest six *fedayeen* – guerrillas harassing troops between the ceasefire of November 7 and the Anglo-French withdrawal on December 22.

In the early morning of December 10, after leaving guards in the flat, he drove alone through the almost empty streets of Port Said to battalion HQ to organise a relief for his guards and then set out again for the flat. His vehicle was found abandoned and he was never seen alive again. From what Army Intelligence could piece together later, it seems he left his vehicle to prevent an Egyptian putting up a propaganda poster. A crowd gathered, his pistol was seized and he was bundled into a car.

When I went to interview his sister she arranged for me to meet one of Anthony's friends, Stephen Hartley, who was also a National Service lieutenant in the West Yorkshires. He remembers patrolling near the Port Said docks at 7.30 that terrible morning. "A message came through from HQ asking if we'd seen or heard anything of Anthony. After that we all began to search, from house to house and flat to flat."

Mrs Tarran said her father opposed the search. "He did everything he could to stop it. He even spoke to Anthony Eden and said the kidnappers would probably panic and do something, which of course is exactly what happened." Lt Moorhouse, bound and gagged, suffocated in the cupboard of a house abandoned during the search.

Just before Christmas, hopes of his survival had been raised. An officer of the UN peacekeeping force believed he had been shown the British officer when he was led blindfolded to a secret destination. It was a cruel hoax. "That was awful for us," said Mrs Tarran. A former Conservative MP, Colonel Cyril Banks, who knew Colonel Nasser, went to Egypt for the family, seeking information. "We had a cable from him on Christmas Day," said Mrs Tarran. "It told us: 'Prepare yourselves for the worst.' It happened 50 years ago, but the memory of it is still distressing."

* * *

During the second week of December 1956 Sir Edwin Herbert, President of the Law Society, spent four days in Port Said on behalf of the Government in order to carry out an independent enquiry into the degree of damage and casualties suffered by the Egyptians as a result of the Allied invasion of the city. This came about after MPs had questioned earlier ridiculously low official estimates of the number of Egyptians who had been killed and wounded.

On his return from Egypt on 15 December Sir Edwin quickly assembled his findings which were released as a white paper on the 21st less than a week later. He estimated that a 'reasonable estimate' of Egyptian dead was 650 and wounded some 2,100.

The built up area of Port Said at that time was very small. In a Land Rover it would have taken less than a day to drive along, through, in, and out of the whole of the town to view the damage to property inflicted by the British. This was extremely extensive.

Significantly, however, Sir Edwin reported that 'The only damage to the Arab town is the destruction by fire of part of the shanty section at the westerly end and superficial damage by small arms fire for say 100 yards down the streets debouching on Mohammed Ali Street.'

In the aftermath of the Port Said affair it was the duty of General Sir Charles Keightley, who had been Commander-in-Chief of the *Operation Musketeer* forces, to summarise the campaign for Parliament. This was published as a Supplement to the London Gazette Thursday 12 September 1957.

Keightley reported that, 'The damaged property was mainly confined to buildings along the sea front, the burnt out portion of shanty town, the block near the Governate and NAVY HOUSE, both of which had been attacked from the air with rockets. Damage to the main town was remarkably slight.' This last sentence will be referred to later.

Western end of the beach at the back of the Fish Dock.

Another view of properties burning behind the Fish Dock.

The Jetty Casino one fire during the Commando assault.

Another view of the Casino Jetty in flames.

The Standard Oil Company fire on the south of the town. The other fire is probably the Coastguard Barracks.

Another view of the fire at the oil tank farm. The tank was hit accidentally by a stray rocket from a French Corsair fighter. The lower waterway is the Bassin Industrie (Manzala Canal) leading to the inland wharves in the town. On 5 November this served as an escape route for the those retreating from the Paras at El Gamel airfield. (Guy Smith)

The site of the burnt out tank at the Standard Oil tank farm at the southern end of the Bassin Abbas Hilmi. (Guy Smith).

View of two of the storage tanks that managed to escape the inferno. Note the scorched trees. (Guy Smith).

Beach huts set on fire by naval gunfire as seen by 40 Commando coming ashore on 6 November 1956. (Guy Smith).

View from behind the beach where 40 and 42 Commando came ashore on the morning of 6 November 1956. This photograph was probably taken the following day. The area is now secure but smoke is still rising. (Photograph Huy Walters.)

View eastwards of the beach and stilt huts towards the mouth of the canal and the back of the Fish Dock. (H. Pickering)

One of the buildings along the Port Said beach. (Photograph Ray Rudkin).

The 'flats' and the burnt-out Shanty town. Note the same buildings in a slightly different view in the following photograph. (Photograph Edgar Coleborn).

The burnt out Shanty Town. As the Commandos were passing through the beach huts area into the town on the morning of 6th November a nearby Egyptian self-propelled Russian SU-100 anti-tank gun on the edge of Shanty Town was giving them problems. One of the destroyers lying off the coast was called up to deal with it. The resulting gunfire set the area alight. (Photo Dr Sandy Cavenagh).

An oblique view of the damage at Shanty Town. (unknown contributor).

Locals viewing the remains of their homes in Shanty Town. (unknown contributor).

Salvaging what they can. (unknown contributor).

Refugee Port Said lady and her family. (Photograph Guy Smith).

Elderly lady sat viewing what is left of her bedroom furniture. Abbas Mosque in the background. (Guy Smith).

Lady salvaging some of her possessions from the ruins ... or looting? (Photograph Guy Smith).

The sender of this photograph thought it was something to do with food distribution. (Photograph Guy Smith).

Man-drawn handcart and 'pushers' with salvaged belongings under watchful eye of tank crewman at a crossroads on the Rue el Mahroussa. The Abbas Mosque minaret on the right-hand skyline. (Thomas Gilkes)

More salvaged belongings, horse-drawn this time. (Brian Adams).

One of the Egyptian casualties of the attack on Port Said. (Dr Yahia Al Shaer).

Identifying dead bodies following the ceasefire. (Dr Yahia Al Shaer).

Some of the young victims of the invasion. Russia supplied a large consignment of weapons to Egypt. Anatoli Tchikov, the Soviet consul in Port Said, distributed these to all and sundry, including children, telling them over loudspeakers, 'Fight on people of Port Said! Russian help is coming! Tonight London and Paris will be destroyed by atomic rockets.' (The Suez Crisis and the united Nations, Jean-Marc Pierre). The children treated these lethal weapons as toys and killed and wounded many of their own people including their own young friends. (Photograph Dr Yahia Al Shaer).

Wounded Egyptian prisoners waiting to be repatriated by train to El Cap. (Photograph Brian Adams).

Searching for what might be left in discarded used food cans. (Unknown contributor).

An interesting time for some. Note the sailors on shore leave. (Trevor Cook).

This is now the position to examine part of General Keightley's report to the government again. On page 5335 (Hansard) Keightley wrote, 'The damage to property was mainly confined to buildings along the sea front, the burnt out portions of shanty town, the block near the Governate and NAVY HOUSE, [seen on previous pages] both of which had been attacked from the air with rockets.

Damage to the main town was remarkably slight.'

View along street from more or less ground level in front of a building. (Photograph Brian Stidwell).

The same view as in the previous photograph but taken from the flat roof of the building. (Photograph Brian Stidwell).

A row of buildings badly damaged. (Photograph Mick Loder).

Three squaddies posing on the piled up rubble of a destroyed building. (Photograph John Burn).

Another view of the same building with local sightseers. (Photograph Chris Pickering).

Destroyed building on the Rue el Mahroussa. Note the Abbas Mosque minaret further along the road. (Dr Yahia al Shaer).

Wrecked building and view of Abbas Mosque minaret from the Rue Mohamed Aly. Photograph taken from Land Rover. Just moments after this photograph was taken a sniper's bullet removed the wiper motor. (Photograph Tom Dando).

Abbas Mosque minaret on Rue el Mahroussa, the route of 42 Commando on 6 November. (Photograph Tom Dando)

Another building destroyed by rocket fire. (Photograph Ronnie Hulton)

The same building viewed from further to the right. Land Rover and Bedford RL 3-tonner truck. (photograph John French).

A couple of squaddies posing against a background of destruction. (Photograph John Burn).

More shattered buildings in an unknown part of Port Said. (Photograph Dr Yahia al Shaer).

Remnants of a balcony similar to the one across the road now lying burnt out on the ground. (Photograph Chris Pickering).

Destroyed buildings, probably on the route of 42 Commando through the town. (Photograph John Mee).

The same scene. Photo taken from closer in to the building on the left. (Photograph John Mee).

The skeletons of more buildings. Note the 'tower' rising above the other building on the right. (Photograph Gordon Eke).

A later view of the buildings in the above photo with the unsafe 'tower' now demolished by the sappers. (Gordon Eke).

Centurion tank and young boy in what is left of a Port Said street. (Photograph Thomas Gilkes).

Unknown Street. (Photograph Dr Yahia al Shaer).

The remains of an unknown building. (Photograph Ronnie Hulton).

Unknown building in Port Said. (Photograph Dr Yahia al Shaer).

This building in the right foreground is the same one as in the previous photograph. (Photograph Dr Yahia al Shaer).

Another destroyed building in the Abbas Mosque area. (Photograph Dr Yahia al Shaer).

A street of buildings destroyed possibly in the 45 Commando area of operations. (Photograph Brian Stidwell).

Unknown part of town. (Photograph Dr Yahia al Shaer).

Possibly the Shanty Town area of Port Said. (Photograph Mick Loder).

Unknown part of Port Said. Army in residence at bottom right . (Photograph Albert Hallett).

Local resident posing for the camera. Probably 45 Commando's area of action. (Photograph Chris Pickering).

The water in the road suggests this might be a little further to the right than in the previous photograph. (Trevor Cook).

This could be yet further along the same street. Sappers with Commer three-tonner truck. (Photograph Alan J Page).

Unknown building. Probably 45 Commando area (Photograph Chris Pickering).

Unknown area with interested onlooker. (Photograph Chris Pickering).

X-Troop of 45 Commando on patrol. (Photograph Chris Pickering).

Buildings destroyed on both sides of this unknown road. (Photograph Trevor Cook).

Debris of the 'war' in unknown street. Note the minaret showing behind the building. (Photograph John French)

Sappers and what was a building in the Arab Quarter of Port Said. (Photograph Malcolm Green).

An unknown street, possibly in Arab Town. (Photograph Brian Stidwell).

An unknown street (Photograph Brian Stidwell).

Fire-scarred building on the right and rubble from the building on the left. (Photograph Trevor Cook).

A totally destroyed street of homes. (Photograph Malcolm Green).

A house being blown up by the sappers. It was found to be stockpiled with explosives which were deemed too dangerous to be moved. (Photograph Alan j Page).

Afterwards, when most of the smoke and dust had cleared. (Photograph Alan J Page).

The remains of another home. (Photograph Richard Graham).

An unknown building, with shell holes where snipers had been 'holed up'. (Photograph Brian Adams).

Rear of a house where a sniper had been hiding. (Photograph Keith Smith).

The view an Egyptian sniper would have had before his window got bigger. (Photograph Bob Jordan).

Flats close to the beach and the Cathedral. Sniper viewpoints enlarged by shells. (Photograph Edgar G Coleborn).

View of the same frontage taken from the left. (Photograph Ronnie Hulton).

The remains of what appears to be an Art Deco style building. (Photo Tom Dando).

The same building with the locals now out and about. (Photograph Tom Dando).

Different viewpoint of the previous building once housing snipers on 6 November. (Photograph Chris Pickering).

From kiosk to chaos on an unknown street in Port Said. (Photograph Trevor Cook).

A smile for the camera in the ruins of his home. (Photograph Ronnie Hulton).

THE AFTERMATH

Following the Suez Canal crisis ceasefire on 6 November questions began to be asked in the House of Commons about the damage to property and, especially, the cost in Egyptian lives and possibly those of other nationals that had been brought about by the Anglo-French invasion of Egypt, especially in Port Said. As it seemed impossible for anyone to provide accurate figures, with the Egyptians claiming possibly inflated numbers and the British, understandably, trying to minimise their responsibility for the numbers of dead and maimed, it was decided that someone should go out to Port Said and try to ascertain this information. Sir Walter Monckton, who had just changed jobs from Minister of Defence to Postmaster General, was given the responsibility.

On 5 December, following his return, Monckton was questioned in the House of Commons about his findings.

'I went to Port Said on 24th November to see for myself the damage caused by the recent allied operations and to obtain what information I could, in the course of a visit which lasted only 24 hours, about the numbers of Egyptians and other nationals who had died or been wounded as a result of the operations.' ... 'I made a thorough search of Port Said in a Land Rover and flew all over the city in a helicopter at low altitude. I interviewed not only members of Her Majesty's Forces who had taken part in the operations, but also several prominent nationals of other countries, including Egyptians, who were available and willing to assist me. ...'

*'**The vast majority of the buildings in the city were unharmed, as can be seen from the photographs. The fact that the damage is as small as it is in a city of the size of Port Said** ... provides the strongest evidence of the great care taken by the allied forces to minimise damage.' (Bold font added by the author).*

Whereas damage to property can be inspected and assessed, it is more difficult to obtain an accurate estimate of the numbers killed or even of those wounded, and within the limits imposed by the time and materials available to me I could not ascertain a really reliable figure. The information I obtained, however, leads me to believe that the estimate of 540 wounded, previously given, is reasonably near the mark.

It is more difficult to make any assessment of the numbers killed or [who] died from wounds. The number of wounded in military operations is normally several times greater than the number killed, and a figure of the order of 540 wounded would lead me to expect a number of dead of approximately 100, as originally estimated, but various statements made to me lead me to think, that it is at least possible that the figure may well have been higher.' (Hansard, 5 December 1956).

This report was deemed to be far from satisfactory and the figures unrealistic and another was called for. The American Consul in Port Said at the time of the invasion was Mr Anthony Quomo who had estimated figures of between 1,000 and 2,000 Egyptians killed. (Hansard, House of Commons, 11.38 pm, 4 February 1957).

Now it was Sir Edwin Herbert, President of the Law Society who was asked to visit Port Said and with time rapidly running out before the allied forces left the town he arrived there on 9 December and returned on the 15th of the month. Within four days he had written up his findings and the white paper report was presented to Parliament on 21 December. This time the casualty figures had risen with the Egyptian dead given as around the 650 mark and the wounded at 2,100. With the Christmas parliamentary recess coming up it was far too late in the day for questions to be asked.

On 9 January 1957, on advice from his doctor, Anthony Eden resigned as Britain's Prime Minister. He was replaced the following day by the Chancellor of the Exchequer Harold Macmillan, yet another old Etonian and the 17th British premier from this school.

On 15 January 1957, with the British now out of Egypt again and with there being no chance of them trying to return after their recent forced withdrawal, Colonel Nasser felt safe to order that all British assets in Egypt be confiscated and that all shareholders and directors of British and French companies involved in such businesses as banking and insurance must be Egyptian. The same ruling would be extended to other foreign firms within the next five years.

With Egypt having been subjected to so much foreign control for more than a century, and if one views this with an open mind, who could blame Nasser for this decision? It is something the British public of today can no doubt sympathise with as they see the government failing to act on vast untaxed profits being taken out of the country.

In the middle of the afternoon on 28 February in the House of Lords, Lord Killearn rose to lead a debate on the subject of Egypt's seizure of British assets and the expulsion of British passport holders from Egypt. *'...these are the people who have been left as the victims—there is no other word for it—of recent British policy. I put it to your Lordships that everyone of us has the right to protection from his Government. In this particular case, although I cannot say that they have more right to that protection, I would emphasise that we in this country owe something to the British community in Egypt; and I hold strongly—it is a matter of opinion—that we are directly and morally responsible for the situation in which they find themselves. I hasten to add that I supported the British Government policy, but I did not support the failure of it. I will not go into that matter again, but the words I used in this House were that I thought they did the right thing at the wrong time in the wrong way. I still feel that, whatever the rights or wrongs may be, there is no doubt whatever that the people who are paying the price are the British community in Egypt. There can be no doubt about that; nobody can refute it. That being so, if there are certain gaps, as I say, in the machinery that has already been established under the noble Lord, Lord Colyton, and for which we are very grateful, there is a moral duty on me to get up and call attention to them and try to get Her Majesty's Government to remedy those gaps. ... '*

'...First of all, the number of British subjects in Egypt prior to November, 1956, totalled 12,000, excluding 5,000 Cypriots. We do not know quite what happened about the Cypriots—your Lordships remember that there was some talk of their being regarded as Greek citizens. Of these 12,000, 5,000 are Anglo-Saxons, and 7,000 Maltese and others. Of the above, some 1,000 persons were employed by Shell, I.C.I., the banks, et cetera, the British Council and British schools. Some 5,000 persons have already reached the United Kingdom, of whom about 4,500 are receiving aid, 3,000 in camps and 1,500 outside. Approximately 3,000 of these are of Maltese origin. This leaves a number still in transit or still in Egypt—we do not know which. Of the above, some 2,000 to 2,500 are residents—I am coming on to my special point—of substantial means, whose needs and losses cannot, in the terms of its charter, be covered by the Resettlement Board. They have been totally dispossessed and are now mostly in the United Kingdom, most of them without funds, homes or employment. Their incomes were derived from British companies, private family businesses, agencies, et cetera and have been expropriated. They have lost houses, properties, employment, incomes, savings, insurance benefits, stocks and shares—in fact, their entire possessions.

They had substantial assets, now expropriated, in Egypt, but they have nothing in the United Kingdom with which to start reconstructing their lives. ...'

'Incidentally here, in case anybody should think that these persons may eventually be able to get back and resume their occupations—it seems extremely unlikely to me—it may interest your Lordships to know that a new Egyptian law has been passed which prescribes as follows. The personnel of businesses must be 75 per cent Moslems, born in Egypt; 15 per cent. Copts—that is, Christian Egyptians; 5 per cent. nationals of surrounding Arab territories and 5 per cent. Europeans other than British and French. That is not encouraging. ... It really comes to this: all securities held in London for account of British residents, companies and institutions are still blocked.'

'Are Her Majesty's Government aware of what is being done in France? Perhaps not. I was not myself aware of it until late the night before last, when I received a copy of Le Monde of February 24–25. I will read your Lordships the gist of what it says ... French subjects expelled from Egypt. There are approximately 7,000 such persons. Only 20 per cent. of those involved have found re-employment. The Government have so far paid each individual a daily allowance of 800 francs per adult and 500 francs per child, until such time as resettlement is expected. To improve that precarious situation a draft law actually under study foresees an admitted benefit through social legislation"—and so on: It gives various forms of benefit. Then it continues: Moreover, in order, understandably, to safeguard the dignity of those expelled, the amount of 250,000 francs for the head of the family, an additional 100,000 for the spouse and 5,000 francs for each child will be granted to each as an ex gratia payment. This would serve to provide the indispensable minimum required for resettlement—that is, purchase of clothing, et cetera. Finally, advances would he granted on the value of assets abandoned by these persons in Egypt. ...'

Lord Milner of Leeds was the next to rise and commented that '*... the results of the action of Her Majesty's Government has been little less than ruinous to hundreds of British subjects who had homes or businesses in Egypt; and the remarkable thing is that one of the main attempts at justifying the action of Her Majesty's Government was the contention that the action was directed towards the protection of British subjects. I remember that the noble Earl, Lord Home, said on November 1 that we had a duty to protect our citizens and their* *property. The noble and learned Viscount on the Woolsack made a prime point, I believe in the same debate, when defending the legal aspect of the action of Her Majesty's Government, of the fact that self-defence (a rather fallacious ground, I thought at the time) included a situation in which the lives of our nationals abroad were threatened. We intervened, he said, to protect our people. I am not aware that prior to our intervention either the lives or the property of our nationals were being threatened in Egypt. But, in fact, the result of the intervention of Her Majesty's Government was to bring about the very state of affairs which the noble and learned Viscount on the Woolsack had said that the intervention was designed to prevent.'*

Lord Milner went on to say that *'The noble Lord, Lord Killearn, mentioned the very large Maltese population of Egypt who, as British subjects, have been evicted. Do Her Majesty's Government accept any responsibility in respect of those subjects, or what is the position with regard to them? I should have thought it was a responsibility which, directly or indirectly, ought to be assumed. ...can Her Majesty's Government inform the House of the number of refugees who have already come to this country and what amount has so far been disbursed to them, or on their behalf, and whether any limit has been set to the sum which, at any rate for the time being, the British taxpayer unfortunately has to provide, through the action of Her Majesty's Government, in this very proper and humane cause?*

Lord Colwyn informed the House that *'More than half of the employable evacuees have found employment, and I think the rest who can work will find jobs very shortly. But the question is; what is going to happen to the aged, the infirm and the rather difficult cases, of which there are quite a few? I fully realise the necessity of putting these unfortunate people into camps, but most of these camps are 200 miles or more away from London, and some are far from the nearest town or village. I realise that the Government cannot afford to give these people great sums of money, but the 1s. 7½d. a day they receive in the camps, does not go far. I ask your Lordships: is that enough money to enable them to look for jobs and to find homes for themselves and their families?'*

Viscount Massereene and Ferrand said that *'... it is our moral responsibility to compensate completely these unfortunate people. Government officials can be very generous when embarking on some grandiose scheme of doubtful economic value, but when paying compensation to private citizens they can be Fagins personified. We must remember, at all costs, that one of the declared objects of the Government's intervention in Egypt was the protection of British life and property. We are in honour bound to do everything possible for these unfortunate people. If we fail in this, our bounden duty, the possession of a British passport may not be so sought after.' ... 'What, however, is apparent is that every civilised right of property and contract has been broken in Egypt. If we do not stand by these rights, but allow ourselves to be influenced by the hypocritical babble of organisations intent on clouding the issue, we shall do a great disservice not only to ourselves but to the whole of Western civilisation.'*

Lord Jeffreys had this to say: *'It is curious that our country, which was so prompt and generous with its aid to Hungarians, who are, after all, foreigners, should be so dilatory and apparently niggardly over the relief of our own fellow subjects who have been so scandalously treated in Egypt. .... Any assistance in the way of money must obviously come from some Government funds, to begin with, and, fortunately, there is some money ready to hand. Some six months ago Britain froze the £120 million remaining from the £400 million so-called war-time debt. That was a debt incurred in paying the Egyptians, who were making large sums out of the British Forces, for not coming into the war—for that is about what it came to. They did not come into the war on either side; in other words, they completely funked any responsibility. I would here say that that debt was due to quite unnecessary consideration on our part. That £120 million is available and, in my opinion, should be made use of for compensating Britons expelled from Egypt.*

Lord Birdwood reminded the chamber that '*On January 15 Egypt nationalised British and French banks and insurance companies, and at that time it was said that others were to follow within five years. Therefore I suggest that any action we contemplate will probably be watched by others, with some anxiety and extremely carefully. It is true that the Egyptian Government said that they would offer fair compensation; yet in the same breath they referred to these assets as "belonging to the enemy". I find it difficult to believe that assets which, on Egypt's own admission belonged to an enemy, can ever be compensated fairly. I would therefore urge that, if necessary, Her Majesty's Government should use the full powers which I understand they have under the Exchange Control Act to see that those affected do not suffer.'*

Lord Gifford then rose to say that '*.... I feel that these refugees from Egypt are having a raw deal. Many of them own securities held in London, nearly all of which are blocked. These include all classes of War Loan, deposit accounts, current accounts, and even National Savings Certificates. As the noble Lord Killearn, has already said, many of these people subscribed to these Government stocks in response to an appeal to help our war effort, and the noble Lord, Lord Killearn, himself encouraged them to do so. In nearly all cases they now find themselves unable to touch these funds which they badly need for the purpose of re-equipping themselves with the bare necessities of life, buying furniture and getting accommodation. It is not only private people who are suffering in this way—there are many schools, churches and charitable institutions.*

The present hard-hearted attitude, as it appears to these people, is difficult for them to understand and is causing perplexity and deep resentment. I might mention one particular fund which, so far as I know, is still blocked, and that is the balance of the Victory Fund, now amounting to some £65,000. Applications have been made, without result, to the Bank of England so that this money can be used to help refugee children and the staff of schools who have been expelled, many of them after service in Egypt all their lives. If some of these securities and funds were unblocked, I am sure that it would save Her Majesty's Government money, because many of these people who are now having to apply for grants from the Resettlement Board would otherwise be able to use their own funds.'

Lord Colyton continued the debate by saying that '*We must remember that, of the 4,500 British subjects who have so far arrived back in the United Kingdom, nearly 3,000 are still in hostels; so that our first task must be to see how comfortable we can make them there. But we do not want to keep them in the hostels. Our aim is to get them out of the hostels into jobs and into homes; ...'*

The Earl of Gosford responded to all this concern by explaining that *'The Government have every intention of holding the Egyptian Government responsible for their actions, and intend to do everything in their power to pursue the claims of British nationals against the Egyptian Government. Interested parties, both individuals and firms, have been invited by public announcement to send in particulars of their assets in Egypt. As these come in, we shall have a clearer idea of the size of the investment at stake and shall be in a better position to consider the tactics to be used in pursuing against the Egyptian Government any claims that are shown to arise. It would not be sensible for me to disclose in advance of negotiations with the Egyptians either the amount at stake or the tactics to be employed. We are pressing, in the meantime, for the desequestration of British assets now held and for the owners to have access to these assets.'* (Hansard 28 February 1957).

In April 1957 the Suez Canal was at last cleared of its obstructions and opened to shipping again, except that of Israel. The United Nations, which had taken over the clearance of the canal wreckage and made the waterway navigable again, still failed to act on Israel's behalf.

Towards the end of the year President Nasser of Egypt nationalised the remaining British and French assets existing in the country. These included investments in the cement manufacturing industry, phosphates and pharmaceuticals.

On 29 April 1958 the World Bank brokered a number of agreements between representatives of General Nasser, and those of the dispossessed shareholders of the Suez Canal Company, which finally gave the latter some compensation for their losses. With 13 years still left of the 100 years ownership of the canal at the time of Company's seizure the shareholders had claimed £204,000.000 in loss of earnings. They accepted just £28,300,000 in lieu of this revenue. On their side the Egyptians agreed not to pursue a claim for the company's assets outside Egyptian jurisdiction, which was presumably real estate, and also agreed to the continuing existence of the company although it no longer owned a Suez Canal. (International Law in the Middle East: Closer to Power than Justice. Jean Allain, 2004. Page 70.)

On 14 July 1958, in a meeting at the White House in Washington with leaders of Congress, President Eisenhower admitted that the United States [not him] may have been in error '*... when it rushed, in November 1956, to save the Nasser regime in Egypt from the Anglo-French action in the Suez area.*' (16 July 1958, Jewish Telegraphic Agency).

Later on he further admitted that not supporting the Anglo-French move to oust Nasser was the biggest mistake of his foreign policy decisions. His reason for this reappraisal was that he had misread the direction Nasser would take afterwards. He thought he was helping to stabilise the region and that the show of not supporting the tripartite aggression would endear the Arab nations to the United States. What happened was that Nasser became a powerful force in the Arab world which began looking towards the Soviet block without the benefits to America that he had hoped for. In the process his lack of support for Britain and France had weakened these European allies of the United States.

In February 1959 Britain signed an agreement with Egypt in regard to the settling of compensation claims of British nationals who had been living and working in Egypt prior to the Suez Canal crisis during which they had their assets seized, their bank accounts frozen, and were driven out of the country. However, this was only an agreement to negotiate and it took more than a decade before a partial but unsatisfactory settlement was reached. (International Law in the Middle East: Closer to Power than Justice, Jean Allain, 2004. Page 70).

On 24 May 1959, John Foster Dulles, the United States Secretary of State at the time of the Suez Canal Crisis, admitted on his deathbed that he had made a mistake in not supporting the Anglo-French bid to oust Nasser from Power.

At 8.15 in the evening of 12 November 1969 Lord Colyton rose from his bench in the House of Lords '*... to ask her Majesty's Government whether they can make a statement on the failure of the Egyptian Government to honour the terms of the Financial Agreement of 1959* [ten years previously] *concerning British subjects in Egypt. ... Whatever view one may take of the events of the Suez Canal Zone in 1956, one thing is perfectly clear; namely, that among the principal sufferers were the members of the British community in Egypt, many of who were deported at 24 hours' notice, and most of whom had their property nationalised of sequestered. ...*

On February 28, 1959 a Financial Agreement was signed with what had then become the United Arab Republic, designed to restore friendly relations between Britain and the U..A.R. In consequence of this, the U.A.R. paid £27½ million in full and final compensation for Egyptianised property and for certain losses arising as a result of sequestration measures. It was also clearly stipulated that British assets which had not been acquired outright by the U.A.R. but had merely been sequestrated would be restored within a period of three months to their owners or agents. In return, Her Majesty's Government undertook to release the frozen sterling balances, which, after deduction of £28 million belonging to the Sudan, and certain commercial debts, amounted to £75 million. This was carried out within a few days of the signature of the agreement, and the money used by the U.A.R. to settle debts which it had incurred in other countries. Her Majesty's Government used the sum of £27½ million paid by by Egypt to compensate the owners of Egyptianised property, albeit at considerable loss to many of the claimants. But so far as the owners of sequestrated property was concerned, a long, heartbreaking and largely fruitless battle then began to regain what was left of their possessions in Egypt. The administrative difficulties created by the U.A.R., and the ingenuity of their officials, were apparent right from the start. It soon became clear that, even where token releases had been made, the U.A.R., by pleading inter alia lack of funds for effecting transfers across the exchange, would not be meeting its obligations. This distinction immediately created inequalities between those categories of British subjects who had been fortunate enough to have all their assets Egyptianised, and whose claim could therefore be promptly established and met, and those whose assets the Egyptian Government merely claimed to have temporarily sequestered. The latter—and these are the people whose cause I am pleading tonight—were placed in circumstances of particular difficulty, because even at that juncture discriminatory measures were being enforced against British nationals who had held permanent Egyptian residence visas, and who were not granted re-entry permits, even of a temporary nature, to enable them to go there to wind up their businesses. There is no doubt whatever that there was definite discrimination against members of the Jewish community.

We now come to a further stage, when a number of nationals whose assets were purported to be released in 1959 found that they had subsequently be either disposed of by the sequestrator, and the proceeds of the sale set aside, or re-sequestrated. In the case of some 150 to 200 British nationals, these further measures of sequestration and discrimination took place.

Repeated protests and requests for information by Her Majesty's Government between 1960 and 1967 were ignored, but meanwhile the process of spoliation, confiscation, and maladministration went on unchecked. The value of the property thus affected is estimated to have been between £20 million and £35 million in 1956. According to an answer which was given in another place by Mr. Rogers on February 9 of this year it really appears that, unless Her Majesty's Government recognise that the United Arab Republic has no intention of making genuine restitution, they must themselves accept moral responsibility for doing so and take active steps to put an end to this protracted inter-

lude. ... I hope that the Minister who is going to reply will be able to give us some encouragement to think that action will now be taken. But I believe that, come what may, justice must be secured for these unfortunate people who have suffered for 13 years through no conceivable fault of their own.' (Hansard, House of Lords, 12 November 1969).

If the plight of the British refugees from Egypt was bad enough all this time after the Suez Canal affair, that of the Egyptian Jews who were thrown out the country with no one to represent them, must have been horrendous.

On 28 September 1970 President Nasser, a heavy smoker and diabetic who also suffered from arteriosclerosis, died from a heart attack.

14 January 1977 Sir Anthony Eden Died of Liver cancer.

In 1979, 23 years after the Suez Crisis, Israeli ships were finally allowed by the Egyptian Government to traverse the Suez Canal.

In his 2003 book, The Life and Times of Anthony Eden, D R Thorpe made the comment that had Eden succeeded in his Suez-crisis venture it would most likely have ensured that the Arab-Israeli wars of the 1967 and 1973 would not have taken place.

Hindsight is a wonderful thing so it is said, but the one really puzzling question that needs to be asked regarding this whole tragic affair is why so little time elapsed between Nasser's nationalisation announcement on 26 July and the beginning of August when, on Eden's orders, 20,000 Reservists who'd recently done with military service to get on with their lives, were forced to return to the Colours where they were paid a pittance for at least the next four months.

Putting aside for the moment all the rhetoric about Munich, Hitler, Chamberlain, Britain's oil interests, Britain's Middle East politics, and the initial enthusiasm of the general public and even the Labour Party for doing something about Nasser, what possessed Eden to make the decision to take military action so quickly before allowing himself the time to consider the consequences of such a move or evaluate the opinions of all those around him?

Even at this stage he still had a three months buffer to reconsider his decision especially in view of the speed at which support for the venture soon changed to opposition, even hostility, both in Britain and worldwide.

Eden was intelligent enough to have taken advantage of a good education which included a degree in Oriental languages obtained at a time when a degree still meant something. He also had long experience in politics including spells in Foreign Affairs for which he was awarded a knighthood in 1954. So it must have been obvious to him that the Suez Canal would be blocked if Britain made any move to interfere with it. It should also have been obvious that there would be reprisals and that the lives of the thousands of English residents of Egypt would no longer be worth living once the invasion force was withdrawn whatever the outcome. When the French and the Israelis became involved this consideration would include the lives of their residents and non-Israeli Jews too. Was his hate of Nasser so great that none of this mattered to him?

The Suez Canal crisis had erupted out of the action of Colonel Nasser living in the Egyptian capital Cairo and yet Eden allowed the military planners to finally decide on carrying out an assault on the small, quiet, ethnically-integrated cosmopolitan town of Port Said, the one place in the whole of Egypt having the least in common with the rest of the country and little to do with Cairo. 75,000 member of its population, according to the historian Yahia al Shaer, were from other parts of the world who just happened to be living and working there.

It became a tragedy that one man was able to exert his will over the cabinet. Only two members had the courage to let their objections to the invasion take concrete form by resigning their positions though not letting their reasons be known out of loyalty to their party and therefore keeping it in power. Not every politician has the integrity of a Churchill or a Powell.

The cabinet system works against honesty. One person elects the members of the cabinet ... and keeps them there. Rocking the boat endangers one's political future, chosen career, and salary. A dictatorship had worked once, when Churchill was at the helm, but those were special circumstances.

In view of what we now know about Eden's problems with pain and the side effects of his medication, the answer to the question why it all happened could be, as Air Chief Marshall Boyle commented, *'The Prime Minister's gone bananas ...'*

THE ROLL OF HONOUR ASSOCIATED WITH THE SUEZ CANAL CRISIS 1956.

28 LIVES LOST.

Thursday, 4 October	Meredith, G J	Fleet Air Arm, HMS Bulwark
Tuesday, 16 October	Ponsonby, G	Royal Engineers
Friday, 2 November	Hall, Christopher J	HMS Bulwark
Saturday, 3 November	Sheehan E A	RAF
Monday, 5 November	Barnett, T A	3 Battalion Parachute Regiment
Monday, 5 November	Bates, T M	3 Battalion Parachute Regiment
Monday, 5 November	Sumners, R W	3 Battalion Parachute Regiment
Tuesday, 6 November	Wood, J M	3 Battalion Parachute Regiment
Tuesday, 6 November	Dudhill, L	40 Commando
Tuesday, 6 November	Fudge, R J	40 Commando
Tuesday, 6 November	McCarthy, P W	40 Commando
Tuesday, 6 November	Ufton, E A	40 Commando
Tuesday, 6 November	Dennis, D H A	40 Commando
Tuesday, 6 November	Howard, D	42 Commando
Tuesday, 6 November	Price, B J	42 Commando
Tuesday, 6 November	Short, B J	42 Commando
Tuesday, 6 November	Fowler, M J	45 Commando
Tuesday, 6 November	Goodfellow, C E	45 Commando
Tuesday, 6 November	Kizlo, B	Royal Armoured Corps
Thursday, 8 November	Pipe-Wolferstan, A H	Royal Engineers
Thursday, 8 November	Laws, H J	RASC
Friday, 9 November	Morton, G A	6th Royal Tank Regiment
Friday, 16 November	Callus, Carmel,	HMS Ursa
Sunday, 18 November	Hudson, R	West Yorkshire Regiment
Monday, 19 November	Naylor, Clive A	HMS Eagle
Thursday, 13 December	Moorhouse, A G	West Yorkshire Regiment
Sunday, 16 December	Pinkerton, D	The Royal Scots
Sunday, 16 December	Crawford, G	Somerset Light Infantry